STUDIES IN ECONOMIC HISTORY

PREPARED UNDER THE DIRECTION OF

THE COMMITTEE ON RESEARCH IN
ECONOMIC HISTORY
SOCIAL SCIENCE RESEARCH COUNCIL

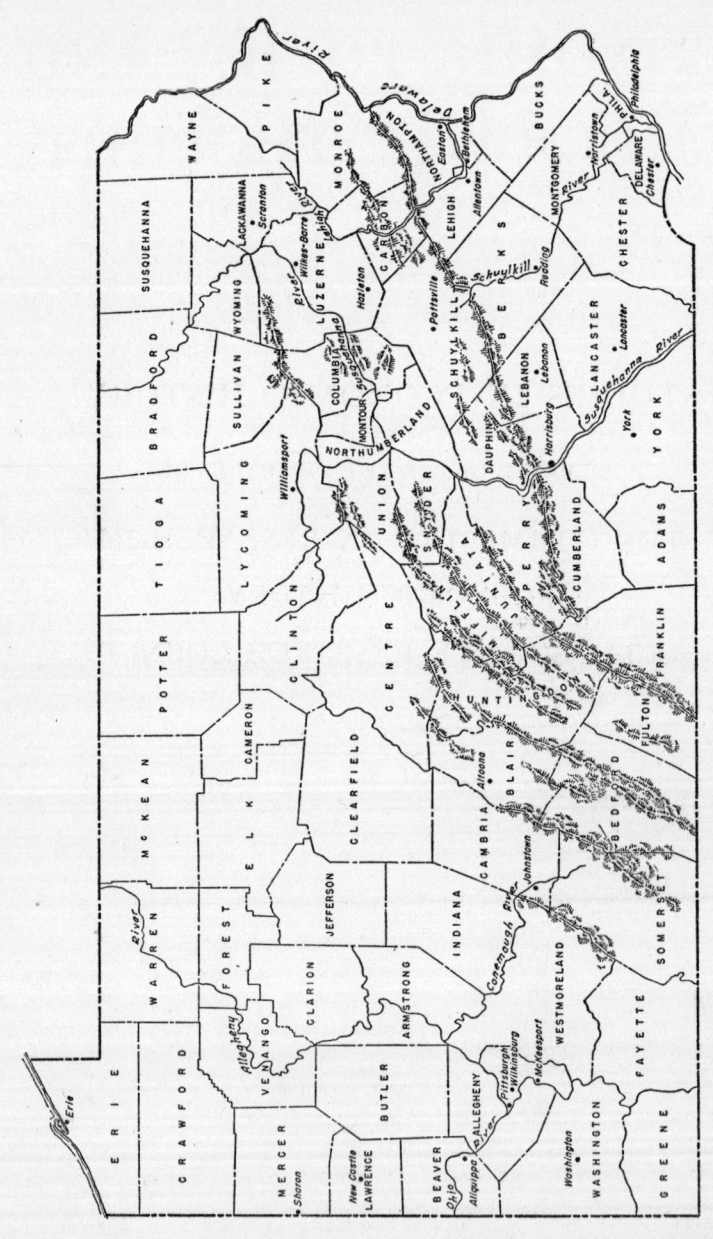

PENNSYLVANIA—POLITICALLY UNITED BUT PHYSIOGRAPHICALLY DIVIDED.

ECONOMIC POLICY AND DEMOCRATIC THOUGHT:

Pennsylvania, 1776–1860

by
LOUIS HARTZ
ASSISTANT PROFESSOR OF GOVERNMENT
IN HARVARD UNIVERSITY

With a Foreword by
BENJAMIN F. WRIGHT
PROFESSOR OF GOVERNMENT
IN HARVARD UNIVERSITY

CAMBRIDGE
HARVARD UNIVERSITY PRESS
1948

COPYRIGHT 1948 BY THE COMMITTEE ON RESEARCH IN ECONOMIC HISTORY,
SOCIAL SCIENCE RESEARCH COUNCIL

ALL RIGHTS RESERVED, INCLUDING THE RIGHT TO REPRODUCE THIS BOOK,
OR ANY PART THEREOF, IN ANY FORM

LONDON : GEOFFREY CUMBERLEGE
OXFORD UNIVERSITY PRESS

PRINTED IN THE UNITED STATES OF AMERICA

FOR STELLA

FOREWORD

Almost all of the great issues of our time, not excluding world peace, are closely related to governmental regulation of economic affairs. No study of recent or contemporary controls imposed by a state government could be confused with a retreat to the ivory tower. But why, it may be asked, go back a century or more to find an aspect of this subject with which to deal? The answer, I think, is a twofold one. We can, in the first place, understand much better the contemporary problems involved in the relations between government and economic life if we realize how long and complex is the history of the attempts to deal with the issues there involved. Beyond this ever-present reason for being concerned with the development of political controls, there is a special reason in this instance. In the latter part of the nineteenth century there was a generally accepted view that the period between the Revolution and the Civil War in the United States was one of laissez faire, an era of sturdy individualism in which governments, both state and national, allowed free range to the inventiveness and energy of private persons. Many scholars, along with judges, legislators, and less disinterested advocates of non-intervention, have continued to hold this view of the formative years of the Union, and that assumption has markedly affected both our political thinking and our legislative history. As Professor Hartz demonstrates, the assumption is not entirely correct. Some previous scholars have, to be sure, believed that this period was not accurately characterized as one of laissez-faire theory and practice, but they have not provided us with evidence adequate to demonstrate the defects in the more usual assumption.

There seem to be two principal presuppositions to the common belief, the first stemming from an interpretation of the Revolutionary heritage, the second from an interpretation of American federalism.

Apparently most of those who have written or talked about the period have concluded that because during the Revolution there was great emphasis upon the rights of the individual it was therefore a period in which there was a pervasive distrust of governmental action. It is evident that there was an acceleration of both the theory and the practice of individualism so far as concerns civil, legal, and political rights. There was also a strong and effective opposition to the belated English mercantilist policies. But just because the American Revolution led to the adoption of bills of rights, to the beginnings of a broader suffrage, and to opposition to the Navigation Acts, it does not follow that the Revolution led to the adoption of laissez-faire theory any more than it led to the popularity of philosophical anarchism. It is not sufficient to point out that Adam Smith's *Wealth of Nations* was read by some men in this country. Nor is it sufficient to demonstrate that a few persons accepted the principle of the free market as defended by Smith. As Professor Hartz shows, Benjamin Franklin was a convert, but Franklin's views seem, in this respect, not much more representative of the usually accepted ideas of the day than does his belief in the desirability of a unicameral legislature. Those bookish attempts at interpretation which stop with the citation of one or two authors, ignoring the large number of more representative theorists, frequently lead to misunderstanding of the climate of opinion which in fact existed.

Another source of misunderstanding seems to stem from the nature of American federalism. It is obviously true that the national government intervened little in economic affairs before 1887 or 1890, but it does not follow that there was correspondingly little state intervention, nor that those who advocated a neutral national government were at the same time opposed to state action. Thomas Jefferson is ordinarily classified as one who believed in a minimum of government. This is correct so far as his attitude toward the functions of the national government is concerned, but it is not an accurate statement of his view of state responsibilities. He advocated a "frugal" national government which would intervene but rarely, but he urged and worked for a variety of statutory reforms in Virginia — changes in the existing property system, the establishment of free public schools, a state university, a dispensary or clinic, and the construction of public works. Even as the belief in natural rights did not always result in the conclusion that nature should be allowed to take its course in economic life, so the belief in a relatively inactive national government did not lead to a belief that the states should be similarly inactive.

Professor Hartz has shown how great was the variety of activities pursued by the state of Pennsylvania in the two or three generations following the Revolution. Through its charter policy, its joint ownership of mixed corporations, its public works program, and its regulation of economic activities, it took a leading rather than a quiescent role in the development of the state's resources and enterprises. On the basis of the evidence here presented it seems reasonable to conclude that governmental participation was as great, perhaps greater, in Pennsylvania in 1830 as in 1930, if one takes into account the scale and range of economic development.

Though the study deals with many aspects of the legislative and administrative history of Pennsylvania's participation in economic affairs, the emphasis is upon the climate of opinion in which that participation existed. There was in the period a great deal of theoretical discussion of the problems involved. Various aspects of this material have been studied by scholars dealing with particular segments of economic activity or intellectual history. None, as far as I know, has attempted to bring the various strands together so that we may see the unified pattern of the whole. What emerges is not a series of summaries of views concerning state aid and regulation but rather an interesting and significant theory of the relation of the public will to community life, a statement of the principles of democratic state action.

Before about 1850 there was extremely little theoretical opposition to governmental intervention in economic life. After 1850 the principle that it is the responsibility of the state to promote and to regulate did not die quickly. In the opinion of Chief Justice Black of the Pennsylvania Supreme Court in the leading Sharpless Case (1853) we find the statement that it is a "public duty" to participate in the development of the railroads. "It is a grave error," says the Chief Justice, "to suppose that the duty of a state stops with the establishment of those institutions which are necessary to the existence of government. . . . To aid, encourage, stimulate commerce, domestic and foreign, is a duty of the sovereign, as plain and as universally recognized as any other." Here is an authoritative statement of the principle of state interventionism which contrasts sharply with the doctrines more usually associated with the courts in the nineteenth century. It is significant evidence that the point of view so frequently expressed by judges of the Supreme Court of the United States later in that century is not altogether consistent with the doctrines accepted in the state courts a little earlier. And, for that matter, the opinions of Justice Field, one of the high priests of laissez faire on the Supreme Court, are not always consistent in this respect with the opinions of Field as Chief Justice of the California Supreme Court a few years earlier.

One final observation. We have heard much in the last few decades about the desirability of closer relationships among the several social sciences. Some of that discussion, as well as some of the attempts to achieve this desirable end, has apparently proceeded on the assumption that all one needs to do is to put a slice of each discipline alongside a slice of other disciplines in order to bring about cross fertilization. Such a method seems more likely to lead to sterility than to fertility, and I would suggest that we need more studies in which the author takes a problem which is not neatly enclosed within the limits of a single discipline — if there is such a problem — but rather one which involves a number of related disciplines, and then draws on all of the materials which are useful for his purposes. This, it seems to me, Professor Hartz has done. It is a matter of no concern whether the result should be classified as a study in history or economics or politics. What is important is that the subject has relevance and that the author has made use of materials and of methods which are not the exclusive possession of any one discipline or subject.

BENJAMIN F. WRIGHT

Harvard University

PREFACE

In the following chapters I have tried to trace the emergence and decline of a certain theory of economic policy which appeared within the framework of democratic ideas during the early years of American history. Though I have not hesitated to explore relevant institutional problems at length, I have been centrally concerned with this theory — the struggles out of which it arose, the doctrinal techniques by which it was perfected, the opposing ideas which served to undermine it, even the reasons why we in our own time have, as I believe, often failed to grasp its importance. The "laissez-faire" cliché has done much to distort the traditional analysis of our early democratic thought. I have not only attempted to show that it embodies an erroneous interpretation: I have also tried to suggest how and why it came to appear.

In writing this book I have vastly increased my indebtedness to Professor Benjamin F. Wright who has kindly consented to introduce it to readers and who, as my tutor at Harvard, aroused my interest in the field of American political and legal ideas. Professor Wright suggested the study of Pennsylvania as a broadly typical example of state development, and throughout its preparation gave me, as always, the finest encouragement, counsel, and criticism. I am grateful also to another of the many students whose work in American thought he has guided, Professor J. Alton Burdine of the University of Texas, for gracious permission to utilize certain materials appearing in his thesis on regulatory legislation in Pennsylvania submitted at Harvard in 1939.

My other debts are also great. Throughout this work I gained much from discussions with members of the Committee on Research in Economic History under whose auspices it was carried on. Their help in connection with both the form and substance of the book — especially the help of Professor Arthur H. Cole of Harvard and Professor Edward C. Kirkland of Bowdoin College — was of that excellent kind which makes possible the effective collaboration of men from different disciplines in the study of common problems. Professor William A. Dunaway of Pennsylvania State College brought to a reading of the manuscript his expert knowledge of Pennsylvania history, and my teachers and colleagues in the Department of Government at Harvard, Professor Arthur N. Holcombe and Professor Merle Fainsod, read the manuscript in an earlier draft and offered valuable suggestions for its revision. Miss Ruth Crandall and Mrs. Winifred Carroll Ferguson did careful work in editing the manuscript and in checking footnotes, and Miss Crandall prepared the index. My wife contributed not only technical assistance in research but a wonderful sort of encouragement from beginning to end.

The help of these friends, despite busy schedules, was invariably given with patience and generosity. It is a pleasure to thank them all.

Louis Hartz

Littauer Center
Cambridge, 1947

EDITOR'S NOTE

The ensuing study of politico-economic thought and action in Pennsylvania during the period 1776–1860 constitutes one of four similar inquiries which the Committee on Research in Economic History has promoted. Others were intended to examine the experiences of Massachusetts, Georgia, and Illinois over these same decades — or, in the last case, from settlement onward to the Civil War. That relating to Massachusetts, written by Professor and Mrs. Oscar Handlin, appeared too recently for Professors Wright and Hartz to take into account.

Arthur H. Cole
*Chairman, Committee on
Research in Economic History*

CONTENTS

FOREWORD vii
PREFACE xi
LIST OF MAPS xvii
LIST OF CHARTS xvii
LIST OF TABLES xvii

PART ONE
GOVERNMENT AND THE ECONOMY

I. THE THEORY OF BUSINESS AND POLITICS

    1. The Significance of State Policy 3
    2. The Colonial Era and After 4
    3. Some Economic Attitudes 9
    4. Constitutions, Parties, and Political Thought . . 21

PART TWO
THE STATE AS PROMOTER AND ENTREPRENEUR

II. THE CORPORATION

    1. The Pattern of Charter Policy 37
    2. The Idea of Sectional Interest 42
    3. Corporations and the State 51
    4. Individual Enterprise and the Parties . . . 56
    5. The Anti-Charter Doctrine 69
    6. The Role of Government 79

III. THE MIXED CORPORATION

    1. The Growth of Investment 82
    2. Profit, Promotion, and Control 89
    3. Issues in Local Investment 104
    4. The Sharpless Case 113

5. From Court to Constitution 122
6. The End of Mixed Enterprise 126

IV. THE PUBLIC WORKS

1. Early Attitudes Toward State Ownership . . 129
2. The Campaign of 1825 131
3. Public Spending and Pump Priming . . . 142
4. Administration: Theory and Practice . . . 148
5. The Struggle Over Liquidation 161
6. The End of Public Works 175

PART THREE

THE STATE AS REGULATOR

V. SOCIAL REFORM AND VESTED RIGHTS

1. Slavery and Indentured Service 181
2. Workers and the State 187
3. The Theory of Labor Legislation 194
4. The Control of Economic Practice: Licensing and Prohibition 204
5. Debtor and Creditor 219

VI. ISSUES IN CORPORATE CONTROL

1. Duration, Repeal, and Alteration of Charters . . 236
2. The Dartmouth College Doctrine: The Case of the Second Bank 243
3. Regulatory Policy 254
4. The Approach to Enforcement 262
5. The Inalienable State Power: The Case of the Pennsylvania Railroad 267

PART FOUR

THE MYTH OF LAISSEZ FAIRE

VII. ECONOMIC POLICY AND DEMOCRATIC THOUGHT

1. The Policy Pattern 289

2. The Theory of State Action 297
3. The Attack on the State 309

APPENDICES

I. Report on Auction of State Mixed-Enterprise Holdings, 1843 323

II. Message of Governor Porter to the Legislature on the Public Creditors and Mixed-Enterprise Banking, 1842   328

III. Report of the Auditor-General on Administrative Abuses in the Repair of the Juniata Branch of the State Works in 1838 330

IV. Claims and Awards for Damages under the Board of Appraisers of the State Works, 1840 . . . 332

V. Payments under Act of 1838 Authorizing Bounties for Silk Production 333

TABLE OF LEGAL CASES 334

BIBLIOGRAPHY 337

INDEX 357

LIST OF MAPS

Pennsylvania — Politically United but Physiographically
Divided . . . . *Frontispiece*

Public Works of Pennsylvania, 1840 154

LIST OF CHARTS

1. Special Charters issued to Business Enterprises by Pennsylvania, Annually, 1790–1860 39

2. Value of Stock held by Pennsylvania in Mixed Corporations, by Types of Enterprise, at Five-Year Intervals, 1800–1860 . . . 87

3. Value of all Stock held by Pennsylvania in Mixed Corporations, at Five-Year Intervals, 1800–1860 89

4. Dividends received by Pennsylvania on all State-held Stock and on State-held Bank Stock, at Five-Year Intervals, 1800–1860 91

5. Expenditures for and Gross Revenue from Public Works in Pennsylvania, with State Loans, and Revenues from Taxation and Licenses, Annually, 1830–1850 150

6. Organization of the Public Works Administration in Pennsylvania, 1844 158

LIST OF TABLES

1. Corporate Charters for Business Purposes by Special Act, 1790–1860 38

2. Bank Charter Bonuses, 1833–1840 54

3. Popular Vote on the Anti-Investment Amendments, 1857 . 125

4. Popular Vote on the Sale of the Main Line, 1844 . . . 163

5. Discharges of Imprisoned Debtors in Philadelphia, 1827–1830 222

6. Popular Vote on the Reservation Amendment, 1857 . . 241

PART ONE

GOVERNMENT AND THE ECONOMY

I

THE THEORY OF BUSINESS AND POLITICS

1. The Significance of State Policy

THIS STUDY is an inquiry into American conceptions of the proper relationship between government and economic life during the period from the Revolution to the Civil War. It is based on developments in a single state — Pennsylvania. The reason for this emphasis lies not merely in the fact that the national problems of the period have been studied with some degree of thoroughness while the state issues have been badly neglected, but also in the more important fact that the disproportionate degree of attention given to the former has not infrequently led to distorted interpretations of politico-economic thought prior to the Civil War. For during that period by far the greatest amount of governmental activity in economic life was initiated not by the national government, but by the state governments. It is in the doctrines and attitudes which clustered about state activity, which had for the most part a local orientation and which were developed mainly by men whose names have been forgotten, that the substance of the original American conception of the legitimate sphere of governmental action in economic life is to be found.

This is not perceived at once in an age which has come to accept the national government as the central agency of public action in the economic sphere. Yet it must be remembered that during most of the period between the Revolution and the Civil War the American economy was notably lacking in that national integration which is one of its most obvious characteristics at the present time. Economic life was predominantly agrarian and commercial, and it was not until after 1850 that corporations of genuinely national significance began to push problems of federal action into the foreground.[1] Moreover the legal basis of state economic action was taken for granted. Despite the significant restrictions which

---

[1] Cf. Fainsod and Gordon, *Government and American Economy*, pp. 5 ff.

the federal Constitution imposed upon the states, it reserved to them, both by implication in the enumerated powers of the national government and by the express provision of the Tenth Amendment, a large authority to deal with economic issues. "The powers reserved to the several States," Madison wrote in the forty-fifth *Federalist*, "will extend to all the objects which, in the ordinary course of affairs, concern the lives, liberties, and properties of the people, and the internal order, improvement, and prosperity of the State." [2]

2. *The Colonial Era and After*

It is commonly recognized that the colonial period, governed by the mercantilist principle, accepted a broad sphere of action for the state in the economic field. An examination of the Pennsylvania evidence reveals the usual pattern of trade regulations: price fixing, market regulations, inspection measures, labor controls, wharfage provisions.[3] The principles which rationalized this economic policy were so firmly entrenched that they were usually taken for granted not only in official discussion, as in the pronouncements of the governors and lieutenant governors of the Province,[4] but also in such unofficial writings as those of Pastorius and Thomas Budd. Thus in 1685 Budd put forth a scheme for governmental regulation of Pennsylvania's economic life, involving the construction of public storehouses, compulsory production of flax and hemp, and industrial education, without once considering the question whether this scheme lay within the rightful province of the state.[5] Certain phases of mercantilist theory underwent significant modification as a result of the new environment which the colonists found, but the principle of state control and promotion of enterprise remained dominant throughout the colonial period.[6]

The repudiation of the idea of economic policy, however, has

---

[2] *The Federalist*, p. 290.
[3] Pennsylvania, *Colonial Records*, I, 343–53; *Pa. Archives*, 4th, I, 475; Giesecke, *American Commercial Legislation before 1789, passim.*
[4] Cf. *Pa. Archives*, 4th, I, 428, 475, 674.
[5] Budd, *Good Order in Pa. and N. J.*, pp. 41 ff.
[6] E. A. J. Johnson, *American Economic Thought in 17th Century*, p. 11.

sometimes been dated from the coming of the Revolution.[7] The Revolutionary theory has been characterized by one student as a theory of "free trade."[8] Another has written: "To the Founding Fathers control of production and distribution of commodities by means of any political agency whatsoever would have seemed the complete nullification of all they were fighting for."[9] Statements such as these usually identify doctrines of natural right directed by the colonists against British trade restrictions with an emergent economic liberalism which assailed the general idea of state economic policy. The appearance in the same year of the greatest documents of Thomas Jefferson and Adam Smith symbolizes a colonial attack not only upon imperial oppression but upon the principle of state action in economic life. Nor can it be said that this interpretation is entirely the product of logical deduction; prior to the Revolution America was not wholly impervious to the movement of liberal economic thought. Pennsylvania, in the career of Benjamin Franklin, provides a striking example of its influence. About 1767, as a result of contact with French economic theorists and Adam Smith, Franklin deserted an earlier faith in state control and embraced the theory of unhampered economic development. "I find myself," he wrote, "inclin'd to adopt that modern [view] which supposes it best for every Country to leave its Trade entirely free from all Incumbrances."[10]

Yet the case of Franklin was a marked exception. While the Revolutionary writings relied heavily upon the idea of natural law, that idea was rarely used in a Smithian or physiocratic sense to assail the principle of state economic policy. No one can doubt the heavy reliance upon the "laws of our nature" and the "immutable maxims of reason"[11] placed by the two foremost Pennsylvania theorists of the Revolution, John Dickinson and James

---

[7] Cf. Hartz, "Laissez-Faire Thought in Pa., 1776–1860," *Tasks of Econ. Hist.*, III (1943), 66–77.

[8] Callender, "Early Transportation and Banking Enterprises of the States," *Quarterly Jour. of Econ.*, XVII (1902–03), 111.

[9] J. Dewey, *Freedom and Culture*, p. 55.

[10] Quoted in Eiselen, *Pa. Protectionism*, pp. 9–10. See also Wetzel, *Benjamin Franklin*, pp. 38–40.

[11] Dickinson, *Writings*, Memoirs of Historical Society of Pa., XIV, 262. *See also* B. F. Wright, *American Interpretations of Natural Law*, pp. 71–78, 84–86, 281–86.

Wilson. But these men were centrally concerned with a question of imperial politics rather than with a question of economic regulation versus free trade. Dickinson's attack upon the Stamp Act in the 1760's was not an attack upon the principle of taxation: it was an attack upon taxation without representation and without consent. He defended as compatible with "perfect liberty" the tradition of economic policy as a whole — even earlier measures designed for the enrichment of the mother country such as the ban on manufactured goods.[12] Wilson was only peripherally aware of the free-trade theory; in 1774, in one of his essays, he remarked briefly that such doctrine was "the opinion of some Politicians." When, in line with the deepening of the theory of resistance, he rejected the idea of colonial allegiance to Parliament, he suggested that the power to regulate commerce be "intrusted to the king, as a part of the royal prerogative." [13]

What the imperial crisis generated in Pennsylvania was not a widespread repugnance for the principle of economic policy but a growing belief in the need for utilizing that principle exclusively for colonial ends. The immense vigor of Dickinson's *Late Regulations*, instead of carrying him over into an attack upon state economic action in general, led him instead to suggest that the colonists embark upon a program of economic policy for their own interest. "Great Britain gives us an example to guide us," he wrote, "SHE TEACHES US TO MAKE A DISTINCTION BETWEEN HER INTERESTS AND OUR OWN." [14] Nor was this emphasis upon native interest entirely novel. As far back as the seventeenth century, despite the pronouncements of royal executives, Budd had shown an astonishing lack of interest in the economic welfare of Britain. The principal justification which he offered for his plan of industrial education and textile production was that it would permit Pennsylvania to undersell Britain in the neighboring colonies.[15]

It is clear, moreover, that during the period of war the idea of

---

[12] Dickinson, *Letters From a Farmer in Pa.*, p. 51.
[13] J. Wilson, *Selected Political Essays*, p. 81 fn; B. F. Wright, *Source Book*, pp. 42 ff; McIlwain, *The American Revolution*, pp. 141, 188.
[14] Dickinson, *Late Regulations Respecting Colonies*, pp. 41-42.
[15] Budd, *Good Order in Pa. and N. J.*, pp. 47-48.

state economic action was abolished neither in theory nor in practice. The radical elements in east and west which came to power during the Revolution thoroughly democratized the state government under the slogan of the "natural, inherent, and inalienable" rights of man, extending the suffrage, reapportioning representation, and providing for the annual election of legislators.[16] But it was precisely these groups which, in their attempt to meet the complex economic problems of the war period, initiated such measures as the fixing of prices, the regulation of mercantile practices, the abolition of the liquor trade, the promotion of manufactures, and the confiscation of property. Much of this legislation we shall have occasion to deal with in subsequent chapters. The defense of price fixing and property confiscation, two of the most radical exertions of state power, were, indeed, characteristic indices of those in favor of the "levelling" constitution of 1776. It is true that the policy of confiscating Loyalist lands was less severe in Philadelphia than in New York or Boston, but a trade in confiscated property did exist.[17] Divesting the Penn proprietors of their estates was defended by the Radicals on the ground that the proprietor and his successors had been but popular trustees and that the private ownership of such large estates was dangerous to the liberties of the people. An indemnity of one hundred and thirty thousand pounds sterling was granted the Penns for their loss, but it was emphasized that the payment of that indemnity was not recognized as a legal necessity.[18]

Late in 1776 the Radicals opposed the recommendation by Congress of price-fixing measures to the states. But to interpret this position as indicating an opposition to the propriety of price fixing as an economic measure is to fall into an error characteristic when issues of federalism mingle with those of economic policy. The Radicals opposed Congressional action on the ground that it would infringe upon the police power of the states, and their position reveals nothing of their attitude concerning the rightness or

[16] *Constitutions of Pa.*, pp. 232 ff.; Selsam, *Pa. Constitution of 1776*, pp. 176–203.
[17] Pennsylvania, *Statutes at Large*, IX, 204–206, 208–12, 324, 330–31, 408–10; East, *Business Enterprise in Revolutionary Era*, pp. 220–21, 226; W. Bell, "Social History of Pa., 1760–90," *Pa. Mag. of Hist. and Biog.*, LXII (1938), 305–306.
[18] *Statutes at Large*, X, 33–39; Brunhouse, *Counter-Revolution in Pa.*, pp. 79–80.

wrongness of price regulation.¹⁹ Their views on the latter score became clear in 1778, after the British evacuation, when as Continental currency depreciated and prices rose a popular committee for regulating prices was appointed by a Philadelphia town meeting, and the legislature enacted measures against forestalling. Agitation against merchants led to outbursts of popular violence, and the militia threatened the use of arms against them. The mercantile opposition to price regulation was associated in the minds of the Radicals with the opposition of eastern merchants to the new democratic constitution; economic control and political democracy became sister principles of the Radical position; and an antagonism between import merchants and consumers which had festered prior to the Revolution became a basic theme in Philadelphia politics. Philadelphia's price-fixing policy was, under the guidance of Christopher Marshall who had been a leader in its development there, soon duplicated in other areas of the state, including the counties of Chester, Berks, York, and the Paxton district of Lancaster.²⁰

In many of its most important aspects, to be sure, Radical economic policy was a failure. Not only was it unable to solve the currency problem, but its efforts at price fixing and the elimination of monopolizing were largely futile. Persistence in an arbitrary price schedule when the economic situation fluctuated daily, failure to work out an over-all price system, which at an early time led to open resistance by tanners, curriers, and cordwainers, the administrative futility of enforcement by popular committees, all meant that prices continued to soar and paper to depreciate, developments which produced more anger than sober consideration on the part of the Radicals.²¹ Moreover in 1780, just as an acceptable currency was launched, the conservative forces in the state began to re-emerge; and the next decade saw a reaction which, culminating in the Constitutional Convention of 1790, discredited not only some of the extreme Revolutionary measures

---

[19] *Ibid.*, p. 26.
[20] *Statutes at Large*, IX, 177, 387–88, 421–22; East, *Business Enterprise in Revolutionary Era*, p. 199; Brunhouse, *Counter-Revolution in Pa.*, pp. 26, 68 ff., 73 ff.
[21] *Ibid.*, pp. 82 ff.; Cf. W. R. Smith, "Sectionalism in Pa. During the Revolution," *Pol. Sci. Quarterly*, XXIV (1909), 227–31.

of political democratization but some of the measures of economic regulation as well. In 1783 the Council of Censors, an agency set up by the Revolutionary constitution to review legislative acts, declared that many of the latter were not only "absurd and impossible" but also violated constitutional protections of property.[22] In the price-fixing area many measures became dead letters on the statute books or were revised in light of the view expressed by the Council of Censors. The preamble to an enactment of 1793 which revised one of the measures declared that "doubts have arisen whether the same does not infringe the equality of rights established by the constitution of this commonwealth."[23] But it is unwarranted to assume on the basis of this trend that the principle of state economic policy had lost its dominance.

The fate of that principle can be known only by an intensive examination of politico-economic thought during the period which followed.

3. Some Economic Attitudes

Though a balanced account of the ideas generated by the complex economic development of our period would require a volume in itself, it is necessary to select here for a preliminary word certain ideas which, in the peculiar setting of Pennsylvania history, came to have an important influence upon attitudes toward governmental action. Outstanding among these was an ideology of regional self-interest produced by intercity rivalries for domestic trade which intensified on the seaboard after the decline of foreign commerce in the latter eighteenth and early nineteenth centuries.[24] With the passing of the age of the great shipping fortunes of Stephen Girard and Thomas Cope, the merchants of Philadelphia turned increasingly to competition with Baltimore for the western trade.[25] During the turnpike era, owing to the high cost of transportation over the Alleghenies to Pittsburgh, the proximity of

---

[22] *Proceedings Relative to Calling Conventions of 1776 and 1790*, pp. 66 ff.

[23] Cited in R. Bull, "Constitutional Significance of Early Pa. Price-Fixing Legislation," *Temple Law Quarterly*, XI (1936–37), 314; *Dallas' Laws*, III, 447. For the continuation of price-fixing objectives into the later period, cf. *infra*, p. 206.

[24] Tyson, *Commerce of Philadelphia*, pp. 44–46, 666; Freedley, *Philadelphia Manufactures*, p. 76; *United States Gazette*, Jan. 25, 1825.

[25] Cf. Plummer, *Road Policy of Pa.*, p. 40.

Baltimore to the Susquehanna, and the building of the National Road which also favored Baltimore, Philadelphia was constantly handicapped in this competition. With the building of the Erie Canal, New York appeared as a new competitor for the trade of the West, and in an effort to frustrate both the merchants of that city and of Baltimore, Pennsylvania constructed its own canal-rail line across the state.[26] The economic failure of this system, owing again largely to the high cost of trans-Allegheny shipment, had scarcely been demonstrated before the advent of the railroad age brought new threats in the form of the Boston and Albany, New York and Erie, and Baltimore and Ohio railroad projects.[27] Philadelphia replied with the Pennsylvania Railroad whose immediate success came as a source of the profoundest relief to the mercantile interests of that city.

Yet it is of the utmost importance to observe that the aspirations of Philadelphia's merchant class were not identical with those of the state as a whole. Quite apart from the fact that they could clash with the aspirations of other groups in the east,[28] they encountered strong antagonisms on sectional grounds. The northeastern counties in the state found their natural trade outlet not in Philadelphia but in adjacent regions in New York.[29] The northwestern counties, as they emerged to economic importance, also fell easily in the commercial path of New York; their proximity to Lake Erie placed them within the range of every effort made by New York City to reach the West.[30] In the southern and western portions of the state there were ties to another of Philadelphia's vigorous competitors — Baltimore. The rich grain-growing counties of Bedford, Franklin, Cumberland, and York, close to the northern counties of Maryland, found a comparatively easy outlet to Baltimore via the Susquehanna.[31] In the extreme west attachments to Baltimore did not, it is true, crystallize significantly until

---

[26] Cf. *infra*, pp. 129 ff.
[27] Cf. E. R. Johnson *et al.*, *Domestic and Foreign Commerce*, I, pp. 235–37; *House Journal, 1822–23*, p. 654.
[28] Cf. *infra*, pp. 106–107.
[29] For evidence of this trade relation, see Bradsby, *Bradford County*, pp. 207 ff.; McKnight, *Northwestern Pa.*, p. 613.
[30] See *Hunt's Merchants' Mag.*, XXVII, (1852), 634.
[31] Cf. Klein, *Pa. Politics, 1817–1832*, p. 20.

the forties; prior to that time the state works united Pittsburgh with Philadelphia in a common interest.[32] But in 1846, when the Baltimore and Ohio Railroad announced Pittsburgh as its objective, the entire western section of the state greeted the announcement with great enthusiasm, and for Pittsburgh, which feared that otherwise the B. and O. might connect with Wheeling or Parkersburg farther south, the alliance with Baltimore appeared as a matter of commercial survival. Inevitably the most bitter antagonisms were evoked in the west when Philadelphia sought to frustrate the Baltimore project,[33] and these were intensified during the fifties by Philadelphia's reliance upon projected extensions of the Pennsylvania Railroad which ran counter to the commercial ambitions of Pittsburgh and by the discriminatory rate schedule for domestic shipping adopted by the Pennsylvania as it began to compete with other lines in the Central States.[34] The record is plain that commercially Pennsylvania was not a single state during our period but a collection of states, that centrifugal forces were constantly at work to isolate the merchants of Philadelphia from their political compatriots.

It is hard for a later age, accustomed to a comparatively mild chamber-of-commerce mentality, to appreciate the intensity of the passions which the regional rivalries of this period evoked. "We can and will baffle the attempts of our neighbors," insisted Samuel Breck of Philadelphia in 1818 at the conclusion of a pamphlet calling for increased canal construction. "We have a *motive* in the defence of our *property*."[35] Describing a railroad mass meeting in 1848, the editor of the *Pittsburgh Daily Gazette and Ad-*

[32] *Pa. Archives*, 4th, IV, 343; Crall, "Rivalry Between Pittsburgh and Wheeling," *Western Pa. Hist. Mag.*, XIII (1930), 237–47. See also *Facts Respecting Inland Navigation*, pp. 13–14.

[33] Cf. J. Clark, Jr., "Railroad Struggle for Pittsburgh," *Pa. Mag. of Hist. and Biog.*, XLVIII (1924), 3–8; W. Wilson, *Pennsylvania Railroad*, I, 2–4; *Proceedings in Relation to Pennsylvania Railroad*, p. 14.

[34] In connection with the Hempfield extension of the Pennsylvania, cf. Tyson, *Commerce of Philadelphia*, p. 75; *North American*, Feb. 3, 1853; *Public Ledger*, Feb. 8, 10, 1853; in connection with the Sunbury and Erie, cf. Sunbury and Erie Railroad Company, *Report* (1853), pp. 3–4; *Report to Philadelphia Board of Trade*. On rate discrimination, cf. *Report to Board of Trade*, p. 3; *Legislative Record, 1861*, pp. 501 ff.; *infra*, p. 270.

[35] Breck, *Internal Improvements by Pa.*, pp. 80–81.

vertiser wrote: "We believe no other subject matter whatever, unless it was akin to a revolution when men felt their religious or civil liberties were at stake — could have collected such a gathering."[36] Maps were circulated and geography publicized to an extent that the colonial period had never known. A variety of conclusions could of course be drawn from a single map, but the respect which mileage statistics elicited was universal and sometimes well-nigh religious. Conscious of the fact that the Quaker City was a shorter distance than either New York or Boston from the trade centers of the Ohio Valley, Philadelphians spoke the language of a divinely inspired imperialism: "It thus becomes an obligation imposed on us by a kind Providence" to build the Pennsylvania Railroad.[37]

But how did the idea of regional competition jibe with the idea of economic nationalism which Pennsylvania's own Mathew Carey was preaching so vigorously at the same time? On the plane of popular enthusiasm questions of consistency are usually not important. Yet some of the competitive publicists were embarrassed by the growth of nationalism, and they went out of their way to disclaim "the ugly genius of rivalry," to repudiate "invidious comparisons" and "unworthy jealousies" and efforts to excite "unreasonable state feeling."[38] In other cases an even more elaborate rationalization was developed. I know of no one in Pennsylvania who argued with Benjamin De Witt of New York that "every state may be considered in relation to matters of this kind as a distinct country and people."[39] But there were similar efforts, based on the principle that intense economic competition among the states was the surest guarantee of national well-being: "No state performs her duty well to the Union that does not well perform her duty to herself."[40] Mr. Justice Lowrie of the Pennsylvania Supreme Court admitted that "state patriot-

---

[36] *Pittsburgh Daily Gazette*, Mar. 18, 1846, cited by Crall in *Western Pa. Hist. Mag.*, XIII (1930), 251.

[37] Philadelphia Committee of Seven, *Address*, p. 7. This committee was selected at a town meeting in behalf of the Pennsylvania Railroad. See *Proceedings in Relation to Pennsylvania Railroad*.

[38] *United States Gazette*, Feb. 11, 1825; Tyson, *Commerce of Philadelphia*, p. 59.

[39] Quoted in Durrenberger, *Turnpikes*, p. 47.

[40] *United States Gazette*, Feb. 11, 1825.

ism" is "selfishness," but insisted that it was "the very form of selfishness that is at the bottom of all national glory." [41] Jeremy Bentham was in bad repute in the America of this age, but the doctrinal accommodation worked out between the nationalist and competitive ideas amounted to a kind of natural harmony-of-interests doctrine projected on a regional plane.

Yet even this ingenious creation was hardly enough. For within the state as within the nation the concept of patriotic solidarity was assaulted by the reality of a mass of conflicting sectional ambitions. This ideological problem was not solved quite so well as the other. Theoretically it could be dealt with easily enough by another application, within a more circumscribed area, of the harmony-of-interests principle. But there were barriers blocking that way out. The reality of conflict, for one thing, was far too blatant. No smooth dialectic of ultimate harmony was going to convince Philadelphia that the impulse of the northern counties to ship via the New York and Erie would actually redound to her benefit when the tracks of that road obviously led to New York; nor was that dialectic going to make the Hempfield Railroad popular in Pittsburgh when it threatened to cut off from that city a major portion of the Ohio River trade. Strategic forces were at work, moreover, which kept constantly alive the conflict between state solidarity and sectional preoccupation. Confronted with a group of sections always in danger of being wooed into the path of other seaboard cities, it was inevitable that Philadelphia should propagandize them heavily with such slogans as the "true-hearted Pennsylvanian" and "our commonwealth one and indivisible." [42] Occasionally this evoked nationalist replies to the effect that "we ought not to forget how much the states depend on one another," [43] but such replies were handicapped in their development by the fact that the cities and counties which presented them also found good uses to which the doctrine of state solidarity could be put. Thus Pittsburgh insisted, when the Pennsylvania Railroad set its

---

[41] Quoted in *Report to Pittsburgh Board of Trade*, p. 10.
[42] *Proceedings in Relation to Pennsylvania Railroad*, pp. 6, 7. Cf. *Legislative Record, 1858*, p. 214; Corn Exchange Association, *Second Annual Report*, p. 9; Philadelphia Board of Trade, *Report, Delegates to Warren Convention*.
[43] *Speech of Gibbons*, p. 3.

termini farther west, that Philadelphia interests were flouting the obligations imposed upon them by Keystone patriotism.[44]

The truth is that the idea of regional self-interest had no area around which it could effectively come to a focus. If it could be used on the state level it could also be used on the sectional level, and if it could be used there it could also be invoked to rationalize the ambitions of one hamlet as against another within a section. There was danger, indeed, that by virtue of this deteriorating logic the ideology would finally resolve itself into a theory of individual competition on a simple atomistic plane. Such a resolution was hardly what any of its protagonists desired. It is true that their appeal was, in the last analysis, directed to the self-interest of the individual either as a member of the state, the section, or the city; but it was their most ardent and perennial theme that the realization of that self-interest hinged upon communal action. Nor is this hard to understand. Every effort to shape the routes of commerce called for large-scale capital investments — investments which grew greater in magnitude as railroads replaced turnpikes and canals — and only collective participation could raise these funds. Moreover the returns on such investments, whether direct or indirect, were scheduled so far into the future that skepticism and timidity were bound to arise. It was inevitable, therefore, that the competitive propaganda should place heavy emphasis upon the concept of communal responsibility, that it should lift its objective from the material plane of self-interest to the loftier plane of public spirit.[45] "As individuals," declared Job Tyson in a plea during the fifties for action to regain Philadelphia's lost position in the field of foreign commerce, "we are connected with the community in which we live by a thousand ligaments, which none but a sojourner with his property and his hopes at a distance, can repudiate or sever. The merchant of Philadelphia who employs his capital or shipping in New York, like him who imports his merchandise into that metropolis, acts in forgetfulness of an original duty to himself and his neighbor. . . ."[46]

[44] *Legislative Record, 1858*, p. 313; *Report to Pittsburgh Board of Trade*, p. 1.
[45] Freedley, *Philadelphia Manufactures*, p. 89.
[46] *Commerce of Philadelphia*, p. 171.

Other notions of peculiar relevance to the idea of state economic policy derived from the growing industrialization of the state. It is true that the ideology of regional competition engendered what one journalist called in 1818 a "merchantilmania" [47] which retarded somewhat popular enthusiasm for the industrialization movement. But the growth of that enthusiasm was demonstrated in the rise of Pennsylvania's ardent protectionist ideology, whose development was also a measure of the state's rejection of Franklin's free-trade theory. If the first tariff act of 1789 was viewed with some suspicion, the depression that followed the War of 1812 solidified protectionist sentiment; the agricultural interest thereafter regularly favored a strong tariff policy and the increasing power of the iron and coal interests made the protectionist demand vehement.[48] The only disciple of note whom Franklin had in Pennsylvania after 1812 was Condy Raguet, an acute analyst with practically no influence. His brave attempts to popularize the classical dogmas and to publicize the limitations of the new industrialism [49] were overwhelmed by the voluminous writings of Mathew Carey and the campaign against pre-industrial biases which he led. The circulation of Raguet's *Banner of the Constitution* never exceeded 1,600, and by the end of 1832 he admitted that he could not see "the slightest prospect of any abandonment for many years to come of the American System. . . ." [50]

The economic theory for which the state became famous during this era, which centered about the voluminous writings of the Careys, was of course directly related to the protectionist movement.[51] Behind the younger Carey's repudiation of Ricardian rent

---

[47] The term was used by the editor of the *Pittsburgh Daily Gazette*, Nov. 17, 1818, cited by Crall in *Western Pa. Hist. Mag.*, XIII (1930), 242.

[48] Eiselen, *Pa. Protectionism*, p. 25 and *passim*. See also remarks of the House Committee on Agriculture in *House Journal, 1832–33*, II, 450. For legislative resolutions calling for a protectionist policy on the part of the Pennsylvania delegation in Congress, see *Pa. Laws 1823–24*, p. 241; *1827–28*, p. 496; *1830–31*, pp. 505–506; *1831–32*, pp. 625, 644–45; *1832–33*, pp. 484–85, 486; *1836–37*, p. 398; *1844*, p. 601; *1846*, pp. 511–12.

[49] Cf. Raguet, *Free Trade*; *Banner of the Constitution*, Apr. 25, 1832, *et seq.*

[50] Quoted in Eiselen, *Pa. Protectionism*, pp. 95–96. Cf. Publicola, *Thirteen Essays on Policy of Manufacturing*.

[51] Cf. Teilhac, *Pioneers of American Economic Thought in 19th Century*, pp. 93 ff.; Rowe, *Mathew Carey*; M. Carey, *Autobiography*; Kaplan, *Henry Charles*

theory and the bleak population doctrine to which it was allied, behind his ideal of a diversified economy governed by the imperative of reducing distance between producer and consumer,[52] there was the same environment which produced the popular doctrine of protectionism.[53] Yet the influence of his technical theory upon popular attitudes has often been exaggerated. Apart from his protectionism, he was ready to rely upon the classical harmonies for economic well-being,[54] something which, as we shall see, public opinion was unprepared to do. In general, indeed, formal economic theory had limited popular influence. By 1834 Mathew Carey was ready to give up issuing pamphlets on monetary questions on the ground that few read or understood them, and in 1835 Charles Ingersoll asserted that not three members of the Pennsylvania legislature had read George McDuffie's report or Albert Gallatin's writings on the Second Bank.[55] Yet, as our period drew to a close, the increasing complexity of economic life had produced a perceptible conviction in the popular literature that business was a kind of science. "The laws of trade and business are as fixed and certain as the laws of the universe," declared the *Ledger* in 1857, "and the principles of them once correctly comprehended there is very little danger of failure in their application."[56] Edwin T. Freedley in his *Practical Treatise on Business* declared in 1852: "There is no great social evil that I can think of, that will not disappear when the laws that make industry most productive are understood. . . ."[57] This view of the nature of

---

Carey; Rezneck, "Industrial Consciousness in U. S., 1760–1830," *Jour. of Econ. and Business Hist.*, IV (1931–32), 784–811.

[52] A systematic exposition of Carey's system is to be found in his *Principles of Social Science*.

[53] Henry Carey himself had investments in a paper mill and in the Schuylkill coal lands, both of which brought decreasing returns prior to the tariff of 1842 and increasing returns once that measure had gone into effect. Kaplan, *Henry Charles Carey*, pp. 46–47; Eiselen, *Pa. Protectionism*, pp. 176–77.

[54] For a brief period in the thirties, prior to his conversion to protectionism, Henry Carey had actually espoused the classical free-trade theory which his father had fought. See his *Rate of Wages*.

[55] Catterall, *Second Bank of U.S.*, p. 266. For Pennsylvania's contribution to monetary theory, see H. Miller, *Banking Theories in U.S. before 1860*.

[56] *Public Ledger*, Mar. 16, 1857.

[57] Freedley, *Treatise on Business*, p. 32.

business knowledge cropped out again and again in popular controversy.[58]

Still other attitudes which came to have a significant impact upon the idea of state action were generated by the pattern of boom and recession which is among the most familiar phases of the economic history of the period. While its aftermath crippled early improvement companies,[59] the post-Revolutionary boom associated with speculation in public securities and land did not lead to results so disastrous as those which followed the boom of the second decade of the nineteenth century engendered by the War of 1812, a new improvements drive, and pressure for expanded credit facilities from newly settled regions. The Banking Act of 1814 created forty-one banks.[60] In the ensuing crash farm bankruptcies were as bad as those in the mercantile and manufacturing fields where, as Raguet put it, the factories which the war had nurtured fell under a "universal suspension." [61] The agricultural population was less heavily involved in the famous boom of the thirties which was associated with new industrial investment and a precipitous expansion of government borrowing for public works.[62] Unwilling to embark upon effective taxation,[63] the state was able to bolster its financial position momentarily in the mid-

[58] See *infra*, pp. 120, 170–171, 173, 272, 312.

[59] M. Carey, *Internal Improvement of Pa.*, pp. 11–12; Ringwalt, *Transportation Systems in U.S.*, pp. 45 ff.; Durrenberger, *Turnpikes*, p. 45.

[60] *Pa. Laws, 1813–14*, pp. 154–73; Holdsworth, *Financing an Empire*, I, 314; Knox, *History of Banking in U.S.*, pp. 445 ff.; Ashmead, *History of Delaware County National Bank*, pp. 7–12.

[61] *Senate Journal, 1819–20*, pp. 221 ff. Condy Raguet was the chairman of the Senate committee which investigated the panic of 1819. See also *Niles Register*, XVII (1819–20), 18–21; Day, *Historical Collections of Pa.*, p. 51; Simons, *Social Forces in American History*, p. 166.

[62] *Pa. Archives*, 4th, VI, 347, 353 ff.; 606 ff.; Hutcheson, "Philadelphia and Panic of 1837," *Pa. Hist.*, III (1936), 182–94; Brown Brothers and Company, *Experiences of a Century*, pp. 32 ff.; McGrane, *The Panic of 1837, passim*.

[63] See Worthington, *Finances of Pa.*, pp. 32–75; *House Journal, 1828–29*, II, 553. In 1831 a limited increase in personal property taxation was imposed, but for a state which had borrowed over thirteen million dollars in both permanent and temporary loans at rising interest rates during the preceding three years, the measure was clearly inadequate. There is evidence to indicate that it was enacted mainly for the propagandistic purpose of fortifying faith in state credit. *Pa. Laws, 1830–31*, pp. 206–209; Hammond, *Financial Affairs of Pa.*

thirties by extracting vast financial concessions in return for chartering the Second Bank and by utilizing its share of the surplus revenue.[64] The failure of the United States Bank led to a collapse of state credit; [65] in 1842 certificates were issued to meet public interest payments, and a vigorous tax program was finally initiated.[66] The finances of local governments rather than those of the state were mainly involved in the speculative movement and panic of the fifties which in Pennsylvania, as elsewhere, was related to the freezing of circulating capital in railroad projects. Though a legislative committee reported in 1858 that conditions were "sad to contemplate," the crisis of that time was of relatively short duration.[67]

The ideological effect of the speculative movements is an imponderable thing, though when viewed against the comparatively quiet background of the colonial era its reality can scarcely be denied. "A young man who went to any of our large cities penniless," wrote a contributor to the *Christian Review* concerning the boom of the thirties, "was considered a blockhead if he did not report himself worth one or two hundred thousand dollars in a few years." [68] Yet it is in the reaction which the boom mentality

[64] *Pa. Laws, 1835–36*, pp. 36–47; Bourne, *Surplus Revenue of 1837*, pp. 99–103; cf. Trotter, *Financial Position of States with Public Debts*, p. 171.

[65] Abroad the 5 per cent stocks of the state, which had sold for 115 in 1833, would not sell at all in 1839. *Hunt's Merchants' Mag.*, XX (1849), 260.

[66] *Pa. Laws, 1842*, p. 486; *Niles Register*, LX (1841), 212. In 1844 a tax measure was enacted which included levies on all personal incomes save those of farmers, and a board of revenue commissioners was created to make systematic triennial assessments. *Pa. Laws, 1844*, pp. 497–503; Snyder, *Taxation in Pa.*, pp. 12–13. A sinking fund for the liquidation of debt was established in 1849 and was embodied in the state constitution in 1857. — *Legislative Documents, 1852*, pp. 758 ff.; *1857*, pp. 606 ff.; *Constitutions of Pa.*, pp. 166–67.

[67] *House Journal, 1858*, p. 45; *Hunt's Merchants' Mag.*, XXXVIII (1858), 148–50; *Pa. Archives*, 4th, VII, 741; Van Vleck, *Panic of 1857*, pp. 105–106.

[68] Quoted by Worthington, *Finances of Pa.*, pp. 39–40. Cf. *Pa. Archives*, 4th, VII, 342; Pennsylvania, *Proceedings and Debates of the Convention of 1837–38*, III, 50. The fourteen closely-packed volumes of Proceedings and Debates of the Constitutional Convention of 1837–38, together with two volumes of Journals, comprise one of the most elaborate records of its kind during our period in American history, and represent a basic source for the study of fundamental political ideas in Pennsylvania. The Convention, consisting of 133 delegates selected on the basis of senatorial and legislative representation, provided an opportunity for the full expression of a diversity of viewpoints. The *Proceedings and Debates* will hereafter be cited as *Convention Proceedings*.

evoked that perhaps its greatest doctrinal contribution is to be found. Pennsylvanians were deeply humiliated over the breakdown of public credit. Abroad, where bondholders of thirteen countries held some two-thirds of the Keystone debt, the name of the state became a convenient synonym for blighted faith.[69] "Every foreign poetaster, scribbler, and smatterer," wrote a commentator in *Hunt's Merchants' Magazine* in 1849, "sneers at American slavery and Pennsylvania repudiation."[70] If Wordsworth's sonnet "To the Pennsylvanians," did not rank with the best of his creations, the well-known letters of the Rev. Sidney Smith must surely be given a place among the most cutting polemics of the period.[71] They did more to inspire a sense of state pride than volumes of Philadelphia's commercial literature on the true-hearted Pennsylvanian. An editorial writer in the Philadelphia *Press* did not choose his words very well, but his point was clear enough: "There is a sensitive feeling among our people against this charge of Repudiation which amounts almost to intensity."[72] Governor Porter, under whose leadership the credit of the state was restored, settled into history as the acknowledged prophet of a new ideology in which the concepts of state honor, contract morality, and puritanic self-denial were mingled.[73]

The reaction which followed in the wake of private speculation was not dissimilar. Every business recession witnessed its ordeal of spiritual purification; the speculative life was vigorously renounced and respect was paid to the maxims of "morality" which had been violated during the frenzy of the previous time.[74] But this reaction rarely gave birth to anything in the nature of a

---

[69] Cf. McGrane, *Foreign Bondholders*, pp. 62–68; D. Dewey, *Financial History of U.S.*, p. 244; Worthington, *Finances of Pa.*, pp. 59–60.

[70] *Hunt's Merchants' Mag.*, XX (1849), 256.

[71] "I never meet a Pennsylvanian at a London dinner," wrote Smith to the *London Chronicle*, "without feeling a disposition to seize and divide him. . . . How such a man can set himself down at an English table without feeling that he owes two or three pounds to every man in the company, I am at a loss to concede; he has no more right to eat with honest men than a leper has to eat with clean men. . . ." Quoted by McGrane, *Foreign Bondholders*, p. 59.

[72] Philadelphia *Press*, Sept. 1, 1857. Cf. Tyson, *Commerce of Philadelphia*, pp. 8–9, 14; *Doylestown Democrat*, Aug. 18, 1847.

[73] Cf. McClure, *Old Time Notes of Pa.*, I, 36; Armor, *Governors of Pa.*, p. 388.

[74] See *Pa. Archives*, 4th, VI, 268; *infra*, p. 78.

medieval attack on the spirit of avarice; it rarely produced a fundamental negation of the acquisitive drive which had motivated the boomtime conduct. It was usually directed at the uses to which that drive was put; it called for its discipline in the service of solid, productive objectives; it posited labor and thrift as the only routes to wealth. Thus the Philadelphia *North American* in a very penetrating essay published during the crisis of 1857 in which it remarked, rather sadly, that "there is something in the American character or organization which gives a peculiar intensity to all our feelings and actions," coined the concept of "legitimate business" as a guide for popular conduct.[75] And the *Ledger*, defending the principle of "honest toil" as against the principle of "lucky chance," concluded that "a course of lectures on the Philosophy of Business, by some competent person, would do more good to the great body of our citizens than probably upon any other subject."[76] In a word, the hero who usually emerged from the anti-boom philosophy was not St. Simeon but Poor Richard.

This leads us to a final observation. Over our period, as has often been pointed out, the acquisitive ideal attained a higher place in the hierarchy of social norms. It is true that business publicists like Tyson and Freedley were still a step or two from embracing the survivalist doctrine of a later age. Freedley could not conclude a classic argument to the effect that ". . . to get money" is a "religious duty" without reference to three limitations on the acquisitive passion: the rules of civilization, the moral law, and the discountenance of honorable men.[77] In developing his theory of regional competition, Tyson was compelled to brand that shortsighted self-interest which discouraged communal action as "a degrading and ignoble passion, the attribute of native meanness, or the mark of a man without a soul."[78] It is true also that each panic found the corporate captain cast in the villain's role, absorbing popular passions when they were not turned inward along lines of puritanic self-criticism. It is impossible to read the

[75] *North American*, June 20, 1857.
[76] *Public Ledger*, Mar. 16, 1857. Cf. Rezneck, "Depression and American Opinion, 1857–1859," *Jour. of Econ. Hist.*, II (1942), 6–7.
[77] Freedley, *Treatise on Business*, pp. 31, 60–61.
[78] Tyson, *Commerce of Philadelphia*, p. 60.

literature without observing how vital a part the attack on the banking "aristocrat" in 1819 and 1837 and on the railroad capitalist in 1857 played in the reaction pattern of those periods.[79] Yet in the end the new men of business won more glory than they lost. Not only, for all of their waste and fraud, were their results impressive, but they were the evidence of reality for a multitude of individual aspirations: "There was not a man who did not speak like a Croesus," wrote Joseph C. Neal, describing the Pottsville coal boom of 1829," . . . even your ragged rascal could talk of his hundreds of thousands." [80]

Some indication of the growing symbolic importance of the entrepreneur is to be found perhaps in the flood of panegyric which in 1832 followed the death of Stephen Girard, a public benefactor who, as the records showed, had persistently violated the banking laws of the state.[81] Within the space of two years Stephen Simpson of Philadelphia was able to publish not only a leading textbook for the labor movement [82] but also a biography of Girard which was as intense in its eulogy as anything emanating from the most conservative portions of the press.[83]

4. Constitutions, Parties, and Political Thought

Significant change characterized the political setting of the period as well as the economic. The conservative drift which led to constitutional alterations in 1790 involved also ratification of the federal Constitution and the supremacy of the Federalist party.[84] With the collapse of the Federalists, however, the Democratic party became practically the only party in the state. "When I say parties," remarked a Pennsylvanian in 1820, "I mean a division in the democratic ranks." [85] An effective anti-Democratic opposition did not appear until 1835 when Jackson's attack upon

---

[79] See *Senate Journal, 1819-20*, p. 223; *Convention Proceedings*, VI, 28, 35 ff.; *North American*, Oct. 23, 1857; *infra*, p. 58.
[80] Quoted, Freedley, *Philadelphia Manufactures*, p. 81.
[81] Cf. *House Journal*, 1822-23, p. 621.
[82] Cf. *infra*, p. 195.
[83] *Stephen Girard*. Cf. Schlesinger, *Age of Jackson*, pp. 201-202.
[84] Cf. Brunhouse, *Counter-Revolution in Pennsylvania*, pp. 191-229; Ferguson, *Early Western Pa. Politics*, pp. 101 ff.
[85] Quoted, Klein, *Pa. Politics*, p. 71.

the Second Bank split the Democratic party, and a newly arisen coalition of Whigs and Anti-Masons won control of the state government.[86] This coalition was also strong in the Constitutional Convention of 1837–1838 which, transferring a number of offices from the appointive to the elective category, reduced the large patronage put at the disposal of the governor by the Convention of 1790.[87] But the eclipse of the Democrats was momentary. With the deterioration of the Anti-Masonic movement, leadership of the opposition fell into the hands of the Whigs, and alone they could not destroy the supremacy of a reunified Democratic party under the guidance of such astute politicians as James Buchanan. In 1839 the Democrats returned to power and, save for two brief periods thereafter, they remained in control of the state until the Civil War.[88]

Party organization in Pennsylvania was weakened by three factors which were mainly responsible for the state's failure to establish a clear-cut party division until the thirties.[89] One of these was a vigorous sectionalism whose economic basis I have already discussed. It was enhanced by the geographic barrier of the Alleghenies, by inevitable psychological differences between the older civilization of the southeast and the more newly settled regions of the state, and by the concentration of German elements in the former and Scotch-Irish in the latter. Another obstacle to effective party organization, one especially important prior to the reduction of gubernatorial patronage in 1837–1838, was the difficult position of the only man who could provide effective party leadership — the governor. Fearful of his constitutional prerogatives, party leaders hesitated to nominate effective men for the executive office. Factional criticism of gubernatorial appointments was strong and local bossism flourished.[90] A third factor

---

[86] Mueller, *Whig Party in Pa.*, p. 22. For the Democratic split on the bank question, see also Martin and Shenk, *Pa. History Told by Contemporaries*, pp. 549–50; Meigs, *Charles Jared Ingersoll*, p. 186; Schlesinger, *Age of Jackson*, p. 203; for the Anti-Masonic Party, Geary, *Third Parties in Pa., 1840–60*, pp. 1–25.

[87] Mueller, *Whig Party in Pa.*, p. 34; *Convention Proceedings*, III, 179 ff.

[88] Dunaway, *History of Pa.*, pp. 438–90.

[89] In the analysis of party development to follow, I have drawn on the penetrating interpretation of Klein, *Pa. Politics*, pp. 353–68.

[90] *Ibid.*, pp. 25–26.

went deeper: there was comparatively little conflict in the state over the large objectives of public policy, especially over those which were of party significance on the national plane and which could solidify competing state organizations on established lines. The inception of a state system of public works, though it generated a minor fear of national competition, did not shake the faith of the vast majority of Pennsylvanians in the need for a federal system as well. I have already commented upon the unanimity of pro-tariff sentiment, especially after the depression that began in 1815. And in so far as the issue of the Second Bank was concerned, an issue which did much to re-establish party conflict on a national basis at an earlier time in other states, it was not until Jackson's attack of 1832 that an appreciable division of opinion appeared. Largely because of pride in the bank's establishment in Philadelphia there was a favorable attitude toward it.[91]

Yet this set of biases was thoroughly in line with the Hamiltonian-Whig tradition. Why, then, was the Democratic party practically the only party in the state prior to 1832 and after that time the party with unquestionably the largest support? While the answer to this question is partially to be found in a deterioration of the quality of conservative leadership after the age of Wilson, Morris, and Rush, due in part to the expanding opportunities of business enterprise, the most acute students of Pennsylvania history agree that Democratic supremacy is to be explained largely in ideological terms. It was supported by the evocative power of certain dogmas which reversed the party allegiance which a simple economic determinism would have dictated for the state, a power deriving in large measure from the early inception of virtual manhood suffrage.[92] The mass base of political

[91] Prior to Jackson's attack on the bank, Pennsylvania was considered the "stronghold" of that institution. Catterall, *Second Bank of U.S.*, p. 65.

[92] The constitution of 1790 provided for a tax qualification for voting, but since no general state tax was levied at that time or for several decades thereafter, this provision was usually met by paying small property or road taxes levied by counties. Virtual manhood suffrage was thus secured some forty years before such action was taken in many other states. *Constitutions of Pa.*, p. 197; Klein, *Pa. Politics*, p. 34; *Hazard's Register*, XIII (1834), 97. An effort was made in the Constitutional Convention of 1837 to abolish the tax qualification, but owing largely to the innocuous character of the requirement, it failed. *Convention Proceedings*, III, 113–34; Bartlett, *Pa. Politics in Jacksonian Period*, pp. 126–29.

life in Pennsylvania meant that equalitarian slogans always had a profound, even mystical appeal there. The vaguest atmosphere of aristocracy was a decisive political handicap, and with the emergence of Jackson the state found a symbol behind which its passion for the commoner was unified with a vengeance. The sheer force of this passion, coupled, to be sure, with a sufficient vagueness in Democratic platforms on crucial issues, made it possible for Democratic politicians to sell their party to the state on the very issues of the tariff, internal improvements, and, prior to 1832, the Second Bank. It was a passion which, as Philip Klein has said, put "an end to rational thinking"; [93] it involved a worship of Jackson which Malcolm Eiselen has properly depicted as a "mad infatuation." [94]

The historian of the Whig party in Pennsylvania recognizes that the weakness of the party was traceable mainly to a vague aristocratic reputation which it had, not to the specific points in its program.[95] The Whigs themselves knew this. They tried to steal their opponents' equalitarian thunder by branding the Jacksonian administration itself as "Federalist" — an epithet which, as Joseph Hopkinson bitterly said, was sufficient by itself to ruin political careers [96] — and by claiming to be the true party of Jeffer-

[93] Klein, *Pa. Politics*, p. 360.
[94] Eiselen, *Pa. Protectionism*, p. 270.
[95] Mueller, *Whig Party in Pa.*, pp. 245–46. There was a general tendency for the wealthier of all occupations and regions to gravitate toward the opposition to the Democratic party, but generalizations attaching a hard-and-fast economic or occupational character to the party alignment of the later period are dangerous. An analysis of the membership of the Convention of 1837 reveals no significant differences between the occupational affiliations of the Democrats and those of their opponents. The *United States Gazette* presented the following statistics (cited in Mueller, *Whig Party in Pa.*, p. 34):

	Democrats	Opposition
Farmers	27	29
Lawyers	16	24
Physicians	6	4
Merchants	4	5
Manufacturers	3	3
Surveyors	4	0
Artisans	5	1
Editors	0	1
Gentlemen	1	0
Total	66	67

[96] *Convention Proceedings*, IV, 305. Cf. Konkle, *Joseph Hopkinson*, pp. 175 ff.

son. But this strategy, save in 1840 when the Whigs capitalized on the appeal of Harrison, was of limited value. It was the Democratic party which cashed in most heavily on the spell that was cast by the equalitarian slogans.

An ideology so influential calls for further analysis. In strict theoretical terms the concept around which it revolved was the concept of natural law. That idea was impaled on the first page of the constitution of 1776 and it stayed there despite all subsequent changes. But what persistent references to the "law of nature" and to "natural right" actually meant to Pennsylvanians in the nineteenth century it is hard to say. As often as not the Lockean apparatus which began with a state of nature and proceeded through contract to government was taken for granted; primary emphasis was placed upon the perfection of related concepts. The most significant of these was the idea of popular sovereignty which, appearing in the theory of "community" developed in the Revolutionary constitution,[97] reached its fullest stage of development in the early years of the nineteenth century when a new conception of the "will of the people" began to take shape — one of those slogans of "magical power" of which Klein has written so acutely in his study of that period. Only rare spirits, die-hard exponents of the old Philadelphia Federalism like Hopkinson or a forthright Democratic politician like James Porter, had the courage to challenge it. In the Constitutional Convention of 1837 Hopkinson shouted: *"The will of the people of Pennsylvania!* Who could put himself in opposition to it? But this cry has been repeated so often; it has come forth on such petty questions and occasions, that it has lost its potency; it has, indeed, if I may say so, become almost ridiculous." [98]

Strategically this line of criticism was futile. The new symbolism of the popular will was not to be demolished by challenging

---

[97] *Constitutions of Pa.*, p. 231.
[98] *Convention Proceedings*, IV, 304. Porter declared: "It has been . . . 'the people,' 'the people,' 'the people,' 'the people,' with scarcely words enough between, to connect them together. I am tired of this unceasing and nauseating repetition. If we are to have nothing but Paddy Carey played to us, in the name of goodness let us have it with some variations." *Ibid.*, III, 415.

the precision of its meaning, nor was its strength impaired by the looseness with which it was used. For one of the sources of its appeal lay precisely in the fact that no one clearly knew what it meant, and when this can be said of an idea, the politician who would destroy it is wasting his time by insisting on logical perfection. We are accustomed to emphasize pragmatic elements in the American doctrinal tradition; we tend to neglect the sweeping intuitions which it also contains. After a study of the literature of this period the conclusion is inescapable that the "people" had become, in a real sense, a mystical entity in the popular consciousness. The analytic ground of the assailants of the concept was as strong as their strategic ground was weak: it is easy to sympathize with Thomas Biddle when he confessed that he was "at a loss" to understand what the idea meant.[99] For the unified, morally infallible entity which the age somehow visualized as the popular will, which spoke in decisive positive and negative tones, was mainly myth. If such an entity has ever existed in politics, surely it did not reside in the Pennsylvania of this period. Where was it to be found amid deep-rooted sectional conflicts? Amid the factional struggles of a highly decentralized party system? Amid the growing complexity of the pressure-group pattern after the inception of the railroad age? Political reality may have involved a basis of underlying general agreement, but on top of that was not a single transcendent popular will but a flourishing plurality of separate, partial, and perennially conflicting wills. The Will of the People had no more reality in a political sense than Philadelphia's "true-hearted Pennsylvanian" had in an economic sense.

This gap between myth and fact had significant repercussions. For the prevalence of a transcendent concept of the popular will served inevitably to discredit the real popular will as it actually found expression in the politics of the time. The political parties, sectional pressures, and interest-group activities out of which public policy necessarily emerged bore on their face the evidence of partial interests which they were intended to serve. They were bound to appear rather bleak when set alongside an all-embracing entity like the Will of the People. Thus a familiar dualism in

[99] *Ibid.*, III, 382.

American thought: though the party system enlisted the fervent energies of the people, they viewed it as a pernicious institution and its "politicians" as men of suspect employment. The politicians themselves did not hesitate to cash in on their own disrepute. In the Convention of 1837, where caucus control and political barter of the Thaddeus Stevens variety were dominant procedures,[100] fierce assaults upon "the spirit of party"[101] were commonplace. The theoretical mechanism involved here was sharply illuminated by one of Hopkinson's contemptuous remarks: that a "search into this humble devotion to the people" revealed that it was "neither more nor less than a devotion to a party. . . ."[102] If it was bad strategy to challenge the Will of the People head-on, it was always good strategy to argue that men like your opponents could never represent so glorious a thing.

Sectional aggrandizement faced a greater ideological obstacle in the concept of a transcendent popular will than it faced in the concept of a unified state economic interest. Sectionalism in the legislature was branded as "public or local corruption"[103] and the omnibus charter bills which implemented it were, after heavy criticism, explicitly abolished by the Constitutional Convention of 1837.[104] One member dared to suggest that "man is imperfect"[105] and might always be wedded to sectional interest, but the environment was hostile to his realism. The lobby technique was discredited beyond doctrinal salvation.[106] A minor effort was made in the fifties to justify the Pennsylvania Railroad lobbyists on the ground that they performed a necessary informational service for the legislature,[107] but it was a miserable failure. Especially after

[100] Cf. Bartlett, *Pa. Politics in Jacksonian Period*, p. 120.

[101] George Woodward of Luzerne perceived this paradox which was rarely examined objectively: "But what have we listened to . . . but appeals from principle to party, and from whom do they come, but from those who, of all others, have been the most clamorous in their denunciations of party." *Convention Proceedings*, II, 387. See also *ibid.*, II, 590; *Hazard's Register*, XVI (1834), 167–68; *North American*, Oct. 24, 1857.

[102] *Convention Proceedings*, IV, 305.

[103] *Ibid.*, XIV, 16.

[104] Article I, Section 25, of the constitution of 1838 provided: "No law hereafter enacted shall create, renew, or extend the charter of more than one corporation." *Constitutions of Pa.*, p. 146.

[105] *Convention Proceedings*, IX, 33.

[106] Cf. *ibid.*, VI, 92.   [107] *Legislative Record, 1857*, No. 82, p. 6.

the work of Biddle's lobbies in obtaining a state charter for the Second Bank in 1835, the "borer," "middle-house-men," and "lobby-member" concepts [108] ranked among the blackest in the whole political literature.

Equipped with this analysis, we are better able to understand another significant ideological manifestation of the period: why its thinking was extremely reluctant to institutionalize the concept of the popular will. The real procedures by which political institutions operated were in permanent conflict with the impossible standards which that concept posed. Neither the legislature nor even a constituent convention was definitely accepted as the people's true agent. This problem was excellently highlighted in 1825 when a proposal for convention was voted down in a plebiscite mainly on the ground that its powers had not been sufficiently circumscribed.[109] What was most striking about this situation, however, was not the state's distrust of the convention technique, but the manner in which the original movement for a plebiscite was opposed. A legislative committee solemnly declared that "all power is inherent in the people" and thence proceeded to the conclusion that "the measure for a call of a Convention . . . should originate with the people themselves, and not with their representatives, whose powers are limited and defined." [110] But this was a question, not of a convention, but of a plebiscite to decide whether one should be called. Who had the power to make such an initial move unless the legislature did? If the legislature did not represent the "people themselves" enough to do even this, how was that fabulous entity ever to express itself? The opponents of the plebiscite were clearly worshiping a people which had no real political existence. The only solution to the problem they posed was, conceivably, some extra-legal outpouring of the popular mind. Not only was this a fantastic expectation, but all known extra-legal techniques labored, as I have already demonstrated, under discredit as a result of the ideology of the popular will itself.

[108] See *Convention Proceedings*, V, 575; VI, 92; *Legislative Record, 1857*, No. 77, p. 6; No. 95, p. 1; *Public Ledger*, June 4, 1857.
[109] Cf. Akagi, "Pa. Constitution of 1838," *Pa. Mag. of Hist. and Biog.*, XLVIII (1924), 307. [110] Quoted in *ibid.*, p. 306.

Yet the relative prestige enjoyed by each of the three branches of government was at least partially determined by its symbolic proximity to the Will of the People. This was illustrated in national politics by the growth of presidential power during the time in which Jackson was visualized as the personal embodiment of that idea. But however vigorously Pennsylvania joined in the worship of Jackson, it is evident that the dogma of the popular will operated in a curiously different way in state politics: there it called for a curtailment of executive authority. Joseph M. Doran of Philadelphia County, one of the outstanding Jacksonians in the state, announced in the Convention of 1837 that the assembly had been called "for the express purpose of depriving the Executive of a considerable portion of his enormous power." [111] Yet if the work of this convention reflected the unwillingness of the state to embody its conception of the popular will in the governor, it also revealed an unwillingness to embody it either in the legislative or judicial spheres of government. Most of the power of which it deprived the governor it granted directly to the people through the expansion of the category of elective offices.

There were unchallengeable limits to the workability of the elective principle. Even if one did not share the fear of some that a multiplicity of elections would lead to a dangerous "weariness and disgust" [112] among voters, a line had to be drawn somewhere. It is hard not to conclude that the most meaningful contribution to the solution of this problem in the Convention of 1837 was made by a conservative faction of the Whig-Anti-Masonic coalition. The ideas presented by John Sergeant, the Whig president of the convention, are illustrative of the faction's point of view. Sergeant insisted on a basic distinction between "political" and "civil" offices, arguing that the elective principle should govern in the first category while the appointive principle should govern in the second. Civil offices, he maintained, called for special qualifications of which the general public could not be an adequate judge. Confronted with the reform emphasis upon popular sovereignty and the social contract, Sergeant pulled out of nowhere a fundamental contract of his own — a contract of only incidental political

[111] *Convention Proceedings*, III, 390.   [112] *Ibid.*, III, 512.

significance — in which civil servants implicitly guaranteed to society a brand of effective work which could not be achieved save by their selection on an appointment basis.[113]

But the issue was hopelessly confused by the appearance of the Will of the People. Nor did Sergeant's effort to link up his position with Lockean doctrine do much to allay its impact. Every effort to fashion a doctrinal category for the non-elected expert was interpreted as an insult to the popular sovereign and as a threat to free institutions. "To say that the people are incompetent," declared Thomas Earle, "would be to establish the monarchical principle that the people are unfit to govern, and we ought then to reform the Constitution by establishing a monarchy." [114] Closely related to such reasoning was the emergence of the rotation-in-office concept as a "sacred" [115] idea in democratic thought. In the Convention of 1837 this concept made its most significant appearance in connection with a drive to impose a constitutional limit of two terms on the gubernatorial office, but it was also a source of controversy with respect to minor offices as well. Continuous occupation of office was branded as a principle of tyranny and inefficiency. Tyranny was possible because steady office holders were "leagued, active, and organized," possessing control over propaganda and party machinery. Inefficiency was traceable to "slackness" which appeared when a man had remained too long in office.[116]

A comparison of the business and political ideologies selected for discussion here, as they evolved independently, suggests significant trends. One of these is to be seen in attitudes toward the qualifications for success in business as compared with governmental enterprise. In this connection one's first impulse might be to draw a striking contrast between the concept of an amateur political intelligence as revealed in rotation doctrine and other phases of democratic theory, and the concept of specialized busi-

---

[113] *Ibid.*, III, 385, 386. A similar theory was put forth by Ezra S. Hayhurst of Columbia County. *Ibid.*, III, 375.
[114] *Ibid.*, III, 560.
[115] Harrisburg *Democratic Union*, June 18, 1845.
[116] *Convention Proceedings*, III, 204, 400, 401, 411, 412.

ness knowledge as developed by such men as Freedley, Tyson, and the editorial writers of the *Ledger*. The contrast is important, but it must not be drawn too simply. The ideology of money-making was not without its own peculiar democratic faith in the amateur, as the boom psychology reveals; nor was the theory of government wholly without some understanding of the function of the expert, as the ideas of Sergeant and others whom we shall later encounter show. The question is one of the tenacity with which these biases got hold of thinking, the areas of activity to which they were extended, and the different frames of reference which prevailed in the political and business fields. Political thought, not inexplicably in light of the general triumph of democratic ideals, was gradually overwhelmed by an exaggerated belief in rotation and the joyous acceptance of inexperience, and even specialized administrative personnel were not exempted from the impact of these attitudes. Business thought, quite apart from the conscious ideologists of a new business science, was never overwhelmed in such a way, despite the mass faith in opportunities for sudden wealth which, largely because of the growth of corporate operations, began to appear during our era. In the halcyon world of the fifties it may have been believed that anyone could win a fortune by investing in railroad securities, but it was not believed that the mandates of natural law required the annual election of locomotive engineers.

A remarkable self-consciousness concerning their divergent attitudes toward business and governmental enterprise was shown by the debaters in the Constitutional Convention of 1837. There Sergeant, in an attack on the application of the elective and rotation principles to minor administrative offices, referred for support to the procedures of business life. "Suppose that a man having a large estate, were to establish a registry and recorders' office for himself, and employ a man to conduct it for him, his functions would be the same, and the duties of his office the same as of the public officer. Would he establish rotation? Did you ever hear of a man fixing a time when he would discharge a useful agent, and that, too, with a certainty that he could not get a better?" [117] Earle

[117] *Ibid.*, III, 387.

replied that the length of service to which the appointment system led was itself a departure from business practice. "Do we employ a journeyman, or a mechanic, or a laborer, for a long term of years? No man in this Convention, or in the State, would do it." But Earle's heaviest reliance was placed on the democratic doctrine discussed above; the requirements which it set down, he argued, sharply separated the political from the business fields.[118]

If conceptions of business and political competence were evolving along different lines, a contrast is also to be seen in the nature of the respective symbolic positions which the politician and the economic entrepreneur were destined to attain before the close of our period. The gradual expansion of the prestige of the business captain which I commented upon earlier appeared simultaneously with a secular decline in the prestige of the politician. It is erroneous, however, to interpret this contrast as deriving inherently from differing views of business and political qualifications. As much booming optimism was marshaled behind the notion of an amateur political intelligence as was marshaled behind the notion of a specialized business science: if Freedley could envision an economic millennium once the rules of enterprise were mastered, Doran could envision a political millennium once the Will of the People was given full expression.[119] Yet if both dreams shared rather pathetically the excessive ebullience of the time, it is clear that Doran's was by far the more futile of the two. And that for a pair of reasons. The popular will which he worshiped was, from the outset, a politically unreal thing. Its unreality served, as I have already suggested, to disparage the very governmental machinery that it could have strengthened, served to make an object of criticism the very politician whose prestige it could have bolstered. This much at least could be said of Freedley's hope: the hot-blast principle was not an ideal laid up in heaven; if its mastery did not bring economic salvation, it at any rate visibly increased the production of iron.

Doran's vision was the falser of the two for another reason. Not only did all institutional efforts to lend expression to the Will of

[118] *Ibid.*, III, 411 ff.
[119] *Ibid.*, III, 390 ff.

the People become enmeshed in party, sectional, and interest-group mechanics and thus become discredited by the very ideal they sought to serve, but many such efforts were designed in fact, as Sergeant warned, not to improve governmental action but to make it worse. However excellent the principles of rotation or election may have been as applied to legislative, gubernatorial, or even judicial offices, they clearly had serious shortcomings in the administrative field. The offices of auditor-general and state treasurer were thrown into the electoral whirlpool, but after a long period of rotating personnel in these positions, a Senate committee had acquired a good deal of evidence to prove its contention that ". . . by the present mode of doing business, the condition of the public claims and collections can never be known." [120] It was in the realm of administration, more clearly than anywhere else, that the age was misled by the glamour of its democratic dreams.

[120] *Legislative Record*, *1857*, No. 32, p. 1.

PART TWO

THE STATE AS PROMOTER AND ENTREPRENEUR

II

THE CORPORATION

1. The Pattern of Charter Policy

IN AN environment of economic change such as that which prevailed between the Revolution and the Civil War the ancient promotional role of the state could scarcely be liquidated. The growth of protectionism was not the only evidence of the failure of Franklin's free-trade theory. The government of Pennsylvania was faced by movements for promotional action to which it had to respond. The ideological ancestry of these movements lay in the colonial doctrines I have already examined, and it is this bond of historic continuity which largely accounts for the fact that the promotional idea was rarely justified at length in philosophic terms. The literature is filled, to be sure, with myriad references to such concepts as "the fostering hand of the state"; the promotional principle had a well-established niche in gubernatorial messages and official documents.[1] But the measure of its continuing significance is not to be elucidated by a cataloguing of these hackneyed pronouncements. It is to be grasped by an examination of the public policies for which it served in considerable measure as an implicit rationalization and by an examination of the controversies they engendered.

Economically the most important among them was the policy of chartering business corporations.[2] While the legal basis of the corporate form extends back in Anglo-American history to the sixteenth century, only one incorporation for business purposes is on the Pennsylvania records for the entire colonial epoch: The Philadelphia Contributionship for the Insuring of Houses from Loss by Fire, chartered in 1768.[3] The small-scale character of

---

[1] Cf. *House Journal, 1809*, p. 519; *1803*, p. 519; *1823–24*, p. 598; *Pa. Archives*, 4th, IV, 6; V, 150, 864; VII, 516, 788; *Legislative Record, 1857*, No. 77, p. 6.

[2] For detailed analysis of the development of charter provisions in Pennsylvania, see *infra*, pp. 254 ff.

[3] Davis, *Earlier American Corporations*, II, 234 ff. Cf. Blandi, *Maryland Business Corporations, 1783–1852*, pp. 9–10.

colonial enterprise, the localization of business relations as a result of poor means of communication, limited supplies of capital and labor — these factors, as Davis has pointed out, discouraged the exploitation of the corporate instrument for economic purposes prior to the Revolution.[4] After that time, however, charter policy gradually established itself as one of the primary concerns of American state governments and expanded steadily throughout the pre-Civil War epoch. Between 1790 and 1860, apart from incorporations under general laws, the Pennsylvania legislature granted 2,333 charters for business purposes. A surface view of the expansion of charter policy in the state is presented in the graph on the following page.

Well over half of the business charters granted by special act of the legislature from 1790 to 1860 were concerned with transportation. This emphasis is brought out clearly in the statistics below.[5]

TABLE I

CORPORATE CHARTERS FOR BUSINESS PURPOSES BY
SPECIAL ACT, 1790–1860

Type	Number	Per Cent of Total
Transportation	1,497	64.17
Banks, etc.	168	7.20
Insurance	260	11.14
Manufacturing, etc.	180	7.72
Water	65	2.79
Gas	75	3.21
Miscellaneous	88	3.77
Total	2,333	100.00

Statistics of direct legislative charter grants provide a fairly accurate view of trends in charter policy during this period, de-

[4] Davis, *Earlier American Corporations*, II, 5–6.

[5] Here and in the following graph I have utilized the pioneer statistical research and classification of W. Miller, "Business Corporations in Pa., 1800–60," *Quarterly Jour. of Econ.*, LV (1940–41), 150–60. For the period 1790–1800 I have utilized the Communication of the Secretary of the Commonwealth to the Constitutional Convention, June 29, 1837, listing all acts of incorporation passed by the legislature since 1776, in Pennsylvania, *Journal of State Convention, 1837–38*, I, 339–496. Miller's classification "Miscellaneous" includes seventeen different kinds of business

spite the enactment of certain general incorporation measures which endowed executive officers or courts with chartering authority. Those measures were of limited scope. It was not until 1874 that a general measure covering virtually all types of business corporations was enacted.[6] As early as 1791, to be sure, a general law for literary, charitable, and religious corporations was passed [7]

CHART I.

SPECIAL CHARTERS ISSUED TO BUSINESS ENTERPRISES BY PENNSYLVANIA, ANNUALLY, 1790–1860.

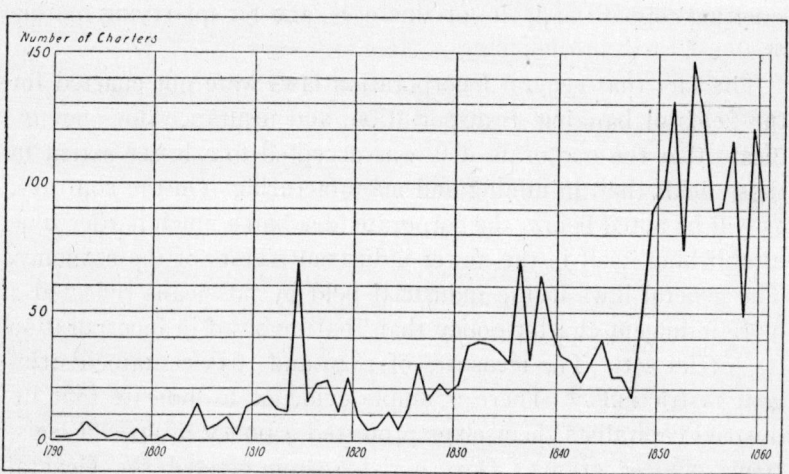

and later extended to include beneficial associations and fire-engine companies.[8] But in the economic field general incorporation measures did not begin to appear until the third decade of the nineteenth century. All of them reflected the rise of manufacturing and mining to a prominent position in the economy of the state.

---

as follows: market companies, 29; telegraph companies, 10; hotel companies, 10; mineral spring companies, 8; meadow companies, 8; boom companies, 5; commercial companies, 3; land companies, 2; ice companies, 2; warehouse companies, 2; guano companies, 2; fur company, 1; salvaging company, 1; street sweeping company, 1; health institute, 1; amusement grounds company, 1; butchers and drovers association, 1. W. Miller in *Quarterly Jour. of Econ.*, LV (1940–41), 154.

[6] *Pa. Laws, 1874*, pp. 74–107.
[7] *Statutes at Large*, XIV, 50. Cf. *House Journal, 1806*, p. 49.
[8] *Pa. Archives*, 4th, VII, 853–56.

A growing recognition of the potentialities of the anthracite trade was mirrored in an enactment of 1836 for the incorporation of companies for the manufacture of iron with coke or mineral coal.[9] In 1849 a general law "to encourage manufacturing operations" provided for the incorporation of companies manufacturing woolen, cotton, flax, or silk goods, iron, paper, lumber, or salt.[10] This measure was extended in 1850 to companies manufacturing glass,[11] in 1851 to companies manufacturing salt goods and to printing and publishing firms.[12] Two years later it was further extended to include companies formed for mining coal, mining and smelting copper, lead, tin, or zinc ores, and for quarrying marble or slate.[13]

The fact that general incorporation laws were not enacted for the fields of banking, transportation, and insurance does not indicate that the corporate idea was accepted to a lesser extent in those fields than in mining and manufacturing. On the contrary, as will be noted below, the corporate idea had a much harder time establishing itself in the newer industrial sectors of the economy. The general laws in the industrial field by no means reflected a more indulgent charter policy than that involved in incorporation by special acts. The measures of 1849 and 1853 contained stringent restrictions.[14] There is ample evidence to indicate that industrial capitalists themselves preferred a policy of special legislative charter grants. Governor Johnston greeted the General Manufacturing Act of 1849 with enthusiasm, predicting that it would lead to the early "erection of large establishments in many places,"[15] but five years after its enactment not a dozen companies had been incorporated under it.[16] In the four years follow-

[9] *Pa. Laws, 1835–36*, pp. 799–807; later amended to include charcoal, *ibid., 1853*, pp. 778–79. Cf. *Pa. Archives*, 4th, VII, 29.

[10] *Pa. Laws, 1849*, 563–69. Cf. *Hunt's Merchants' Mag.*, XXI (1849), 124; *Pa. Archives*, 4th, VI, 854–56.

[11] *Pa. Laws, 1850*, p. 627.

[12] *Ibid., 1851*, pp. 511–16.

[13] *Ibid., 1853*, pp. 269–70, 637–38. For other extensions of the measure, see *ibid., 1854*, pp. 215–16; *1856*, p. 7; *1859*, pp. 337–38; *1860*, pp. 343, 629. Cf. *House Journal, 1853*, II, 66 ff.; *1857*, p. 702.

[14] Cf. *infra*, p. 257.

[15] *Pa. Archives*, 4th, VII, 394.

[16] *Ibid.*, VII, 649.

ing the passage of the mining measure of 1853 only one application for a charter had been made under it and in that case operations had not commenced.[17] At the same time capitalists and promoters sought repeatedly to extract from the legislature special charters with more lenient provisions.[18]

When viewed in light of this evidence, the failure of the legislature to enact general laws for the incorporation of companies in the transportation, banking,[19] and insurance fields reflects in fact a more indulgent and flexible policy there. But that failure may be attributed partially also to a difference in the nature of the group conflicts in the two economic spheres. While single industrial charters were usually of limited, local import, individual charters in banking and transportation often involved major questions of sectional adjustment and public policy which seemed to call for direct legislative judgment. This distinction was formally recognized by the House committee of 1854 which recommended the extension of the provisions of the General Manufacturing Act of 1849 to mining industries: "Corporations of a local character, and which would not affect the interests of large sections of the State, or produce an injurious conflict of interest and feeling, may be safely entrusted to the courts; while those of a more general character, such as the incorporation of railroad companies, and other incorporations which might be named, should only be suffered to have an existence by the usual and solemn means from an act of Assembly." [20]

[17] *Ibid.*, VII, 649. The scant use made of the early general acts in the industrial field is probably the most relevant factor as regards the question raised by Miller of the "economic consequences" of the measures, and confirms the wisdom of his judgment that special-charter figures provide a substantially accurate picture of incorporation trends. See W. Miller in *Quarterly Jour. of Econ.*, LV (1940–41), 153, fn. 1.

[18] *Pa. Archives*, 4th, VII, 649.

[19] This generalization excepts a Free Banking Act passed in 1860. *Pa. Laws, 1860*, pp. 459–71. It is significant that this measure experienced the same type of rejection as that accorded the first general industrial incorporation measures of the period. Only nine banks were ever incorporated under its provisions, and within three years after its enactment only three such banks had been formed. Successful pressure to obtain special charters from the legislature not requiring the securing of circulation by deposit of government securities was the cause of this. Knox, *History of Banking in U.S.*, pp. 459–610.

[20] *House Journal, 1853*, II, 66. The report of this committee contains an excellent survey of previous general incorporation legislation.

Another reason for the limited reliance upon general incorporation laws during this period is to be found in a characteristic reluctance of the legislature to delegate authority in the economic field. In the charter program as elsewhere this attitude brought with it a fluctuating policy and an immense waste of legislative time. With a precipitous rise in the number of charter grants during the fifties the need for a more adequate system of general incorporation became acute. In 1858 Governor Packer warned the legislature, as some of his predecessors already had done, that "no reasonable industry" could flourish under a policy of special acts characterized by "great lack of consistency and principle."[21] It was the inadequacy of legislative action as well as the gradual broadening of the accepted economic sphere of incorporation which finally accounted for the general incorporation measure of 1874.

2. *The Idea of Sectional Interest*

One of the most important principles governing the evolution of charter policy was the principle of sectional aggrandizement. Why this factor should appear in extreme fashion in the charter field is partially explained by the high percentage of charters which were granted for transportation purposes. It was inevitable that the pattern of sectional commercial rivalries described in the previous chapter should be reflected perennially in alignments over charter grants. The historic triangle of Philadelphia, Baltimore, and the west offers a striking example of this. During the twenties Baltimore interests with the support of the Susquehanna counties pressed for the chartering of a Baltimore and Susquehanna Railroad Company which would enhance the river trade with Maryland. Their efforts were repeatedly frustrated by the work of Philadelphia representatives in the legislature.[22] During the for-

---

[21] *Pa. Archives*, 4th, VIII, 13–14. Cf. *ibid.*, VII, 714, 840–41. For a typical case, trace the legislative career of the charter of the Hazelton Coal Company: *Pa. Laws, 1835–36*, pp. 129–32; *1843*, pp. 140–41; *1840*, pp. 403–404; *1853*, pp. 28–29.

[22] Cf. *House Journal, 1828*, II, 542 ff.; M. Carey, *Internal Improvement of Pa.*, p. 31. During debates on legislative representation in the Convention of 1837, the fact that Philadelphia legislators "from year to year" had "united, as in a phalanx, against the project of the Baltimore and Susquehanna Railroad" was bitterly remarked upon by delegates from the Susquehanna counties. *Convention Proceedings*,

ties the struggle entered a more acute phase. Anxious to make itself the terminus of the Baltimore and Ohio, Pittsburgh, with the aid of the southwestern counties, had powerful lobbies at Harrisburg seeking to push through a charter grant for the Maryland project. Equally powerful lobbies were on hand representing Philadelphia which sought to frustrate the ambitions of the Baltimore and Ohio and extract instead a charter for the Pennsylvania Railroad.[23] A delicate compromise was the result. In 1846 the legislature granted a concession to the Baltimore and Ohio permitting it to extend its tracks from Cumberland to Pittsburgh, but this grant was to be void if the Pennsylvania Railroad should be initiated within a year.[24] It was the latter provision which largely accounted for the peculiar intensity of the stock subscription drive for the Pennsylvania, a drive which ended a year later with a gubernatorial declaration invalidating the Baltimore charter.[25] Subscriptions were canvassed from house to house, mass meetings were held, press support was widely utilized.[26]

This conflict also provides an extreme example of the ideology turned up by sectional rivalries in the charter field. So intense was the sectional feeling in the west in 1846 that there were repeated threats that if the Baltimore and Ohio were not given a right of way to Pittsburgh the western counties would secede from the state and form "a new trans-Alleghenian commonwealth."

II, 75–76. Thaddeus Stevens of Adams County declared: "It cannot be denied by any one, that no matter how the members of the city and county of Philadelphia stand as to democracy or aristocracy, no matter how hostile they may be on the question of party politics, the moment they come into the House of Representatives, and get officers elected, that moment you hear no more of party on any question in which the interests of that city are concerned, but they go fifteen votes in a solid phalanx, for every measure which will benefit Philadelphia in the least. *Ibid.*, II, 64.

[23] McClure, *Old Time Notes of Pa.*, I, 128 ff; J. Clark, Jr., "Railroad Struggle for Pittsburgh," *Pa. Mag. of Hist. and Biog.*, XLVIII (1924), 3–12; W. Wilson, *Pennsylvania Railroad*, I, 2–4; Armor, *Governors of Pa.*, pp. 417–19.

[24] *Pa. Laws, 1846*, pp. 448–53, 312–26. In order to nullify the Baltimore and Ohio right of way the Pennsylvania was compelled to attain a stock subscription of three million dollars and to have thirty miles or more of track under contract for construction by July 30, 1847. *Ibid.*, p. 449.

[25] *Pa. Archives*, 4th, VII, 189–92.

[26] See *Public Ledger*, Jan. 28, Feb. 4, May 7, Oct. 10, 12, 13, 15, Nov. 14, 19, 27, 1846; *Proceedings in Relation to Pennsylvania Railroad*, pp. 9, 14, 17; Philadelphia Committee of Seven, *Address*, p. 11; Cleveland and Powell, *Railroad Promotion and Capitalization*, p. 187; idem., *Railroad Finance*, p. 20; *infra*, pp. 105 ff.

The new state was to comprise twenty-two counties with McKean, Clearfield, Huntingdon, and Bedford on its eastern border.[27] Philadelphia publicists branded this talk as "The Pittsburgh Lunacy" and as "treason," and poured forth a stream of the state-pride ideology which had always been effective against the Baltimore and Susquehanna during the twenties. There was much blasting of "foreign corporations, foreign inducements, and foreign interests."[28] At Harrisburg a protagonist of the west declared that such language was fit only for "a confederacy of sharpers" and sought to mobilize national pride against state pride.[29] It will be observed at once that this ideological pattern amounts to nothing more than a duplication of the larger theory of sectional interest which we examined in the previous chapter. The matter of charter competition was so integral a part of that theory that the two cannot be separated. The only novel variant in the Philadelphia-Pittsburgh contest of 1846 was the introduction of the state-credit ideology. Eastern publicists sought to exploit anti-repudiation sensitivities by arguing that since Philadelphia shouldered a large proportion of the state tax burden any barrier in the way of its commercial expansion might plunge the commonwealth again into bankruptcy.[30]

Had all sectional differences over transportation charters reached an intensity equal to that achieved by the Pittsburgh-Philadelphia rivalry in 1846, the evolution of charter policy would have been unbearably hectic. But the commercial interests at stake in the generality of charters, especially those concerned with bridges, turnpikes, and canals, were of more limited scope. The legislative process, moreover, provided a characteristic solution to the con-

---

[27] *North American*, Mar. 19, Apr. 16, 1846. The *North American* called this period one of "war feeling" between Pittsburgh and Philadelphia. *Ibid.*, Mar. 5, 1846.

[28] *Ibid.*, Mar. 27, Apr. 16, and especially "Treason Seldom Triumphs," Feb. 28, 1846. Cf. *House Journal, 1828*, II, 542.

[29] *Speech of Gibbons*, p. 3. Gibbons was a young senator from Philadelphia who believed that both the Pennsylvania and the Baltimore and Ohio should have equal rights. His position evoked bitter antagonism among his constituents and blighted his career for nearly a quarter-century. *North American*, Mar. 5, 1846; McClure, *Old Time Notes of Pa.*, I, 130.

[30] The *North American* predicted that the state debt would be repudiated within three years if right of way was given to the Baltimore and Ohio. Feb. 28, Mar. 27, 1846.

flicts they engendered — the log-rolling principle. Speaking of charter policy Charles Ingersoll remarked: "No one deems it wrong to take and give for his county or district, and jobbing in legislation is as common as in stocks. Exchanges of local advantages are the levers that move the whole commonwealth." [31] Due to an ideological rationale which I have already analyzed, this procedure was branded as a "dangerous system," [32] but it must not be assumed that the constitutional abolition of omnibus charter bills in 1837 seriously vitiated its operation. Prior to that time, it is true, the log-rolling principle was blatant on the face of the statute books; James Dunlop was substantially correct when he said that ". . . bridges and turnpikes are put in such a mass that they cannot be resisted." Single measures commonly mingled as many as five different transportation charters, their geographic distribution serving as conclusive evidence of the sectional combination that had been involved in their enactment.

Opposition to abolishing such measures came mainly from sparsely populated districts having limited legislative representation; it was based on the argument that without the opportunity to attach their charters to measures embracing charters of more influential counties such districts would be unable to push them through. A charter policy despotism was envisaged in the legislature by Philadelphia, Lancaster, Chester, Allegheny, Berks, Bucks, York, Montgomery, Washington, and Westmoreland counties. Other counties were warned that they "might as well decline elections" since they would be unable to have their charters granted.[33] But if the results of the abolition measure did not vindicate the hopes of its champions, neither did it vindicate the fears of its opponents. As Thomas Cunningham astutely observed in the Convention of 1837, charter log-rolling was inherent in the process of legislative grants and was bound to persist even if single measures were required for them.[34] Statute records after 1838 do not show that small districts fared more poorly than before, nor

[31] *Convention Proceedings*, XIV, 16.
[32] *Ibid.*, V, 612.
[33] *Ibid.*, IX, 154 ff.
[34] *Ibid.*, IX, 39. Cf. *Pa. Archives*, 4th, VII, 751, 840, 841.

do legislative debates show that less importance was attached to the bargaining power of their votes.

The overshadowing importance of the sectional principle in the evolution of charter policy is to be perceived also in alignments on bank charters which, together with transportation grants, made up over 71 per cent of all franchises enacted by the legislature prior to the Civil War. In certain aspects the operation of the sectional principle in the banking field was closely related to its operation in the transportation sector. This was due to an established legislative practice which frequently incorporated into bank charters requirements for assisting specified transportation companies. Such assistance usually took the form of stock subscriptions, loans, or outright grants of money.[35] The practice inevitably called into play the usual pattern of sectional transportation ambitions. It reached its apogee in the charter granted to the Second Bank in 1835 which called for stock subscriptions as follows: [36]

Baltimore and Ohio Railroad Company	$200,000[37]
Williamsport and Elmira Railroad Company	200,000
Monongahela Navigation Company	100,000[38]
Cumberland Valley Railroad Company	100,000
Warren and Pine Grove Railroad Company	20,000
Warren and Franklin Turnpike Road Company	15,000
Warren and Ridgeway Turnpike Road Company	5,000
Johnstown and Ligonier Turnpike Road Company	10,000
Snow Shoe and Packersville Turnpike Road Company	20,000
Roseberg and Mercer Turnpike Road Company	5,000
Total	$675,000

[35] See *infra*, p. 258; Holdsworth, *Financing an Empire*, I, 167; Cook, *Philadelphia National Bank*, p. 81.

[36] *Pa. Laws, 1835–36*, p. 43. The subscriptions were to be made if requested by the companies within a year after the passage of the charter. Cf. Cleveland and Powell, *Railroad Promotion and Capitalization*, pp. 113, 227.

[37] This subscription was not to be made until a Maryland law had been enacted permitting the state of Pennsylvania or any of its chartered companies to intersect by railroad and unite with the Baltimore and Ohio at any point in Maryland. Moreover the funds were to be subscribed only for work on that portion of the road stretching from Connellsville to Pittsburgh. *Pa. Laws, 1835–36*, p. 43.

[38] Half of this amount was to be subscribed at the opening of stock books; the remainder after an additional one hundred thousand dollars had been invested. *Ibid., 1835–36*, p. 43. Cf. Crumrine, *Washington County*, p. 387.

The charter also provided for grants of financial assistance in the following amounts: [39]

Chambersburg and Bedford Turnpike Road Company	$ 20,000
Somerset and Bedford Turnpike Road Company	20,000
Somerset and Mount Pleasant Turnpike Road Company	20,000
Robbstown and Mount Pleasant Turnpike Road Company	8,000
Washington and Williamsport Turnpike Road Company	8,000
Mount Pleasant and Pittsburgh Turnpike Road Company	5,000
Washington and Pittsburgh Turnpike Road Company	15,000
Bedford and Stoystown Turnpike Road Company	10,000
Stoystown and Greensburg Turnpike Road Company	12,000
Greensburg and Pittsburgh Turnpike Road Company	12,000
The state road from the White Horse Tavern on top of the Allegheny Mountain to the Virginia state line in Greene County	9,000
Total	$139,000

It is doubtful whether the Second Bank would have been chartered without these sectional concessions.[40] "Evidently all the hobbies and local schemes in the State," wrote William Graham Sumner, "clustered around this big carcass and fought with one another for slices of it." [41]

Yet the sectional aims engendered by this linkage of finance and transportation policies were of marginal importance compared with a type of geographic alignment which manifested itself peculiarly in the bank charter program. This was the historic rural-urban division of interest which characterized the growth of that policy throughout the nation prior to the Civil War.[42] During the opening years of the nineteenth century this alignment turned up in controversies over a policy of branch banking which the legislature authorized the Bank of Pennsylvania and the Bank of

---

[39] *Pa. Laws, 1835–36*, p. 44.

[40] Porter said of the Second Bank charter: ". . . no man can doubt, that the bill would not have been passed, but for the provisions contained in it for various internal improvements, and for the advancement and support of the cause of education." *Convention Proceedings*, V, 565. Cf. William B. Reed to Nicholas Biddle in Biddle, *Correspondence*, pp. 258–61.

[41] Quoted, Holdsworth, *Financing an Empire*, II, 497.

[42] For a discussion of this alignment in Pennsylvania, see *Senate Journal, 1819–20*, pp. 224–25.

Philadelphia to pursue.[43] With the growth of speculative fever in the interior counties the legislature soon observed there an "unbounded thirst" [44] for independently chartered institutions. This thirst, as a Senate committee later reported, was allied to the hopeful delusion that the chartering of banks would of itself create capital. Rural areas "fancied that much of the prosperity of the cities was to be traced to the establishment of banks, and that if that were the case, there was no reason why the country should not participate in their advantages." [45] The branch system was condemned as a technique for draining discount and loan profits from areas that produced them, as an instrument for achieving a credit despotism of the urban over the rural interest.[46] The establishment of independent banks in rural regions would not only break the grip of the cities but would enhance tax receipts by creating new taxable wealth and would actually serve as an insurance against credit overexpansion: a "most effectual remedy" for overexpansion would be found "in the rivalship which an increase in the number of banks to a proper extent is calculated to create." [47]

These were the premises that led to the ill-fated Banking Act of 1814, and after the fiasco that followed it some of them experienced a considerable eclipse in the popular mind. The notion that banks could create wealth in rural areas was branded as a "fallacy," [48] hard labor being pointed to in good puritanic fashion as the sole producer of that object. The notion that interbank competition could be relied upon to prevent overexpansion was coun-

[43] *Statutes at Large*, XVII, 961–62. Cf. *House Journal, 1827*, II, 803; Holdsworth, *Financing an Empire*, I, 136; Chapman and Westerfield, *Branch Banking*, p. 38. Branches of the Bank of Pennsylvania were established at Harrisburg, Reading, Easton, Lancaster, and Pittsburgh. Knox, *History of Banking in U.S.*, p. 443. D. Dewey, *State Banking before Civil War*, p. 137; *Pa. Laws, 1809–10*, p. 27.

[44] *House Journal, 1809*, p. 747.

[45] *Senate Journal, 1819–20*, pp. 224–25. Cf. H. Miller, *Banking Theories in U.S. before 1860*, p. 20.

[46] *House Journal, 1809*, p. 748.

[47] *Ibid., 1807–1808*, p. 198. "An extravagant emission of bank paper will be prevented by the fear of being called upon for specie, and partiality in the distribution of loans, destroyed by the anxiety each will feel to secure itself the best customers." *Ibid.* See also *ibid., 1809*, p. 520; *1811*, p. 345.

[48] *Convention Proceedings*, I, 199; VI, 85 ff. Cf. H. Miller, *Banking Theories in U.S. before 1860*, p. 34.

tered by the argument that since they would "all invite customers" an increase in the number of banks automatically endangered financial stability.[49] Yet neither the sectional demand for a wider distribution of banking capital nor the faith in interbank competition disappeared in policy debate. Both of these ideas began to flourish in a somewhat different setting when, after New York embarked upon its free-banking program in 1838, a movement to adopt the same scheme got under way in Pennsylvania as in other states and was eventually victorious in 1860.[50]

In the Convention of 1837, where the rural-urban division had persistently appeared during the consideration of restrictions on the legislative power to charter banks,[51] the free-banking proposal was championed mainly by a radical anti-bank group which was coming to recognize the futility of its objectives.[52] Free banking was criticized as the road to heightened state indebtedness and the creation of excessive amounts of banking capital,[53] but the demand for broader sectional allotment of banking capital to which it was allied was hard to counter. A House committee reporting negatively on the scheme in 1856 said that it was "not insensible to the fact that the banking capital of Pennsylvania is unequally and perhaps unfairly distributed over the state. Out of the $22,000,000 of banking capital in the Commonwealth, $12,000,000 of it is concentrated in Philadelphia; while in Pittsburgh there is but $3,060,700, and in the northern and central portions of the State, the disproportion is equally as great. . . ."[54] The idea of interbank competition was somewhat more tenable in

[49] *House Journal, 1815–16*, pp. 159–63.
[50] Permissible capitalization under the Free Banking Act of 1860 was set at a minimum of fifty thousand and at a maximum of one million dollars. State and national securities were to be deposited against note issues with the auditor-general. *Pa. Laws, 1860*, pp. 459–71; Holdsworth, *Financing an Empire*, II, 583.
[51] *Convention Proceedings*, IX, 154.
[52] Earle of Philadelphia County was the chief defender of Free Banking in the convention. *Ibid.*, I, 384; VI, 94. Cf. Chapman and Westerfield, *Branch Banking*, p. 54.
[53] Muhlenberg, *Remarks on Free Banking*. Muhlenberg also held that a free-banking act would be a violation of the constitutional provision against extending the charter of more than one corporation in a single measure. *Ibid.*, p. 5. See also Myers, *Remarks on Free Banking*, Pennsylvania House Committee on Banks, *Report*, p. 3 ff; *Pa. Archives*, 4th, VII, 206, 741.
[54] Pennsylvania House Committee on Banks, *Report*, p. 5.

connection with free banking than it had been in connection with the Banking Act of 1814, but as the history of the operation of the free-banking system shows it was again a fallacious starting point for the solution of the banking problem.[55]

An additional word is necessary concerning the foreign corporation aspect of the sectional idea. The bias against outstate corporations which the logic of Philadelphia's commercial position compelled her to propagate in the transportation field manifested itself elsewhere as well. In the banking field the influx of varied currencies from adjoining states was always a primary factor conditioning the effectiveness of state policy,[56] but in a purely competitive sense the foreign corporation factor had special implications there. Fear of a reliance upon outstate institutions, involving Pennsylvanians in all of their weaknesses and none of their profits, was, especially during the early period, a strong consideration in the expansion of bank charter policy.[57] In 1835 Biddle played heavily upon the state's anxiety to retain Philadelphia as the banking "seat" of the nation,[58] and it has been argued that a controlling motive in the grant of a charter to the Second Bank was the appearance at that time of New York's plan for a great fifty-million-dollar bank.[59] In the insurance field the competitive idea was at least equally significant. Prior to 1812 incorporated marine insurance capital amounted to less than 8 per cent of the capital involved in Philadelphia's import-export trade,[60] a situation which was blamed for heavy reliance upon British insurance offices "to whom we have, in fact, paid a tax." [61] Such de-

[55] Cf. *supra*, note 19; Edwards, *Finance Capitalism*, p. 142.
[56] See *supra*, note 19.
[57] *House Journal, 1807*, II, 138; I, 197.
[58] *Proceedings, Stockholders of Bank of U.S.*, p. 37. Cf. Biddle, *Correspondence*, pp. 260–61.
[59] Holdsworth, *Financing an Empire*, II, 495. Cf. *Niles Register*, XLIX (1835–36), 162.
[60] *House Journal, 1812–13*, pp. 42–43. These figures were presented by a House committee which recommended the renewal of the charter of the Pennsylvania Insurance Company. It took cognizance of the war situation in the following resolution: "That, although at the present time, commercial enterprise is considerably checked by the risks attending a maritime war with a great naval power, it is the more necessary to encourage a trade with neutral nations, by affording ample means for insuring ships and merchandise." *Ibid*.
[61] *Ibid., 1809*, p. 80.

pendency in time of loss was branded as unseemly and dangerous.[62] Not only was this argument presented to expand insurance charter policy, but it accounted also for the maintenance throughout the entire period of statute restrictions on foreign corporation agents which were more stringent in the insurance field than in any other.[63]

3. *Corporations and the State*

Important as sectional conflict was, it represented only one of the types of tension which the charter program produced. Another was generated by a divergence of interest between the state itself and the corporations it chartered. This antagonism appeared most clearly in the transportation field where after 1825 the state launched its greatest public enterprise program. It must not be imagined, however, that prior to that time the state shouldered no obligations in transportation; until 1791, indeed, it assumed them almost completely. The call for transportation improvements after the Revolution produced a series of enactments by the General Assembly which provided for the construction and operation of turnpikes and bridges by public officers at public expense.[64] It was only when it became clear that public construction was insufficient to meet transportation needs and when pressure was put upon the legislature by the Pennsylvania Society for Promoting the Improvement of Roads, that the state was ready to share with the corporate system the job of building transport facilities. Begun in the Philadelphia area in 1791 with the chartering of a road to link the Schuylkill and the Susquehanna, the turnpike charter program was gradually extended after 1803 to remoter regions of the state.[65] Despite the simultaneous operation of public and corporate facilities during this period, however, little competitive conflict appeared. To be sure there was opposition to corporate facilities on the part of trans-

---

[62] Cf. *ibid.*, *1803*, pp. 88–89; *1808*, pp. 489–90; *1809*, pp. 510–11; *1810*, p. 135; *1811*, p. 157; Huebner, "Marine Insurance in U.S.," *Annals of American Academy of Pol. and Soc. Science*, XXVI (1905), 252; Oviatt, "Fire Insurance in U.S.," *Annals of American Academy of Pol. and Soc. Science*, XXVI (1905), 162.

[63] See *infra*, p. 261.

[64] Plummer, *Road Policy of Pa.*, pp. 43–45; Durrenberger, *Turnpikes*, pp. 39–40; Jenkins, *Pennsylvania*, III, 260–61.

[65] Plummer, *Road Policy of Pa.*, pp. 46–52; Jenkins, *Pennsylvania*, III, 261–67.

porters who wanted toll-free state lines.[66] But this alignment is to be distinguished from one involving direct competition between state and corporate enterprises.

Such competition naturally came to the fore when the state embarked upon a much expanded public works program in the twenties, one in which the revenue objective was of primary importance not only for the purpose of redeeming investment but for the purpose of straight public profit making.[67] It reached a high degree of strategic importance in debate over charter policy. "Whenever a railroad measure was introduced," asserted Representative Longacre in retrospect in the late fifties, "the hue and cry was raised that it was intended to divert trade from the Public Works. . . ."[68] Debate over this issue reached its highest point of intensity when the chartering of the Pennsylvania Railroad was considered. Fear that the road might cripple the state works was, as Governor Bigler put it, "the very first and most formidable difficulty which presented itself in the way of this enterprise."[69] The defenders of the project argued that it would actually throw added business to the Columbia Railroad, a part of the state line, and that the increased value of property adjacent to the Pennsylvania's tracks would net the state in tax revenue an ample remuneration for any trade she might lose.[70] Despite these arguments the charter of the Pennsylvania did not pass the legislature without a provision for a tax on its tonnage to compensate for possible losses to public works.[71]

If we inquire more closely into this episode we shall discover a revealing linkage between corporate-state rivalry and the sectional principle. If the defenders of the state interest in 1846 were distinguished from their opponents by a heightened patriotism, it is curious that they should appear mainly in the western counties where the ambitions of the Pennsylvania Railroad encountered

[66] Cf. *House Journal, 1803–1804*, p. 384; *1821–22*, pp. 824–26.
[67] See *infra*, pp. 138–39.
[68] *Legislative Record, 1857*, No. 47, p. 3.
[69] *Pa. Archives*, 4th, VII, 737.
[70] *Proceedings in Relation to Pennsylvania Railroad*, p. 11; Philadelphia Committee of Seven, *Address*, p. 37; *Pa. Archives*, 4th, VII, 737.
[71] See *infra*, pp. 267 ff.

strong opposition on grounds of sectional interest as well. Dubious about the economic worth of the Pennsylvania Railroad compared with the Baltimore and Ohio from their point of view, those counties realized that any loss in the traffic of the public works would have to be compensated for by taxes which they would partially have to shoulder. This feeling was especially keen in the southwestern area which derived little benefit from the works and which viewed a decline in their traffic as the prelude to even heavier tax payments for value not received.[72] The truth is that corporate-state rivalry in transportation was largely a façade behind which the sectional principle operated: in this context the sectional ambitions embodied in charter requests clashed not only with the customary commercial jealousies of other sections but with the financial stake those sections had in the state works. In this logic lay, moreover, one of the reasons for the declining consideration given to the state interest during the forties and fifties. With the heightening of the railroad fever, scarcely a city or a section in the state failed to hitch its commercial fate to one or more railroad projects. Sectional pressures in the legislature overrode state interest. After the chartering of the Lebanon Valley Railroad, a road which ran practically parallel with the Columbia line of the state system, Representative Thorn remarked: ". . . two or three more railroads could not work very much more injury to the Public Works." [73]

Conflict between state and corporate interest also appeared in the banking field. This was due partially to the large stockholdings which the state, in line with a mixed corporation policy which we shall examine later, had in certain established banks. Since revenue from these holdings was an important source of state income, fear of impairing it emerged automatically as a consideration in the chartering of rival banks and persisted until the state investments were liquidated in 1837. Confronted with an increasing number of petitions for new bank charters toward the close of the first decade of the nineteenth century, a legislative committee remarked: "Upon such applications the stake the commonwealth

[72] See *infra*, pp. 268 ff.
[73] *Legislative Record*, *1857*, No. 47, p. 3.

already has in . . . existing institutions ought always to be kept in view." [74] A striking example of the effect of this consideration is to be found in a controversy that developed in 1803 when the industrial and commercial growth of Philadelphia led to petitions for the chartering of the Bank of Philadelphia.

At that time the state held twenty-five hundred shares of stock in the existing Bank of Pennsylvania amounting at par value to one million dollars and bringing into the state treasury dividends of eighty thousand dollars annually.[75] Moreover, owing to provisions in the charter of the Pennsylvania Bank, that institution served as the official deposit agency for state funds. In light of these facts a House committee reported unfavorably on the chartering of the Bank of Philadelphia, arguing that the existing public interest must be protected, "especially" in an institution "where the property of the state is lodged. . . ."[76] Involved in the corporate-state interest pattern here was of course the simple principle of intercorporate competition. The Bank of Pennsylvania offered to pay the state $200,000 outright on the condition that the Bank of Philadelphia be denied a charter.[77] The result was that when the Philadelphia bank finally did win its charter it was compelled to pay $135,000 to the state as a bonus for the privilege.[78] The bonus principle in the banking field, originating with this con-

TABLE 2

BANK CHARTER BONUSES, 1833–1840 [78a]

1833	$ 102,297.90
1834	42,506.17
1835	66,608.99
1836	1,719,673.12
1837	1,290,250.00
1838	227,053.53
1839	103,875.03
1840	105,214.25

[74] *House Journal, 1807–1808*, p. 197.   [75] *Infra*, chap. III.
[76] *House Journal, 1803–1804*, p. 252.
[77] Holdsworth, *Financing an Empire*, I, 136.
[78] *Statutes at Large*, XVII, 684. Cf. *House Journal, 1822*, p. 588; Holdsworth, *Financing an Empire*, I, 136; Cook, *Philadelphia National Bank*, pp. 33–35.
[78a] Data for this table were taken from the *Annual Reports of the Pennsylvania Auditor-General*.

troversy, accounted for a sizeable portion of state income, especially during the banking expansion of the thirties.

The establishment of the bonus practice gave an affirmative twist to the state interest *vis-à-vis* charter policy which contrasts sharply with the negative pressure produced by public-corporate competition; it served not only to counteract that preoccupation with protecting state investments which tended to discourage the chartering of new banks but gave the state, traditionally dominated by a strong anti-tax bias, a vested interest in the expansion of bank charter policy after public bank stockholdings had been liquidated. But bonus revenue was not the only stake the state had in the granting of new bank charters. Banks were compelled to lend sums to the state, usually in amounts up to 5 per cent of capital stock at 5 per cent, if requests for such loans were made.[79] The charter granted to the Bank of Pennsylvania, the first state bank to be incorporated, required it to lend to the state $500,000 at interest not to exceed 6 per cent for the purpose of establishing a loan office for the assistance of farmers.[80] The revenue to be derived from both the bonus and the loan policies became especially attractive during the thirties when monetary needs for construction of public works rocketed, and there is little doubt that the banking overexpansion of that period is in some measure traceable to them. The most extreme application of these policies, as of others in the banking field, is to be found in the charter granted to the Second Bank in 1835 which extracted for the state a bonus of two million dollars, temporary loans of one million annually, and a permanent loan of six millions.[81] With the onset of the panic of 1837, bank bonuses fell under heavy criticism as instruments for legislative bribery and were branded as worthless quantities of paper by which the state was deluded.[82] Governors

---

[79] See *infra*, p. 258.

[80] Cf. *infra*, note 84; *House Journal, 1820–21*, pp. 356–57.

[81] *Pa. Laws, 1835–36*, p. 42. See also Biddle's remarks in *Proceedings, Stockholders of Bank of U.S.*, p. 37; John McKim, Jr. to Nicholas Biddle in Biddle, *Correspondence*, p. 265. The Girard Bank was permitted to increase its capital from $1,500,000 to $5,000,000; it paid a bonus of $250,000. *Pa. Laws, 1835–36*, p. 133.

[82] *Convention Proceedings*, XIV, 23 ff. For a defense of the bonus principle as a source of state revenue at this time, cf. *ibid.*, XIV, 57.

Ritner and Porter both called for the abolition of the bonus system.[83] In 1842 a measure was enacted permitting the imposition of more limited fees for the enrollment of charters. This act abolished the old bonus practice and embraced not only banking but industrial corporations.

4. *Individual Enterprise and the Parties*

Analysis of the intersectional and state-corporate interest patterns has directed our attention mainly to the fields of transportation and finance. Analysis of a third alignment in the evolution of charter policy, the corporate-individual pattern, will direct our attention to other fields. In this connection it is worth recalling that, despite Pennsylvania's industrial pre-eminence, less than 10 per cent of the charters granted by the legislature during our period were for industrial purposes. The smallness of this percentage is not to be interpreted as indicating that the promotional principle was accepted to a lesser extent in the industrial area than in transportation. Not only does the strong protectionist sentiment of the age prove that this was not the case, but the idea is refuted by the maintenance on the state level of two additional policies. One of these, which flowered during the early decades of the nineteenth century, involved granting state loans to industrial entrepreneurs who could not raise sufficient capital. In 1809 William M'Dermett of Bedford County received a loan for the extension of his steel works on the ground that "works of public importance deserve public encouragement."[84] The other was a

---

[83] *Pa. Archives*, 4th, VI, 301.
[84] *House Journal, 1808*, pp. 311–12; *Statutes at Large*, XVIII, 1037. See also *House Journal, 1804*, p. 273; *1808*, p. 881; *1812–13*, p. 661; *1817*, p. 653; *1822*, p. 233. For a loan of three hundred pounds to an individual who had perfected a method of converting bar iron into steel, see *Dallas' Laws*, II, 454–55; a loan of two hundred pounds for calico printing and bleaching, *ibid.*, II, 704; a loan of six hundred dollars for casting hinges, weights, and the like, *Pa. Laws, 1812–13*, p. 182; also *ibid., 1810–11*, pp. 34–35. Loan provisions varied in so far as interest, time, and security were concerned. There was pressure during the period prior to the close of the War of 1812 for the state to purchase certain inventions. *Pa. Archives*, 4th, IV, 671; *House Journal, 1812–13*, p. 661. For a brief period loans were also granted in the agricultural field. In 1793 the state established a loan office on the basis of a provision in the charter of the Bank of Pennsylvania requiring it to lend five hundred thousand dollars for that purpose. The measure allocated the funds regionally, providing that county commissioners were to apportion county allotments among

liberal policy of incorporating associations for purely promotional objectives in industry and in agriculture, a policy that expanded with the growth of such associations after 1819 when a number of them were organized to express the state's heightened protectionist ardor.[85]

It was the defense of "individual enterprise" that rationalized the limitation of the industrial charter program. And behind it was the economic fact of the early entrenchment in manufacturing and mining of a multiplicity of small entrepreneurs. Quite apart from legalistic ideas concerning the injustice of incorporating firms to compete with small operators, the defense of individual enterprise produced a vigorous criticism of the corporation on purely economic grounds. This criticism drew heavily on the contention that the corporation's employment of agents without a direct entrepreneurial interest in its fate served to make it less effective than the individual operator.[86] The "resistless power" of the individual, as Governor Shunk put it in 1842 in a message vetoing the incorporation of the Pennsylvania Railroad Iron Manufacturing Company, could furthermore be frustrated by the utilization for monopolistic purposes of the legal privileges attached to the corporate device.[87] Though this line of argument developed in its

---

wards, districts, and townships. Applications for loans were made to county treasurers; loans were limited to a maximum of three hundred dollars and a minimum of one hundred. Mortgages on real estate served as security; county commissioners were authorized to reject defective collateral; loans were limited to a third of the value of the mortgaged premises which were required to be free as to title prior to the loan. Six per cent interest, repayable in seven yearly installments, was provided for. The Loan Office was abolished in 1794. *Dallas' Laws*, III, 414–21; 519–21.

[85] Eiselen, *Pa. Protectionism*, p. 52; *Pa. Laws, 1806–1807*, pp. 68–73; *1811–12*, p. 104; *1819–20*, pp. 51–54; *1823*, pp. 206–208; *House Journal, 1806*, p. 79. In certain cases, as, for example, the Pittsburgh Manufacturing Association and the Philadelphia Domestic Society for the Encouragement of Manufactures, limiting trading privileges were permitted. For the incorporation of agricultural promotional associations, see Breck, *Internal Improvements by Pa.*, pp. 29–30; Bidwell and Falconer, *Agriculture in Northern U.S.*, pp. 184, 189; *Hazard's Register*, XIV (1834–35), 313, 321; IX (1832), 100; *Niles Register*, XVII (1819–20), 7; XXXII (1827), 225; XXXIV (1828), 17; *House Journal, 1824*, II, p. 130; *1823*, pp. 592–98; *1822*, p. 803; *1821–22*, p. 506; *1805*, p. 105; *Pa. Archives*, 4th, V, 156, 551; *Pa. Laws, 1822–23*, pp. 223–27; *1819–20*, pp. 51–54.

[86] Cf. *Pa. Archives*, 4th, VI, 36; VII, 558.

[87] *Ibid.*, VII, 153–61. During the legislative session 1830–31 the House Committee on Corporations remarked in reporting negatively on the incorporation of the Germanville Glass Manufacturing Company of Wayne County: "No company

pure form in the industrial field — where mines, furnaces, forges, and rolling mills could be labeled as ordinary businesses not calling for corporate action — it must not be assumed that it was wholly absent in the fields of transportation and banking. It asserted itself partially in reactions against corporate mismanagement in those fields, especially during depression periods. For example the crisis of 1857, which culminated a period of unprecedented promotional corruption in transportation, witnessed an intense denunciation of the separation of ownership from management which the corporate system involved. "Certain fat and lazy officials, railroad presidents, brokers, and contractors" [88] received stern polemical treatment from communities that had been swayed by their sales talk. The Supreme Court lamented the fact that the directors of the Northwestern Railroad Company had "but little pecuniary interest in" it "beyond the salaries liberally voted to some of their number." [89]

An excellent case study of the doctrine produced by the industrial corporate-individual alignment is afforded by the coal trade. Charter policy there was conditioned by a peculiar set of circumstances which had their origin in the second decade of the nineteenth century when few capitalists recognized the potentialities of the anthracite trade and when the technical difficulties involved in it seemed immense. Early anthracite canals failed largely because of the hazards of navigating mountain streams.[90] The first charters given by the legislature were primarily for transportation purposes; mining privileges were added as an additional inducement for capitalists to venture upon the undertakings. "Mining privileges have never been granted where mining alone was the object of association," declared a Senate committee in 1834, "but

---

can prosper that is exposed to the competition of individuals upon a *perfect* footing of equality. The employment of agents and the natural carelessness of men who perform a duty with no feeling of direct interest are such drawbacks upon profits as must in such case necessarily ruin a corporation, even where others prosper. All experience has shown that the only safety of companies is in monopoly; and the instinct of self-preservation directs all their energies to that point." *House Journal, 1830–31,* II, 652.

[88] *Pittsburgh Union,* quoted in Philadelphia *Press,* Sept. 1, 1857.
[89] *County of Lawrence* v. *The Northwestern Railroad Company,* 32 Pa. St. Rep. 144 (1858).
[90] Bogen, *Anthracite Railroads,* pp. 8–9.

for considerations of a secondary nature, and as inducements to companies to accomplish what have been regarded as greater public objects." [91] In 1818 the legislature, in line with this policy, chartered the Lehigh Navigation Company, granting to it the sole jurisdiction of the Lehigh River for a distance of eighty-three miles and combining in its charter both mining and transportation privileges.[92] A decade later, with the influx of individual operators into the coal areas, this monopoly became a matter of serious argument. The Lehigh company, under the effective management of Josiah White, discouraged the competition of individual miners by charging prohibitive rates for transportation over the Lehigh, and it maintained its own coal prices at a level which evoked criticism in Philadelphia.[93] In 1832 and 1834 there were conventions of protest on the part of the individual operators.[94] At the same time an increasing number of applications for mining charters were coming before the legislature.

A vigorous debate over charter policy ensued. Owing to the unprecedented sums of Philadelphia capital which were made available for mining investment after 1825, individual operators contended that the corporate system was no longer needed for the exploitation of coal resources. "The truth is," declared George Taylor, a Pottsville writer, in 1833, "that the argument about want of capital in the Coal Trade is exploded, and has become perfectly futile and inapplicable." Arguing that upwards of five and a half million dollars had been expended by individuals in the trade, Taylor asserted that additional amounts of capital could

[91] Pennsylvania Senate Committee on Coal Trade, *Report*, p. 44. The committee referred to the union of mining and transportation privileges as a "great and radical error." *Ibid.*, pp. 19, 47. This remained a difficult problem in industrial charter privileges until the end of the period. Cf. *Legislative Record, 1856*, pp. 317 ff.

[92] *Pa. Laws, 1817–18*, pp. 197–205; *Hazard's Register*, III (1829), 302; Bogen, *Anthracite Railroads*, pp. 8–9; Brenckman, *Carbon County*, p. 79; *Report upon Coal Trade*, p. 17.

[93] Bogen, *Anthracite Railroads*, pp. 20 ff; Jones, *Anthracite-Tidewater Canals*, pp. 19–20. Cf. *Extract Relative to Lehigh Navigation*; *Correspondence between Lehigh Company and Beaver Meadow Company*; Lehigh Coal and Navigation Company, *Report*.

[94] Cf. "Report of Nescopeck Valley," *Report upon Coal Trade*, p. 99; *Proceedings, Convention Interested in the Connexion of Susquehanna and Lehigh Rivers*, pp. 4–16.

easily be obtained when necessary.[95] After a thorough investigation of the Lehigh monopoly, a Senate committee, headed by S. J. Packer, agreed that the coal trade "can now be brought entirely within the controul of individual means." [96] Only individual enterprise, it was argued, could attain the most economical division of mining labor. The owning of lands, the working of them, the transportation of coal, and its sale were four distinct functions that a single business unit could not combine effectively.[97]

Moreover the corporate system led inevitably to monopoly and high price schedules.[98] In this connection intermittent periods of overproduction which characterized the evolution of the coal trade were branded as subtle conspiracies on the part of corporate operators. Since corporations could negotiate their paper for longer periods than individuals, they overproduced deliberately in order to ruin unincorporated competition by flooding the market.[99] In light of a secular rise in coal demand and the British experience, the Senate committee of 1834 feared the emergence of monopoly even if the trade was left entirely to individual operators: "It may become necessary for the purpose of preserving divisions of labour, and to keep down monopoly, for the Legislature to authorize limited partnerships, with limited capital, limited parcels of lands, and so restricted in other respects as to promote the very objects for which individual coal dealers now so laudably and legitimately contend. That even corporations could be erected, and with these advantages, cannot be doubted." [100]

Absenteeism provided another line of argument. The charge that the coal corporation was governed by a "distant board of directors" was advanced to challenge its economic adequacy,[101]

---

[95] Taylor, *Effect of Incorporated Coal Companies*, pp. 6–7. Cf. Schalk and Henning, *Schuylkill County*, p. 106.
[96] *Report upon Coal Trade*, p. 45.
[97] Taylor, *Effect of Incorporated Coal Companies*, pp. 5, 7–9; *Pa. Archives*, 4th, VII, 36–37.
[98] *Report upon Coal Trade*, p. 19; Taylor, *Effect of Incorporated Coal Companies*, p. 19. Cf. *House Journal, 1806*, p. 50; *Convention Proceedings*, VI, 83; *Pa. Archives*, 4th, VI, 388.
[99] *Report upon Coal Trade*, p. 63; Taylor, *Effect of Incorporated Coal Companies*, pp. 19–23.
[100] *Report upon Coal Trade*, p. 46.
[101] Taylor, *Effect of Incorporated Coal Companies*, p. 9.

but the argument had larger social implications as well. Individual dealers contended that a "community growing up under an incorporate company differs from that created by individual operators," since in the former case civic improvements and the living conditions of the workers were neglected. Communities at Mauch Chunk, Carbondale, and Tamaqua were declared to consist "only of the servants and laborers of the companies," while communities at Port Carbon, Minersville, and other areas worked predominantly by individual producers were lauded as examples of civic progress.[102] Corporations were blamed, finally, for the speculation evil. Governor Ritner asserted in 1837 that they were usually motivated "by some plan to dispose of a particular tract of land to great advantage, and not by intention of real investment" in the field.[103]

The argument of the corporation defenders was based mainly on the capital issue, and they insisted that it be viewed in terms of the coal trade's inevitable expansion. That expansion was bound to make it increasingly difficult for the individual producer to survive; his entrenchment would serve only to retard the growth of the trade.[104] Far from contributing to the speculative movement, argued Marcus Bull of the North American Coal Company, the corporate device was actually an insurance against it: the credit of the corporation was reduced equally with the reduction in the personal liability of its stockholders and in many cases to an even greater extent. "By this necessary connexion of cause and effect, the public is guarded against loss in a much more perfect manner than it can be from individuals whose capital is not known, and to the state of whose affairs no access can be had, as can generally be done in the case of corporations."[105] Moreover, fraudulent transactions were undertaken less frequently by cor-

---

[102] *Ibid*, p. 26. Cf. *Legislative Record, 1856*, p. 319.

[103] *Pa. Archives*, 4th, VI, 387; Taylor, *Effect of Incorporated Coal Companies*, p. 24.

[104] Testimony of Lehigh Navigation Company, *Report upon Coal Trade*, pp. 55 ff; of James Wilde, *ibid*., pp. 65 ff; of William Milnes and John White of the North American Coal Company, *ibid*., pp. 70, 90, 92; of Delaware and Hudson Coal Company, *ibid*., pp. 112 ff; M. Bull, *Mining Operations of North American Coal Company*, p. 6.

[105] *Ibid*., p. 7.

porations than by individual producers, since "such measures with them require too many accomplices to admit of frequent success, whilst no such restraint exists with individuals." [106] Miners employed by corporations were assured of steadier work than those employed by individual dealers, and nothing was more unjust than the charge that corporations led to pernicious labor conditions. "They have been to this region," declared William Milnes of the Schuylkill area, "what the sun is to the solar system — its life and being." [107]

However shoddy some of these arguments may have been, the reply of the corporation defenders was obviously sound in substance. Economically the state gained nothing from the comparatively slow evolution of its industrial charter policy.[108] In so far as the coal trade was concerned, it was unfortunate that debate about the advisability of the corporate system should have gotten itself entangled with the specific issue of the Lehigh monopoly. Undoubtedly the practices of that monopoly were interfering with the development of mining in the state, but they were scarcely a sound basis for discrediting the corporate technique. Overproduction and speculation were problems traceable at least as much to the individual mining operator as to the mining corporation, and a fluctuating tariff policy which was partially responsible for both could not legitimately be blamed on the charter principle. Despite the heavy criticism of industrial corporations, however, the general industrial incorporation laws, enactment of which began in 1849, testify to a somewhat broadened acceptance of the charter principle in the industrial area prior to the close of our period.

Is any fundamental conflict to be found in the charter field in terms of party alignment? Such conflict is often attributed to the Democratic-Whig division, the former party being interpreted as opposed to the charter program and the latter as defending it.

---

[106] *Ibid.*

[107] Testimony, *Report upon Coal Trade*, pp. 66, 72, 82. In 1853 the coal lands in the Pottsville area were owned by six corporations and about sixty individuals, only twenty-five of whom were resident in the region. Schalk and Henning, *Schuylkill County*, I, 109.

[108] Cf. V. Clark, *Manufactures, 1607–1860*, pp. 266–67.

Since prior to the middle thirties the Democratic party in Pennsylvania had no significant formal opposition, it is impossible to arrive at any definite conclusions on this score for the first three decades in which charter policy unfolded on any appreciable scale. We know only that that policy did expand despite the dominance of the Democrats. Democratic legislatures were responsible for the great Banking Acts of 1814 and 1824 and they were responsible for an increase of over 100 per cent in the number of charters granted during the third decade of the nineteenth century compared with the first. More adequate comparative data became available in 1835 when Democratic supremacy momentarily ended and a Whig-Anti-Masonic coalition seized control of the governorship and the House. Yet the figures for that year do not show the decisive increase in the number of charter grants which the traditional party interpretation would seem to call for. On the contrary the number of charters granted in 1835 was 14 per cent below the number granted during the previous year when the Democratic party was in control not only of the governorship but of both branches of the legislature as well. It is true that the infamous charter of the Second Bank was granted during the reign of the anti-Democratic coalition, but that charter was also authorized by the Senate in which the Democrats continued to hold a majority of five.[109] The following year witnessed a sharp increase in the rate of legislative charter grants, but this increase must be attributed to the speculative upsurge which followed the chartering of the Second Bank. In this connection it is more meaningful to compare the number of charters granted during the boom peak of 1814 under Democratic dominance with the number granted in 1836. There is no significant difference. Seventy charters were granted under coalition supremacy in 1836, sixty-nine were granted under Democratic supremacy in 1814.

The truth is that the party formula has only the most limited value as an explanation of conflict over charter policy. And the reasons for this are not hard to find. The importance of sectional motivation in the charter program tended always to withdraw the issue from the party struggle. The Democratic legislature which

[109] Holdsworth, *Financing an Empire*, II, 496; Mueller, *Whig Party in Pa.*, p. 26.

enacted the Banking Act of 1814 could scarcely be expected to pursue a rigorous anti-charter policy when the sectional demand for additional banking facilities had reached its full intensity. Nor is it surprising that the charter granted to the Second Bank in 1836 was authorized by a Senate under Democratic control. The hero in the White House might assail the bank, the Pennsylvania senators at Washington might suddenly determine to oppose it,[110] but the vast concessions to sectional and state ambition which Biddle made at Harrisburg overrode formal party antagonism. The process was always at work. The twenty-two western counties of the state did not secede during the great east-west controversy over the Pennsylvania Railroad in 1846, yet it is obvious that if either of the parties had become involved in that contest the result would have been an organizational split of disastrous proportions.[111] In a state where on other counts as well sectional passions were constantly hampering party unification, the pursuit of a rigorous anti-charter policy was simply an impossible political adventure.

Moreover the desire for bonuses and loans from newly chartered banks which facilitated the overexpansion of the thirties was felt no less intensely by the Democrats than by the Whigs. The drive for expansion of public works was sectional and not party in character; the anti-tax philosophy was a state and not a party creation. Finally lobby techniques at Harrisburg contributed to the removal of charter policy from the area of party conflict. While this factor manifested itself most clearly in connection with the railroad promotionalism of the forties and fifties,[112] it was not unimportant during the earlier period. The $128,000 which George Handy, a director of the Second Bank, spent on legislative pressure in 1835 was spent, we may be sure, with little consideration for party lines.[113]

It is possible that in the industrial field, where considerations of

---

[110] Catterall, *Second Bank of U.S.*, p. 339.
[111] *The Daily Keystone and People's Journal*, a Democratic paper, attempted unsuccessfully to make a party issue out of the railroad controversy. Mueller, *Whig Party in Pa.*, p. 132. See also Stevens' keen remarks on the relation between the party and sectional motivations, *supra*, p. 43, footnote 22.
[112] Cf. Cochran and Miller, *Age of Enterprise*, p. 78.
[113] *House Journal*, 1842, II, 739 ff.

section and state finance were relatively unimportant, Democratic supremacy resulted in a more stringent charter policy than would have resulted under Whig dominance. The number of industrial charters vetoed by the Democratic Governor Shunk when dealing with a Whig legislature was high.[114] In a broader sense, however, the use of the gubernatorial veto proves little. Governor Snyder, a Democrat dealing with a Democratic legislature, engaged in a charter struggle with that legislature more bitter than any which Shunk experienced. The Banking Act of 1814, one of the most radical and disastrous extensions of the charter program of the entire period, terminated a controversy in which Snyder had twice vetoed the measures of his party colleagues in the legislative branch.[115] A similarly striking conflict between executive and legislature when both were under the control of the Democrats took place during the term of Governor Wolf. Wolf's use of the veto power in the charter field became so extensive that in 1835 he warned the legislature that ". . . a more general application of that power would necessarily bring the Executive and Legislative branches of the Government into collision with each other, and destroy that harmony which is essential to a judicious and prosperous administration of its affairs." [116]

The facts are that legislative-executive conflict was constantly present in the evolution of the charter program, and that it was traceable primarily to the difference in constitutional character of the gubernatorial and legislative functions. State legislators were responsible to the circumscribed interests of section and pressure group; the governor was responsible to a state-wide constituency. The first type of responsibility encouraged a profusion of specific charter grants, the second an over-all view of policy which tended to be more restrictive. This was excellently illustrated by the persistent gubernatorial defense of state invest-

---

[114] *Pa. Archives*, 4th, VII, 153–54. See also *Doylestown Democrat*, Sept. 22, 1847.
[115] *Pa. Archives*, 4th, IV, 805 ff, 836 ff; Armor, *Governors of Pa.*, pp. 319–20; Holdsworth, *Financing an Empire*, I, 314. By 1814 many of the legislators had been pledged to their constituents to vote for the measure despite Snyder's opposition. *Senate Journal, 1819–20*, pp. 226 ff.
[116] *Pa. Archives*, 4th, VI, 235, 234. See also remarks of Ritner on the legislative-executive relationship in the incorporation of loan companies. *Ibid.*, VI, 303.

ments against charters which sectional pressure in the legislature produced for transportation companies competing with the state works.[117] Governor Ritner, a Coalition man, attacked those charters as strongly as any Democratic governor. In a message vetoing a charter for the Harrisburg and Lancaster Railroad Company, Ritner branded the policy pursued by the legislature in this connection as "ruinous." [118]

I have pointed out that the economic criticism of the corporation produced by the corporate-individual alignment in the industrial field was also to be found in the transportation and banking sectors. Yet it is important to emphasize that the correlative plea for reliance upon the individual entrepreneur scarcely appeared in the latter areas. Sectionalism and the state interest, dominant considerations in the development of bank and transportation policy, involved no conflict between the ideas of individual and corporate enterprise. Indeed the sectional principle embraced no criticism whatever of the corporate technique. Concerned exclusively with the geographic area for whose benefit that technique was to be used, it did in fact implicitly recognize the practical need for the charter program. The failure of a strong individualistic argument to emerge in banking and transportation is primarily traceable, of course, to the capital limitations of individual enterprise there. There was some attempt to develop the limited partnership procedure into a substitute for the charter principle, but this effort was unimportant.[119] The truth is that, the challenge of public enterprise apart, the economic necessity of the corporation in banking and transportation soon met only limited denial. This is reflected in a persistent recognition of the need for charter policy in areas beyond the power of individual enterprise

---

[117] See *supra*, p. 53; *infra*, p. 161.

[118] *Pa. Archives*, 4th, VI, 384–85. Cf. *ibid.*, VII, 139–42.

[119] *Pa. Laws, 1835–36*, pp. 143–46. Banking and insurance activities were excluded from the limited partnership procedure. *Ibid.*, p. 143. Considerable optimism accompanied the initiation of this measure. In 1836 Ritner remarked: "The act of Assembly, passed during the last session, relative to 'Limited Partnerships' should . . . prevent the increase of corporation." *Pa. Archives*, 4th, VI, 288. See also *ibid.*, VI, 386. In 1852 Bigler recognized the limitations of the measure as a substitute for the corporate technique. See his message vetoing "An Act to Incorporate the Charlestown Silver Lead Mining Company." *Ibid.*, VII, 554 ff. *See also* Harrisburg *Democratic Union*, Feb. 25, 1845; *Hunt's Merchants' Mag.*, XXV (1851), 752.

to deal with.[120] Governor Wolf declared that this formula laid down "the true line of discrimination." [121] Governor Ritner called it "the good, old and safe rule of legislation in Pennsylvania." [122]

In addition to large capital requirements an element peculiar to the banking area favored the charter principle there: once the paper system was accepted, a necessary means of controlling it lay in the close restriction of banking activity to duly chartered institutions. The prevalent glorification of unincorporated enterprise in the industrial field thus contrasts sharply with a vigorous crusade against unincorporated enterprise in the banking area. Prior to the enactment of the Banking Act of 1814 the repeated refusal of the legislature to charter new banks led to the emergence of a series of unincorporated banking establishments.[123] Four measures were enacted by the legislature to strike at these institutions, setting down severe penalties for the acceptance of their notes by duly chartered banks.[124] There was much talk expressing "decided disapprobation" of the unchartered enterprises; [125] there was none defending them. A defense of their position was not even forthcoming from the unchartered entrepreneurs themselves who, especially as their business expanded, sought desperately for some emancipation from the liability obligations their status imposed.[126] A similar situation developed during the fifties when a variety of private bankers appeared in the state who dealt in the cheap currency of outstate banks. Not only did their operations limit the circulation of the par paper of Pennsylvania banks, but their unincorporated status permitted them to

[120] Cf. *House Journal, 1830–31,* II, 651; *1832–33,* II, 760; *1852,* II, 50; *Legislative Record, 1856,* p. 319; *Convention Proceedings,* V, 529, 610; VI, 85; *Pa. Archives,* 4th, VI, 636, 841; VII, 207–10.

[121] *Ibid.,* VI, 129, 192.

[122] *Ibid.,* VI, 387. Usually coupled with this rule in general discussion was the requirement that charters should be granted only for "objects of importance to the community." *House Journal, 1830–31,* II, 651; *Pa. Archives,* 4th, VI, 635; VII, 36, 93–95; *Report upon Coal Trade,* p. 45.

[123] *House Journal, 1809,* p. 664; *1813,* pp. 196–97; *Senate Journal, 1819–20,* pp. 225–66; *Pa. Archives,* 4th, IV, 826–27.

[124] A summary of this legislation is to be found in *House Journal, 1822–23,* pp. 621–23. See also *infra,* chap. VI.

[125] *House Journal, 1809,* pp. 664–65. Cf. Knox, *History of Banking in U.S.,* p. 443.

[126] *Senate Journal, 1819–20,* p. 226.

escape the taxation and regulation imposed by the Banking Act of 1850. Naturally they were severely criticized.[127]

Opponents of the existing paper system, moreover, did not normally desire a complete abolition of banking enterprises. There was, to be sure, a group with the latter objective, originating during the controversy over the Bank of North America in 1785,[128] which believed that "most men can keep all the money they can handle."[129] Yet this school soon became a fringe of limited importance, and in discussing their plans of impossible reform its members modestly conceded that "we must not do it at once" but "gradually and slowly."[130] With the appearance of the free-banking idea, as I have already noted, they quickly showed a willingness to compromise on that scheme. During the legislative session of 1809–1810 a House committee recognized that the question of incorporated banks was "no longer open to legislative consideration — as they are introduced, the only question then is how far it would be just and right, in the Legislature to extend the privilege . . . ."[131] In 1838 a legislative committee, commenting on the "public and private ruin" which a "total overthrow" of the credit system would involve, declared that "no respectable portion of the community, if indeed any of our citizens, advocate such a policy."[132] A note of nostalgia for eighteenth-century days was, it is true, registered occasionally, just as the passing of individual enterprise in the insurance field was sometimes lamented.[133]

[127] *Pa. Archives*, 4th, VII, 879.
[128] M. Carey, *Annulling the Charter of the Bank of North America*, p. 119 and *passim*; H. Miller, *Banking Theories in U.S. before 1860*, pp. 21, 23, 24; Lewis, *Bank of North America*, pp. 54 ff. [129] *Convention Proceedings*, VI, 88–89.
[130] *Ibid.*, VI, 73; XIV, 55. Cf. Schlesinger, *Age of Jackson*, pp. 336–37, 525–27.
[131] *House Journal, 1809*, p. 519. Virtually the same words are used by a committee in *ibid., 1807–1808*, p. 197.
[132] *Ibid., 1837*, II, p. 847.
[133] During the legislative session 1830–31 a House committee reporting negatively on a Senate bill to incorporate the American Insurance Company of Philadelphia, remarked: "The history of incorporated insurance companies in Philadelphia, is one more of the many examples of the inability of individuals to contend against chartered privileges. Not many years ago, nearly all insurances in our city were effected with private underwriters. With the increase of corporations, private underwriting gradually declined, and is now wholly at an end." *Ibid., 1830–31*, II, 775. Cf. Huebner in *Annals of American Academy of Pol. and Soc. Science*, XXVI (1905), 252; Oviatt in *Annals of American Academy of Pol. and Soc. Science*, XXVI (1905), 157; Fowler, *Insurance in Philadelphia*, p. 48–49.

After pointing out that a half-century earlier it would have opposed bank charters of any kind, the Committee on Banks of the House sighed in 1842: "We must take things as we find them and proceed accordingly." [134]

5. *The Anti-Charter Doctrine*

Despite the extent of its acceptance in fact, however, the charter principle from the outset came into conflict with the democratic theory of the time. An anti-charter philosophy emerged which became one of the most powerful, repetitious, and exaggerated themes in the popular literature. The job of analyzing it is a hard one. For, like so much of the popular doctrine we are studying here, it was far less a disciplined set of ideas than a cluster of glamorous symbols indiscriminately utilized. It is clear, at any rate, that it drew most of its strength from the two main concepts of the democratic theory: the individual and the community. If the idea of "individual enterprise" became insignificant as a challenge to banking and transportation corporations in economic terms, on the philosophic plane it flourished with a vengeance. There it was grounded not on statistics of capital investment or theories about the most economic division of labor but on the natural law doctrine of the Revolution and the various constitutions which embodied it. Corporations were "monopolies" and "aristocracies." Their creation violated rights insured by the "social compact." [135]

Every obvious contrast between individual and corporate enterprise was used to polemical advantage. The corporate characteristic of indefinite duration was a good target, though the early establishment of a policy of limiting the life of charters made the attack upon it somewhat unreal.[136] "A company never dies," a House committee dramatically declared in 1830.[137] It was said that the growth of the corporate system was undoing

---

[134] *House Journal, 1842*, II, 205. Cf. *ibid., 1829*, II, 131.
[135] Cf. *ibid., 1811*, p. 345; *1828*, II, 734; *1829*, II, 701; *1830–31*, II, 651; *Doylestown Democrat*, Sept. 22, 1847; *Convention Proceedings*, VI, 28, 35, 37; *Senate Journal, 1819–20*, p. 223; *Pa. Archives*, 4th, IV, 806.
[136] Cf. *infra*, pp. 236 ff., for limits and duration of charters.
[137] *House Journal, 1830–31*, II, 653.

the work of the state's intestate laws,[138] and in the mining field where corporations were chartered to hold land the reinstitution of a new kind of primogeniture was seen taking place.[139] With the legal recognition of limited liability for stockholders, a new contrast between individual and corporate action was supplied.[140] Occasionally, to some extent because of criticisms of the Dartmouth College principle to which it was allied, the anti-charter theory evoked the cry of communism and dire talk of the "agrarian doctrines of Fanny Wright." [141] But the truth is that the vigorous individualism of the theory itself contributed to a glorification of property rights. Embracing a denunciation of eminent-domain privileges granted to transportation companies, an argument which reached its highest pitch of intensity with the passage of the Lateral Railroad Act of 1832,[142] the anti-charter doctrine assailed the appropriation of private property for corporate purposes. "The doctrine of vested rights," asserted George M. Keim of Berks County, "is a sacred one. . . . It existed before these obnoxious charters were created." [143] Above all it was contended that the granting of corporate privileges in fields where unincorporated entrepreneurs had made investments was itself an infringement upon the property rights of the latter. Ingersoll even went so far as to contend that the mere limitation of individual initiative which the growth of a corporate system presumably involved amounted to an attack on the right of property. The "real and legitimate meaning" of the property right included the prerogative of men "to follow such callings as they prefer." [144]

The defense of the individual against the oppression of charter policy found in constitutional provisions texts of varying value. In connection with the federal Constitution there was the argu-

---

[138] *Pa. Archives*, 4th, VII, 86, 236. Cf. Armor, *Governors of Pa.*, p. 398.
[139] *Convention Proceedings*, VI, 83; *Pa. Archives*, 4th, VII, 37, 559.
[140] Cf. *infra*, pp. 256–57.
[141] Cf. *infra*, pp. 243 ff. *Convention Proceedings*, V, 607, 510, 594; VI, 81; IX, 207.
[142] *Pa. Laws, 1831–32*, pp. 506–508.
[143] *Convention Proceedings*, V, 611. See also *ibid.*, XII, 210; *Pa. Archives*, 4th, VII, 93–95, 251–52; *House Journal, 1832*, II, 509–10; Plummer, *Road Policy of Pa.*, pp. 49–50.
[144] *Convention Proceedings*, XIV, 21. Cf. Meigs, *Charles Jared Ingersoll*, pp. 199 ff.

ment that the chartering of banks by the state violated two provisions of Article I, Section 10: the clauses that forbade states to emit bills of credit and that prohibited them from making anything legal tender but gold and silver coin.[145] The Declaration of Rights of the state constitution of 1776 stated, "That government is, or ought to be, instituted for the common benefit, protection and security of the people, nation or community; and not for the particular emolument or advantage of any single man, family, or set of men, who are a part only of that community."[146] This provision, however, could not be taken as disparaging charter policy, since in a subsequent section of the constitution of 1776 the legislature was explicitly empowered to "grant charters of incorporation."[147] In the Constitutional Convention of 1790 an attempt was made to insert a provision that "perpetuities and monopolies are contrary to the nature of a republican government, and ought not to exist." Though this proposal was defeated by the decisive vote of 44 to 12,[148] the convention did include in the Declaration of Rights of the constitution a provision that was eventually worn threadbare by the anti-charter ideologists. Originally appearing in the Revolutionary constitution, this provision listed among the "natural, inherent and inalienable rights" of men the equal power of "acquiring, possessing, and protecting property."[149] "By this section," declared Governor Shunk in 1842, "the power of the Legislature to make distinctions among the citizens, in regard to the acquisition . . . of property, is . . . clearly prohibited . . . ."[150]

When it moved from the concept of the individual to the concept of the popular community, the anti-charter doctrine tapped an ideological source of equal strength. It would be futile to attempt a precise definition of the concepts of "people" and "sovereignty" as they were constantly hurled against the charter

[145] Cf. *House Journal, 1842*, II, 205; Harrisburg *Democratic Union*, Mar. 8, 1845; *Convention Proceedings*, V, 438; I, 193. For replies to these arguments with the citation of judicial precedent, see *ibid.*, V, 533 ff.
[146] *Constitutions of Pa.*, p. 233.
[147] *Ibid.*, p. 237.
[148] "Minutes of Grand Committee," *Minutes of the 1789 Convention*, pp. 89-90.
[149] *Constitutions of Pa.*, p. 232.
[150] *Pa. Archives*, 4th, VII, 154. See also *ibid.*, VII, 88, 236.

program. In the heated debates of the Convention of 1837 Walter Forward declared that he "would be pleased by some one's defining what is meant by sovereign power." [151] No one satisfied his request. Yet certain meanings of the sovereignty concept seem clear enough. In part it obviously referred to public privileges such as monopoly, eminent domain, and tax-exemption rights often granted to corporate bodies,[152] in part to the chartering of foreign corporations held to be unwarranted intruders,[153] and in part also it simply meant that the functions for which corporations were chartered were functions properly within the sphere of the state itself. Ingersoll summarized these meanings, especially the last, when he said of state legislators that "they grant the whole sovereignty over the currency, the highways, and other property of the sovereignty." [154] It is scarcely necessary to point out that this argument had implications for outright state enterprise, and these were richly elaborated in other policy fields which we shall examine later. Thus a House committee in 1830, providing a formula for the governance of charter policy, included within it the rule that charters should be granted only when it had been proved "that it is inexpedient for the state to proceed in the undertaking as a public measure." [155]

If my earlier analysis of the community idea is correct, another reason for the immense appeal of the sovereignty symbol in the anti-charter theory may be perceived. Did not the corporation, quite as much as parties or pressure groups, represent one of those lesser sovereignties which the symbolic exaltation of the popular sovereignty served always to derogate? Certainly a trace of this logic, not unfamiliar in the history of political doctrines, is to be found in the lament that corporations would "in due time rule the commonwealth," [156] that they were coercing the press and dominating the electorate, that they were proliferating lobbyists, "hungry cormorants" and "small parasites" whose presence in

[151] *Convention Proceedings*, XIV, 11.
[152] See *infra*, p. 278.
[153] Cf. Pennsylvania Senate Committee on Foreign Corporations, *Report*, p. 5.
[154] *Convention Proceedings*, XIV, 8. Cf. *Pa. Archives*, 4th, VI, 841.
[155] *House Journal, 1830–31*, II, 651.
[156] Cf. *Pa. Archives*, 4th, VII, 86; VI, 192, 636; *Convention Proceedings*, VI, 93.

the legislature was constantly adduced to attack the corporation, especially during the era of railroad capitalism.[157] An element of the same logic is to be seen in a distinction between corporations under monarchical and democratic systems which became one of the clichés of the anti-charter doctrine and which was occasionally invoked to assail the adoption of British corporation precedent by American courts. If corporations were instruments by which the power of a king had been limited, surely in Pennsylvania they were instruments by which the power of the people was limited.[158] Porter insisted upon the inapplicability of the McIntosh doctrine in Pennsylvania since "in this country sovereignty is vested in the people themselves, and whatever power is granted to corporations, is so much abstracted from the people themselves." [159] And it was on the basis of the same principle that Shunk, curiously enough, was able to say of corporations: "They are behind the times, they belong to an age that is past." [160]

Since the contention that charter grants impaired popular sovereignty was so basic a part of the anti-charter dogma, it was inevitable that the dogma should assail the legislature as betraying the constituent trust in its development of a charter program. Ingersoll built an elaborate theory on this idea. Quite apart from sovereign privileges which were granted to corporate bodies, the mere fact that they had an existence longer than that of the legislature which chartered them was sufficient to condemn charter policy. If, as Hamilton argued, the chartering power was an attribute of sovereignty, this power belonged not to the legislature but to the people in their constituent capacity. In Britain the creation of corporations was in theory an act of the crown, and the annexing of personal intangibility to them by the common law was a corroboration of the executive authority. In Pennsylvania, however, no royal prerogative existed, and if the chartering power had indeed been transplanted to American soil, it took

---

[157] *Legislative Record, 1857,* No. 82, p. 5; *1856,* p. 217. See also *Pa. Archives,* 4th, VI, 723-24; VII, 37-38; *Convention Proceedings,* VI, 425; *Doylestown Democrat,* Sept. 22, 1846.
[158] *Convention Proceedings,* VI, 28, 82.
[159] *Ibid.,* I, 58.
[160] *Pa. Archives,* 4th, VII, 207-208.

root, owing to the theory of inalienable constituent sovereignty, "in the popular not the legislative soil." [161] In practice Ingersoll's theory would have required a constituent vote every time a charter was granted. Fantastic as his own elaboration of the idea was, the anti-legislative implication of the sovereignty argument did bear some fruit in practice in the Constitutional Convention of 1837 which, reacting against the charter granted to the Second Bank in 1835, imposed certain limits upon the legislative chartering power. The abolition of omnibus charter bills and the requirement of six months' notice for the extension of bank charters [162] which the Convention enacted terminated a debate in which more radical proposals had been considered. One of these, curiously opposed both on the grounds that it would lead to excessive laxity and excessive stringency in charter policy, called for the action of two successive legislatures before a charter might be granted.[163] Another asked for a two-thirds vote for the passage of bank charters.[164]

The popular defense against the anti-charter doctrine was remarkably weak. Occasionally the very impersonality of the corporation was bravely defended, mainly in the banking field, as a method of release from the pettiness and conniving of the indi-

---

[161] *Convention Proceedings*, XIV, 6–12.

[162] For the abolition of omnibus charter bills, see *supra*, chap. I, p. 27; for the requirement of notice, *Constitutions of Pa.*, p. 145: "No corporate body shall be hereafter created, renewed, or extended, with banking or discounting privileges, without six months' previous public notice of the intended application for the same in such manner as shall be prescribed by law." Article I, Section 25. See also *Convention Proceedings*, XIV, 171.

[163] Dickey of Beaver County argued that since the proposal would divide responsibility for charters between two legislatures neither would be impelled to adopt a circumspect policy in granting them. Chandler of Chester County argued that because of the natural tendency of legislatures to postpone action on unpleasant subjects, the two-legislature requirement would lead to a persistent passing of the buck, with the result that "few charters would ever be passed." The first criticism drew the reply that since it was just as difficult to get a bill through one house after it had passed the other as it was to get an original bill through, the proposal if adopted would not lead to a prolific charter policy. The proposal also encountered opposition on the ground that it would send capital to other states and would, especially in the banking field, lead to the destruction of business confidence. *Ibid.*, IX, 105, 121, 133, 138, 146, 154.

[164] This proposal was attacked on the ground that it violated majoritarian principles; it was defended as "a voluntary restraint assumed by the people for their own benefit." *Ibid.*, I, 379, 386; V, 528.

vidual operator. More frequent emphasis was placed upon the breadth of economic participation which the corporate system made possible. "Who are those monopolizers and aristocrats, sir," asked George Chambers of Franklin County, "who own the banks, but the people?" [165] The cry of the "widows and orphans, frail old women and toddling children" [166] went forth across the state, weaker now than it was eventually to become, but convincing enough to inspire the shrewd proprietors of the Lehigh Navigation Company, faced during the early thirties with an acute need for public relations work, to disseminate figures on the dispersion of stock ownership in the company and to generalize vaguely on the number of the aged and the young which the figures included.[167] There is little doubt that with the mass promotional techniques developed during the railroad capitalism of the forties, a wider enlistment of community resources was achieved by the corporate system.[168] But the popular-participation argument, however ingeniously developed, was not enough to counter the highly involved legalism of the anti-charter theory. It was confronted by the righteous puritanism of the contention that the man of moderate means could by his own hard work derive a higher return on his capital than he could by investing it in corporate enterprises,[169] by the counter-charge that corporate ownership was in fact almost invariably concentrated in the hands of a few,[170] and by the assertion that even if ownership was widespread, control was concentrated — the last argument being linked to a criticism of the use of proxies in stockholder voting.[171]

[165] *Ibid.*, I, 378; IX, 206, 124. Marcus Bull of the North American Coal Company declared: "They [corporations] are not *aristocratic*, but truly *republican* in principle. . . . No particular political, mental, or moral requisites are necessary; all that is required is the adequate funds, and with these it is believed that any stock may be purchased." *Mining Operations of North American Coal Company*, p. 7. Chambers asserted: "They are democratic in their associations and purposes, being alike open to all who may choose to become stockholders." *Convention Proceedings*, XIV, 59. See also *ibid.*, I, 385; VI, 125; XIV, 55, 57.

[166] *Ibid.*, I, 378.

[167] J. White, *Circular*; White and Hazard, *To Members of the Legislature*; Lehigh Company, *To the Committee on Corporations of the Senate*.

[168] Cf. Cochran and Miller, *Age of Enterprise*, p. 68; Edwards, *Finance Capitalism*, pp. 147–48; Sipes, *Pennsylvania Railroad*, p. 11.

[169] *Pa. Archives*, 4th, VII, 87–88.

[170] *Ibid.*, VII, 87.   [171] See *infra*, pp. 255–56.

A puzzling aspect of unreality characterizes the anti-charter theory when studied in the setting of actual policy developments. It is evident that the theory flourished long after there was any hope of its acceptance either by the legislature or the judiciary. Though the Supreme Court sometimes criticized the expansion of charter policy, it always upheld its constitutional validity: ". . . it seems scarcely necessary to say that monopolies are not prohibited by the constitution; and that to abolish them would destroy many of our most useful institutions." [172] The principle of the eminent domain grant, which evoked so much of the vested rights legalism of the anti-charter doctrine, was also consistently upheld: the right of eminent domain might "be exercised by the government through its immediate officers or agents, or indirectly through the medium of corporate bodies." [173] The abolition of the charter program by the legislature was out of the question; in another breath Governor Shunk, one of the most vigorous of the anti-charter ideologists, could recognize the practical need for charters,[174] and he would probably have been impeached had he acted on the anti-charter principles he so often and so flamboyantly professed. Why, then, when charter policy was irrevocably entrenched and expanding, should the popular literature be dominated by an ideology which denied the legitimacy of the very principle of a charter grant?

The conclusion is inescapable that the anti-charter dogma thrived by virtue of an ideological rationale largely independent of policy considerations. Its intense equalitarianism, its involvement in the democratic theory of the time, made it an excellent polemic for orators and politicians, even though interest pressures in the state dictated an expansion of charter policy. In the mass-based political life of Pennsylvania the independent importance

---

[172] *Case of the Philadelphia and Trenton Railroad Co.*, 6 Wharton 25, 46 (1840). Cf. remarks of Chief Justice Tilghman, *Washington and Pittsburgh Turnpike Co.* v. *Cullen and Crane*, 8 Serg. and Rawle 517, 521 (1822); *Schuylkill Navigation Co.* v. *Thomas*, 13 Serg. and Rawle 431, 433 (1825).

[173] *City of Pittsburgh* v. *Scott*, 1 Pa. St. Rep. 309, 314 (1845). See also *Harvey* v. *Thomas*, 10 Watts 63 (1840); *Harvey* v. *Lloyd*, 3 Pa. St. Rep. 331 (1846); *Hays* v. *Risher*, 32 Pa. St. Rep. 169 (1858). Cf. Porter's remarks, *Convention Proceedings*, XII, 207 ff; also *House Journal, 1832*, II, 509–10.

[174] Cf. *Pa. Archives*, 4th, VII, 36.

THE ANTI-CHARTER DOCTRINE

of ideology is not to be underestimated. Democratic supremacy, as I suggested in the previous chapter, rested largely upon it: the state was as ardently wedded to the American System as any in the Union, and it was mainly by monopolizing the equalitarian ideology that Democratic politicians were able to win elections.[175] As an integral part of that ideology, the anti-charter doctrine reflected the strategic logic by which the Whigs were handicapped. It was developed widely by the Democrats. Though in fact the charter question was scarcely a party issue, Democratic politicians tirelessly branded their opponents as believers in "monopoly" — a principle "dear to the hearts of the Federal Party."[176] The Whigs sought to make what political capital could be made out of a pro-corporate argument, but occasionally they reacted to the criticism just as they reacted to the damning "Federalist" epithet itself: they repudiated it. They sought themselves to exploit the power of the great anti-charter symbols just as they sought to exploit the force of the other equalitarian slogans to which these were allied: they defended individual enterprise, hated aristocracies, assailed impairments of sovereignty.[177] This had the effect of lifting the anti-charter symbols, as a similar rationale lifted the other equalitarian slogans, to a position of broad acceptance. But the strategy of the Whigs in this connection was no more successful than their attempts to claim that they were the true party of Jefferson. The nemesis of an aristocratic reputation haunted them to the end.

Nor did this party strategy go unobserved. In 1837 Joshua F. Cox of Somerset bitterly remarked that the Democrats operated on the principle that the "very salvation of their party depended upon keeping up the cry of 'monopoly' — 'monopoly.' " And he asked a relevant question: "Can it be possible that a party which believes banks to be monopolies can go on so rapidly creating them?"[178] It was embarrassingly relevant in 1837. For only two years earlier a Democratic Senate had authorized a state charter

---

[175] Cf. *supra*, pp. 23–24.
[176] *Doylestown Democrat*, Sept. 8, 1847.
[177] Cf. remarks of Ritner, *Pa. Archives*, 4th, VI, 287–88, 301, 386–88; of Pollock, *ibid.*, VII, 938.
[178] *Convention Proceedings*, IX, 168, 169.

for the Chestnut Street Monster. It had authorized it, as I have already pointed out, owing to precisely the forces that made it impossible for the Democrats or any other party to pursue in practice the radical theoretical anti-charterism which their party professed: the pressure of section, of lobby, of public investment need. Once the mistake of the Second Bank charter had become clear, this gave the Whigs one of their best opportunities to turn anti-charterism against the Democrats. M. B. Lowry, a Democratic member of the legislative committee investigating the charter of the Second Bank, indignantly declared that the Whigs had "charged their own high offences upon the Democratic Party which from principle and sound policy has uniformly contended in opposition to it [the Second Bank]." [179]

When seen as a portion of the democratic religion of the state, the radicalism of the anti-charter doctrine is better understood in relation to the fact of an established charter policy. The peculiar status of the anti-charter symbols is perhaps best demonstrated in the fact that the corporate idea, as it sought to broaden the sphere of its acceptance, was compelled itself to appropriate their appeal. The main unfolding of this remarkable development is to be found in the period after the Civil War, but its origins are clearly discernible in the epoch we are examining here. A consideration of it will bring us to an important point of view from which we have not yet considered the anti-charter ideology — its historic development. From a developmental standpoint the doctrine did not have a laborious career. It emerged astonishingly full-blown in the controversy over the Bank of North America in 1785.[180] The intensity of its manifestation, however, is easily linked up with the alternation of boom and recession. Like the puritanic theme it flourished during depression periods, and the linkage between the two ideologies was demonstrated again and again by the charge that corporations were vehicles of boom immorality.[181] It entered

---

[179] Quoted, Mueller, *Whig Party in Pa.*, p. 79.

[180] See M. Carey, *Annulling the Charter of the Bank of North America*, p. 123 and *passim*.

[181] *Senate Journal, 1819–20*, p. 223; *House Journal, 1830–31*, II, 651; *Convention Proceedings*, V, 613; VI, 65, 85. In an attempt to reply to this argument Chandler claimed St. Luke as favoring banking corporations: "Wherefore then gavest not

upon the first stage of a secular decline during the last two decades of our period, particularly during the fifties when the rate of charter grants experienced, as our figures have shown, a marked expansion. I use the word "decline" to characterize this development, but actually some of the main anti-charter concepts persisted and even expanded in importance in the literature of this late period. The decline of the theory was revealed in an inner deterioration of its conceptual integrity; the concepts remained, but their meaning began to change, and change radically. They began slowly to be appropriated by the corporation itself.

The fate of one crucial concept will suffice to illustrate this development — "individual enterprise." Quite apart from its use in the attack on the economic value of the corporate device, this concept was at the heart of the entire natural law and constitutional challenge of the charter principle. In certain controversies of the forties and fifties, however, it began to appear as a righteous description of corporate as well as unincorporated enterprise. The highly evocative antithesis of the previous time — the individual versus the corporation — gradually blurred. This blurring of concepts, this appropriation by the corporation of the doctrinal dynamite of its opponents, is the historic manifestation in symbolism of the coming-of-age of corporate enterprise in the state. The most complex ideological shift of the entire period, it marks, as we shall see in subsequent chapters, the slow beginning of a new era of popular thought not only regarding charter policy but regarding the whole relationship between state and economic life.

6. *The Role of Government*

What was the larger meaning of the anti-charter doctrine for the role of government in the economic field? Was it, to use common terminology, a "laissez-faire" doctrine embracing a "physiocratic" conception of natural harmonies? It is not hard to see why

---

thou my money into the bank, that, at my coming, I might have regained mine own with usury." He contended that stock gambling was traceable not to the corporate system but to a species of popular ignorance which public education would eliminate. *Ibid.*, VI, 111. It was also held that banking corporations had a "moral influence" on society because they encouraged punctuality in payments. *Ibid.*, VI, 125 ff; H. Miller, *Banking Theories in U.S. before 1860*, pp. 21 ff.

this question might be answered in the affirmative. The theory contained a persistent indictment of "monopoly" and an equally persistent reference to the principle of "nature." Yet the impression which these terms convey is liable to be deceptive. It is evident of course that a species of faith in the competitive principle was central to the anti-charter doctrine. But it is dangerous to identify that faith with the natural law ideas. For those ideas remained ideas of political right, not ideas of a pervasive economic harmony in the Smithian or physiocratic sense. It was not Smith, for all his antagonism to the corporate device, nor lonely domestic classicists such as Franklin, Pelatiah Webster, and Raguet who were the idols of the anti-charter polemicists, but Locke and the Revolutionary theorists. There were, to be sure, exceptions to this rule: in rare instances Smith's anti-corporate argument was quoted [182] and Governor Shunk, as a result of obscure influences, loved to talk of that "perfect harmony, . . . so kindly provided by Him who rules all things." [183] But such exceptions provide no more accurate a guide to the use of the nature concept among the generality of anti-charter polemicists than the physiocracy of Franklin provides to its use among Revolutionary theorists. For the vast majority of the former it seems clear that the natural law idea evoked the vision not of an automatic market but of the Declaration of Rights of the state constitution.

But did not the anti-charter ideology represent a wholesale criticism of state economic action in a purely political sense? A thorough combing of the doctrine will turn up at least a few highly quotable phrases of the broader type. "Too much legislation is more to be dreaded than the entire want of it," lamented the Packer Committee in 1834. "The maxim is true that 'the world is governed too much.'" [184] In criticizing charter policy Governor Wolf liked to refer to "that republican simplicity" upon which the democracy of the state was predicated.[185] Add to these statements

---

[182] Cf. *House Journal, 1806*, p. 51; Taylor, *Effect of Incorporated Coal Companies*, p. 4.
[183] *Pa. Archives*, 4th, VII, 208–209, 236–37.
[184] *Report upon Coal Trade*, p. 46.
[185] *Pa. Archives*, 4th, VI, 192. Governor Porter also adopted the same phrase. *Convention Proceedings*, VI, 655.

the far more elaborate defense of "individual enterprise" and "vested rights," and is not the sum practically identical in appearance with latter-day doctrines assailing the principle of public action in economic life — with doctrines ordinarily described as "laissez-faire" in meaning?

Again appearances tend to be misleading. Equally challenging questions can be asked on the other side. Was not the fear that economic power might rival the authority of the state pivotal in the anti-charter doctrine? Did not the use of the sovereignty concept in this connection actually adumbrate the legitimacy of state as opposed to corporate enterprise? Did not the transfer of the equalitarian idea directly into the economic field have a meaning deeply antagonistic toward the unbridled exercise of economic prerogatives — as the charge of communism which it sometimes evoked made clear? Do "laissez-faire" theories ordinarily elicit the communist charge? Was not the "individual enterprise" slogan, moreover, directed against the corporation? Do modern champions of "individual enterprise" ordinarily seek the abolition of the corporate system?

The full significance of these questions cannot be seen in the limited area of policy and theory we have so far examined. For the anti-charter dogma was bound up with other doctrines evolving simultaneously in connection with other policies. It cannot be understood apart from these, and nothing is more unfortunate than the practice of viewing it independently. When studied in its historic setting, the doctrine assumes a role which is in many respects the precise antithesis of that in which the "laissez-faire" interpretation has traditionally cast it. Instead of serving as the spearhead of a broad anti-governmental philosophy, it served as a kind of barrier to the elaboration of such a philosophy. For, as we shall see in subsequent chapters, it was not until the doctrine had entered upon its deterioration phase, late in this period, that a wholesale ideological assault upon state economic action was able to emerge.

III

THE MIXED CORPORATION

1. The Growth of Investment

"A CORPORATION IN LAW," asserted the Packer Committee of 1834, "is just what the incorporating act makes it. It is the creature of the law, and may be moulded to any shape or for any purpose that the Legislature may deem most conducive to the general good." [1] The plasticity of the corporate device in America was nowhere better illustrated than in the history of its mixed corporation variant. Pennsylvania's mixed enterprise policy was initiated as early as 1793 and it persisted until the close of our period when two state actions were taken which gradually abolished it. The first of these was a legislative measure in 1843 [2] which provided for the liquidation of most of the state stockholdings; the second was a constitutional amendment in 1857 which forbade public investment in business corporations.[3]

Mixed corporation policy first appeared in the banking field. In chartering the Bank of Pennsylvania, the state subscribed twenty-five hundred shares at a par value of one million dollars.[4] Holdings in bank stock were increased in 1803 when the Bank of Philadelphia was chartered. Three thousand shares were taken in the stock of that bank at a total value of three hundred thousand dollars.[5] In 1810, as a result of the accession of new shares in both the Pennsylvania and the Philadelphia banks and as a result of a subscription to the stock of the Farmers' and Mechanics' Bank, the government of Pennsylvania held 7,364 shares of bank

---

[1] *Report upon Coal Trade*, p. 46.
[2] *Pa. Laws, 1843*, p. 182.
[3] *Constitutions of Pa.*, pp. 166–67.
[4] *Statutes at Large*, XIV, 377–78. To finance the subscription all public stock of the United States in the state treasury, all unappropriated funds and a loan from the Bank, at 6 per cent, were utilized. Cf. Holdsworth, *Financing an Empire*, I, 133; D. Dewey, *State Banking before Civil War*, p. 6.
[5] *Statutes at Large*, XVII, 126, 491. Unless otherwise indicated all subsequent statistics on mixed corporation investment and dividends are taken from the *Annual Reports of the Pennsylvania Auditor-General*.

stock amounting at par value to $1,990,793.⁶ By 1815 the total had risen to $2,108,700.⁷ After that year the amount of bank stock held by the state remained static until 1843 when the entire investment was liquidated at public auction.

Mixed enterprise policy was extended to transportation in 1806. A House committee recommended the enactment of a bill authorizing the governor to subscribe on behalf of the state one-fifth of the shares in all turnpike companies incorporated during the legislative session of that year. The state investment was to be paid after construction was completed, and the state was "to participate in the profit and the controul" of the roads. The committee argued against the retroactive application of the investment principle on the ground that many turnpikes previously chartered were launched without due regard to their importance to the community.[8] Despite this qualification, however, the bill recommended by the committee was rejected by the legislature as too broad in its application. Subscriptions by the state were not made generally, but were specifically provided for in charters of favored turnpike corporations.[9] A year later another legislative committee, urging the extension of mixed enterprise policy, pointed out the necessity of limiting its application only to "such great leading roads" as "promise to be of . . . general utility." [10]

In 1810 the state investment in turnpike corporations amounted to only $61,937. By 1820, however, the investment in this field totaled over one million dollars, and during the next two decades it increased over 100 per cent, amounting in 1843 to $2,320,312. The average state investment in fifty-six mixed turnpike corporations listed by the auditor-general in 1825 was $32,309.[11] Though actual state investment sometimes exceeded actual private investment, as in the case of the Bellefonte and Phillipsburg company

---

[6] Cf. Cook, *Philadelphia National Bank*, pp. 35, 81; *House Journal, 1807–1808*, I, 197.

[7] Cf. *Hazard's Register*, V (1830), 6.

[8] *House Journal, 1806–1807*, p. 398.

[9] Cf. *Pa. Laws, 1807–1808*, pp. 85–86; *1810–11*, pp. 256–59; *1815–16*, pp. 138–39; *1820–21*, pp. 101–30; Durrenberger, *Turnpikes*, p. 48; John, "Centre Turnpike Road," *Publ. of Hist. Soc. of Schuylkill County*, II, 4, 522–23.

[10] *House Journal, 1807–1808*, I, 316.

[11] Cf. Durrenberger, *Turnpikes*, p. 50.

and the Butler and Mercer company, private subscriptions exceeded on the whole state subscriptions. The reports of certain turnpike companies to the legislature in 1821 revealed that $1,861,542 of their stock had been subscribed by the government, while $4,158,347 of it had been subscribed by private investors.[12] The general sale of state-held stock which got under way in the summer of 1843 cut deeply into the public turnpike investment. Within two years the state had virtually duplicated in reverse the development of the previous twenty: by 1845 turnpike holdings had dropped to $1,510,042. With the enactment of the constitutional amendment of 1857 the possibility of new investments was automatically precluded. At the outbreak of the Civil War, the remainder of earlier investments amounted to something more than one and a quarter million dollars.

The mixed bridge corporation also appeared in the second decade of the century; by 1815 state bridge holdings totaled $182,500. Between 1815 and 1840 there was a rapid expansion of investment in this area, which paralleled the expansion of turnpike investment. By 1840 state subscriptions to the stock of bridge corporations added up to $514,350. The average holding in bridge corporations was usually larger than that in turnpike corporations, owing to the comparatively greater capitalization of the former, but the difference was not uniform throughout the period and it was not a striking one. In the eleven mixed bridge corporations in existence in 1820, the state subscription averaged $34,727, approximately $1,200 more than the average investment in turnpike corporations during that year. In 1825, however, the average bridge subscription exceeded the average turnpike subscription by less than three hundred dollars.

Though in certain bridge companies the state held the major part of the capital stock, as in the Northumberland Bridge Company, and in others roughly 50 per cent, the actual state investment fell short of equaling the investment of private stockholders. In twenty-five companies reporting to the legislature in 1822, private subscriptions of stock amounted to $1,629,200, while state

[12] *Hazard's Register*, II (1828), 298. Cf. Durrenberger, *Turnpikes*, p. 102.

subscriptions totaled only $382,000.[13] The sale of state-owned stocks begun in 1843 struck an even harder blow at the mixed bridge corporation than at the mixed turnpike corporation. As in the banking area, the state had completely liquidated its bridge holdings by 1845. A few investments in bridge stock were made subsequently, but the constitutional amendment of 1857 prevented any effective resurrection of the mixed bridge corporation in Pennsylvania. In 1860 only nine thousand dollars' worth of bridge stock was held by the state.

In canal and navigation companies state investments rose from a total of $50,000 in 1820 to a total of $645,269 in 1840. Though such companies were fewer in number, their average capitalization was greater than that of either turnpike or bridge corporations, and the average state holding in their stock exceeded in value average holdings in either of the latter. Three state investments totaling $185,000 were listed in this field in 1825. On the whole, actual private investments exceeded actual state investments by a considerable sum in canal and navigation companies, though there were exceptions such as the Monongahela Navigation Company in which the state had, by 1828, subscribed $30,000 worth of stock as against a private subscription of $18,360. In the same year the Schuylkill Navigation Company reported a private subscription almost nineteen times greater than the state subscription; the Union Canal Company reported a private subscription nine times greater; and the total private investment in eight companies was $1,416,510 as against a total state investment of $130,000.[14] Though the sale of stocks in the early forties reduced state holdings in canal and navigation companies from $645,269 to $190,657, a more significant recovery was subsequently made in this field than in either the turnpike or bridge fields. In 1860 total state holdings stood at $325,532. Even this figure, however, represented only a little more than 50 per cent of the state investment at its 1840 peak.

The history of state investment in railroad companies ran a

---

[13] *Hazard's Register*, II (1828), 297.
[14] *Ibid.*, II (1828), 300.

different course. The railroad investment program did not get under way in any major form until the forties, and its liquidation did not set in until the fifties. While state investments in other areas declined precipitously from 1840 to 1845, railroad investments expanded. By 1850 they amounted to $643,456, an increase of more than $300,000 over the 1840 figure. The continuation of the state's policy of stock liquidation during the later period, however, hit the mixed railroad corporation particularly hard. By 1855 the state railroad investment had fallen to $460,179; in 1860 it totaled only $181,647, about one-third of the aggregate holding in 1850.

The state railroad investment program, even at its height, was of minor significance compared with investments by cities and counties. The mass of public railroad investment took place on the local plane. Nor did this involve the introduction of a new principle as far as mixed enterprise was concerned in Pennsylvania. Cities and counties had traditionally subscribed to the stock of local corporations. An accurate picture of this procedure is difficult to present when subscriptions were made without legislative authorization, owing to the loss and confusion of local records.[15] State statute volumes, however, reveal with a fair degree of clarity the process as it evolved under legislative authority. "The first trace we find of this principle," Governor Bigler once wrote, "is in the form of authority to county commissioners, to make subscriptions to specific objects. Next we find a few instances of the extension of it to the municipal authorities. . . ."[16] Counties operated in the bridge field at the very outset of the nineteenth century,[17] and in 1816 the House Committee on Roads and Inland Navigation reported favorably on a general measure permitting county commissioners "to subscribe for stock in any turnpike road in which the citizens of the county may be supposed to feel a general interest."[18] A general measure was not adopted, however, and authorization was given in specific cases. The form of authorization varied. In certain instances the number of stock shares or

[15] Cf. *ibid.*, I (1828), 408.
[16] *Pa. Archives*, 4th, VII, 528.
[17] *Hazard's Register*, I (1828), 408.
[18] *House Journal, 1815–16*, p. 365.

CHART 2

VALUE OF STOCK HELD BY PENNSYLVANIA IN MIXED CORPORATIONS, BY TYPES OF ENTERPRISE, AT FIVE-YEAR INTERVALS, 1800–1860

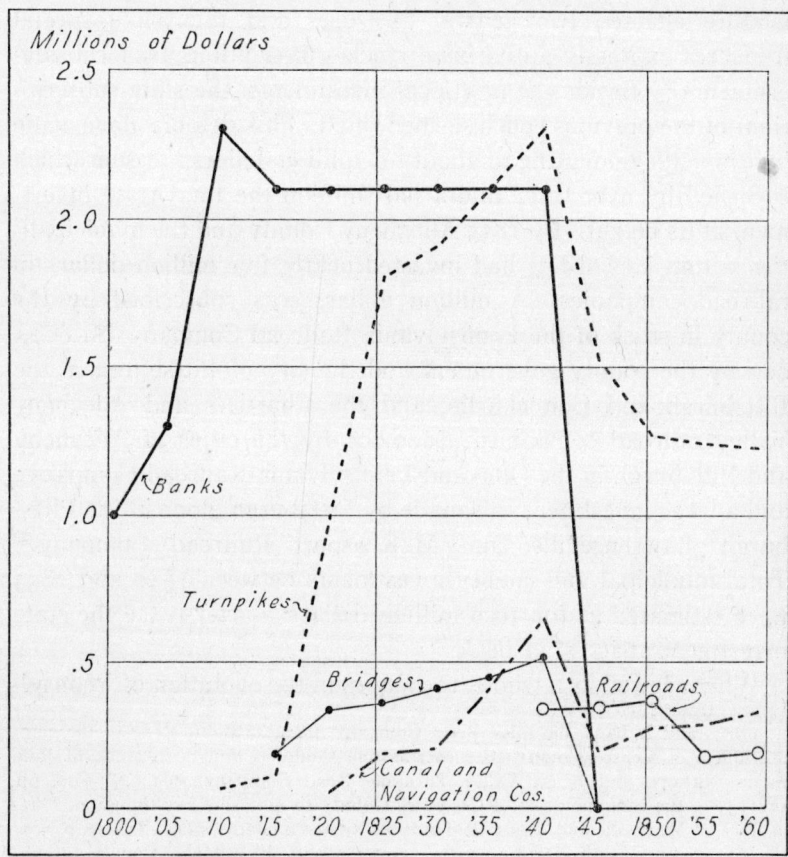

the total amount of subscription was expressly set forth; in others no limits were provided for.[19]

It was inevitable that local governments should dominate public railroad investment. The amounts of capital required for railroad

---

[19] For authorization to the commissioners of Potter County to subscribe 140 shares of stock at fifty dollars each in a company chartered to build a road from Jersey Shore to Coudersport, see *Pa. Laws, 1829–30*, p. 63; to the commissioners of Huntingdon County to subscribe one thousand dollars in stock of the Huntingdon,

construction were unprecedented, but the powerful intrastate competition which centered about the railroad question made it impossible for the state government to embark upon a comprehensive program of stock subscription. Between 1846 and 1860 the legislature enacted two general measures and thirty-five special measures expressly authorizing stock subscriptions by local governments.[20] Beside the new local investments, the state subscriptions of the previous epoch seemed small. Philadelphia alone made investments amounting to about ten million dollars,[21] a sum which exceeded by over three and a half million the total state investment at its height. By 1855 Allegheny County and the municipalities within its borders had invested nearly five million dollars in railroad companies. A million dollars was subscribed by the county in stock of the Pennsylvania Railroad Company; $1,600,000 by the county government and the city of Pittsburgh in the Pittsburgh and Connelsville, and the Chartiers and Allegheny Valley railroad companies; $600,000 by the cities of Allegheny and Pittsburgh in the Ohio and Pennsylvania Railroad Company; and a large investment was made by Pittsburgh alone in the Pittsburgh, Lawrenceville, and McKeesport Railroad Company.[22] Total municipal and county investments between 1840 and 1853 were estimated at fourteen million dollars — over twice the state investment at its 1843 peak.[23]

When viewed as a whole, the stages in the evolution of Pennsyl-

Cambria, and Indiana Turnpike Road Company, *ibid.*, *1830–31*, p. 1; to the commissioners of Centre County to subscribe one thousand dollars in stock of Bald Eagle, Nittany, and Brush Valley Turnpike Road Company, *ibid.*, *1835–36*, pp. 512–13; to the commissioners of Crawford County to subscribe five thousand shares in stock of Meadville and Titusville Turnpike Road Company, *ibid.*, *1836–37*, p. 327; for an unlimited authorization to the commissioners of Venango County to subscribe stock in the Shippenville and Emlenton Turnpike Road Company, *ibid.*, *1829–30*, p. 67.

[20] Cf. *Pa. Archives*, 4th, VII, 528 ff., 652 ff.

[21] 47 Pa. St. Rep. 192 ff. (1864); *Public Ledger*, Jan. 8, Feb. 5, 8, 10, 25, Mar. 1 1853; *North American*, Jan. 8, 11, 1853; Philadelphia Common Council, *Report, Special Committee in Relation to the Sunbury and Erie Railroad*, pp. 9 ff.; Philadelphia Committee on Railroads, *Report, passim*; Sunbury and Erie Railroad Company, *Report*, pp. 3–4.

[22] *History of Allegheny County*, pp. 575–76; Allegheny Valley Railroad, *Report*, p. 10; Cleveland and Powell, *Railroad Promotion and Capitalization*, p. 206.

[23] This is the estimate of Chief Justice Black. *Sharpless et al.* v. *Mayor of Philadelphia*, 21 Pa. St. Rep. 147, 158 (1853).

vania's mixed corporation policy seem clearly defined. Total state investment, beginning at the million mark in 1800, expanded steadily until a high point was reached in 1843 — $6,171,416. The sale of stocks initiated in 1843 cut the state investment down

CHART 3

VALUE OF ALL STOCK HELD BY PENNSYLVANIA IN MIXED CORPORATIONS, AT FIVE-YEAR INTERVALS, 1800–1860

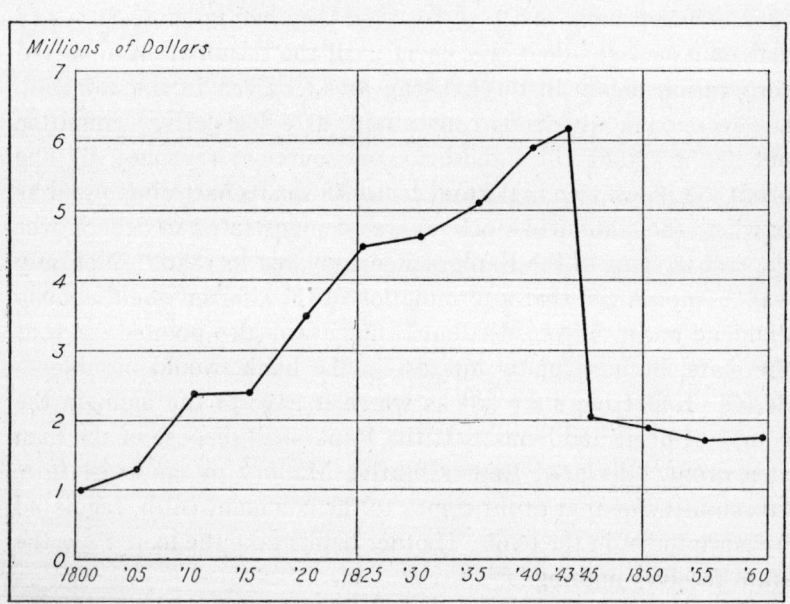

to about one-third of its previous size, and a fairly steady decline took place thereafter. By 1860 aggregate state holdings had dropped to $1,746,546. Local investment, which got under way in 1846, expanded spectacularly until 1857 when its continuance was prohibited by constitutional amendment.

2. *Profit, Promotion, and Control*

Three principal motives governed the execution of mixed corporation policy. The first to appear was the motive of public profit. In the older states of the North and South banking enterprises needed no governmental aid, since an adequate supply of foreign capital was always available and the business of banking was considered an unusually profitable field of investment.[24] The rejected overtures made by the state to the Bank of North America in 1793 were made primarily with the profit motive in mind.[25] Annual dividends on state bank investments rose from $99,500 in 1805 to $309,433 in 1815.[26] The crisis of 1819 reduced dividends sharply and, though the amount of bank stock held by the state remained static until the liquidation of 1843, dividend returns never again equaled those of 1815. By 1820 they had fallen to $123,527 and remained at about that level until the termination of mixed corporation policy in the banking area.[27] Even in the twenties, however, bank dividends constituted, as a legislative committee put it, the state's "first and principal source of revenue." [28] The profit motive was an important factor in the rechartering of banks in which the state held stock, as was demonstrated in debate over the rechartering of the Bank of Pennsylvania in 1830.[29] Not only was it emphasized that a termination of the charter would abolish dividend receipts from that bank, but it was also pointed out that the state, because of its interest in the bank, would be able to derive profit from state stocks which it gave to the bank in the course of projected loans. "If the Bank shall dispose of the loan at a profit," declared Representative Mallory in the legislature, "three-fifths of that profit comes to the commonwealth, regulated by her interest in the bank. If other banks take the loan . . . the state receives nothing." [30]

The revenue motive was not of comparable significance in the

---

[24] Callender, "Early Transportation and Banking Enterprises of the States," *Quarterly Jour. of Econ.*, XVII (1902–03), 159; D. Dewey, *State Banking before Civil War*, p. 33.

[25] Holdsworth, *Financing an Empire*, I, 133; Lewis, *Bank of North America*, p. 81.

[26] In 1816 dividend receipts on bank stock amounted to two-fifths of the entire state revenue. Cf. Holdsworth, *Financing an Empire*, 143; D. Dewey, *State Banking before Civil War*, pp. 33, 37–38.

[27] The chartering of other banks in Philadelphia in addition to the Bank of Pennsylvania and the Bank of Philadelphia was undoubtedly another factor which reduced dividend returns in the banking field. Cf. Report of House Committee on Ways and Means, *House Journal, 1822*, pp. 818, 588.

[28] *Ibid.*, p. 818.

[29] *Pa. Laws, 1829–30*, pp. 86 ff; *Hazard's Register*, V (1830), 81–85.

[30] *Ibid.*, V (1830), 82.

Chart 4

DIVIDENDS RECEIVED BY PENNSYLVANIA ON ALL STATE-HELD STOCK AND ON STATE-HELD BANK STOCK, AT FIVE-YEAR INTERVALS, 1800–1860

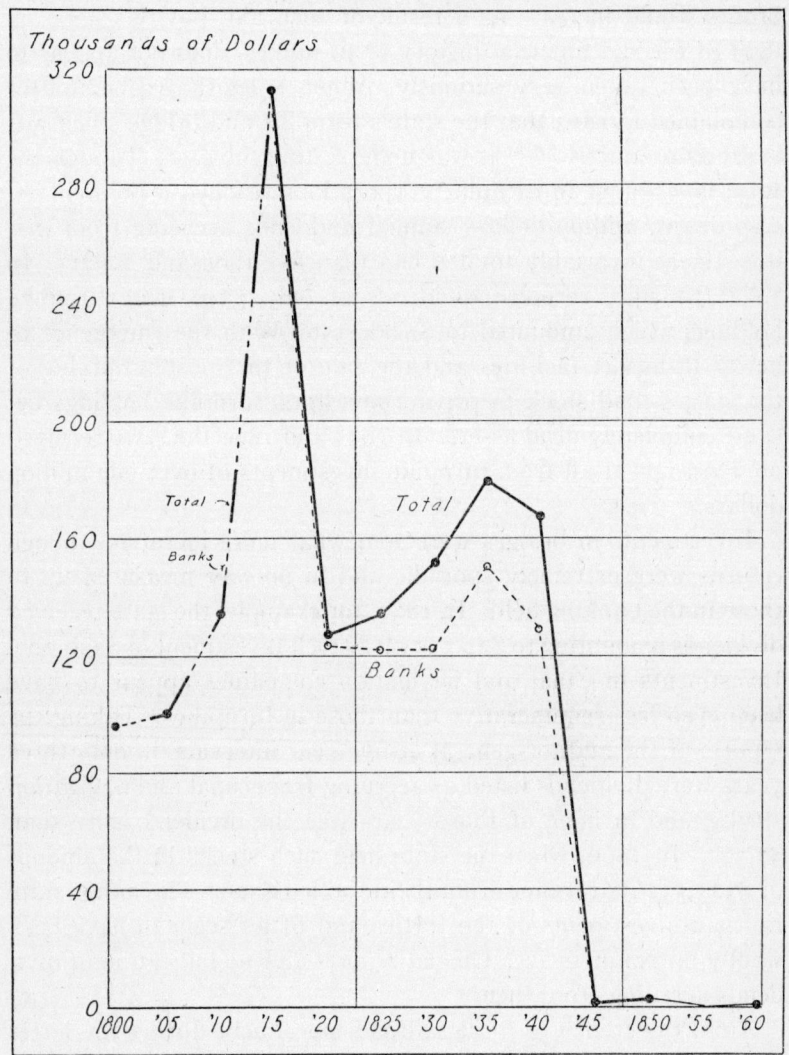

transportation field, though legislative efforts were constantly made to secure the greatest possible dividend returns from investments in transportation corporations. Early legislative committees recommending state aid to turnpike companies suggested that profits would increase as a result of such aid, but this hope, in light of the sad financial history of turnpikes, does not appear to have been taken very seriously. When a legislative committee complained in 1823 that the state's turnpike and bridge stock was "very unproductive," [31] it was understating the case. Though the state investment in turnpike corporations reached a point in excess of two million dollars, annual dividends accruing from that investment invariably totaled less than five thousand dollars. In 1825 the state received dividends of only $540 from turnpike holdings which amounted to $1,809,356. With the emergence of newer transport facilities and the sale of the most profitable of the state's road stock to private investors, turnpike holdings became completely dead assets. In 1855 and 1860 the state received no dividends at all from turnpike investments of over one million dollars.

Investments in bridges were somewhat more lucrative, though returns were extremely sporadic and in no way measured up to those in the banking field. In 1830, for example, the state received dividends amounting to $20,135 on a stock investment of $400,000. Investments in canal and navigation companies appear to have been even less remunerative than those in turnpikes. Taking the reports of the auditor-general at five-year intervals, in only three years were dividends listed as accruing from canal and navigation stocks, and in none of those years was the dividend more than $7,500. In 1860, when the state held such stocks in the amount of $325,532 its revenue from them totaled $306. The minor state railroad investments of the forties and fifties seem to have been wholly unremunerative. Official reports give no indication of dividends accruing from them.

Amid the frenzy of local railroad investment during the latter forties and fifties, railroad promoters promised great dividends to counties and municipalities. The promoters of the Pennsylvania

[31] *House Journal, 1822*, p. 819.

Railroad predicted immediate returns of 10 per cent on the stock subscribed by Philadelphia.[32] Instead of deriving revenue, however, counties and municipalities found themselves facing bankruptcy as a result of investments. During the panic of 1857[33] almost all railroads failed to pay interest on local bonds issued in return for stock, the Pennsylvania being a notable exception. Half of Philadelphia's stock holdings were characterized by a justice of the Supreme Court as "worthless."[34] In Allegheny County, many of whose bondholders lived outside the county so that action could be easily taken against them, the Democratic Convention of 1857 flatly refused to embark upon the "imposition of taxes for railroad purposes."[35] Except for bonds issued to the Pennsylvania Railroad, the county repudiated by issuing new bonds at lower interest rates.[36] A historian of the county remarked in 1889: "The disgrace, bad as it was, did not last long, and the people can now look back upon it with a profound consciousness that honesty is the best policy. . . ."[37]

A second objective behind mixed enterprise policy was promotional. This aim was particularly important in transportation, both because of the riskiness of that field as an area of private investment and because of its relation to the interstate and intercity commercial competition of the period. It was, as Governor Bigler once remarked, of overshadowing significance in the local investment movement of the forties and fifties,[38] when the promoters of the Pennsylvania could insist that municipal investment was a matter of commercial "life and death" to Philadelphia, and the Connelsville promoters could propagandize Pittsburgh and

---

[32] *Public Ledger*, Nov. 27, 1846. Cf. Cleveland and Powell, *Railroad Promotion and Capitalization*, p. 207.

[33] A good account of railroad stagnation at this time is to be found in *Pennsylvanian*, Aug. 22, Sept. 1, 1856. See also *History of Allegheny County*, p. 575.

[34] *Pennsylvania Railroad Company* v. *The City of Philadelphia*, 47 Pa. St. Rep. 189, 192 ff. (1864).

[35] *Philadelphia Press*, Sept. 1, 1857; *Pennsylvanian*, Sept. 5, 1857.

[36] *History of Allegheny County*, pp. 575-76. Cf. *Public Ledger*, June 13, 1857.

[37] *History of Allegheny County*, p. 575. McClure remarked of Allegheny politics at this time: "Men climbed into Congress and into the State senate and house as repudiation leaders. . . ." *Old Time Notes of Pa.*, I, 143. See *infra.*, p. 120.

[38] *Pa. Archives*, 4th, VII, 652.

the western counties with similar language.³⁹ Yet the arguments they used had been developed years before in connection with state investment. Petitions coming to the legislature in 1806 from Northumberland, Luzerne, and Lycoming counties, which pleaded for an extension of mixed enterprise policy to the transportation field, warned that unless this was done trade, population, and capital would drift to other regions where better transport facilities were to be had. They pointed to the "dispirited and exhausted" condition of unaided turnpike corporations, branded a reliance upon them as an inequitable "system of individual sacrifices," and insisted that "one great end of all congregations of men in political society" was to perform by the "combined efforts of the whole" that which was beyond the capacity of individuals.⁴⁰

Reporting favorably on these petitions, the House Committee on Roads and Inland Navigation presented three immediate benefits to be derived from public investment in turnpike and canal companies: (1) The incentive for private investment would increase, since the motive of enhancing property values by means of constructing transportation facilities — what the committee called "the indirect indemnity in the rise of other property" — would act with "increased force" upon property owners. (2) Commerce would expand, and the return to all stockholders would be proportionately greater. (3) The state, being financially interested in the corporations, would take more stringent action in protecting them against the evasion of toll payments.⁴¹

There is no doubt that the early reliance upon private transportation companies was a failure. The number of "paper" transportation corporations on the statute books was always high; in 1828 turnpike building lagged almost a thousand miles behind the statute figure, and rail and canal projects had realized scarcely more than one-fifth of the mileage authorized in charters. Abundant as capital supplies may have been, the required transport facilities could not be sustained by the hope of indirect re-

---

³⁹ *Public Ledger*, Nov. 27, 1846, Feb. 8, 1853; *Legislative Record, 1857*, No. 77, p. 6.
⁴⁰ *House Journal, 1806*, pp. 392 ff; *1807–1808*, I, 312–16. Cf. *ibid.*, *1822–23*, p. 316; *Pa. Archives*, 4th, IV, 786.
⁴¹ *House Journal, 1806*, p. 396.

wards on the part of merchants and landowners. In terms of direct earnings early transportation companies were unsuccessful: in 1806 there was not a twenty-mile turnpike in the state which produced 5 per cent for its proprietors. The devastating effect of speculative booms, changing technological problems, limited traffic in interior regions, toll evasions, all contributed to this condition.[42] Yet once mixed enterprise policy was initiated, these factors militated also against the success of enterprises owned jointly by the government and private investors. The great expectations of early mixed enterprise enthusiasts were not realized. Despite the warnings of early legislative committees, moreover, the state made many investments in corporations whose objectives were purely local. One needs only to examine the statute books to see that sectional barter again and again prevented the state from concentrating its aid on strategically crucial lines.

There was also the matter of fraud — an "almost inevitable consequence" in some cases, as William Smith, a sympathetic contemporary observer of mixed enterprise investment, admitted.[43] The governor was empowered to refuse licenses to mixed corporations in which proceedings had not taken place according to law, but with an executive staff inadequate for the immense economic responsibilities that the state assumed, he was naturally unable to check matters thoroughly, and in 1830 Governor Hiester was himself compelled to call for a legislative investigation of mixed enterprise frauds.[44] Excessive subscriptions of stock by the state and the incautious outlay of public funds were, as Smith noted, the two mistakes which made fraud by private promoters possible. Nor were these mistakes avoided during the local investment movement of the last two decades of our period, when the Supreme Court pointed out that precautions against them were "totally inadequate to protect the public." [45] The Harrisburg and Millerstown Turnpike Company in the state program and the

---

[42] *Ibid., 1806*, p. 395 ff; *1807–1808*, I, 313; *Hazard's Register*, I (1828), 405–406; Durrenberger, *Turnpikes*, p. 114.

[43] *Hazard's Register*, I (1828), 410.

[44] *Pa. Archives*, 4th, V, 379.

[45] *County of Lawrence v. Northwestern Railroad Company*, 32 Pa. St. Rep. 144, 149 (1858).

Northwestern Railroad Company in the local program provide two extreme examples of the victimization of government. In the former instance, where the charter provided that a public subscription would be made only after twenty-five thousand private shares had been subscribed with a payment of three dollars on each, the president of the company faked 24,994 of the required shares and succeeded in spending forty thousand dollars of state money before a legislative investigating committee exposed his operations and delivered a tirade against the menace of "fictitious stock." He had freely announced that the "state subscription would make the road, and more than make it." [46] In the latter instance the Northwestern directors, after faking a large portion of the required private subscription in order to obtain funds from Philadelphia and other localities, distributed twenty-two thousand dollars to themselves for their own services and voted to release their treasurer from responsibility for accounting for private funds that had never been collected.[47]

A final mixed enterprise objective, as noted earlier, was the partial guidance of corporate policy by the state. A necessary supplement to the profit and promotional aims, it was also conceived as significant in its own right. Ordinarily three techniques were used for selecting state directors in mixed enterprises: direct election by the legislature; [48] appointment of certain executive officers as ex officio members of the board in mixed corporation charters; [49] appointment by the governor or auditor-general.[50]

[46] *House Journal, 1827–28*, II, 739 ff, 901–30. Cf. *ibid.*, 1822–23, pp. 508–509.

[47] *County of Lawrence* v. *North-Western Railroad Company*, 32 Pa. St. Rep. 144, 149–50 (1858). For fraudulent techniques used in connection with the Pittsburgh and Erie, see *House Journal, 1853*, II, 578.

[48] For legislative election of state directors for the Bank of Pennsylvania and the Bank of Philadelphia, see *House Journal, 1813*, pp. 207–12; *1812*, p. 258; and other volumes of *House Journal, 1800–1843*. See also Cook, *Philadelphia National Bank*, pp. 33, 81.

[49] This was a comparatively rare procedure and was limited to the transportation field, the outstanding example of it being in connection with the Union Canal Company. The auditor-general, the state treasurer, and the secretary of the Commonwealth were the officials appointed. Cf. *Pa. Laws, 1820–21*, pp. 102–103.

[50] Cf. *ibid., 1823–24*, p. 235; *1825–26*, p. 324; *1826–27*, pp. 187–88; *House Journal, 1833*, II, 721. On the local level the control factor was taken with varying degrees of seriousness. Prior to the boom in railroad investment legislative acts

The first technique was used almost exclusively in the banking field where, because of its stake in dividends and in privileges such as borrowing and deposit rights, the state took control responsibilities more seriously than elsewhere.

Yet even in the banking field administrative mistakes were manifold. Despite the example set by the national government in the Bank of the United States, the legislature persistently failed to provide in charters for a number of state directors proportionate to the size of state investment. Since such provision was not made in terms of total capitalization permitted in charters, the disparity turned out to be even greater in terms of actual capitalization. The act of 1793 chartering the Bank of Pennsylvania provided for a state subscription of one-third of all authorized stock but it provided for the election of only six directors by the legislature as opposed to nineteen by private investors.[51] In the rechartering act of 1830 the total number of directors was reduced to sixteen and the state was permitted to appoint four.[52] In actual operation the disparity between state investment and state board representation was striking. Three-fifths of the actual stock investment in the Bank of Pennsylvania was held by the govern-

---

authorizing local subscription usually did not provide expressly for public representation on directorates, though in certain cases this was done. For the election of managers for the Hanover and Carlisle Turnpike Company by the commissioners of Cumberland and Adams County, see *Pa. Laws, 1834–35*, p. 213; for the election of managers for the Schuylkill Bridge at Norristown by the commissioners of Montgomery County, *ibid., 1850*, p. 470. With the expansion of local railroad investment more detailed provisions appeared. A supplement to the charter of the Pennsylvania Railroad Company permitted local governments subscribing to the capital stock of the company to elect one director for each ten thousand shares subscribed but the number thus elected was limited to three for each municipality. On the basis of these provisions Allegheny County had two representatives on the board until 1859 when its holdings were liquidated, and the city of Philadelphia had three representatives there until 1879 when its stock was sold. Subscriptions by two municipal districts of Philadelphia, Spring Garden and Northern Liberties, meant that each of these had one member on the board until 1854 when they were consolidated with the city of Philadelphia. Since the city already had the maximum permissible representation on the board, the consolidation of the districts with it meant that the total public representation was reduced. See Schotter, *Pennsylvania Railroad Company*, pp. 23–24; Pennsylvania Railroad Company, *Annual Reports*, 1849, *et seq.*; *Pa. Laws, 1853*, 331–36.

[51] *Statutes at Large*, XIV, 369.

[52] *Pa. Laws, 1829–30*, p. 86. Cf. Holdsworth, *Financing an Empire*, I, 148. For under-representation of the state in the Bank of Philadelphia, see Cook, *Philadelphia National Bank*, p. 81.

ment in 1835, yet its representation remained limited to four directors.

The control problem in the banking field did not become serious, however, until the latter twenties when the state, having embarked upon its system of public works, was compelled to make increasingly heavy financial demands upon the banks. The banks were placed in a difficult position, since the fashion in which the state proceeded to execute the works program was not designed to inspire confidence in its credit. In 1829 the legislature authorized a permanent state loan of $2,200,000. Neither the Bank of Pennsylvania nor the Bank of Philadelphia made a bid for this loan. The banks were eventually persuaded to offer the state a temporary loan to meet the immediate demands of creditors, but the reaction against their policy was intense.[53] In the Bank of Pennsylvania tensions had long been developing between state and private directors, and the failure of the loan of 1829 precipitated an open clash. Five state directors publicly charged the private officers of the bank with malpractice and with deliberately causing the loan of 1829 to fail.[54] The latter replied by accusing the state agents of engaging in "pertinacious, persevering, and indiscriminating opposition" to any important measures that they proposed, and of violating not only established rules for conducting business but "ordinary courtesies" as well. Declaring that the trouble lay in an *"assumed* diversity of interest" between the state and private stockholders which had no basis in fact because of a common concern with profits, they pointed to dividends received by the state as "evidence of able and faithful management" — an argument which implicitly admitted that public directors had little influence on policy.[55] A joint investigating committee of the House and Senate, while vindicating the private directors in certain respects, emphasized that because of "the paucity of their number" the state directors were "mere specta-

---

[53] *House Journal, 1828–29*, II, 553. "It was also the impression that mismanagement of the institution in stock operations had so diminished its means, that it possessed little capital for banking business." *Ibid.*, II, 533. Cf. D. Dewey, *State Banking before Civil War*, p. 38.

[54] Holdsworth, *Financing an Empire*, I, 143–44.

[55] *Hazard's Register*, V (1830), 38 ff.

tors instead of active promoters of" the public interest. The committee urged an increase in the proportion of state directors, citing the Bank of the United States as an example to follow, but this objective was not achieved.[56]

A more serious conflict took place in 1842, a year of general banking depression and financial embarrassment for the state. With the closing of the Girard Bank, the state called upon the Bank of Pennsylvania to provide one million dollars of its notes for the payment of interest on state loans. The confidence of other banks in the Bank of Pennsylvania was damaged; they rejected its notes, and it was compelled to close its doors.[57] The legislature thereupon authorized an assignment to be made, but the wording of its provision for the election of assignees was thoroughly confused, especially in regard to the number of votes permitted to the state. It was not clear whether the state was to have one vote for each share of stock held, in which case it would clearly dominate the election, or whether it was to be limited by the usual voting scale, in which case the election would be dominated by private stockholders.[58] A bitter fight over this issue between Job Man, the state treasurer, and the private directors broke up election proceedings. Insisting that the position of the directors was " a dangerous encroachment on the rights of the State," and that "the Legislature never intended to surrender the entire control of three-fifths of the stock owned by the state, to the Stockholders owning two-fifths thereof," Man elected on his own authority a set of assignees which included Governor Porter.[59] This move, as well as a separate election by private stockholders, was voided in July by the Supreme Court which referred the assignment measure back to the legislature for improvement.[60]

This did not end debate. The measure also contained a provi-

[56] *House Journal, 1828–29*, II, 553, 558–63. Cf. *Pa. Archives*, 4th, VI, 620–21; *Convention Proceedings*, IX, 147.
[57] *Commonwealth* v. *Bank of Pennsylvania in Equity*, 3 Watts and Serg. 173, 184 (1842); Pennsylvania, *Message of Governor in Relation to Permanent Loan*.
[58] *Pa. Laws, 1842*, pp. 202–205.
[59] *The Commonwealth* v. *The President, Directors and Company of the Bank of Pennsylvania*, pp. 4–6; *Commonwealth* v. *Bank of Pennsylvania in Equity*, 3 Watts and Serg. 173, 175 (1842).
[60] *Ibid.*, p. 173.

sion which granted the state priority in the assignment when it was to be made, and the validity of this provision was argued out in a separate case. By the narrow margin of three to two the court held that the state was entitled to preference on the ground that the bank served as a deposit agency for state funds and was therefore in the position of trustee for the government.[61] In a long dissenting opinion Justice Kennedy insisted that it was a violation of equity principle to distinguish between public and private deposits, especially in light of the fact that the state owned part of the bank's stock and derived profits from it. In various *obiter dicta*, some of them satirical, he assailed generally the role of the state, anticipating criticisms of government action that were to emerge later. He rejected the notion, which no one save himself had presented, that the state was entitled to preference because its agents were invariably incompetent compared with individual businessmen and could not "be got to use the same degree of vigilance" as they in financial matters.[62] The upshot of the entire controversy was that no assignment was made; the Bank of Pennsylvania reopened after other banks advanced the state funds to meet its interest payments.[63] But the conflict evoked sharp criticism of mixed enterprise policy in the banking field. Governor Porter, blaming private interests for all the difficulties that had arisen, declared that the state was practically impotent in the determination of the policy of the banks and derived no benefit from the partnership.[64]

In transportation enterprises control responsibilities were even less effectively discharged. In many cases the legislature failed completely to provide government directors, an omission due largely to the dominant importance of the subsidy motive in the transportation field. Yet problems were bound to arise to heighten interest in control, as was evidenced in the case of the Susquehanna Bridge Company in 1820 when the interest of the state as a

---

[61] *Ibid.*, pp. 193–95.
[62] *Ibid.*, pp. 209.
[63] Holdsworth, *Financing an Empire*, I, 186.
[64] *Pa. Archives*, 4th, VI, 620–21. For a characteristic conflict between public and private directors in the Bank of Philadelphia in 1837, see *House Journal, 1837–38*, II, 256–57. Cf. *ibid., 1822*, p. 588.

stockholder was jeopardized by certain dubious financial claims against it. A legislative committee lamented its lack of information concerning the affairs of the company, while a belatedly appointed government agent, Benjamin Ober, insisted that those affairs were confused beyond salvation.[65] Control also became a matter of concern as a result of repeated petitions to the legislature by mixed transportation companies for assistance in discharging legitimate debts. In 1827 the House Committee on Ways and Means indignantly denied a number of these petitions on the ground that the state had not been represented on company boards when the debts were incurred.[66] Yet it was difficult for the state to pursue a hands-off policy once mixed enterprise investments had been made. There was constant pressure for the outlay of funds in an effort to salvage those already expended,[67] and on the basis of that consideration the state frequently paid mixed corporation debts or guaranteed interest on mixed corporation loans.[68]

Concern with control was also increased by the scantiness of

[65] The company had been endowed with banking privileges which were subsequently revoked. When the banking activities were wound up, stockholders in the banking department held that the original bridge department, in which the state held 90,000 shares of stock, was heavily indebted to them. *Ibid., 1820–21*, pp. 31, 158; *1821–22*, pp. 451–54. With the elimination of banking privileges, bridge stock depreciated 60 per cent; the state was urged to restore the privileges on the ground that it "would be benefitted more than $50,000 as the stock would immediately rise to par." *Ibid., 1821–22*, p. 967.

[66] *Ibid., 1827–28*, II, 890–91. State investments in the petitioning companies amounted to $1,800,000, a sum greater than the total of individual subscriptions.

[67] See remarks of the auditor-general on this problem, *ibid., 1832–33*, II, 551.

[68] See *Pa. Laws, 1820–1821*, p. 125; *1821–22*, p. 53; *House Journal, 1812*, p. 571 ff; *1821–22*, pp. 824–26; *1830–31*, II, 638; *Pa. Archives*, 4th, V, 845 ff. In most cases debt assumption was justified on the ground of the state investment already made or on the ground of the public necessity of the works involved, but there were instances also in which it was justified as a procedure preliminary to the freeing of the roads from toll. Cf. *House Journal, 1821–22*, pp. 824–26; *1832–33*, II, 551. Moreover the state sometimes guaranteed interest on investments in transportation corporations or on loans made to them. Cf. *Pa. Laws, 1820–21*, p. 102; *1833–34*, pp. 198–99; *1840–41*, p. 53; *1854*, pp. 688–702. Governor Wolf heavily criticized this practice, arguing that interest guarantees in private corporations should be superseded by the mixed corporation technique since this would "at least give it [the state] the advantage of being represented in the direction and management of the construction of the work and the expenditure of the money." *Pa. Archives*, 4th, VI, 234. In light of the poor administration of the state's control policy in the mixed corporation field, especially as regards transportation companies there, Wolf's remarks seem optimistic.

dividends on transportation investments. In 1826 the auditor-general was instructed by the legislature to "address a circular" to managers of mixed turnpike enterprises in order to determine whether toll discrimination was taking place.[69] He reported that some companies greeted this circular with "total silence," while others that did reply failed to supply adequate information.[70] Aroused, the legislature directed the auditor-general to appoint state managers in all turnpike companies in which the government held at least half the stock.[71] It was discovered that of fifty-five companies only four were charging stage owners the tolls required by law, the estimated loss to the state in dividends being ten thousand dollars annually.[72] In a few instances, as on the Stoystown and Greensburg road, the appointment of state managers succeeded in changing corporation policy.

On the whole, however, the state managerial policy was a failure. In the cases of the Northumberland Bridge Company, the Harrisburg Bridge Company, the Wilkes-Barre Bridge Company, and the Centre Turnpike Road Company, private directors simply refused state agents admittance to board meetings. State directors appointed for the Harrisburg Bridge Company reported that, though they had "heretofore mentioned to several directors of our appointment," they were entirely ignored. Messrs. Swetland, Muench, and Hobart, other state agents, complained of the same treatment: ". . . the managers refuse to let us act."[73] Though some private directors rationalized their resistance by drawing legal distinctions or vaguely invoking the Dartmouth College doctrine,[74] such theorizing was scarcely needed. The state had evaded responsibilities for control too long to assert itself successfully by the sudden appointment of a series of directors.

---

[69] *House Journal, 1826–27*, II, 484.

[70] *Ibid.*, II, 728.

[71] This act limited to five the number of directors in mixed turnpike and bridge corporations in which the state held as much as half of total stock subscribed and required the auditor-general to appoint two of these. It is a characteristic example of the state's persistent refusal to require representation proportionate to its stockholdings. See *Pa. Laws, 1825–26*, p. 324; *House Journal, 1826–27*, II, 699.

[72] *Ibid.*, II, 728.

[73] *Ibid.*, II, 701, 703–704.

[74] *Ibid.*, II, 40, 42, 44.

What was needed both in banking and in transportation was a comprehensive rebuilding of mixed enterprise administration, the development of consistent policies for the appointment of directors, and the integration of the new system smoothly into the prevailing executive organization. In light of the general character of administrative policy during our period, however, this was clearly too much to ask.

There is little doubt that disillusionment with mixed enterprise administration was one of the reasons for the sweeping stock liquidation measure of 1843. More important reasons, however, were the state's grave financial condition and the rise to power of a Democratic administration, under the leadership of Porter, that was determined to remedy it. Porter, who bitterly resented his failure to get financial aid from the banks, recommended stock liquidation as a source of revenue as early as 1839.[75] There appears to have been some belief in postponing the sale until better prices could be obtained for the stocks. It was held, however, that such postponement was unfair to the creditors of the state.[76]

[75] *Pa. Archives*, 4th, VI, 620–21, 839. Cf. Pennsylvania, *Message of Governor in Relation to Permanent Loan*; Chapman and Westerfield, *Branch Banking*, p. 52. Porter recommended that if, owing to the drop in the value of state bank stocks as a result of the prevailing depression, a sale would involve too great a sacrifice for the state, the legislature should annul the charters of the mixed corporation banks and divide their assets among state and private stockholders. *Pa. Archives*, 4th, VI, 621. The following table indicates the precipitous drop that took place in the value of the state bank stocks between 1839 and 1842.

Value of Bank Stock Owned by Pennsylvania on Specified Dates *

	Bank of Pennsylvania	Philadelphia Bank	Farmers' & Mechanics' Bank	Total
No. of shares held by state	3,750	5,233	1,708	
Par value	$1,500,000	$523,300	$ 85,400	$2,108,700
Value on				
Mar. 7, 1839	1,860,000	567,780	105,896	2,533,676
Jan. 8, 1840	1,537,500	520,683	93,513	2,151,696
Jan. 6, 1841	1,545,000	523,300	89,670	2,157,970
Jan. 3, 1842	600,000	251,184	51,240	902,424

* *House Journal, 1842*, II, 29.
[76] *North American*, Oct. 17, 1843.

Stocks in the following amount were sold in 1843:

Bank Stocks	$2,108,700
Bridge Stocks	524,350
Turnpike Stocks	803,833
Canal, Railroad, and Navigation Stocks	755,500
Total	$4,192,383

The stock of only one corporation, the Farmers' and Mechanics' Bank, was sold at par value. The price which the state received for all stocks sold was $1,319,730, a loss, compared with their par value, of $2,872,652. The remainder of state-held stock, amounting at par value to $1,986,797, was not sold, either because of the lowness of the offers received or the absence of any offers at all. The greater part of the stock of the Philadelphia and Pennsylvania banks was purchased by the banks themselves, thus consolidating ownership among existing private stockholders and ending completely mixed enterprise in banking.[77]

3. Issues in Local Investment

The mixed enterprise activities of the state up to the forties failed notably to evoke legalistic discussion of the proper sphere of government in economic life. Criticism of the policy was concerned with its practicability, and even the vigorous liquidation movement of the early forties confined its doctrine within that limit. The legitimacy of the mixed corporation was pervasively taken for granted. With the emergence of local railroad investment in the late forties, however, the ideological setting began to change, and by the close of our period the theory was strong that mixed enterprise investment was not only inexpedient but that it violated basic democratic and constitutional norms as well. Since

---

[77] The Bank of Philadelphia bought 3,919 shares of its stock out of a total of 5,333 shares held by the state; the greater part of the state loan held by the bank was sold to provide funds for this purchase. No stock was sold for less than one dollar per share. The sale commissioners were Evans Rogers, James Clarke, and Job Man. "Report of Commissioners for Sale of State Stocks," *House Journal, 1844*, II, 28–46; *Public Ledger*, Oct. 24, 25, 1843; Holdsworth, *Financing an Empire*, II, 575; Cook, *Philadelphia National Bank*, p. 106. A special law of 1843 rechartering the Farmers' and Mechanics' Bank of Philadelphia required that bank to purchase all of its stock then held by the state at par value of fifty dollars a share. *Pa. Laws, 1843*, p. 310.

the new doctrine fundamentally altered attitudes toward the mixed corporation, its development must be traced in some detail. The first step on the road to its elaboration was taken in Philadelphia in 1846 when controversy arose over a municipal subscription to the stock of the Pennsylvania Railroad Company.

It was not until after the Pennsylvania's charter had been secured that its promoters began to popularize the idea of municipal investment. Resolutions passed at the first town meetings held in behalf of the railroad made no allusion to it.[78] Shortly before the opening of stock books, a meeting was held which called for a municipal subscription of two and a half million dollars to be made after a previous subscription of a similar amount had been received from private sources.[79] It was also proposed, in order "to remove any possible objection on the score of responsibility" that the subscription question be voted on in a municipal plebiscite.[80] These proposals were rejected by one branch of the city councils, and passed over without action by the other.[81] Charging that the councils had been antagonistic to a scheme "consistent with representative government," the railroad promoters proceeded themselves to poll opinion, and discovered of course that popular sentiment was "overwhelming[ly]" in favor of subscription. In July the measure again came up in the councils, committees of both branches reported in its favor, but it failed of passage by a tie vote in the Common Council.[82] In the fall elections none of the Whig councilors who had opposed subscription were renominated. Whether or not the machinations of the promoters were responsible for this fact, as anti-subscription Whigs like Horace Binney charged, it made municipal investment practically certain. The Whigs were traditionally dominant in Philadelphia, and the opposition to them had just been split by the emergence of the Know-Nothing Party.

[78] Cf. *Proceedings in Relation to Pennsylvania Railroad*.
[79] C. Binney, *Horace Binney*, pp. 244–45.
[80] "Address to Friends of Pennsylvania Railroad," *Public Ledger*, Oct. 10, 1846.
[81] *Ibid.*, Oct. 10, 1846; C. Binney, *Horace Binney*, p. 245.
[82] *Ibid.* It was reported by the promoters that upwards of sixty thousand Philadelphians were in favor of subscription while only one hundred and thirty-three opposed it. *Public Ledger*, Oct. 10, 1846.

Yet as the campaign developed the subscription issue cut across party lines.[83] "Anti-Railroad" and "Railroad" slates were formed, each of which included representatives of the three parties.[84] A decisive majority of the men elected were in favor of subscription.[85] Two and a half million dollars were subscribed, and this amount was subsequently increased to four million.[86] In 1847 a bill was introduced in the state legislature expressly authorizing this subscription on the part of the city, but it failed to pass and the subscription was made without legislative authorization.[87] A year later, however, the legislature was induced to enact a measure retroactively authorizing the Philadelphia subscription, and also authorizing the cities of Pittsburgh and Allegheny, and the County of Allegheny to make similar investments.[88]

Beneath the confusion of party lines which the railroad slates produced in the elections of 1846, a situation described by the *Public Ledger* as a "curious affair," [89] there was a deeper economic conflict. The merchants of the city were heavily in favor of subscription, and the railroad promoters did not find it difficult to enlist the support also of the professional, manufacturing, and laboring interests. Their strongest opposition came from the holders of real estate upon whom the tax burden of investment would necessarily fall.[90] In debates in the Common Council over

[83] Cf. *Whig Anti-Subscription Council Ticket*; C. Binney, *Horace Binney*, pp. 247–48; Geary, *Third Parties in Pa.*, pp. 103 ff.

[84] There were five separate tickets in this campaign: the regular Whig, the Democratic, the Native, a Railroad ticket composed of Whigs and Democrats, and an anti-Railroad ticket formed of Whigs, Democrats, and Natives. *Pennsylvanian*, Oct. 10, 1846; *Public Ledger*, Oct. 10, 13, 15, 1846; *North American*, Oct. 13, 1846; Mueller, *Whig Party in Pa.*, p. 132.   [85] *Public Ledger*, Oct. 15, 1847.

[86] Duane, Hood, and Myers, *Digest of Acts and Ordinances of Philadelphia*, pp. 193–94; C. Binney, *Horace Binney*, pp. 251–52. For other railroad investments by Philadelphia, see Duane, Hood, and Myers, *Digest of Acts and Ordinances of Philadelphia*, pp. 194–97.   [87] C. Binney, *Horace Binney*, p. 252.

[88] *Pa. Laws, 1848*, pp. 273–76; *Pa. Archives*, 4th, VII, 528–29.

[89] *Public Ledger*, Oct. 10, 1846.

[90] Read, *Opinion*, pp. 29–30; *Public Ledger*, Oct. 12, Nov. 27, 1846. A debt of ten million dollars and a 500 per cent increase in the tax rate was envisaged. *Whig Anti-Subscription Council Ticket*. There was a fear that the railroad if successful would serve to increase the value of property in adjacent districts rather than in Philadelphia proper where the taxes would be levied. "We have no faith in the golden dream of so many that the rents of Market Street, and Front Street, and Water Street, are to advance until the value of the freehold capital shall be doubled." *Fellow Citizens of Pa.*

the second subscription proposal, the idea was even presented that only holders of real estate were entitled to decide whether a subscription should be made, since other groups were not directly involved in shouldering its expense.[91] A circular published at the time insisted upon a distinction between the rights of "property" and the rights of persons arguing that the former were the dominant consideration as far as the decision on the subscription proposal was concerned.[92]

Such doctrine provided, of course, an excellent polemical target. When railroad publicists condemned it as "monstrously inconsistent with the foundation principles of Republicanism," they were able to identify it with the theory of a landed property qualification for voting which had been discredited in the state in 1776. "Is it possible that at this day, and in this community, we are to be told that a man's civil rights are to be measured by the extent of his *property*, and that he is only to be allowed a voice in the government which he supports in *proportion* to the amount of his bonds, mortgages, and real estate?"[93] Moreover property taxes were shifted to rents, and rents were paid by precisely the groups to which the anti-subscription theorists would deny a voice in the decision concerning investment. The man of easy fortune "who leads a life of leisure by means of a patrimonial . . . income"[94] was not to be preferred to the enterprising worker or trader upon whom he was, in the last analysis, economically dependent. Indeed it was this relation of dependency which made it imperative for real-estate owners themselves, if they pursued their self-interest, to favor the subscription measure. For without the Pennsylvania Railroad Philadelphia would be bested in commercial competition by Baltimore, New York, and Boston, and this defeat would mean that population would drift away from the city and that real-estate values would fall.[95]

[91] *Public Ledger*, Oct. 10, 1846.
[92] Read, *Opinion*, p. 26; *Public Ledger*, Oct. 12, 1846. During debate over subscription in the Common Council it was argued that Council members owning stock in the Pennsylvania Railroad would be voting money into their own pockets by the subscription measure. *North American*, Nov. 6, 1846.
[93] *Public Ledger*, Oct. 12, 1846. For a reply to this argument, see *Fellow Citizens of Pa.* [94] *Public Ledger*, Oct. 12, 1846.
[95] *Ibid.*, Oct. 10, 1846. Cf. Philadelphia Committee of Seven, *Address*, p. 37.

There was also the question whether the Pennsylvania Railroad would in fact be successful. Its promoters might have encountered less antagonism from propertied interests had it not been for various unsuccessful railroad projects, such as the Reading and Norristown, and Danville and Pottsville railroads, which cluttered up transportation history in the vicinity of Philadelphia.[96] Indeed, as was pointed out in the Select Council, the latter road had itself urgently solicited municipal investment.[97] When such examples were presented, the railroad publicists could point in reply to other kinds of municipal improvement which had been effective,[98] but they did not deign to base their case exclusively on this argument, or even upon the evidence of such outstate projects as the Boston and Albany road or the Erie Canal which they so deeply feared.[99] They appealed to principles of risk and enterprise which lay at the "root of all internal improvement" [100] and without which no progress would be made. An anti-subscription circular by Binney was placed in the same category with "Anti-Gas" remonstrances which had come to the councils in 1833 to oppose municipal gas lighting and which were now ranked among the "politico-economical curiosities of the age." [101]

On the score of expense the railroad promoters cleverly inverted the argument of their opponents and reasoned from the principle of diminished rather than increased taxation. Clearly the former idea, if followed to its logical conclusion, would lead to the abolition of all civic improvements and services.[102] They contended, moreover, that the interest which the Pennsylvania would pay to the city on its subscription — 5 per cent annually — would itself take care of interest on bonds floated to subscribe to the stock of the road. This was apart from the great dividends the city was promised on its investment.[103] But even if these consid-

[96] Cf. Read, *Opinion*, p. 25; *Fellow Citizens of Pa.*
[97] *Public Ledger*, Nov. 14, 1846.
[98] Wharton, *Letter to Toland and Elliott*, p. 27. An interesting parody of this letter is to be found in John Doe, *Letter to Jones, Smith, and Black.*
[99] *Public Ledger*, Oct. 10, 12, 1846; Philadelphia Committee of Seven, *Address*, pp. 11, 15–16, 37.
[100] *Public Ledger*, Oct. 12, 1846.
[101] *Ibid.*; C. Binney, *Horace Binney*, pp. 250–51.
[102] *Public Ledger*, Oct. 12, 1846.
[103] *Ibid.*, Nov. 27, 1846.

erations were not present, the "honor and integrity" of Philadelphia, not to speak of its whole economic future, had become linked to the realization of the Pennsylvania road, and in such a setting even immediate possibilities of profit or loss ought not to be important.[104]

The argument thus far, with the possible exception of the taxation issue, was not much different from earlier discussions of mixed enterprise policy. A more legalistic note was introduced, however, by the contention, buttressed by learned opinions from Horace Binney and John M. Read, that investment was in itself an invalid exercise of municipal power. A hot argument developed in which Thomas Pettit, Thomas Wharton, and John Sergeant sought to demonstrate the validity of subscription. Taking place prior to the state act of 1848 authorizing local investment in the Pennsylvania, this argument was concerned exclusively with the following point: *whether the city could subscribe without express authorization by the state.* It is thus highly important to observe that even those who challenged the legitimacy of investment at this time admitted that it could validly be made if the powers of the municipal corporation were expressly enlarged for that purpose by the legislature.

The evidence of this admission is to be found everywhere in the anti-subscription argument. An anti-subscription councilor warned his colleagues in October of 1846 against passing a subscription ordinance "unless they could lay hands on an express Act from the Assembly giving power to do so." [105] The admission of state power was revealed in the fact that practically the entire argument of Read and Binney was concerned with interpreting the provisions of the Philadelphia charter of 1789, concerned, as Read later put it, with elucidating the powers which "the framers of the charter . . . intended" to grant to the city.[106] Binney

[104] *Ibid.*, May 7, 1846. Cf. *ibid.*, Nov. 27, 1846; *Pennsylvanian*, Oct. 10, 1846. For this type of reasoning in connection with Philadelphia's subscription to the Sunbury and Erie, see *North American*, Jan. 8, 1853.
[105] *Public Ledger*, Nov. 14, 1846.
[106] *Pennsylvania Railroad Company* v. *The City of Philadelphia*, 47 Pa. St. Rep. 189, 192 (1864). See also Read, *Opinion*, p. 4.

said: "I deny the power of the City . . . unless she has it by her charter, by *express grant*, or it is an incident to the execution of some act of government of the City within her corporate powers." [107] This admission was also brought out in connection with the act of 1846 incorporating the Pennsylvania Railroad Company. The first section of that act, in providing for commissioners to open stock books for the company, declared that "it shall be lawful . . . for all firms, co-partnerships and bodies politic and corporate, by themselves or by persons duly authorized, to subscribe for shares in said stock." [108] Pettit, Wharton, and Sergeant cited that part of the provision which noticed "bodies politic and corporate" as evidence that the legislature had, by the very act of incorporating the Pennsylvania Railroad Company, expressly granted to municipalities the power to subscribe to its stock.[109] Binney denied this in a long argument. But his denial was devoted exclusively to the presentation of a different interpretation of the legislative proviso.

Binney insisted that a brief clause hidden away in an incorporation statute provided neither the place nor the language in which so "high and solemn" a purpose as that of extending the powers of a municipal corporation could be effected. Moreover, the presence of the phrase "duly qualified" in the legislative proviso showed that it was not intended to grant power of subscription to any persons or corporations other than those qualified to subscribe previous to its passage. Any other interpretation would mean that the act of 1846 dissolved all regulations previously enacted for the control of corporations, partnerships, and individuals, in order to attract subscriptions to the Pennsylvania road, a view that was "disrespectful to the Legislature." But even if the purely formal power to subscribe had thus been granted to the city, asserted Binney, that grant did not touch the related question whether the city had authority to borrow and tax for the purpose of effectuating subscription. The answer to this question

---

[107] H. Binney, *Opinion*, p. 8. Wharton declared that the issue hinged on whether "distinct and express authority must be obtained from the Legislature." *Letter to Toland and Elliott*, p. 6.   [108] *Pa. Laws, 1846*, pp. 314–15.
[109] Wharton, *Letter to Toland and Elliott*, pp. 5–6. Cf. Read, *Opinion*, p. 4; H. Binney, *Opinion*, pp. 7–8.

was to be found exclusively in the provisions of the municipal charter.[110]

The defenders of subscription declared that the power to tax and borrow for that purpose was granted in the preamble of the Philadelphia charter of 1789 which referred to the inadequacy of the old charter of 1701 as regards the "promotion of trade, industry, and happiness," and in the sixteenth section of the new charter which permitted the city to enact all ordinances as "shall be necessary or convenient" for its "government and welfare."[111] This was a better legal case than any to be derived from hidden clauses in the act of 1846, and it was only by resorting to an involved argument that the anti-subscription theorists were able to counter it. They denied that references in the charter of 1789 to the inadequacy of the earlier document had the effect of extending the powers of the city in any way: those references were concerned, insisted Binney, only with the need for making more effective the execution of powers previously granted.[112] Moreover the welfare clause of the sixteenth section of the new charter was not to be interpreted as granting any but the ordinary powers of government: "*Government* and *welfare* go together, the one as the instrument, the other as the object." Hence it was not enough to demonstrate that the subscription was "speculatively for the welfare of the City";[113] it was necessary to demonstrate that it was a measure involved directly in its government.

The last argument was a tortured one to say the least, but it was related to another which made more sense: that the government of the city was confined to its geographical limits. Since the construction of the Pennsylvania Railroad was to begin not at Philadelphia but at Harrisburg one hundred miles away, it was argued that a subscription to its stock by the city was not as Councilor Gilpin put it, within the range of "proper municipal legislation."[114]

[110] *Ibid.*, pp. 6–8. For a similar line of argument, see Read, *Opinion*, pp. 4 ff.
[111] *Statutes at Large*, XIII, 193; *Public Ledger*, Nov. 14, 1846; Wharton, *Letter to Toland and Elliott*, p. 10.
[112] H. Binney, *Opinion*, p. 12. Cf. Read, *Opinion*, pp. 13–20.
[113] H. Binney, *Opinion*, p. 15. Cf. Wharton, *Letter to Toland and Elliott*, pp. 16–17.
[114] *Public Ledger*, Nov. 14, 1846. Read assailed the idea of the city's uniting "a private enterprise with its ordinary municipal functions." *Opinion*, p. 26.

The pro-subscription writers denied that the line of municipal interest could be drawn at the city limits, emphasizing the undeniable stake that Philadelphia had in the Pennsylvania road despite the beginning of its construction at Harrisburg.[115] Binney admitted that actions beyond city limits were necessarily involved in some actions of government within those limits, such as the building of outcity sewers, but he was unwilling to grant, on the basis of his identification of welfare with government, that subscription ranked among them. Here his implicit admission of the power of the state to authorize subscription came out clearly. For he built his argument limiting city action to city limits on the ground that the outcity field was the proper domain of the state. "If the body corporate desire a power to operate by their by-laws beyond their limits, or to govern their freemen *within* in regard to things *without*, they must seek it in the only source from which such power can be derived, the Legislature of the State." [116]

Whatever may have been the legal merit of the anti-subscription case, it contained an unmistakable element of novelty. It did not, to be sure, challenge the legality of the entire traditional policy of local investment, since the major portion of that policy had been executed under express legislative authority. But there were cases, such as the city's investment in the Philadelphia Ice-Boat and the Schuylkill Water-Works, which had been unauthorized by the state.[117] These were heavily emphasized by such pro-subscription men as Sergeant and Tyson, and the reply of their opponents to this citation of precedent was clearly the weakest part of the anti-subscription case. Sometimes this reply consisted of pointing to the previous history of state authorized investments

---

[115] Wharton, *Letter to Toland and Elliott*, pp. 20 ff; *Public Ledger*, Nov. 14, 1846.

[116] H. Binney, *Opinion*, p. 19. Wharton insisted upon a distinction between the powers of the greater municipal corporations such as Philadelphia and smaller ones such as the districts of Southwark, Northern Liberties, and Spring Garden. *Letter to Toland and Elliott*, pp. 14–16.

[117] Duane, Hood, and Myers, *Digest of Acts and Ordinances of Philadelphia*, pp. 297 ff, 657 ff. See also *Stiles* v. *Jones*, 3 Yeates 491. Wharton also placed heavy emphasis on a report of the Committee on City Property of the Councils in 1836 which recommended the erection of a tobacco warehouse in the following words: "Whatever tends to the general prosperity of the citizens of Philadelphia, must promote the proper benefit of the Corporation. . . ." Wharton, *Letter to Toland and Elliott*, pp. 21, 27. See also *Public Ledger*, Nov. 14, 1846.

as evidence that such authorization was always conceived as necessary; sometimes it consisted of drawing distinctions between the previous unauthorized investments and the investment in the Pennsylvania Railroad Company on the basis of the criterion of functions integral to the internal government of the city; sometimes it consisted of an expressed hesitation to discuss previous municipal investments on the ground that inviolable property rights had already resulted from them.[118] But it seems clear that even the anti-subscription publicists appreciated the novelty of their argument in the thought of the state. They were forced to say, with Binney, that "no wrongful exercise of power in other cases, can furnish the least colour of defence to an exercise of it in this case." [119]

The judiciary did not decide this controversy; it was settled by the legislative measure of 1848 authorizing local subscriptions to the stock of the Pennsylvania Railroad and the financial measures necessary to implement them. The passage of this act cut the whole ground from under the legalism of the anti-subscription groups. For they had themselves admitted again and again that express legislative authorization could validate local investment. Their case had been a shortsighted one. If they had hoped that the legislature would remain impervious to the pleas of the railroad promoters for an authorizing act, they had misjudged utterly the pressure politics which the new age of railroad capitalism was initiating. Having been compelled to construct a fairly novel doctrine, they had constructed it on a foundation that vanished with a single act of the legislature.

4. *The Sharpless Case*

But the ingenuity of the anti-subscription theorists was not exhausted. The battle over subscription was soon fought out in other communities as well; the fear of property owners throughout the state deepened with the expansion of the local investment program. "It is a life and death question with us," declared a

---

[118] *Ibid.*, Nov. 14, 1846; Read, *Opinion*, p. 22; H. Binney, *Opinion*, p. 32.
[119] *Ibid.*; cf. John Doe, *Letter to Jones, Smith, and Black*, pp. 5, 7.

member of the anti-investment group in Pittsburgh.[120] And when the results of the program began clearly to appear, a revulsion against it set in among virtually all groups fully as intense as the mania which had engendered it. In 1853 the anti-subscription forces, inspired now by a fervor that was religious in character, appeared before the Supreme Court in an attempt to prove that the local investment program was unconstitutional. This case, in which arguments were presented by attorneys from both Philadelphia and Pittsburgh, centered about a subscription initiated by Philadelphia on legislative authorization to the stock of the Philadelphia, Easton and Water-Gap Railroad Company and the Hempfield Railroad Company.[121]

Neither of these roads was to have tracks in Philadelphia. The Hempfield road was to be laid from Greensburg in Westmoreland County to a point near to West Newton in that county and thence by connections with other roads to Wheeling, Virginia. At its nearest point the projected road was about three hundred miles from Philadelphia. Its objective was to serve as a feeder line for the Pennsylvania Railroad, and thus to secure to Philadelphia the trade of the northeastern section of the state. The interest of Philadelphia was conceived not only in general commercial terms, but in terms also of its stock in the Pennsylvania Railroad and the increased profits upon it which the building of the Hempfield road would produce.[122] Sharpless and three other property owners of Philadelphia sought an injunction preventing the mayor of the city from going through with the subscription. Chief Justice Black described the case of *Sharpless* v. *the Mayor of Philadel-*

---

[120] Williams, *Argument*, p. 1. By 1853 Pittsburgh's railroad debt per capita had mounted to $34, Philadelphia's to $20. Cochran and Miller, *Age of Enterprise*, p. 80. Governor Bigler asserted that the "violent controversies" which preceded subscription in certain cases were themselves destructive of the value of bonds issued for subscription purposes. This was especially true in the case of county subscriptions which frequently involved a sectional alignment as well as the traditional alignment of real property owners versus mercantile groups. "The people in one section of a county may derive valuable advantages from the construction of a public work, whilst those of another section, equally taxed for payment of interest and principal of debt, so contracted, may possibly realize no benefit at all." *Pa. Archives*, 4th, VII, 653. For comment of Governor Pollock, see *ibid.*, VII, 794. See also *Legislative Record*, *1861*, p. 386.

[121] Cf. *Pennsylvanian*, Mar. 28, Aug. 3, 1853; *Public Ledger*, Feb. 5, 1853.

[122] *Sharpless et al.* v. *Mayor of Philadelphia*, 21 Pa. St. Rep. 147, 148 (1853).

phia as "beyond all comparison, the most important cause that has ever been in this Court since the formation of the government." [123]

The new anti-subscription case was a bold one. It denied the legitimacy of local investment even when that investment was expressly authorized by the legislature. Such a contention was not presented in the debate of 1846 and it amounted to a decisive repudiation by the anti-subscription groups in Philadelphia of their position at that time. Doctrinally, therefore, it was not inconsistent for John M. Read, who had denied the legality of subscription in 1846, to appear as a leading attorney for the Philadelphia, Easton, and Water-Gap Railroad in 1853. Read himself pointed out the logic of his position in a statement published in the *Pennsylvanian*.[124] Moreover, the issue in 1846, which centered about the true meaning of the Philadelphia charter, involved at most certain common law rules respecting charter interpretation; it did not involve a constitutional issue. The debate of 1853, on the other hand, concerned no longer with elucidating the true intention of the legislature but with evaluating the legitimacy of that intention, directly involved provisions of the state constitution.

The first phase of the anti-subscription argument sought to prove that measures authorizing local investment involved unconstitutional extensions of both state and local power. It was contended that the legislature, owing to the express grant to it of the law-making authority in Article I of the constitution, could not delegate that authority to county or municipal corporations. Correspondingly, counties and municipalities had no constitutional right to receive such power when delegated; their purposes were for "local government only."

But what was to indicate the dividing line between the "appropriate functions" of the local corporation and functions "entirely foreign" to it? [125] The answer to this question in 1853 was vaguer than the answer which had been given in 1846. The earlier doctrine, preoccupied with the single subscription to the Pennsyl-

---

[123] *Ibid.*, p. 158. See Konkle, *Thomas Williams*, I, 224 ff.; Konkle, *Chief Justice Lewis*, p. 178.
[124] *Pennsylvanian*, Mar. 15, 1853.
[125] *Ibid.*, July 27, 1853; cf. Williams, *Argument*, p. 5.

vania, had been content to define municipal purposes mainly in terms of objects geographically located within city limits. The case of 1853, however, having in view a wider range of subscriptions, some of them for roads directly connecting with local boundaries, was unwilling to place so large an emphasis upon the geographical factor. Attorney Thomas Williams of Pittsburgh said that "there is, and can be, in fact, no safe or definable limit if we once overstep the boundaries of the district"; but he insisted, too, that "even within them, there is no safety but in a rigid adherence to the original object, scope, purpose, and design of the corporation." [126]

The railroad attorneys, relying upon the long tradition of state authorized local investment in Pennsylvania, insisted that the right to enlarge the powers of municipal corporations "has never been questioned." [127] Once the promotional function of the state was accepted, moreover, its application became "clearly a subject of legislative and not judicial discretion." [128] But even if the matter were one for judicial review, the geographical limit upon municipal action was unsound. Smith, McCulloch, Paley, and Phillips were invoked to prove that the approaches to a city were of vital importance to its citizens; Read emphasized that Philadelphia's investment in the Pennsylvania Railroad was partially dependent for its success on the Hempfield line, quite apart from the fact that that line had the larger significance for the city of warding off the commercial threat of Baltimore.[129] Finally the railroad attorneys took the offensive with the positive argument that counties and municipalities were the best agencies for executing mixed enterprise policy, since the allocation of such power to them served to strengthen community self-government. An "anti-centralizing" theory was developed by Attorney Alexander Dallas which appealed to traditional symbols of local pride.[130]

[126] *Ibid.*
[127] Read, *Argument*, p. 23.
[128] *Ibid.*, p. 12.
[129] *Ibid.*, pp. 12–14, 30.
[130] *Public Ledger*, July 29, 1853. Cf. *Pennsylvanian*, July 29, 1853: "In the spirit of this theory I ask the Court who are the best judges of the interests, wants, wishes, and resources of the city of Philadelphia? . . . Why has this great metropolis been incorporated, and its citizens trusted ever since its foundation, with vast powers of independent self-government . . . ?"

A second anti-investment argument went deeper. This was that taxation for public investment was levied upon groups opposed to it and was therefore a violation of the equal right of acquiring, possessing, and protecting property, guaranteed in Article IX of the state constitution.[131] This argument was associated with a criticism of the initiation of subscriptions solely on the judgment of county or city officers. In certain cases, as for example in Philadelphia County, members of the state legislature automatically became county commissioners. This procedure combined in the same hands the state power of authorization and the local power of subscription. Moreover it was contended that councils in the cities were not fully representative: council members were members of the municipal corporation only in their capacity as citizens and not in their capacity as municipal officers. "In the cities of Philadelphia and Pittsburgh," declared Williams, "the 'citizens' are integral members of the corporations, and the Councils are not."[132] But it must not be assumed that the taxation argument failed to touch those subscriptions that had been initiated, as in the case of Reading,[133] on the basis of direct popular vote. For the equal right of possessing property, secured in the constitution, was a right that could not be infringed even by an express vote of the majority. Thus the argument was not long in branching off into a strong attack upon the despotism of majorities. "Men can no longer consider their property their own," lamented Attorney B. H. Brewster, "if the majority can get authority from the Legislature to tax, and mortgage without limitation, and this the majority cannot do."[134]

It was here that the full measure of the novelty of the anti-investment case began to appear. For the taxation argument logically denied the legitimacy not only of state authorized local investment but of investment made by the state government in its own right as well. *The constitutionality of the entire mixed enterprise tradition as it had evolved since the late eighteenth century*

---

[131] *Public Ledger*, July 29, 1853; *Pennsylvanian*, July 29, 1853; Williams, *Argument*, p. 7.
[132] *Ibid.*, p. 30. Cf. *Pennsylvanian*, Mar. 15, 1853; *Public Ledger*, Feb. 25, 1853.
[133] Montgomery, *Berks County*, p. 457.
[134] *Pennsylvanian*, July 27, 1853. Cf. Konkle, *Thomas Williams*, I, 275.

was thus challenged for the first time. If Brewster could ironically maintain that local subscription was based on the idea of "benefiting the unwilling, and enriching them in spite of themselves," [135] with how much greater irony might the same argument be leveled against the mixed enterprises of the state government whose distribution had notoriously been governed by sectional log-rolling in the legislature! Few local investments, as the railroad attorneys pointed out, could compare with many of those in terms of the distance between the point at which the tax burden fell and the point at which benefits were received. Equally relevant was the experience of the state in the public works field. There a debt far in excess of mixed corporation indebtedness had been incurred, and the program of taxation initiated to help liquidate it had been keenly felt. Yet many of the works built by the state were wholly of local import.[136] The anti-investment theorists replied with a very tenuous distinction between mixed enterprise taxation and public works taxation, admitting that the latter involved "nothing . . . which violates the principal of equality." [137]

Brewster and Williams knew that they were challenging an investment function which had been established for decades and that their case had little if any precedent. This was why they furiously denounced any effort to treat the question "as a question of mere power" [138] and sought to lift the argument to a philosophic plane. They assailed mixed enterprise investment as a species of Skidmorian socialism, as an expression of the "popular despotism of Rousseau" and the "arbitrary tyranny vindicated by Hobbes." [139] In their effort to limit the legislature they appealed to the higher law theories of Coke, Blackstone, Kent, Vattel, Locke, and Marshall. "Natural justice," "the great God of Nature," "public liberty," "eternal justice," "universal law," "Magna Charta," "higher matters," "right inherent, inalienable, indefeasible," "natural right," "divine law," "private right," "the

---

[135] Williams, *Argument*, p. 1.
[136] Read, *Argument*, p. 11.
[137] Williams, *Argument*, p. 19.
[138] *Ibid.*, p. 14. Cf. *ibid.*, p. 7.
[139] *Pennsylvanian*, July 27, 1853.

law of laws" — these were the most important slogans in the anti-investment case. The issue was not one, Brewster declared grandly, for the precedent splitting "subtlety of the criminal lawyers." It was one "for statesmen, for men who are capable of taking a broad and comprehensive view of the genius of the government — its scope and purposes — the great objects proposed to be accomplished, and the great rights intended to be secured." [140]

The railroad attorneys treated such talk with contempt. "This is all very well in the theories of politics," said Read, "but it can maintain no standing among the exact rules of legal science." [141] Again and again Read and Dallas confronted their opponents with precisely the precedent that embarrassed them.[142] Read discussed public investment not only in Pennsylvania but in Britain, France, Canada, and twenty-two other states in the Union which were relying upon a policy of municipal subscription. *"It is too late, therefore, upon any abstract ground, depending upon the mere theory of our form of government, or what is sometimes termed the genius of our institutions, to deny those powers to the Legislature of an independent sovereign State of this great confederacy. Our institutions are the products of centuries of civilization, and what has been done at all times .... cannot now be stigmatized as violating the inalienable rights of man, or the first principles of natural justice."* [143]

The railroad attorneys were on weaker ground when argument shifted to the question of the practical wisdom of continuing mixed corporation policy. Their contention that the results of local investment had been "extremely fortunate" was a hollow one, and the example of the Pennsylvania Railroad Company which they cited was conspicuous for its loneliness. They insisted that insufficient private capital was available for the task of railroad con-

---

[140] Williams, *Argument*, pp. 7, 8, 9, 13, 14, 53; *Pennsylvanian*, July 27, 1853. Cf. Konkle, *Thomas Williams*, I, 234.

[141] *Pennsylvanian*, July 29, 1853.

[142] The anti-investment case, asserted Dallas, was based on the idea that the "people were always untrue to the foundations of our polity." *Public Ledger*, July 29, 1853.

[143] Read, *Argument*, pp. 15–22 (italics mine).

struction particularly after losses capitalists had sustained in the United States and the Girard banks, in the banks of the southwest, and in canal projects that were now unproductive. Since the credit of the state had been exhausted by the public-works system, the only remaining source of aid lay in counties and municipalities. Moreover an invalidation of public investment would not only stop railroads under construction, but it would nullify public borrowings under the entire mixed corporation policy: ". . . it will be the last time," warned Read, "that a Pennsylvania loan, of any kind, will be negotiated in a foreign market."[144] The anti-investment attorneys replied with a lurid analysis of the graft and financial recklessness that characterized local mixed enterprise, pointing out, quite rightly, that local repudiations were in any case inevitable.[145] They also appealed to "politico-economical science" and to "laws of trade" which could not "be violated with impunity" to demonstrate that private enterprise was "adventurous enough to outrun at all times the actual necessities of the country."[146]

It is important to observe that these higher laws of economics were as novel in the history of mixed corporation thought as the higher laws of politics that were so crucial a part of the anti-subscription case. Both bring to mind similar appeals which played roles of varying importance in the anti-charter doctrine.[147] But while there they were used against the incorporated company, it is clear that in the anti-investment theory they were used in its behalf. For the withdrawal of public investment in the transportation field in the fifties meant inescapably an exclusive reliance upon the private corporation. Implicitly Brewster and Williams were presenting a defense of the corporate system. Nor is this altered by the fact that corporate attorneys were their main opponents; corporate interests desired to maintain the flow of public funds, even if this meant disparaging the strength of the corporation and disseminating doctrine which, amusingly enough, evoked the charge of Skidmorian socialism. The glorification of

[144] *Ibid.*, pp. 24, 31. Cf. *Pennsylvanian*, July 29, 1853.
[145] Williams, *Argument*, pp. 1, 49.
[146] *Ibid.*, p. 50.
[147] Cf. *supra*, chap. II.

business enterprise in the anti-investment theory stands, moreover, in striking contrast to the concern for the "dispirited" condition of corporate entrepreneurs which led to the extension of mixed enterprise policy to the transportation field in the early years of the century, and is itself a measure of the growth of corporate transportation enterprise since that time. Whether in economic fact that enterprise had reached a point where it could readily dispense with public investment is a difficult question. It has been argued that public investment was actually of little economic advantage to the railroads.[148] The Pennsylvania Railroad, though it did not purchase the Philadelphia stock holdings until 1879, was at any rate an outstanding example of the new strength of the transportation corporation.[149]

If Brewster and Williams appropriated the higher law doctrine of the anti-charter theory and implicitly utilized it in behalf of the corporation, they did the same thing with the individualism of that theory. Why, specifically, was unrestrained (corporate) enterprise so effective? It was because of the profit motive, the fear of insolvency, the close connection between the entrepreneur and his work, restraints which were "taken off" when government entered the field.[150] But were these not precisely the factors which the anti-charter theory traditionally found wanting in the corporation as compared with individual enterprise? Williams, speaking generally of "private enterprise," completely obscured the elementary distinction between incorporated and unincorporated businesses on which the anti-charter ideology rested. In the process the corporation was implicitly transformed from a villain into a hero, from a soulless entity into an enterprising individual. In the defense of business enterprise made by the anti-investment theorists, more of which we shall discuss below, we find, in short, precisely that blurring of the anti-charter concepts and that appropriation of those concepts in behalf of the corporation itself which, as I suggested in the previous chapter, was the historic evidence of the collapse of the anti-charter argument. In the mixed

---

[148] Cleveland and Powell, *Railroad Promotion and Capitalization*, p. 232.
[149] Schotter, *Pennsylvania Railroad Company*, p. 24; C. Binney, *Horace Binney*, p. 255.
[150] Williams, *Argument*, p. 50.

enterprise setting we can note another characteristic of that collapse: in the process of their appropriation by the corporation the anti-charter symbols were used also against the government.

5. *From Court to Constitution*

The decision of the court in the Sharpless Case sustained the constitutionality of local subscriptions.[151] Chief Justice Black wrote the majority opinion, Justice Woodward concurring. Justices Lewis and Lowrie dissented, but wrote no opinions. Woodward agreed with the anti-subscription attorneys that local investment did not come "within or near that class of objects which we have been taught to consider as municipal purposes," [152] but he refused to invalidate subscription laws on the ground that the question was not one of constitutional significance. The Chief Justice, on the other hand, asserted that the making of railroads was a "public duty." He surveyed the entire history of the state's investment activity; "from the earliest times" that activity had been carried on "in pursuance of laws which no one ever doubted to be constitutional." He declared: "It is a grave error to suppose that the duty of a state stops with the establishment of those institutions which are necessary to the existence of government: such as those for the administration of justice, the preservation of the peace, and the protection of the country from foreign enemies. . . . To aid, encourage, and stimulate commerce, domestic and foreign, is a duty of the sovereign, as plain and as universally recognized as any other." [153]

The "grave error" which the Chief Justice described is perhaps as adequate a definition as any of that amorphous concept known

---

[151] *Sharpless et al.* v. *Mayor of Philadelphia*, 21 Pa. St. Rep. 147, 159–75 (1853). Though the court did not expressly commit itself on the validity of local subscriptions unauthorized by the legislature, it was subsequently held that its decision "left no doubt that if the question had depended on the original charters" of the municipal corporations alone the decision would have been unfavorable to subscription. *Pennsylvania Railroad Company* v. *The City of Philadelphia*, 47 Pa. St. Rep. 189, 194 (1864). Cf. subsequent remarks of Black, *Legal Intelligencer*, Sept. 9, 1858: "No lawyer doubts that a borough can only subscribe to a railroad when expressly authorized by law to do so." *See also* C. Binney, *Horace Binney*, p. 253.

[152] *Sharpless et al.* v. *Mayor of Philadelphia*, 21 Pa. St. Rep. 147, 182 (1853).

[153] *Ibid.*, pp. 169–71. Cf. Brigance, *Jeremiah Sullivan Black*, p. 34; Konkle, *Thomas Williams*, I, 229 ff.

as "laissez faire" which is often alleged to have governed the thinking of the period before the Civil War. But for our purpose the significance of Black's remarks lies less in his own vigorous repudiation of the concept than it does in his insistence that the opposite notion was "plainly" and "universally recognized." The Chief Justice's historiography was as sound as Woodward's was fallacious. The obvious evidence of decades was at hand to prove that the anti-subscription argument was incomparably a *pièce d'occasion*. In 1857 Justice Lowrie, who dissented in the Sharpless Case himself admitted the fact in an engagingly simple way. In the case of *Commonwealth* ex rel *Thomas* v. *Commissioners of Allegheny County* [154] he declared in connection with subscriptions made by Allegheny County: "Newspapers and public meetings freely discussed the subject, and the hopes of the people bore down all doubt about their right to enter upon the adventure, and it was only when it was discovered to be unsuccessful that any respectable number became awake to the question of the constitutionality of their proceeding." [155]

Defeated in the courts, the anti-investment groups began to work for constitutional amendments abolishing the mixed enterprise activities of both state and local governments. Such amendments had already been enacted in Ohio, Illinois, and New York.[156] The measures introduced in the legislature in 1855 read as follows:

> The credit of the commonwealth shall not in any manner or event be pledged or loaned to any individual, company, corporation, or association, nor shall the commonwealth hereafter become a joint owner or stockholder in any company, association, or corporation.
>
> The commonwealth shall not assume the debt, or any part thereof, of any county, city, borough, or township, or of any corporation or association, unless such debt shall have been contracted to enable the State to repel invasion, suppress domestic insurrection, defend itself in time of war, or to assist the State in the discharge of any portion of its present indebtedness.
>
> The legislature shall not authorize any county, city, borough, township, or corporated district, by virtue of a vote of its citizens or

[154] *Commonwealth* ex rel *Thomas* v. *Commissioners of Allegheny County*, 32 Pa. St. Rep. 218 (1858). [155] *Ibid.*, p. 234.
[156] *Pa. Archives*, 4th, VII, 653; Persons, *Government Experimentation in Business*, p. 90.

otherwise, to become a stockholder in any company, association, or corporation, or to obtain money for or loan its credit to any corporation, association, institution, or party.[157]

Public opinion was so widely in favor of these measures that their passage by the legislature and their ratification by the people met no important opposition. The *Pennsylvanian* asserted that they were "reforms permeated with the very incense of Democracy," but it was impossible to make a party issue of them. They belonged to a series of nine amendments which were introduced in the legislature simultaneously.[158] Two of the others called respectively for the limitation of future state debt to a maximum of seven hundred and fifty thousand dollars and for the establishment of a sinking fund for the liquidation of existing debt.[159] Another was designed to reduce Philadelphia's representation in the legislature; opposition to it occasionally involved a general disparagement of the amendment series. In 1856 Senator Price of Philadelphia argued that the fundamental law was a "venerable instrument" and "should be seldom changed." He admitted that the amendments abolishing mixed corporation investment were intended to serve a desirable purpose, but he argued that the "sober second thought of the people" would henceforth secure the state against the investment evil without constitutional change.[160] In 1857, however, when the legislature approved the

[157] *Legislative Record, 1855, passim.*
[158] Cf. *Legislative Record, 1856*, pp. 334, 413, 438.
[159] The indebtedness provision read as follows: "The State may contract debts to supply casual deficits or failures in revenues, or to meet expenses not otherwise provided for, but the aggregate amount of such debts, direct and contingent, whether contracted by virtue of one or more acts of the general assembly or at different periods of time, shall never exceed seven hundred and fifty thousand dollars, and the money arising from the creation of such debts shall be applied to the purposes for which it was obtained, or to repay the debts so contracted and to no other purpose whatever." An additional provision, however, permitted the state to "contract debts to repel invasion, suppress insurrection, defend the State in war, or to redeem the present outstanding indebtedness of the State; but the money arising from the contracting of such debts shall be applied to the purpose for which it was raised or to repay such debts, and to no other purpose whatever." *Constitutions of Pa.*, p. 166.
[160] *Legislative Record, 1856*, p. 336. Cf. *Philadelphia Press*, Oct. 12, 13, 1857. The *Ledger* remarked that the danger of tampering with the constitution was "supposed to be the weakest and most vulnerable point" in the case in favor of the amendments. *Public Ledger*, Oct. 14, 1857.

amendments for the second time, the vote in the Senate was 24–7 in their favor, in the House 78–12.[161]

TABLE 3
POPULAR VOTE ON THE ANTI-INVESTMENT AMENDMENTS
1857

	For	Against		For	Against
Adams	2,668	492	Lancaster	4,993	29
Allegheny	5,560	431	Lawrence	939	189
Armstrong	38	27	Lebanon	1,289	63
Beaver	1,650	1	Lehigh	527	450
Bedford	2,443	112	Luzerne	3,922	535
Berks	7,721	827	Lycoming	1,786	40
Blair	408	62	M'Kean	(no returns)	
Bradford	1,304	45	Mercer	1,076	216
Bucks	3,027	387	Mifflin	1,289	104
Butler	847	168	Monroe	109	57
Cambria	1,048	169	Montgomery	4,906	903
Carbon	501	10	Montour	614	36
Centre	1,223	93	Northampton	2,195	154
Chester	8,702	256	Northumberland	1,592	36
Clarion	1,444	355	Perry	2,235	112
Clearfield	313	196	Philadelphia	7,172	193
Clinton	566	47	Pike	425	13
Columbia	2,182	62	Potter	413	1
Crawford	1,508	173	Schuylkill	4,366	233
Cumberland	3,792	1,256	Snyder	690	193
Dauphin	2,279	495	Somerset	1,006	41
Delaware	2,162	207	Sullivan	265	20
Elk	28	247	Susquehanna	2,837	282
Erie	965	21	Tioga	2,471	27
Fayette	1,063	159	Union	417	12
Forrest	10	3	Venango	1,065	34
Franklin	5,243	122	Warren	389	114
Fulton	262	164	Washington	1,544	526
Greene	525	112	Wayne	1,479	2
Huntingdon	1,357	61	Westmoreland	4,149	385
Indiana	725	185	Wyoming	308	4
Jefferson	549	744	York	2,732	822
Juniata	1,350	138			
			Total	122,658*	13,653

* The total of this column should be 122,663.
[161] *Harrisburg Telegraph*, Sept. 25, Oct. 3, 1857.

6. The End of Mixed Enterprise

It will be observed that the amendment series, with its limitation on state debt and its sweeping prohibition of the pledging of public credit for corporate purposes, was designed to outlaw not only mixed enterprise investment but the state's policy of guaranteeing corporate loans and its policy of large public works undertakings. This meant that the doctrine rationalizing the amendments represented a wider attack upon governmental action than that presented by the anti-investment attorneys before the Supreme Court in 1853. Repudiating all public investment policies, C. R. Buckalew who defended the amendments in the Senate in 1856, spoke philosophically of the "general nature, design, and results of constitutional government." Declaring that the inner propensity of all governments was to usurp and abuse power, he indicted the legislative branch as "the main offender," on the ground, curiously enough, that it was least responsible to public opinion — a charge which emphasized the sectional and corporate pressures that had dominated investment policy since the eighteenth century.[162]

In this broader setting the anti-governmental themes developed by Brewster and Williams in the Sharpless Case came fully into their own. This was especially true of the individualistic and higher law arguments, originally fashioned by the anti-charter polemicists to denounce the corporation but which were now utilized to defend what was in fact an exclusive reliance upon the corporation in the transportation field and to attack governmental interference. The *Pennsylvanian* saw the amendments bringing the state "back to those evident duties which it was designed she should discharge." The spectacle "of a State descending from her corporate position to become a partner in all the small companies or associations" within its boundaries impressed the editors of that journal as "degrading to the financial position of the Commonwealth."[163] The *Public Ledger* felt no less deeply about the

---

[162] *Legislative Record, 1856*, pp. 344–46.
[163] *Pennsylvanian*, Aug. 26, 1857.

matter. Once the amendments were ratified, it sighed its relief in a series of articles on the true function of government — admitting, however, that "as a general rule" little was to be gained by tinkering with the constitution.[164] It theorized upon the "keenness of self-interest," compared "private individuals" with public officials much to the derogation of the latter, and hinted of a beneficent mechanism which guaranteed that the "interest and enterprise of individuals or private companies" would alone accomplish all necessary tasks when the time was "ripe and ready." Surveying the situation in Washington, France, Mexico, and other regions of the world, the *Ledger* concluded that money above all was something in which governments should deal as little as possible; "only men of great mercantile intellect and skill" could be trusted with it.[165]

Governments that undertook everything from the sale of tobacco to the construction of railways were "absolute" governments, sharply to be distinguished from the democratic type. Under such governments "people invariably lose their interest . . . and their enterprise of spirit." The *Ledger* drew a striking parallel between an established religion and a policy of governmental action in economic life: the maintenance of the entrepreneurial motive was likened to the "self-culture of the religious spirit . . . upon the universality of . . . [which] hangs the life of nations." Without going further into the extremely philosophic views of the *Ledger*, the following summary of its position may be quoted: "The *only legitimate objects* [italics the *Ledger's*] of a government are much fewer and simpler than are commonly supposed, and the more closely States confine themselves to these, the greater will be their prosperity. The chief object of government is simply to defend the weak from the aggressions of the strong, by maintaining the equal rights of all. It is not for a government to make itself into a bank, or canal, or railroad company, or all combined, any more than it is to assist one sect of religion to establish itself at the expense of all others. But its aim should be simply to remove all obstruction, and allow every grand

---

[164] *Public Ledger*, Oct. 15, 17, 1857.
[165] *Ibid.*, Oct. 17, Dec. 14, 1857. Cf. *ibid.*, June 6, 1853; Sept. 22, 1857.

and useful institution to develop itself and grow freely by its own inherent energies unmolested." [166]

It is interesting that the *Ledger* admitted that its own italicized conception of the legitimate function of government was not one "commonly supposed" to be valid. But if it rejected public opinion as a guide, whence did it derive its conception of the only legitimate objects? It did not derive it from the holding of the chief justice in the Sharpless Case. There the state's master guardian of the fundamental law had specifically presented the *Ledger's* view in order to reject it as a grave error. It did not derive it from any subsequent decisions of the court. In every succeeding case dealing with the problem the Sharpless holding was sustained. "Several changes have taken place in the membership of this court since that case was decided," declared Justice Woodward in 1858, "but at no time since could a different judgment have been obtained." [167] Some might assert, as Read asserted in the Sharpless argument, that what men commonly suppose to be the legitimate sphere of government *is* the legitimate sphere: "Mankind settle these questions for themselves, by a logic which is superior to the closest lucubrations of the speculative philosopher." [168] But for the editors of the *Ledger*, as for the anti-subscription theorists in 1853, this was an intolerable positivism. They had attained to that higher level of insight which was gradually transforming a mixed enterprise policy accepted since the late eighteenth century into a policy which violated the first principles of democracy.

[166] *Ibid.*, Oct. 17, 1857.
[167] *Commonwealth* ex rel. *Thomas* v. *Commissioners of Allegheny County*, 32 Pa. St. Rep. 218, 232 (1858).
[168] Read, *Argument*, p. 4.

IV

THE PUBLIC WORKS

1. Early Attitudes Toward State Ownership

IF MIXED enterprise policy had been extended to the transportation field during the first decade of the nineteenth century mainly in recognition of the fact that the corporate system alone could not achieve its transportation objectives, it was clear by the third decade of the century that a supplementary policy of public investment was also failing to achieve them. Yet the economic ambitions which those objectives reflected grew stronger with each year that passed. With the deepening of seaboard competition for the West the sensitivity of Philadelphians became increasingly delicate. In dark moments during the twenties they saw the approach of commercial isolation and decline, their own state split up among rival imperialisms — New York capturing the trade of the Easton area, Albany at the gates of Pittsburgh, Baltimore victorious in the Lancaster region.[1] Not unnaturally the belief began to grow that if the charter and mixed enterprise policies were failing to ward off these commercial threats, some other policy must be found that would.

The notion that the government itself might undertake the job did not emerge quickly. During the period immediately following the Revolution, the state had, it is true, assumed complete responsibility for turnpike construction and maintenance.[2] But its increasing reliance upon charter policy after 1790 demonstrated that it had little desire to shoulder transport obligations completely. In debates which had accompanied the evolution of the mixed corporation idea, the possibility of outright state ownership and control had been considered. The reaction to it had been

---

[1] For typical expressions of the attitude of Philadelphians toward this competition, see *United States Gazette*, Jan. 4, 25, 26, 28, Feb. 10, 11, 16, 28, Mar. 1, 7, May 24, June 1, 3, 7, Aug. 19, 26, Sept. 5, 6, 1825; *Poulson's Daily Advertiser*, Jan. 11, 28, Mar. 14, 22, 23, May 6, 1825.

[2] See *supra*, p. 51.

negative. To some extent this was due to habits and prejudices inherited from abroad. Though on the Continent state ownership and operation of turnpikes and canals had been accepted, in Britain, where larger amounts of private capital were available, the idea had not attained great strength.[3]

But foreign experience, while constantly referred to in discussion, was not the dominant consideration. Certain specific arguments were leveled against state ownership during the early period. One of them reflected the fear that a policy of state ownership would, as a House committee put it in 1806, "beget incurable jealousies"[4] among the various localities in Pennsylvania, that sectionalism would wreck the program. A second consideration was the financial one. By 1820 mixed enterprise investment had already reached appreciable proportions; to embark upon a wholesale program of public ownership would entail expenditures that seemed prohibitive.[5] Finally it was argued that the mixed enterprise program, combining both public and private vigilance, was more effective than outright state ownership. Alone public officials would be influenced by considerations of graft, the contractors whom they employed would make their work as protracted and expensive as possible, and there would be no concentration of responsibility.[6]

These criticisms, concerned entirely with the practicability of state ownership, did not challenge the *right* of the state to own and operate transportation facilities. It was implicitly assumed that the state could rightfully own any facility in existence, either for the purpose of making the facility free or for operating it at a profit. This was clearly demonstrated by most of the charters of turnpike, bridge, and canal companies; the state reserved the privilege of purchase "after a limited time, either with a view to revenue or for the purpose of making them free."[7]

---

[3] See *Facts Respecting Inland Navigation*; Smith, *Canal Navigation in Pa.*, p. iv.
[4] *House Journal, 1806–1807*, p. 394.
[5] *Ibid., 1807–1808*, p. 315; *1806–1807*, p. 304.
[6] *Ibid.*, pp. 304–95. See also *ibid., 1807–1808*, p. 315.
[7] See *ibid*. For examples of such reservation clauses, see *Dallas' Laws*, II, 330–32; IV, 27–28; *Pa. Laws, 1810–11*, pp. 119–34; *1812–13*, pp. 239–45. Committees for the appraisal of the works in case of purchase were provided for. They consisted

2. The Campaign of 1825

As interstate competition for the western trade deepened in intensity, as the movement from turnpikes to canals and railroads made ever increasing amounts of capital necessary for transportation development [8] and thus highlighted the inadequacy of private efforts, particularly as the Erie Canal program got under way in New York,[9] the antagonism toward outright governmental entrepreneurship began to wane. By 1826 the state had come to believe that public ownership was sound. A shift in view was discernible as early as 1818, when Senator Breck published an influential pamphlet in which he maintained that if necessary the state itself must undertake the job of uniting the eastern and western sections of Pennsylvania by means of a canal.[10] Soon a host of other notable men appeared in support of the public works idea. In the legislature Dr. William Lehman began unceasingly to urge the need for immediate action.[11] A movement developed in behalf of state ownership which had the passion of a religious campaign.

Behind this movement was the Pennsylvania Society for the Promotion of Internal Improvements, an organization formed in Philadelphia in 1824. It derived its original support mainly from the east.[12] Chief Justice William Tilghman of the Supreme Court presided over one of its first mass meetings, and Nicholas Biddle acted as secretary. Other prominent members of the society were the indefatigable Mathew Carey, Benjamin Chew, Josiah Randall,

---

usually of representatives of both the corporation and the government. For an act of purchase, see *ibid.*, *1811–12*, pp. 178–80.

[8] For the gradual change in public attitude as a result of this development, see *Comparative Calculations on Internal Improvements*; *United States Gazette*, Feb. 11, Sept. 5, 1825; *Poulson's Daily Advertiser*, Mar. 22, 1825.

[9] For the strong influence of the example set by New York, see M. Carey, *Internal Improvement of Pa.*, pp. 18–36; Tyson, *Commerce of Philadelphia*, p. 13; *House Journal, 1823–24*, p. 165.

[10] Breck, *Internal Improvements by Pa.*, pp. 75–78 and *passim*.

[11] Cf. *House Journal, 1817–18*, pp. 619–27; *1823–24*, pp. 163–70.

[12] The society had at the outset forty-eight members. It was supported by their contributions and "donations by public spirited citizens and liberal corporations." Pa. Society for Internal Improvements, *First Annual Report*. For data on the organization and activities of the society, see also Pa. Society for Internal Improvements, *Address*; Strickland, *Reports on Canals, Railways, Roads*; *Poulson's Daily Advertiser*, Mar. 24, 1825.

Judge Thomas Duncan, Charles J. Ingersoll, William J. Duane, and Thomas Biddle.[13] It was not long before this group broadened the base of its support both vertically and horizontally. Subcommittees were set up in each county, pamphlets were circulated, and the co-operation of newspaper editors throughout the state was used to good effect. Petitions urging the construction of a canal across the state [14] began to flood the legislature. The society sent William Strickland, a Pennsylvania engineer, to Europe to study schemes of canal communication developed there. He returned with a collection of detailed blueprints for the use of the legislature.[15]

In 1825, the society called a canal convention in Harrisburg.[16] The idea of a convention encountered opposition. One of the strongest arguments leveled against it — a commentary on the limited extent to which pressure group activity was rationalized — was the argument that the convention would somehow usurp the power of the legislature.[17] But the convention nevertheless served to accelerate appreciably the public works movement. From 46 of the 50 counties in the state 117 representatives gathered in Harrisburg. The *Pennsylvania Intelligencer* reported that men from the following professions made up the bulk of the membership: lawyers, 47; farmers, 30; merchants, 16; manufacturers, 7; physicians, 7; innkeepers, 3; mechanics, 2.[18] In the year that

---

[13] *Poulson's Daily Advertiser*, Jan. 28, 1825; M. Carey, *Internal Improvement of Pa.*, p. 13.

[14] Cf. Pa. Society for Internal Improvements, *Address*; *Poulson's Daily Advertiser*, Apr. 22, 1826.

[15] Cf. Strickland, *Reports on Canals, Railways, Roads*. The Society instructed Strickland as follows: "In your examination of the canals of Europe we request you will always bear in mind the fact that the great capital which is ever at the command of those who there undertake such works, and the immediate and profitable use to which they can be applied, have induced those who have executed them to regard their cost of less importance than we are compelled to consider it here." Quoted in Pa. Society for Internal Improvements, *First Annual Report*, p. 31. This distinction was emphasized as early as 1805 when the state was heavily influenced by British procedures. See *Facts Respecting Inland Navigation*, pp. 34–35. See also Tanner, *Canals and Railroads of U.S.*, pp. 11–12.

[16] M. Carey, *Internal Improvement of Pa.*, p. 14. Meigs, *Life of Charles Jared Ingersoll*, p. 153.

[17] Shelling, "Philadelphia and Agitation for Pa. Canal," *Pa. Mag. of Hist. and Biog.*, LXII (1938), 195; *Poulson's Daily Advertiser*, May 6, 1825; *Miner's Journal*, May 21, 1825.   [18] Quoted, *Niles Register*, XXIX (1825–26), 63.

the convention was held, the legislature empowered the governor to appoint five canal commissioners to take necessary steps for "the establishment of a navigable communication between the eastern and western waters of the state, and Lake Erie." [19] These commissioners made three reports. In 1826 the governor urged legislative action and in that year an act was passed providing for the construction of two canals, one from the western end of the Union Canal to the Susquehanna River, another from Pittsburgh to the Kiskeminitas River. Three hundred thousand dollars were appropriated.[20]

The canal convention, with its membership drawn from most of the counties of the state and from widely diverse occupations, had the appearance of representing a united, state-wide opinion. Beneath the surface, however, there were serious tensions. The sectionalism which the earlier critics of governmental ownership had feared revealed itself at once. It was originally proposed that the convention restrict itself to considering only the east-west plan of the society, but the opposition to this idea was so bitter that it was dropped. "That sectional considerations produced this opposition," wrote Mathew Carey, "cannot be doubted. The representatives of those counties not likely to be immediately benefited, strenuously opposed the measure, with all the powers of eloquence. Among the opposition were found all the representatives of Bedford, Cumberland, Franklin, Lancaster, Northampton, Tioga, and York. Berks, Chester, Lebanon, and Lehigh were divided." [21]

Newspapers in the rural regions contended that the program of improvements projected by the Pennsylvania Society would be of

---

[19] *Pa. Laws, 1824–25*, p. 239.

[20] *Pa. Archives*, 4th, V, 657; *House Journal, 1825–26*, I, 310–11; *Senate Journal, 1825*, p. 363; *Pa. Laws, 1825–26*, p. 55; M. Carey, *Internal Improvement of Pa.*, p. 16.

[21] *Ibid.*, p. 14. An economic analysis of the opposition reveals that the first five counties mentioned by Carey exported predominantly agricultural articles and had already established markets in Baltimore and the adjoining counties in Maryland and Virginia. The remaining counties which unanimously opposed the scheme adopted were situated in the northeastern section of the state, a region that the proposed canal would not touch and one that traditionally relied on the New York market. Bishop, "The State Works of Pennsylvania," *Trans. of Conn. Acad. of Arts and Sciences*, XIII (1907), p. 184. Hereafter this study will be cited as "State Works."

assistance only to Philadelphia. "We repeat," wrote the *Miner's Journal* of Pottsville, "the country has nothing to expect from the liberality of the city; the city is as much indebted to the country as the country is to the city and perhaps more so." [22] The sectional alignment that had existed in the canal convention existed also in the legislature when the question of the three hundred thousand dollar appropriation came up in 1826. "The vote in the House of Representatives on the third reading," Carey reports, "was 62 yeas and 32 nays. All the members from Adams, Bedford, Cumberland, Franklin, Lancaster (with one exception), Lehigh, Lebanon, Northampton, Perry, Pike, Union, Wayne, and York, voted against the bill. Berks, Montgomery, Schuylkill, Westmoreland, and Philadelphia County were divided." [23]

A split in the legislature developed early between the "Main Liners" and the "Branch Men." The Branch Men represented the regions that the main canal line did not touch. Though they were ready to support the principle of public works, they refused to vote appropriations for the Main Line unless appropriations were also made to connect their constituencies with it. The Main Liners, on the other hand, wanted the east-west canal completed before branch canals were constructed. Even among the Main Liners, however, there was a serious split during the early period, for the details of the western route had not yet been finally decided upon. They agreed on the route east of the mountains, which had already been mapped out, but some wanted the Main Line in the west to go northward to the Great Lakes while others wanted it to go southward to the Ohio.[24] It is not hard to understand why Carey wrote: "The system was moulded by the prevalence of local interests, in violation of the plain dictates of sound policy." [25]

The sectional factor was not the only barrier to the enactment of a consistent public works program. There were vested interests in the way as well. Turnpike owners throughout the state saw their investments jeopardized by the construction of a canal. The

---

[22] *Miner's Journal*, Oct. 1, 1825.
[23] M. Carey, *Internal Improvement in Pa.*, p. 18.
[24] *United States Gazette*, June 3, 1825; Klein, *Pa. Politics*, pp. 337–39.
[25] M. Carey, *Internal Improvement in Pa.*, p. 16.

same kind of opposition that the Erie Canal met from turnpike proprietors in the Albany-Buffalo region was met also by the Pennsylvania project.[26] Moreover there were wagoners who traveled the turnpikes, and innkeepers who had set up establishments along the way.[27] In addition to these interests opposing the canal, there were certain groups in the farming regions of the east who opposed it also. They feared that the construction of an east-west canal would flood the Philadelphia market with products from the west, and that their favored position there, which was reflected in higher land values, would be damaged.[28]

But if during the previous period the legitimacy of transportation ownership as a function of the state had not been denied, it is not difficult to understand why, in the middle twenties, no such denials were heard either. As the failure of private capital to meet transportation needs became increasingly glaring, even the old criticisms of the practicability of state ownership began to vanish. It was sometimes asserted that the state should wait until the Union Canal was completed,[29] but that plea was not taken seriously. Apart from the sectional consideration, the only argument against the expediency of public ownership which remained important in the middle twenties was the contention that the measure was financially unsound. It was argued that, in addition to creating a great public debt, the building of the canal would destroy an important yearly income derived from tolls on the wagon traffic between Philadelphia and Pittsburgh. Whatever might be the public works revenue in subsequent years, it was pointed out that it could not for some time be relied upon to pay even the current yearly expenses of the works program.[30]

The sectional and financial arguments were answered with vigor. Nothing reveals more clearly than the reply to the sectional argument the peculiar dilemma which, as I noted earlier, the entire theory of regional competition faced: it had no area around which it could come to a stable focus. It is clear that the ideology of

---

[26] *Miner's Journal*, Oct. 8, 1825.
[27] *House Journal, 1824-25*, II, 267.
[28] *Miner's Journal*, Oct. 8, 1825.
[29] *Ibid.*, Aug. 26, 1825.
[30] *Ibid.*; see also *Niles Register*, XXIX (1825-26), 60-61.

local interest which threatened to sabotage the works program was nothing more than the projection upon a more limited plane of precisely the same competitive doctrine which the public works protagonists themselves, in pointing to the threats of Baltimore and New York, utilized to champion that program. Any attack on the theory of local competition was bound to compromise in some measure the doctrinal integrity of the theory of interstate competition. Thus it is not surprising that the works publicists devoted a portion of their time to preaching a principle alien to the competitive dogma, the principle of the indivisibility and the interdependency of the economic community. They sought with intense ardor to prove that no section in the state could fail to profit, either directly or indirectly, from governmental construction of the east-west canal. The farmers of the west would be able to market their produce at Philadelphia as cheaply as the farmers of Lancaster County could during the turnpike era.[31] Land values in the west would rise.[32] Villages and towns and waterworks and mills would spring up "as if by magic."[33] But the farmers of the east would not suffer from this. Philadelphia was a shipping port, and the price of produce there was set by the world market.[34] The new mineral regions would at last be opened to an effective commerce. "The spinner of cotton at Flat-rock, and the worker of marble and soap-stone in Montgomery, or slate in York, will exchange their commodities for the iron of Huntingdon, the timber of Cambria, and the salt of Westmoreland."[35] Manufacturers would be vastly benefited. Emigrants from abroad would settle in

[31] *United States Gazette*, Mar. 1, 1825.
[32] *Ibid.; House Journal, 1824-25*, II, 266. The Pennsylvania Society estimated that the proposed improvements project would bring a rise in land value of from three to five dollars an acre. *Poulson's Daily Advertiser*, Mar. 22, 1825. See also issue of Jan. 11, 1825; *House Journal, 1829-30*, II, 226.
[33] *United States Gazette*, Mar. 1, 1825.
[34] "Will it make one cent a barrel of difference to a farmer east of the Susquehanna, whether the western farmer sends his flour by a flat-bottomed boat to New Orleans or by a canal boat to Philadelphia, to be shipped off? It cannot. The products of the country must be exported from some sea-port, and it surely cannot injure any person in the east of our state, to have Philadelphia do a vast deal more business, and New York, Baltimore and New Orleans, proportionally less. . . . To the people of the adjacent counties, we would say, 'Is not her prosperity your prosperity? . . . If she sinks, will not you suffer?'" *House Journal, 1824-25*, II, 268.
[35] *Ibid.*, p. 269.

Pennsylvania.[36] Every group would gain from the prosperity of every other.[37] This was demonstrated by the experience of every foreign country and every state in the Union that had embarked upon the building of canals.[38]

It is worthy of special notice that an important argument advanced in favor of public works was that they would provide expanded opportunities for the unemployed and the poor. Nor was this a new notion among Pennsylvanians. In executing mixed corporation policy, the employment objective had been considered. Thus during the depression of 1819 a Senate committee headed by Raguet explicitly recommended an expansion of public investment as one method by which the state might reduce unemployment.[39] When the campaign for state ownership got under way, the employment objective was elaborated upon, the protagonists of the works reiterating that "the execution of the canal will give employment to many of the labouring poor." [40] In line with their general optimism, they foresaw the speedy elimination of poorhouses and poor taxes.[41] It is true that the *Mechanics Free Press*, the organ of Philadelphia unions, was not always sympathetic toward the public works idea,[42] but this is to be explained largely by the fact that the unions were composed of specialized urban craftsmen who could see but slight benefit for themselves in the growth of opportunities largely for unskilled labor in other sections of the state.

It is impossible to separate the emphasis upon the indivisibility of the economic community, which found expression in the works theory, from the financial doctrines that accompanied it. For what was actually emerging was a full-fledged theory of state spending

---

[36] *Poulson's Daily Advertiser*, Mar. 14, 1825. For an early presentation of the emigration argument, see Smith, *Canal Navigation in Pa.*, p. 3.

[37] *United States Gazette*, May 24, 1825; *Miner's Journal*, Feb. 4, 1826.

[38] *Ibid.*

[39] The committee also pointed out that investments might be more profitable for the state at a time when the price of labor was low. *Senate Journal, 1819–20*, p. 235.

[40] *Hazard's Register*, II (1828), 325. For the belief of the House Ways and Means Committee in the desirability of public works as an instrument for the elimination of unemployment, see *Hazard's Register*, III (1829), 190. For the arguments of the Pennsylvania Society for the Promotion of Internal Improvements in this connection, see *Internal Improvements*, pp. 6–7; see also *Poulson's Daily Advertiser*, Mar. 14, 1825; *Niles Register*, XX (1821), 85.

[41] *Poulson's Daily Advertiser*, Mar. 14, 1825.

[42] *Mechanics Free Press*, Oct. 17, 1829, Mar. 27, 1830.

in the public interest. When it was contended that the construction of the works would create a dangerous debt, three arguments were presented in reply: tolls and profits would be so abundantly forthcoming in later years that the debt could be paid off easily; the increase of trade which would attend the execution of the works would produce a large amount of new taxable resources; and even if the works project should be a failure financially, it was not in the last analysis to be judged in financial terms.

In connection with the first of these ideas the enthusiasm was vast. Not only was it believed that tolls would produce sufficient revenue to meet the cost of the works, but it was also believed that they would provide a great surplus of revenue which would eliminate the necessity of taxation and support the public school system. The Pennsylvania Society declared: "These tolls will, at no distant day, form a sinking fund for the redemption of the debt created from the completion of canals, and ultimately support the government, and relieve the state from the burden of taxation." [43] A House committee declared that "the tolls will support the government, and educate every child in the commonwealth." [44] The opponents of the canal pointed to Britain where dividends on canal stocks did not lend support to such roseate expectations; they were answered by the assertion that errors had been made in Britain's canal policy and that these would not be duplicated in Pennsylvania.[45] There can be no doubt that one of the strongest feelings in connection with the works was the feeling that they afforded to the government not only an opportunity to enhance the commerce of the state, but an opportunity to make great profits as well.[46] The older reliance on the private profit motive in the transportation field gave way to enthusiastic visions of public profit, free public services, and reduced taxation.

The notion that the state would gain indirectly through an increase in taxable resources was not developed so extensively,

---

[43] *United States Gazette*, Feb. 11, 1825.
[44] *House Journal, 1824–25*, II, 284. See also *United States Gazette*, Mar. 1, Jan. 26, Feb. 16, and Mar. 7, 1825; *Poulson's Daily Advertiser*, Jan. 28, Mar. 14, 22, 1825; M. Carey, *Internal Improvements*, No. I, p. 3.
[45] *Miner's Journal*, Oct. 1, 1825.
[46] See *Hazard's Register*, III (1829), 190.

primarily because it was more complex and did not have the immediate appeal that the revenue-from-tolls argument had. But the public works theorists inevitably fell back upon it, whenever the argument became difficult on other fronts. In the canal convention, where the financial difficulties involved in canal construction were heavily emphasized, a committee tried to demonstrate that auction duties and retail licenses would bring greater amounts to the treasury in consequence of the public works system, and that farmers hitherto unable to pay for unpatented lands would be able to do so if cheap transportation to the Philadelphia market was afforded them. It was estimated that two million dollars would come to the treasury from the farmers.[47] J. L. Sullivan, a pamphleteer, spoke of "an appreciation of property that will have paid in advance the whole cost of the canal." [48]

The publicists in favor of state construction and ownership did not stop with proofs of its practicability. Spurred on by the mounting enthusiasm of the twenties they lifted the issue to the higher plane of moral and political right. At the canal convention Loring insisted that the works would become "the arteries of our political existence," and — something which was badly needed at the time — "great thoroughfares of affection" which would minimize intrastate jealousies. Such facilities should not be used "to pamper the cupidity and enrich the purses of our capitalists"; [49] corporations could not be trusted with them. If the task were left to corporations, declared John Sergeant, ". . . they would make the parts of the line that were least expensive, and at the same time would be most productive of toll, while difficult parts would be left undone, and thus the main object would be frustrated." [50] But, even more important, the corporations would become so powerful that they would dictate political policy in the state. The "calamitous" end result would be that they would "monopolize their benefits in perpetuity," and would possess a portion of the popular "sovereignty"; their powers would always be regarded with "jealousy." [51]

[47] *Miner's Journal*, Oct. 1, 1825. [49] *United States Gazette*, Aug. 26, 1825.
[48] Sullivan, *Canal Policy*, p. 4. [50] *Niles Register*, Sept. 24, 1825.
[51] *United States Gazette*, Jan. 28, 1825; *Miner's Journal*, Oct. 8, 1825; *House Journal, 1824–25*, II, 204.

It is easy to see that we are confronted here with a fusion of the theory of public ownership and the traditional anti-charter doctrine. Sectional motivations cut across party lines in connection with the public works question, an effective anti-Democratic opposition had not arisen by the mid-twenties, and sentiment for some plan of state ownership was reaching overwhelming proportions; but it is still worth noting that in the legislature which voted the first major appropriation for the public works the Democratic party, fountain of the anti-charter ideology, had clear-cut dominance. In the Senate there were 26 Democrats and 7 Federalists; in the House, 77 Democrats and 23 Federalists.[52] In terms of the issue at hand a fusion of the anti-charter and state ownership theories was inevitable. The only alternative to state ownership was continued reliance on the corporate system or on the mixed enterprise program in which, in the transportation field especially, private control was dominant. If the need for state ownership was to be demonstrated, the undesirability of the corporate device as an exclusive reliance had also to be proved. But if the blending of the two theories was dictated by strategic necessity, it was, as we shall perceive more fully below, also logical in a theoretical sense. In our earlier analysis of the anti-charter doctrine we observed the implications it contained for public enterprise, implications which appeared most clearly in the ideas that charter policy granted aspects of "sovereignty" to private companies and that charters should be granted only after it had been found impracticable for the state itself to embark upon the enterprises involved.[53]

What is somewhat paradoxical, however, is the fact that among the most forceful champions of the anti-charter theory in the state ownership discussion of the twenties were men like Nicholas Biddle and John Sergeant. I suggested earlier that that theory was not the exclusive property of any party or any group, but to find conservatives such as these in the ranks of its foremost protagonists is still unusual. Yet the fact can be explained. The

---

[52] Shelling in *Pa. Mag. of Hist. and Biog.*, LXII (1938), 201. Cf. *Hazard's Register*, I (1828), 406; Klein, *Pa. Politics*, p. 357.
[53] See *supra*, p. 72.

commercial and financial interests in the east did not desire to undertake the works project themselves; there had already been failures enough in that field. However strongly it might be contended that an east-west canal would be a profitable venture, private capitalists were perfectly willing to permit the government to reap the rewards of this type of investment. But while eastern commercial interests did not wish to build the canal, they wanted, and that as quickly as possible, some means of tapping the trade of the West before it was monopolized by Baltimore or New York or New Orleans. Hence they were among the foremost agitators for the public enterprise scheme. That they should make use, in their agitational efforts, of anti-charter symbols distasteful to them in other connections is an understandable paradox.

This becomes clearer when we examine more closely Sergeant's arguments in favor of public ownership. Not only are the traditional anti-charter ideas presented, together with an idealized view of the public nature of transportation facilities, but we also find a novel variation of the whole public enterprise theory. Sergeant emphasized the "painful" losses which had been incurred by private capitalists in the construction of the Philadelphia-Pittsburgh turnpike and other turnpikes in the state. Maintaining that the "same ruin" would come to private investors who embarked upon the east-west canal program, he put forth the following social principle: "The public good ought not to be advanced at the expense of individuals." [54] This principle could not play an important part in the propaganda for the public works. For to emphasize the unprofitable character of investments in turnpikes and canals ran counter to the whole stream of argument which sought to demonstrate that the government would not only derive revenue from them sufficient to pay the cost of their construction, but sufficient also to eliminate taxation and support the public school system. The fact of the matter was, and the state soon discovered it, that such visions of revenue were fantastic, and that there was nothing in the experience of New York or Europe to justify them. Sergeant's principle that the public good ought not be furthered

[54] *Niles Register*, XXIX (1825-26), 61.

at the *expense* of individuals was a curious mate for the more popular principle that the public good ought not to be advanced at the *profit* of individuals. One reflected the sad experiences of private capitalists; the other reflected roseate dreams which, partly as a result of effective pressure-group and propaganda activity, were now dominating the mind of the state. One contained a plea for the private corporation; the other contained a denunciation of it. It is a tribute to Sergeant's ingenuity that he could synthesize the two principles into a single theory.

But in 1825 that synthesis was not excessively difficult to achieve. For the ambitions of the commercial east and the enthusiasm of the public at large were directed toward a single objective — state ownership.

3. Public Spending and Pump Priming

The theory rationalizing the public works could not be abruptly ended once the initial victories had been achieved in 1825 and 1826. The works were built piecemeal, there were bitter debates over each extension of the line, and the publicists favoring the program were perennially faced with the job of justifying it before the people of the state. The job became harder as the years went by. For the works program involved expenditures undreamed of originally, and a series of knotty administrative difficulties wholly new in the state's experience. Almost from the beginning the proponents of the scheme were compelled to fight against a mounting disillusionment in the public mind. On the whole the principles of 1825 continued to serve their purpose well enough. But new problems brought forth elaborations of them appreciably extending the pattern of thought which had already been developed. The financial problem became one of the most important: expenditures for public works helped to plunge Pennsylvania into bankruptcy. How to justify this situation, when the most roseate visions of an overflowing treasury had been presented at the outset, became the toughest job of the indefatigable public works theorists.

Actually there was no justifying it. But there was, at any rate, a chance of demonstrating again that the public spending principle was inherently valid. Pennsylvania's experience could be chalked up to an improper understanding of it. In 1832 the Committee of Ways and Means of the House proceeded to re-examine the problem.[55] You could not judge the debt of a government in the same way that you judged the debt of an individual. It was necessary, above all, to avoid this kind of confusion. Traditional political economy was imprecise; it lacked a usable terminology. A distinction had to be drawn between individual wealth and national wealth. Individual wealth was "such an accumulation of property as will enable a man to procure the necessaries and comforts of life without his own labor" — in short, it was an accumulation big enough to retire on, and any man who had to work could not be called a wealthy man. It was an accumulation which could be converted at pleasure into all the commodities necessary for personal living. Now it was clear that, in these terms, no nation could ever be very wealthy. No nation had ever saved up enough to furnish it with the necessaries and comforts for even a month, let alone an appreciable period of retirement; the whole concept of individual wealth became meaningless and absurd when applied to states. National wealth was not the concrete acquisition of goods, but the faculty of acquiring them; it was "the power, rather than the possession." That power was not to be measured by the size of the treasury. Nor did it have any important connection with the balancing of the budget, except for the fact that a state must not sink too deeply into debt. It was to be measured, instead, by the capacity and the functioning of the economic system, by the size of the population, by the productive powers of the community — by the strength of "national industry." Thus any expenditures which increased that strength necessarily increased the wealth of the state, regardless of what the result might be in the treasurer's report. If Pennsylvania spent a million dollars on public works, and thereby increased the productive power of the state by a million and a half, she was the gainer by half a million, "notwithstanding the removal of the specie from her vaults." [56]

[55] *House Journal, 1832–33*, II, 693–707.
[56] *Ibid.*, II, 696.

The individual and the state must therefore be governed by different codes of financial morality. Indeed for the state to embark upon a policy of accumulation would result in the encouragement of idleness and the paralyzing of industry. Even war was often a profitable thing for the state, despite the fact that the money spent in fighting it perished in the using. For war administered "a powerful stimulant to industry." [57] Public works had all the advantages of war without its disadvantages. Moreover the notion of public spending flowed organically from the theory of democracy. The government was an artificial being, created by the people for their own benefit. It was therefore its duty to embark upon a spending policy that would galvanize the productive system. "It is of no importance what amount of liability is incurred, by the corporate artificial agent, provided it promotes the prosperity and happiness of the people." [58] Those who painted dark pictures of posterity struggling with an immense debt which it had not incurred misunderstood the principles of public spending. For the national wealth that spending created was also bequeathed to posterity: posterity was the recipient of all the enduring profits of state investment in the past. Indeed, if Pennsylvania remained inactive in the competition for the trade of the West, subsequent generations would have genuine cause for regret. They would inherit an inferior productive system.[59]

This was 1832. The state had already begun to feel the pinch of public works expenditures, and a taxation program had been initiated, but the situation was far from calamitous. By 1841 the state was on the edge of bankruptcy. The theory of public spending presented in the treasurer's report of that year [60] is a more elaborate one than the House committee had prepared; it is concerned with bigger sums of money, and it contains a stronger polemical note, opening with an attack upon the economic confusions of "the timid politician" and the "cursory observer." [61] But the concepts are the same: there are the same definitions of

[57] *Ibid.*
[58] *Ibid.*, II, 698.
[59] *Ibid.*
[60] *Ibid., 1841*, II, 17–23.
[61] *Ibid.*, II, 17.

individual and national wealth, the same combination of the principles of spending with the principles of democracy, the same view of the debt and posterity's relation to it.[62]

The question of private as opposed to public ownership reappeared in an acute form less than ten years after the public works were begun. Economically the source of the argument was not of great importance. It had to do with the use of railways which the state had constructed from Philadelphia to Columbia and across the Alleghenies. These were the only rail branches in the Main Line, and together they did not add up to more than one hundred and sixty miles of road. Moreover the Columbia branch was mainly involved since there was comparatively little passenger travel on the western railroad. As Governor Wolf emphasized in 1833, the government intended to rely upon private individuals and private companies for providing boats and carrying goods on the state canals.[63] But the railroad problem was not so easily decided. In 1833 the question arose whether the state, having built the Columbia road, should provide the motive power on it as well. The committee of the legislature to which the issue was assigned was at loss for precedent in the matter. All other railroads in the country were owned by private companies, and all of those in Great Britain, so far as the committee knew, were similarly under private ownership.[64] The committee recommended that the motive power be furnished by private companies rather than the state.[65]

However, these recommendations were not warmly received by the legislature, and in 1834 a bill was passed empowering the canal commissioners to put locomotives on the Columbia road and operate them for the profit of the state.[66] This provision continued in practice throughout the history of the public works. The state supplied the motive power, while private firms supplied passenger and freight cars. The state collected its tolls from the

[62] *Ibid.*, II, 20.
[63] *Pa. Archives*, 4th, VI, 134.
[64] *House Journal, 1833–34*, II, 705.
[65] *Ibid.*, II, 712. See also *ibid.*, 1834–35, II, 507.
[66] *Pa. Laws, 1833–34*, p. 508.

companies, leaving them to carry on the transportation business directly with the public. This curious division of responsibility produced a difficult administrative situation on the Columbia road almost from the beginning; it was, as a House committee put it in 1851, "an anomaly." [67] Since it became clear at an early time that the state was not receiving tolls in amounts proportionate to travel on the Columbia road, it was necessary in 1837 to put state agents on the passenger trains to maintain a check upon the number of passengers the private companies carried.[68] Two sets of agents were thus employed. At the outset the private companies objected. But their objections diminished when the public agents discovered, not only that the state was being cheated, but that the companies were being cheated as well by the conductors they employed.[69]

Two divergent pressures were brought to bear on the legislature in connection with the Columbia road. One of them was concerned with liquidating the state's role completely, except as the provider of tracks, as the House committee had urged in 1833. The other was concerned with abolishing all private operations and putting cars as well as locomotives in the hands of the government. The superintendent of motive power on the Columbia road during the forties twice recommended that the latter course of action be taken,[70] and there was a popular movement of considerable strength afoot in its favor. This movement was intensified when it became clear that the private companies were reaping immense profits. Governor Shunk in 1842 declared that the state had spent over four million dollars on the Columbia road and that it was receiving returns of some 3 per cent on its investment, while companies using the road had invested only thirty thousand dollars and were receiving returns of nearly 200 per cent.[71] But

[67] *House Journal, 1851*, II, 357. See also *ibid., 1834–35*, II, 507; W. Wilson, *Pennsylvania Railroad*, I, 20 ff; Sipes, *Pennsylvania Railroad*, p. 7; Tanner, *Canals and Railroads of U.S.*, p. 113 ff. "The management of [the Philadelphia and Columbia Railroad] differs from that of any other, except that of the Allegheny Portage, in this country or Europe." *Hunt's Merchants' Mag.*, XIII (1845), 130.
[68] *House Journal, 1837–38*, III, 60.
[69] *Ibid.*
[70] Harrisburg *Democratic Union*, Sept. 24, 1845; *Pa. Archives*, 4th, VI, 832.
[71] *Ibid.*

the private companies appear to have had an influence at Harrisburg sufficiently powerful to stifle the scheme of complete state ownership.[72]

In opposing public ownership the champions of the private interests revived the idea that had appeared in the state when it had relied mainly on the mixed corporation for the construction of transport facilities: the self-interest of private entrepreneurs was a safeguard of efficient administration.[73] To the extent that the state owned locomotives or cars, they contended, the objective would be to discourage rather than to welcome the use of the Columbia line. For, while private owners who "desire the accumulation of property" would naturally seek to expand traffic, public administrators, who had a fixed salary, could look forward to nothing but increased work as a result of increased custom.[74]

But the ideas now directed against the government were somewhat broader in scope than the ones of the period before 1825. In 1834, the Keating Committee went beyond the matter of expediency to the matter of right: governmental ownership was at war with the precepts of democracy.[75]

> Whatever individuals are equal to, as a general rule, should be entrusted to them, and to them alone. This is so congenial, both to our feelings and the principles of our government, that arguments are unnecessary to satisfy us of its truth. If we allow the state to embark in one enterprize that can be accomplished by her citizens, where shall we stop? Will we allow her to run into everything that can be driven to advantage? If the general government was not in the way, would we allow the state alone to export and import because it may be profitable? Or, would it be policy that she should own all our improvements made by companies, and all our banking institutions, because they may yield a revenue? . . . Or should we go farther yet, and like some government of old, own all the lands within our charter, and farm them out, because it might be to our advantage? [76]

---

[72] "The moment the Canal Commissioners recommend the purchase of cars, the halls of legislation will be surrounded by agents of the companies. This has been done every session. . . ." Harrisburg *Democratic Union*, Sept. 24, 1845; *Pa. Archives*, 4th, VI, 929.
[73] *House Journal, 1834–35*, II, 508; *1833–34*, II, 710.
[74] *Ibid.*, p. 711.
[75] *Ibid., 1834–35*, II, 507.
[76] *Ibid.*

The committee also sought to exploit the anti-executive prejudices of the state, contending that governmental ownership would necessarily involve an increase in gubernatorial patronage.[77]

However self-evident the committee believed these notions to be, it is an important fact that the legislature did not find them so. The extensive pro-governmental theories of 1825 were still fresh in the mind of the state, and those theories had been framed to demonstrate that public ownership was alone compatible with the ideas of democracy. What troubled many legislators was, indeed, the feeling that the state had not gone far enough in the ownership sphere. Monopolistic tendencies crept into the administration of the Columbia line, despite the strong feeling within the legislature and without that free competition among transporters ought to be preserved there.[78] Even the Keating Committee had to admit that "at first blush" governmental ownership seemed most desirable, since "if there must be a monopoly, all would be disposed to yield it rather to the State than to an individual." [79]

4. Administration: Theory and Practice

The original objective of the public works was to link Philadelphia with Pittsburgh.[80] Canal construction was begun at Harrisburg in 1826.[81] But in the following year, when the legislature enacted the necessary measures to continue this work, appropriations were made for four lines of improvement which were not connected with the main east-west line.[82] This was the beginning of sectional barter in the legislature which resulted in undue prolongation of work on the Main Line, and in the construction of various branches which were not unified into a coherent transportation system.[83] Governor Ritner said of the latter that they "are mere disjointed beginnings of an immense whole, whose plan was never perfected and whose present condition is a sad proof of the

---

[77] *Ibid., 1834–35*, II, 509.
[78] *Pa. Archives*, 4th, VI, 832, 928.
[79] *House Journal, 1833–34*, II, 710.
[80] *Ibid., 1825–26*, I, 310–11.
[81] See *ibid., 1834–35*, III, 3.
[82] *Pa. Laws, 1826–27*, p. 192.
[83] Bishop, "State Works," pp. 189–205.

selfishness of sectional jealousy and of log-rolling legislation." [84] The railroads that were built constituted two links in the cross-state chain. One of them was the Philadelphia and Columbia Railroad which extended some eighty-one miles from Philadelphia to the Susquehanna river at Columbia, linking Philadelphia by a combined system of rail and water transportation to Harrisburg. The other, the Allegheny Portage Railroad, began at Hollidaysburg and extended over the highest Allegheny mountains to Johnstown. The remainder of the Main Line was made up of canals and river improvements.[85]

Total public works expenditures, involving original cost, operation expenses, and interest on loans, amounted to $101,611,234.[86] The policy of financing the works was imprudent from the outset. State credit was in excellent condition in 1826 when the first ground was broken at Harrisburg, but within three years, primarily because an adequate fund for the payment of interest on loans was not established, the confidence of banks and capitalists had been seriously weakened.[87] In 1835, when the Main Line was completed, the state debt was $24,589,743.[88] Over $22,000,000 of this amount represented investments in the public works. By this time tolls were producing revenue but the amount of such revenue did not even remotely approximate the large sums which had been expected. In 1835 toll proceeds amounted to $684,357. But the interest payments due in the same year amounted to $1,169,455 — over $400,000 more than toll proceeds and almost as much as the toll revenue and the amount in the interest fund for that year combined.[89] These were obvious danger signals. But they were obscured by the speculative mania of the time, and new programs of work expansion were undertaken. It was only when the 5 per

---

[84] *Pa. Archives*, 4th, VI, 308–309. See also *Hunt's Merchants' Mag.*, XX (1849), 258; M. Carey, *Internal Improvement*, No. II, pp. 1–2.

[85] For general descriptions of the works, see Bishop, "State Works," pp. 189–205; Bowen, *Sketch Book of Pa.*, pp. 69–119; Tanner, *Canals and Railroads of U.S.*, pp. 95–146; *The Canals of Pa.*, Excerpt; M. Carey, *Internal Improvement of Pa.*, *passim*; Armroyd, *Connected View of Internal Navigation*, pp. 84–90.

[86] Bishop, "State Works," p. 229.

[87] See M. Carey, *Internal Improvement*, No. II, p. 1.

[88] *Pa. Archives*, 4th, VII, 10 ff.

[89] Bishop, "State Works," pp. 213–14.

Chart 5

EXPENDITURES FOR AND GROSS REVENUE FROM PUBLIC WORKS IN PENNSYLVANIA, WITH STATE LOANS, AND REVENUES FROM TAXATION AND LICENSES, ANNUALLY, 1830–1850

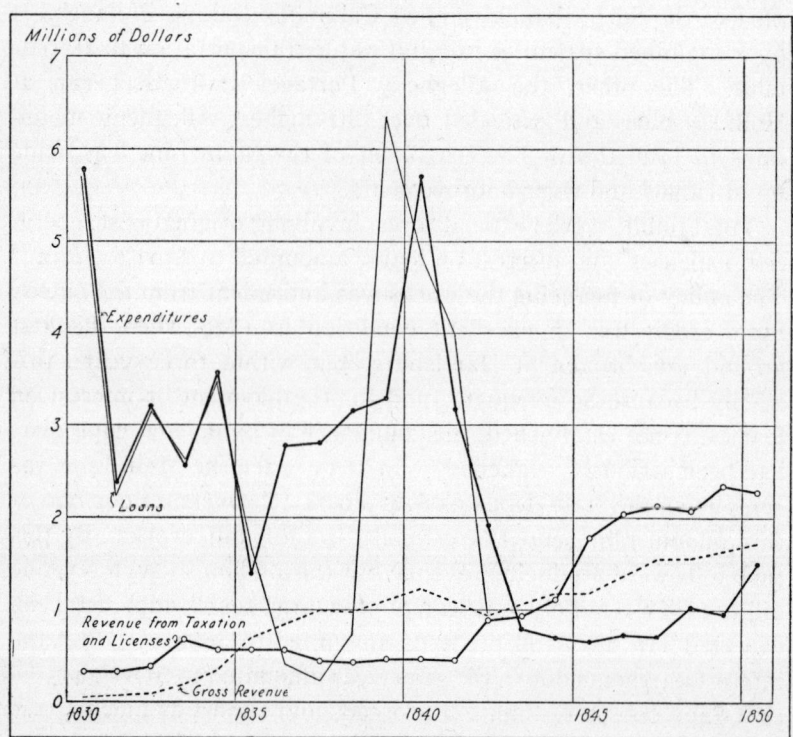

cent stocks of the state would not sell at all that a new psychology appeared and retrenchments were initiated.[90]

Formally the works were under the direction of a board of canal commissioners, an agency which had a hectic administrative history.[91] The early acts of 1824–1827 provided, wisely enough, that the canal board be selected by the governor,[92] since

---

[90] Cf. *supra*, chap. I, p. 17.
[91] For a brief summary of the structural history of the board, see remarks of Governor Porter in 1840, *Pa. Archives*, 4th, VI, 736–40.
[92] Bishop, "State Works," p. 189.

he was the only official under whom responsibility could be effectively concentrated. But the strong anti-executive bias which prevailed prior to 1837 soon interfered with this procedure, and in 1829 the legislature itself appointed nine persons to the board.[93] Inevitably this extended to the administration the political trading that governed appropriations, and an appreciable public opinion shortly emerged which assailed the technique of legislative selection. The appointing power was returned to the governor, but since the situation was still deemed unsatisfactory, the legislature in 1840 enacted a measure which provided that the Senate, the House, and the governor should each select one commissioner. Governor Porter vetoed this compromise measure, rightly pointing out that deadlocks and abrupt administrative changes might easily ensue upon its adoption, and recommended a substitute which was adopted in 1844 — direct popular election.[94] One of the knottiest administrative problems in the state was thus thrown into the lap of the people, and the prevailing democratic ideology was completely satisfied.[95] Yet the measure was clearly unsuited to the immense administrative tasks involved in the works program. The canal board was swallowed up in the bitter electioneering rivalries of the time.

To a people wholly unused to big and expensive administrative agencies, the board was, from beginning to end, a strange and confusing thing. Nor is the chaotic history of its appointment the only evidence of this fact. Since it did not fit into any of the traditional categories of government, there was the persistent fear that it was becoming "an engine of almost unlimited power." A Grand Committee of the legislature, investigating the public works in 1833, admitted that the board would be "paralyzed" without sufficient authority. But "the mind is naturally struck with an idea of the danger which may arise from it," the committee remarked uneasily, "and asks, whether it is all absolutely necessary . . . ."[96] Actually it seems clear that the board, instead of

[93] *Pa. Laws, 1828–29*, pp. 200–201.
[94] *Pa. Archives*, 4th, VI, 736 ff.
[95] See *Niles Register*, LXIV (1843), 128; *Norristown Register*, June 26, 1844; *Pennsylvanian*, Apr. 18, 1844; *Public Ledger*, Oct. 7, 1844; Harrisburg *Democratic Union*, Aug. 16, 1843.   [96] *House Journal, 1832–33*, II, 748.

having too much power, did not have enough. Not only was it unable to enforce its regulations with strong sanctions, but it was compelled to apply to the legislature for the passage of laws which it should have been able to enact as administrative measures on its own initiative.[97] In 1829 the powers of the board over finished portions of the canal were limited to the establishment of tolls, the appointment of collectors and lockkeepers, and the purchasing of ground for sites and toll-houses. Subsequently, when the board was suspected of engaging in discriminations and drawbacks, even the first of these powers was whittled down by a statute binding the commissioners to a fixed scale of tolls throughout each year.[98] The latter measure, as Governor Bigler pointed out in 1855, made it even more difficult for the board "to meet the exigencies in trade and commerce." [99]

If the board lacked sufficient power, it is also true that it failed to use in the most efficient way the power it did have. Centralized in Harrisburg, it could not maintain effective supervision over all works in progress. Control thus drifted down to secondary officers, and lack of uniformity in construction practices was the result.[100] The majority of the Grand Committee of 1833 recommended that the works be divided into three sections and that each section be placed under the control of a separate board of commissioners. It suggested also that a Department of Public Works be created under the direction of a secretary who would be a regular member of the governor's cabinet at Harrisburg.[101] This scheme, involving a decentralizing aspect which would have insured closer supervision of the separate branches of the works and a centralizing aspect which would have produced a better concentration of responsibility, might measurably have solved the administrative problem. But it was presented toward the close of the legislative session of 1833 and the committee itself recognized that no action could be taken upon it at that time.[102] No action

---

[97] *Ibid.*, *1829–30*, II, 230. Cf. remarks of Governor Porter, *Pa. Archives*, 4th, VI, 833.
[98] *Ibid.*, VII, 383.
[99] *Ibid.*, VII, 728.
[100] *House Journal*, *1832–33*, II, 751–52; *Senate Journal*, *1855*, pp. 61–62.
[101] *House Journal*, *1832–33*, II, 751–53. [102] *Ibid.*, II, 752.

ever was taken. In 1850 Governor Johnston was still urging a similar proposal.[103] In a separate report the minority of the committee recommended that the transactions of the board be given greater publicity,[104] but it is hard to see how this measure alone could have produced appreciable improvement.

From what has already been said it is clear that a basic weakness in the works setup lay in the large sphere of power which the legislature insisted upon retaining. At the outset it was apparently believed that the legislature would itself hand down most of the necessary interpretations of public works legislation, and when the canal board was in specific instances forced to assume the interpretative function, the legislature conceded the necessity grudgingly.[105] Yet it is important to observe that the board itself did not always desire to assume clear-cut administrative powers. This was demonstrated in 1829 when its secretary, instead of recommending that sufficient authority be given the board to enact necessary regulations, righteously argued that public works law was "part of the law of the land" and therefore "ought to be passed upon directly by the immediate representatives of the people."[106] The fact is that there were often cases in which the board found it strategic to pass the buck to the legislature, especially in connection with financial claims arising from works construction. During the fifties, for example, when there were protests owing to the withholding of payments to laborers and contractors, the board gladly referred this delicate matter to the legislature for judgment.[107]

It was in the realm of appropriations that the legislative relationship to the works administration presented its major problem. Nor was it entirely one of sectionalism. There was also the factor of sheer irresponsibility. Usually the legislature neglected to appropriate sufficient funds for repairs or it waited until the very end of the session to do so. Since the board lacked power to divert funds allocated for other purposes to the financing of repairs, the

---

[103] *Pa. Archives*, 4th, VII, 381.
[104] *House Journal, 1832–33*, II, 753–56.
[105] *Ibid.*, II, 753.
[106] *Ibid., 1829–30*, II, 225 ff.
[107] See *Senate Journal, 1854*, pp. 481, 482, 649.

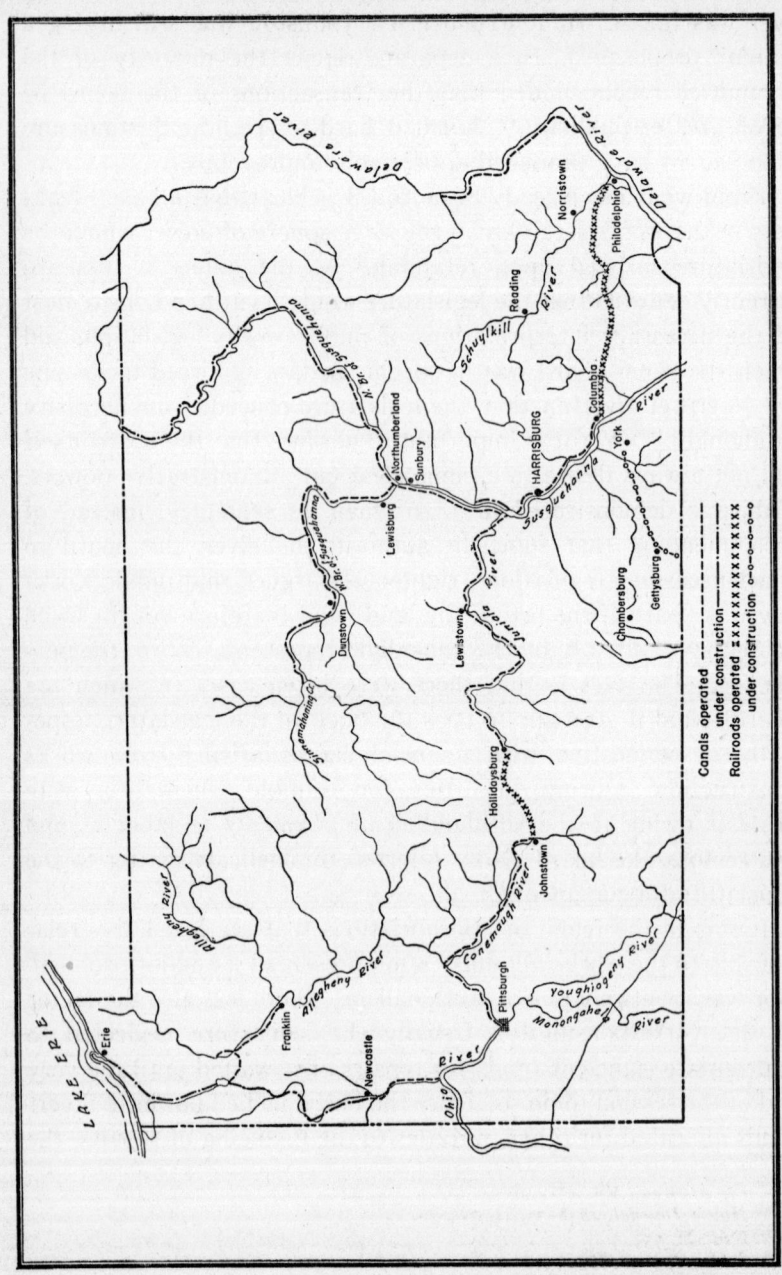

PUBLIC WORKS OF PENNSYLVANIA, 1840.

result was that many necessary repairs were not made in time or not made at all.[108] Yet revelations of financial inefficiency and graft on the part of the board and its inferiors often prompted pleas that the legislature take an even greater hand in the determination of expenditures. A House committee in 1841 contended that if the legislature more actively supervised the letting of contracts its time would be amply paid for by the economies thereby effected.[109] Actually any further extension of legislative authority might well have been disastrous. Remedial actions that the legislature did undertake, such as its frequent committee investigations, were not always generated by the purest motives. While many of the committees honestly desired administrative reform, others, as Governor Porter said in 1842, were prompted by the pressure of dissatisfied contractors upon their representatives at Harrisburg or by the desire to discredit board members for political ends.[110]

Since the board failed to maintain effective contact with various projects under way, a high degree of unchecked power was held by section superintendents whom it appointed. These officials purchased materials, disbursed funds, and selected their own subordinates.[111] In construction they were compelled to operate on a basis of competitive bidding for contracts, but in the matter of repairs they were usually permitted to negotiate directly with contractors of their own choosing. Frequently they negotiated contracts in excess of funds allotted to them, and in 1856 the legislature enacted a measure expressly prohibiting this practice.[112] Each superintendent was permitted to draw on the treasury for a sum equal to a bond posted with the auditor-general,[113] but ways were found to circumvent this limitation. Appreciating the shortness of their tenure, some superintendents paid workers and contractors in their own script, to be redeemed at a future time, a practice branded by Governor Bigler in 1854 as a "mon-

[108] *Pa. Archives*, 4th, VI, 715.
[109] *House Journal, 1841*, II, 587.
[110] *Pa. Archives*, 4th, VI, 833–34.
[111] *House Journal, 1832–33*, II, 752–53; *1851*, II, 356.
[112] *Ibid., 1832–33*, II, 751; *1841*, II, 564; *Senate Journal, 1854*, p. 649; *1855*, pp. 58–62; *Legislative Documents, 1857*, p. 458.
[113] *House Journal, 1832–33*, II, 749; *1840*, I, 226–34.

strosity in the economy of public affairs." [114] In 1854 a commissioner appointed by the legislature discovered $149,377 in unpaid debts on the Main Line and credit certificates so old that the writing on them was scarcely legible. Common workers were at a disadvantage in collecting money, being unable to resort to the bribes and political pressure sometimes used by big contractors.[115] It is difficult to estimate what the total losses to the state were as a result of such malpractice, but it is safe to say that they were not small.

A great deal of power was held also by the engineers upon whose recommendations superintendents normally made disbursements. The engineering department was independent of the superintendents, however, the chief engineer being appointed directly by the canal board with authority to select subordinates for various construction projects. Since his work was usually a mystery to members of the board, who rotated on a political basis, he had considerable independence.[116] Yet a failure on the part of the chief engineer, as on the part of the board, to maintain adequate communication with subordinates meant that the latter actually determined the substance of recommendations upon which superintendents acted. It was this pervasive inability of executives to maintain communication which impelled the Grand Committee to remark in 1833 that "strange as it may sound ... as we descend in the rank of officers, the amount of power vested in each increases." [117]

In the provision of estimates engineers often stated sums that were lower than the situation warranted.[118] The consequence was that when the legislature embarked upon a program it rarely knew the final cost. Since works once undertaken had to be completed if original investments were to be saved, the legislature was often compelled to vote funds far in excess of those originally contemplated. To a considerable extent the bad financial condition

[114] *Pa. Archives*, 4th, VII, 642–43; *House Journal, 1849*, II, 673.
[115] *Senate Journal, 1855*, pp. 61–63. See also *House Journal, 1849*, II, 673; *1840*, I, 234–35; *Hunt's Merchants' Mag.*, XIII (1845), 138; XX (1849), 258–60.
[116] *House Journal, 1832–33*, II, 750–51.
[117] *Ibid.*, II, 750.
[118] *Legislative Documents, 1854*, pp. 332–33; *House Journal, 1832–33*, II, 749.

into which the public works descended may be chalked up to deceptive estimates provided by engineers. But the fault was not exclusively theirs. They knew that they had to deal with a legislature not governed by a consistent policy and that if necessary constructions were to be made, large estimates could not be submitted to it. The situation was aggravated by the mode of selecting engineers. Since the chief engineer was appointed by the board and he appointed his subordinates, political rotation was introduced into the engineering department. A legislative committee in 1841 recommended that the department be made independent of the board,[119] but this objective was not achieved.

It is difficult to generalize concerning the lower brackets of administration, since uniformity of practice was lacking here more than in any other area. It is obvious that the construction and operation of so far-flung a system of works required the appointment of hundreds of lesser officials — foremen, lockkeepers, weighmasters, toll collectors, purchasing agents, cargo inspectors, and timekeepers. The legislature tried by statute to insure delineation of function among these employees; it provided, for example, that lockkeepers should not be collectors of toll as well, and that the disbursing and timekeeping functions should not be joined.[120] Two purposes motivated such action. One was the purpose of so organizing the inferior agencies as to provide a basis for selection according to special capacity. Another was the purpose of preventing fraud, the idea being that a separation of function would mean that the officers would check one another. In some instances, however, these provisions helped to create a superabundance of minor officials, which was a source of severe public criticism.[121]

[119] *Ibid.*, *1841*, II, 589.
[120] *Ibid.*, *1832–33*, II, 749.
[121] *Ibid.*, *1851*, II, 357. A legislative committee of 1836 remarked in connection with the Allegheny Portage Road: "A great want of subordination appears to exist among the officers, few of their duties seem clearly defined or understood. One officer appoints, and another dismisses the same hands and subordinate officers. What one approves another condemns, and the management of the works is, therefore, in a state of constant uncertainty and fluctuation." *Ibid.*, *1836–37*, II, 807. In 1843 Governor Porter declared: "The employment of improper subordinate officers and agents on our public improvements, has been a frequent and just theme of complaint; and I believe in nine cases out of ten, in which these officers and agents have

Chart 6

ORGANIZATION OF THE PUBLIC WORKS ADMINISTRATION IN PENNSYLVANIA, 1844

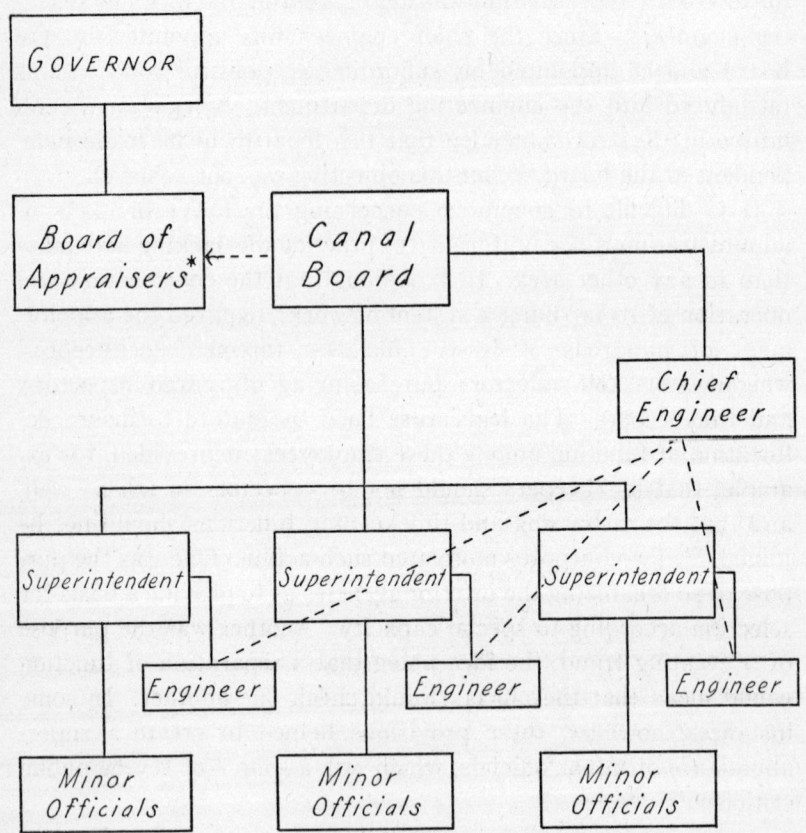

*The Board of Appraisers had appelate jurisdiction in cases of construction damages.

Toll collection was often difficult. Many users of the works tried to evade tolls and the secretary of the canal board reported that "nothing in the moral sense of even the respectable citizens" served to discourage this tendency. However, the record of the collectors themselves was by no means perfect. Tolls were collected which never reached the public treasury. In 1844 there was a delinquency among fifty-five officials of $11,340,109 in this connection, and the state had been compelled to bring suit against seventeen of them for the money they had collected.[122] In some cases, where informal legal pressure was successful in obtaining funds from collectors, the state had difficulty obtaining the money in turn from the lawyers it had employed.[123]

Claims of property owners on the route of the works constituted a serious problem. Early legislation provided for the settlement of these claims by justices of the peace or courts of quarter sessions, relying upon popular juries. This system led to excessive damage awards, especially in those counties which were dissatisfied with the works administration, and in some cases the state was actually compelled to abandon construction plans because of the expense involved.[124] In 1830 the legislature authorized the governor to appoint a board of appraisers to settle property claims, giving the board two spheres of jurisdiction: over permanent damages occasioned by construction, and over fire damages caused by locomotives on railroad sections. Only in the latter sphere, however, did the board have original jurisdiction; in the former it served as a tribunal of last resort for appeals from decisions which the canal commissioners were authorized to make in the first instance.[125] This was a distinct step forward. Economies in damage settlements were immediately effected, and had the board been given sufficient freedom to operate, the claims area would probably have been notable for efficient administration. Unfortunately, however, the board was hamstrung from the outset.

In the first place legislative provisions put no time limit on the filing of claims. Many claims were thus made years after the original damage had been done, when it was difficult to obtain

---

been continued in the public service, they have been backed and sustained by the influence of official friends." *Pa. Archives*, 4th, VI, 971–72.

[122] *House Journal, 1844*, II, 414–16.
[123] *Legislative Documents, 1858*, p. 223.
[124] *House Journal, 1840*, II, 457–58; *1834–35*, II, 550–52; *1829–30*, II, 227.
[125] *Ibid., 1840*, II, 458–60; *1834–35*, II, 550–52.

accurate information, especially since the works personnel was constantly rotating and officials involved in claims disputes were often no longer in the public employ when adjudication took place.[126] Moreover the legislature failed to use language that unmistakably endowed the board with judicial authority; the result was that the board often had difficulty compelling witnesses to testify before it and was criticized for violating the "constitutional right" of trial by jury.[127] It was attacked as a partisan rather than a judicial arm of the state, interested not in justice but in the lowest evaluations of damages, and in truth its harrassed members had to admit that they were "sometimes obliged to act apparently the part of an attorney for the Commonwealth," [128] discovering on their own initiative facts which favored state interest. Finally the legislature, unable to resist pressures to interfere, in many cases revised the decisions of the board, giving greater damage awards, or ordered the board to re-hear cases already settled. This legislative interference evoked bitter criticism from board members who argued that the legislative awards were exorbitant and that legislative interference discredited them in the eyes of the public.[129]

Curiously enough, the unhappy board of appraisers invoked in its own behalf the traditional theory of the separation of powers.[130] Yet it was precisely on this ground that it was weak. To be sure, the traditional theory envisaged a sharp separation of the branches of government, but a quasi-judicial administrative agency was not among them. It was because it failed to fit into any of the older categories that the board encountered much of the criticism leveled against it on constitutional grounds. In a deeper sense the whole of the works administration, including the canal board and its army of subordinates, was a departure from traditional categories. And it was the failure of the state frankly to recognize this, to develop techniques appropriate to an independent administrative service, which was reflected in the chaotic history of the works administration.

[126] *Ibid., 1853*, II, 68; *1851*, II, 356–57; *1840*, II, 460–63. Cf. Konkle, *Chief Justice Lewis*, p. 95.
[127] *House Journal, 1832–33*, II, 753–56.
[128] *Ibid., 1840*, II, 462.
[129] *Ibid.*, II, 465–70.
[130] *Ibid.*, II, 466.

5. The Struggle over Liquidation

During the early forties a movement got under way to sell the public works to private investors, and by 1859 not a single section of the system remained in the hands of the state. The emergence of the sale movement was directly related to the state's financial embarrassment which came to a head in the issuance of interest certificates in 1842. Under the spur of immediate need for funds the state turned to the possibility of works liquidation as it turned to the disposal of its mixed corporation holdings. Maladministration of the works system, moreover, helped to induce disillusionment with public management. As effective corporate enterprises began to appear in the transportation field, that maladministration began to take on greater significance. In an earlier chapter I pointed out that, mainly under the impact of the sectional drive for commercial aggrandizement, railroads were chartered which competed deleteriously with the public works. In 1841 the state treasurer listed this competition as one of the principal causes of the financial crisis. A significant aspect of the relation between the new corporations and the public administration is revealed in the fact that many of them derived personnel from men who had originally gained experience on the state system. President Thomson of the Pennsylvania Railroad Company had previously served as an engineer on the Philadelphia and Columbia line of the works.[131] In 1854 Governor Bigler bitterly remarked that the public system had become "a species of Normal schools for the education of engineers and supervisors to take charge of other improvements." [132] The state could not compete with the drive of the emergent railroad capitalists.

Economically the works were a failure. Even had the system been well administered, technological change would have made it obsolescent; a canal-rail system could not survive in a railroad age. "It was an amphibious connexion of land and water," wrote Job Tyson to a London friend concerning the works in 1852,

---

[131] Sipes, *Pennsylvania Railroad*, p. 11. See also Scharf and Westcott, *History of Philadelphia*, III, 2199.
[132] *Pa. Archives*, 4th, VII, 643.

"happily elucidating the defects peculiar to both modes of transit, with the advantages of neither."[133] The Pennsylvania system could not even compete successfully with the Erie Canal. The route from the Ohio to Philadelphia was, it is true, over two hundred miles shorter than the route to New York provided by the Erie. But the Main Line, stretching over the Alleghenies and involving changes from canal to rail shipment,[134] made the Pennsylvania route less effective and more expensive.[135] A writer in *Hunt's Merchants' Magazine*, surveying the situation, concluded that Philadelphia must give up its dream of commercial greatness and concentrate upon industrial development instead.[136]

The first section of the works was disposed of in 1843. In that year the Erie extension, running from Erie to the mouth of the Beaver river on the Ohio, was not sold but given away to the Erie Canal Company in the bill incorporating that company.[137] In 1844 an act was passed to dispose of the Main Line from Philadelphia to Pittsburgh for the sum of twenty million dollars. A company was authorized for that purpose which would possess two hundred thousand shares of stock at a value of one hundred dollars each. It was also provided at the same time that the Delaware extension of the canal be sold separately.[138] There were no bidders for the Main Line at this time, a fact which was widely attributed to the price that was set for it.[139] In connection with the Delaware line, on the other hand, there was literally a stampede among investors to purchase stock. But they were mainly

---

[133] *Commerce of Philadelphia*, p. 13.

[134] Cf. Bishop, "State Works," pp. 245 ff.

[135] *Hunt's Merchants' Mag.*, XIV (1846), 192. In their report of 1842 the canal commissioners recognized that the high rate of tolls in Pennsylvania was preventing her from competing successfully for the western trade. *House Journal, 1842*, III, 42. See also *Niles Register*, Nov. 15, 1845; Bishop, "State Works," pp. 246–48.

[136] "That Pennsylvania and Philadelphia have not derived nearly so great a benefit in their trade with the west, from the construction of these internal improvements, as has accrued to the state and city of New York, we apprehend no one will doubt; nor, unless the cost of transportation on the Pennsylvania works can be put at an equally low rate with that on those of the neighboring states, can it be doubted that Philadelphia must take her rank among the great manufacturing, rather than commercial cities of the Union." *Hunt's Merchants' Mag.*, X (1844), 320.

[137] Bishop, "State Works," p. 249.

[138] *Pa. Laws, 1844*, p. 554.

[139] Bishop, "State Works," p. 250; Harrisburg *Democratic Union*, Feb. 14, 1844.

THE STRUGGLE OVER LIQUIDATION 163

speculators and gamblers, attracted to the sale by the fact that no cash down payment was required, and the commissioners authorized to make the sale refused to continue proceedings.[140] In 1844 the legislature put the question of sale directly to the

TABLE 4

POPULAR VOTE ON THE SALE OF THE MAIN LINE
1844

	For	Against		For	Against
Adams	2,677	1,555	Lancaster	12,845	1,004
Allegheny	7,761	5,728	Lebanon	2,216	1,675
Armstrong	1,108	1,484	Lehigh	3,283	608
Beaver	2,677	1,652	Luzerne	378	4,438
Bedford	3,187	838	Lycoming	1,509	2,497
Berks	3,559	7,127	Mercer	2,223	2,810
Bradford	1,332	4,185	Mifflin	1,299	1,660
Bucks	3,153	5,007	Monroe	340	1,427
Butler	2,054	1,823	Montgomery	4,154	5,129
Cambria	955	955	McKean	151	498
Centre	1,531	2,474	Northampton	3,166	727
Chester	6,870	4,248	Northumberland	1,058	2,421
Clarion	385	1,931	Perry	1,273	2,106
Clearfield	552	633	Philadelphia City		
Clinton	613	936	and County	21,869	10,196
Columbia	455	3,405	Potter	25	652
Crawford	1,820	2,376	Pike	174	503
Cumberland	4,284	1,553	Somerset	2,753	372
Catron	701	95	Schuylkill	2,353	2,890
Dauphin	2,853	2,293	Susquehanna	686	2,383
Delaware	2,321	1,134	Tioga	221	2,341
Erie	2,684	2,237	Union	1,289	2,113
Elk	62	152	Venango	289	1,097
Fayette	2,707	3,072	Warren	219	1,068
Franklin	6,036	505	Washington	3,937	3,085
Greene	903	2,096	Westmoreland	3,458	3,561
Huntingdon	3,726	2,368	Wayne	202	1,712
Indiana	2,356	870	York	4,500	959
Juniata	970	1,259			
Jefferson	426	675	Total	149,748	124,598*

* The total of the first column should be 146,648. The data are given as presented in *House Journal, 1847*, II, 266.

[140] *Public Ledger*, June 2, 1845; *House Journal, 1844*, II, 107–116.

people. In this referendum a majority of over twenty thousand was returned in favor of disposing of the Main Line.[141]

The intensity of feeling in favor of sale in 1844 was traceable mainly to the acuteness of the state's financial condition. When that condition improved, interest in sale slackened. In 1845 a House committee, reporting against the disposal of the Main Line, declared that in the plebiscite of the previous year "the public mind was very much excited" and that its judgment then should not be taken as final.[142] Moreover, after 1844 an attempt was made at administrative reform which seemed for a moment encouraging.[143] But by the fifties the sale campaign had been revived with intensity. Antagonism toward the new tax burden which the state was bearing and the failure of comprehensive administrative improvement to materialize gave impetus to the sale movement. In the interval the Pennsylvania Railroad Company, which soon became the anticipated buyer of the works, had been chartered.

In 1854 an act was passed which put a minimum of ten million dollars on the price for the sale of the Main Line.[144] But the Pennsylvania was not ready to buy at this price. In 1855 President Thomson of the Pennsylvania communicated with the secretary of state, offering to pay seven and a half million dollars for the Main Line.[145] This offer was strongly criticized as too low, and it was not until two years later that a bill was passed agreeing to it. The measure also contained a provision that if the Pennsylvania paid two and a half million dollars in addition to its offered price, a total of ten million, it was to be permanently released from all state taxation.[146] The sale was negotiated in the summer of 1857. But public antagonism toward a measure so favorable to the company was partially responsible for ousting the Whigs from legislative dominance in the following elections.[147] Heavy lobby pressure had pretty clearly been involved. It was argued "that this

---

[141] *House Journal, 1847*, II, 266.
[142] *House Journal, 1845*, II, 544.
[143] *Pa. Archives*, 4th, VII, 73; Bishop, "State Works," p. 251.
[144] *Ibid.*, p. 254.
[145] *Ibid.*, p. 255; *Legislative Documents, 1856*, p. 47.
[146] *Pa. Laws, 1857*, p. 520.   [147] Geary, *Third Parties in Pa.*, p. 216.

bill was engineered through by the paid borers of the Pennsylvania Railroad Company, who infested the legislative halls, to tell the representatives of the people that they demand the sale of the public works." [148] A year later, when a measure was passed offering the remaining lateral branches of the works to the Sunbury and Erie in return for three and a half million dollars worth of its bonds,[149] opposition legislators complained of a "buzzard roost" of borers and "paid scribblers" and insisted that the time had come to make lobbyists register with the state.[150]

The sale issue cut pretty much across party lines. If the sale measure of 1857 was enacted by a Whig legislature, the sale measure of 1855 had been authorized by a Democratic Senate.[151] Governor Bigler, a Democrat, had urged sale.[152] But the measure of 1857, with its low price and tax exemption, encountered Democratic opposition. Urging a repeal of the measure, the Democrats campaigned in the gubernatorial election of the summer of that year on the platform, "Packer and Repeal," "Wilmot and Sale." [153] But even in this connection the party was not united. The *Pennsylvanian*, probably the state's outstanding Democratic newspaper, was in favor of sale even on the terms of 1857. Once the sale had been negotiated,[154] it hastened to assuage the hard feelings that the "family quarrel" within the party had produced.[155]

A vast amount of theory and debate was produced by the campaign to sell the public works. Up to this time, as I have demonstrated, the state's attitude toward the principle of public ownership had advanced through four fairly well defined stages: (1) The period immediately after the Revolution in which the state assumed complete responsibility for the construction and opera-

---

[148] *Legislative Record, 1857*, No. 77, p. 5; see also *infra*, p. 278.
[149] *Pa. Laws, 1858*, p. 414; *Legislative Record, 1858*, pp. 222 ff.
[150] *Ibid.*, pp. 306, 327, 328.
[151] For an excellent analysis of the party history of the sale measures, see *Legislative Record, 1857*, No. 87, p. 5.
[152] *Harrisburg Telegraph*, May 27, 1857.
[153] Cf. *ibid.*, June 24, July 8, 1857.
[154] Apart from all other expenses, the state had spent $18,578,801 in the construction of the works; it received $11,000,000 in total sale price. Cf. Bishop, "State Works," pp. 278–88.
[155] *Pennsylvanian*, June 24, 1857; *ibid.*, June 18, 19, 1857.

tion of turnpikes. (2) The period from 1791 to 1825 when the state began to rely increasingly upon private and mixed corporations and when complete public ownership was challenged on practical grounds. During this period public ownership was universally acknowledged, as before, as being within the legitimate sphere of state action. (3) The period of the initiation of the public-works system when public ownership was not only accepted as legitimate but was believed by the overwhelming mass of Pennsylvanians to be practical and desirable as well. (4) The period after 1830 when, in controversies over the use of the public railways, the legitimacy of ownership as a governmental function began to be challenged for the first time and in a vague way.

The sale campaign produced a much broader elaboration of the legalistic challenge, lifting it for the first time to a rank of importance. Shadowy as the line is between the legitimate and the expedient in popular thought, we should be neglecting a major ideological turning point if we failed to take note of this development. When a citizens' meeting in Norristown insisted in 1844 that the maintenance of public works was a "sin against first principles," [156] it was speaking a language alien to the criticisms of state ownership dominant during the previous time. Though it did not fully come into its own until the fifties when the sale campaign was revived with a new intensity after it had slackened as a result of financial and administrative improvements, the notion began steadily to grow that public ownership violated some fundamental political or moral law, that it was somehow alien to democratic philosophy — beyond the rightful sphere of state action. "The objects of government should be as few and simple as possible," declared a Select Committee of the Senate recommending the sale of the Main Line in 1854. "To mingle it with business, whether mercantile or mechanical, is inconsistent with its object . . . . The separation of politics and trade would do much to restore our government to its original purity, and would be hailed by every virtuous citizen as the dawn of a brighter day . . . . Governments should be restricted to purely political

[156] *Norristown Register*, Mar. 27, 1844.

powers necessary to the existence of society." [157] A citizen of Adams County who published a series of influential articles in the *Philadelphia Evening Bulletin* demanded that the government restrict itself "to more legitimate purposes." [158] Others said: "The government which degrades itself to be a common carrier of merchandise, a trader, a manufacturer, a broker, departs from its proper sphere, usurps the rights of its citizens . . . ." [159]

Whatever else might be said in behalf of such contentions, it cannot be claimed that they were a traditional part of the thinking of the state. However loudly "first principles" might be invoked, they were derived not from history or tradition but from the contemporary metaphysics of their expounders. When the Senate committee identified the "separation of politics and trade" with the "original purity" of the Pennsylvania government, its history was bad. For while it is true that an epoch existed in the history of the state when it was not the owner of the existing vast system of public works, there had never been a time when it had not owned and operated some facilities and had had heavy investments in others. In a larger sense there had never been a time since the arrival of Penn when politics had been separated from trade. And though there had been a time when it was widely believed that state ownership, and only state ownership, was compatible with the "original purity" of government, there had never been a time when the reverse was true.

Broad legal and philosophical arguments of this type were necessarily vague. They blended with others more or less specific in content. One of them was the sentimental contention, already suggested above, that government soiled its hands when it touched sordid matters of commerce, that its dignity was impaired, as one pamphleteer put it, by "chaffering about tolls and traffic." [160] More important, however, was the argument that public ownership stifled rights of enterprise with which the government could not legitimately interfere. Much was made of the fact that transportation charters had often been denied because the corporations

---

[157] *Legislative Documents, 1854*, p. 335.
[158] McPherson, *Sale of Main Line*, p. 6.
[159] *Norristown Register*, Mar. 27, 1844.
[160] McPherson, *Sale of Main Line*, p. 46.

they authorized might compete harmfully with the state works.[161] In light of the increasing weakness of this barrier against charter policy,[162] the argument was clearly overdrawn. But it gained support from an allied contention that the taxation program which works deficits had imposed upon the state was driving Pennsylvania capital to other regions. And there was always the general argument, a remarkable reversal of the theory which had sometimes discouraged charter grants, that any type of state ownership, by virtue merely of its existence, must serve to compete with non-public entrepreneurs.[163]

These arguments reflected certain economic changes which had taken place since the inception of the public ownership program. The idea that public ownership restricted private enterprise could not seriously have been presented in 1825; then it was well-nigh universally recognized, even by eastern capitalists themselves, that both corporate and mixed-corporate enterprises were too weak to shoulder alone the transportation task. The idea could carry conviction only during a time in which private capital was beginning to demonstrate greater strength. It is revealing that the sale campaign which lapsed after the bankruptcy reaction of the early forties was not revived on an important scale until the Pennsylvania Railroad Company, which soon became the expected buyer of the public works, had been chartered and had demonstrated success. Although that company was technically a mixed and not a private corporation, its effective management was in private hands. The new power of corporate transportation capital was frankly discussed as a justification for the termination of public ownership. In the House in 1857 Mr. A. B. Johnson insisted that what was "proper and right" for the state depended upon the relative strength of the corporate system.[164] Probably the clearest exposition of this line of argument, however, was made by the writer from Adams County who spoke of the state's enterprise program as follows: "However wisely she may have

---

[161] *Ibid.*, p. 45.
[162] Cf. *supra*, p. 53.
[163] McPherson, *Letters on State Canals*, pp. 4 ff; *Legislative Record, 1857*, No. 77, p. 5.
[164] *Ibid., 1857*, No. 87, p. 5.

once thus employed herself, the time for such occupation has disappeared with that growth of wealth, that upheaving of enterprise, and that combination of capital which have made private associations equal to what only a great Commonwealth could have, twenty years since, attempted." [165]

The older criticisms of public ownership were revived with a vengeance. There was all too much evidence to indicate that the fears of graft and sectionalism which had been expressed before 1825 had been confirmed. The canal commissioners were charged with distorting records so that even the undeniable evidence at hand to prove that the state had been inefficient was but part of the real story.[166] "State management," wrote Mr. Edward McPherson of Harrisburg, "has always been premonitory of failure." Certain "fatal defects" were inherent in it. Partisan rather than merit criteria governed the selection of employees; efficiency was impossible.[167] The Select Committee of the Senate of 1854 called the public works system "a vast engine of political power, unknown to the constitution, moved by a common impulse, and operative upon the public mind at any time they are so disposed, in state conventions, and at the ballot-box in a solid column." [168] Even worse was the influence upon the minds and habits of the people that public inefficiency exerted — the "malign influence on morals." Young men of honesty were corrupted by entering the public service; they came to rely upon wire-pulling for the promotion of careers rather than upon the ancient virtues of thrift, saving, hard work.[169] Sale became a matter of conscience as well as a matter of economic necessity, and the expanding philosophy of the *Way to Wealth* contributed its bit to the new anti-governmental movement.

The defenders of the government admitted the need for admin-

---

[165] McPherson, *Sale of Main Line*, p. 46.
[166] *Ibid.*, p. 35: "In other words, the Canal Board have distorted the facts one-third of a million of dollars, on an average, every year."
[167] McPherson, *Letters on State Canals*, p. 4. See also *Norristown Register*, Mar. 20, 27, 1844; *Public Ledger*, Oct. 4, 1844; Harrisburg *Democratic Union*, Aug. 16, 1843; *House Journal, 1833–34*, II, 629.
[168] *Legislative Documents, 1854*, pp. 328–29.
[169] *Ibid.* On the public works as a source of "moral corruption," see also *Legislative Record, 1857*, No. 93, p. 2.

istrative reform. This marked a definite shift from an earlier attitude. In 1836 the minority of a House investigating committee insisted that it viewed "with great pleasure" the administrative developments on the public works, and further asserted: "The public offices and employment under our government belong to the people. No set or faction have an hereditary or prescriptive right to them. It is inconsistent with the genius of our institutions to employ one set of agents during life . . . ."[170] It was not long, of course, before this explicit application of the rotation idea to the public works became impossible. But the new attitude of the pro-governmental groups was by no means untenable, despite the fact that it was usually drowned out by the noise of the opposition. They admitted that the efforts at reform which had been made had not thus far struck "at the root of the evil,"[171] but they insisted that new ones would. Had the works system continued, it is hard to say whether the evidence would have borne them out. Certain lessons had been learned. The reforms of 1842 indicate that, and so, also, does the general thinking of the pro-governmental groups during the period of the forties and fifties. Governor Porter, in recommending a series of administrative reforms in 1854, emphasized that a "business operation to make money" launched by the state in competition with "the efforts of individuals" had never been "contemplated as an office in the organic law of the State," and that new principles were required to execute such an operation with success. He asked for the institution of a career administrative service, so that the works would become "scientific and mechanical work shops."[172] But in the same year the bill was passed which finally transferred the Main Line to corporate enterprise.

A series of highly colored contrasts were presented in which the condition of public enterprise was set alongside that of private enterprise. Even those who were opposed to the sale of the works found themselves deeply influenced by these comparisons. Almost everyone admitted that the works program "set at defiance all

[170] *House Journal, 1836–37,* II, 829, 825.
[171] *Ibid., 1854,* p. 704. See also Harrisburg *Democratic Union,* Mar. 16, 1844.
[172] *Pa. Archives,* 4th, VII, 643.

the laws which govern business men." [173] The Senate committee asked: "In what company or bank, or what railroad, except that of the state would this be possible?" [174] Governor Porter asked: "What . . . would be the condition of the Reading Railroad, the Pennsylvania Railroad, and other similar works, were they required to change their engineers and superintendents at short periods and bring strangers into their employ?" [175] After the sale had been made in the summer of 1857 the *Harrisburg Weekly Telegraph* declared happily that the works would now be operated by the "best businessmen in the state." [176] This was a far cry from the attitudes prevalent in 1825. Then "business principles" in the transportation realm called to mind nothing more savory than the shilly-shallying of the Union Canal Company, paper turnpikes, and a series of mixed-corporation failures.

It is important to observe that the theory which favored the maintenance of state ownership, like that which had rationalized its acceptance, was linked integrally to the traditional anti-charter doctrine. The corporation that would purchase the works would clearly be one of the most powerful in the history of the state, and this fact made it easy for all of the anti-charter concepts to flourish. Democratic Representative Roumfort in 1844 insisted that it would be "a controlling power" alongside which the "public welfare" and the "branches of government" would be impotent. It was predicted by others that the new corporation, "a monopoly of fearful magnitude," would establish newspapers along the whole line of the works, shape political attitudes, and force the repeal of all restrictions upon it. Drawing the hackneyed distinction between corporations under monarchical and democratic systems, still other publicists feared the impact of the new corporation upon the "honest workingman," emphasizing that it would "interfere with the action" of that "individual enterprise" so dear to the anti-charter doctrine.

In this connection, in words reminiscent of Governor Wolf's

[173] *Legislative Documents, 1854*, pp. 328, 336.
[174] *Ibid.*, p. 335.
[175] *Pa. Archives*, 4th, VII, 642.
[176] *Harrisburg Telegraph*, Aug. 1, 1857.

old criticism of charter policy, one legislator lamented that "the true policy of Republican legislators" was fast disappearing.[177] Twenty-two representatives who voted against sale in 1854 insisted that the idea assumed "that the people of Pennsylvania are not capable of managing their own affairs" and substituted an "antiquated doctrine" of corporate paternalism for that of self-government.[178] Until it became clear that the Pennsylvania was to purchase the Main Line, there was a strong fear that the works would fall into the hands of a foreign corporation, and anti-sale theorists utilized the traditional criticism of such corporations for all it was worth. "Was there ever such a thing upon earth," asked Representative Brackenridge in 1844, "as a free and independent state . . . giving foreigners the entire right of way through the heart of her territory?" Roumfort warned against outstate investors who would not hesitate to sabotage the Pennsylvania line for the aggrandizement of their own transport systems.[179] State ownership theory had become so deeply interwoven with the anti-charter theory that in the context of the sale controversy the two cannot be separated. Together they constituted, as earlier, a single politico-economic position — pro-state, anti-corporate.

Occasionally the record of corporate mismanagement was presented to counter the strong contention that public agents were inferior to private businessmen as administrators. In 1844 when the usual contrast between private and public efficiency was presented in the House, Roumfort asked: "Is the gentleman serious in this assertion?" He spoke of the innumerable corporation failures which "now press upon the country with the dead weight of an incubus," of the depreciated shinplasters which had been issued by such companies as the Lehigh Coal and Navigation Company and the Susquehanna and Tidewater Canal Company,

[177] Harrisburg *Democratic Union*, Feb. 14, Mar. 16, 1844. These issues of the *Union* present a transcript of legislative debates on the sale proposal. *House Journal, 1845*, II, 544 ff.

[178] *Ibid., 1854*, p. 704. Fear of corporate power was undoubtedly a factor delaying the sale. The sale measure of 1854 was especially criticized because of the laxness of its restrictions upon the corporation purchasing the works. *Legislative Documents, 1854*, pp. 340–41. See also *House Journal, 1858*, p. 406.

[179] Harrisburg *Democratic Union*, Feb. 14, 1844.

of the devious ways in which corporations were evading the regulatory laws of the state.[180] Logically this would seem to be a powerful argument, and it is curious that it served no more than it did to offset the force of the plea that "business principles" govern public administration. Even the champions of state ownership failed fully to realize its relevance in this precise connection. Behind this peculiar blind spot, one which was to persist in the American politico-economic psychology, there was at work that complex ideological mechanism by which the prestige of the business entrepreneur was rising. Whatever the sins of the corporate captains may have been, it was a profoundly impressive fact that the public works were becoming, as Governor Bigler had put it, a species of normal schools for the training of their employees. The politician had difficulty competing. A group of politicians, in referring to the rotation of personnel on the public works, once presented with unconscious candor their own estimate of themselves: "In mere political stations these changes may be tolerated . . . but in positions which require the incumbent to know something . . . it must be obvious that the services of such should be secure from arbitrary and wanton change." [181]

Allied as it was with the state ownership theory, the anti-charter dogma experienced a major defeat when the public works were liquidated in the fifties. Yet the character of that defeat is to be perceived not only in the actual fact of sale but also in the peculiar fashion in which the meaning of the anti-charter theory was corrupted in the course of the liquidation argument. The defenders of public enterprise argued in classic fashion that corporations owning the works would grind down "individual enterprise." But the sale theorists argued at the same time and with equal vigor, as Representative Augustine said in 1857: "These improvements should be carried on and completed by individual enterprise." [182] Clearly something was happening here to the great "individual enterprise" symbol; in one instance it was being used to attack the corporation, in the other to defend it. None of the sale

---

[180] *Ibid.* See also *infra*, pp. 262 ff.
[181] *Legislative Documents, 1854,* pp. 335-36.
[182] *Legislative Record, 1858,* No. 79, p. 4.

enthusiasts seriously believed that the public works were to be bought by unincorporated capitalists; everyone was aware of the fact that one of the Adams County writer's new "combinations of capital" would make the purchase and all sale measures expressly anticipated this fact. The corporate system was simply beginning to appropriate for its own purposes the rich individualism of the anti-charter theory. Its defenders either spoke in the name of "individual enterprise," or casually obscured the entire distinction between unincorporated and chartered business by speaking of "private or corporate" [183] enterprise with which the state had no right to interfere.

The assumption of the individualist theory by the corporation and the havoc it wrought with the traditional anti-charter theory is clearly revealed in another connection. When the defenders of public enterprise bravely declared that they were ready to infuse "business principles" into the operation of the works, their opponents had a quick retort. Business principles, as Edward McPherson said, were simply incompatible with public enterprise. To be efficient men had to be "personally" interested in the financial success of their work; they had to be spurred to economy by the motive of self-interest. This was demonstrated by the maxims of "political economy" and "religion." [184] But was this not the same type of argument which the anti-charter theory characteristically leveled *against* the corporate system? Did not that theory contend, as a House committee put it in the early thirties, that the corporation's reliance upon agents "with no feeling of direct interest" in their work was sufficient of itself to ruin enterprises? [185] In the anti-charter theory personal self-interest was lacking when a business was incorporated; in the sale theory personal self-interest was lacking when a business was public but eminently present when a business was incorporated. The sale theory appropriated the anti-charter concept for the defense of the corporation — and utilized it against the state. Meanwhile the anti-charter theory, clinging to its original meaning, was defending the state.

[183] See McPherson, *Letters on State Canals*, p. 4; 30 Pa. St. Rep. 9, 17 (1858).
[184] McPherson, *Letters on State Canals*, p. 4.   [185] Cf. *supra*, p.58.

There are a variety of instances in which the "laissez-faire" interpretation of the anti-charter theory is proved to be false but none is so striking as the controversy over the liquidation of the public works during the forties and fifties. If any theory must be given the "laissez-faire" label, surely it is not the anti-charter theory but the new philosophy that had emerged to oppose it. The anti-charter theory was contending for state entrepreneurship on a scale greater than any dared in the subsequent history of the state. It was seeking to demonstrate, despite revelations of great public inefficiency, the superiority of public over private action in the transportation field. Its role stands out sharply, perhaps because by the late forties and fifties the anti-charter element was about all that remained of the romantic and ebullient theory of public ownership which had originated during the twenties. The popular theory of public spending, the new definitions of wealth and debt, the vision of a treasury overflowing with tolls, the hope of abolishing taxes and supplying free public services — all of these had evaporated. The House Committee of Ways and Means, three years after the bankruptcy of 1842, insisted that the future of the works was "full of promise." [186] But there was no resurrecting the old hopes. A new theory was emerging to satisfy the reaction that their collapse had produced. This theory radically whittled down the role of the state, imposed the most Spartan financial restrictions upon its activity, and derogated the reputations of the men in its service.

But it is worth repeating that this theory, like the latter-day attack upon mixed enterprise which it so closely resembled, was not the gospel of the earlier generations. It flowered toward the close of our period and can be understood only in light of the complex economic, political, and administrative developments discussed above.

6. The End of Public Works

Controversy did not cease once the sale measures had been enacted. Immediately after Governor Pollock had advertised the auction of the Main Line in accordance with the provisions of the

[186] *House Journal*, *1845*, II, 546.

Act of 1857, Henry S. Mott, Arnold Plumer, and George Scott, the incumbent canal commissioners, sought to obtain an injunction from the courts restraining Pollock from further executing its provisions.[187] They insisted that it was their duty to protect the public works from impairment and that the measure of 1857 was void because it had been promoted by the "servants, officers, and agents" of the Pennsylvania Railroad Company.[188] The attorney-general and lawyers for the Pennsylvania replied that the canal commissioners had no executive authority, no rights in the public works, and that their status was merely that of "ministerial agents."[189] "There are three departments of government required by the Constitution," declared Attorney Staunton, one of the company lawyers, "— executive, legislative, and judicial. The complainants are mere creatures of legislative authority."[190] In so far as the charge of legislative corruption was concerned, Staunton declared that such indictments belonged in the arena of political debate, not in a court room. Affidavits were presented on behalf of the company denying that it had promoted the sale measure with a view to purchasing the Main Line.[191]

The canal commissioners contended also that the office of governor did not embrace the duty of an auctioneer. Attorney Hirst, one of their counsel, assailed the legislature for "not even choosing a regularly licensed auctioneer, who would not be liable to the law imposing penalties for selling without a license."[192] This was not an impressive argument, and it was vigorously countered by the governor's denial that any decision of the court could obstruct him in the discharge of his duties. The court appears to have been troubled by this denial, and on one occasion Justice Woodward asked counsel for a further discussion of it. "Here a general argument sprang up," reported the *Ledger*, "in which the bench and all the counsel joined for a few minutes; the result of which appeared to be that the governor could not be enjoined."

---

[187] *Mott v. Pennsylvania Railroad Company*, 30 Pa. St. Rep. 9 (1858).
[188] *Ibid.*, p. 12.
[189] *Ibid.*, p. 16.
[190] *North American*, June 18, 1857.
[191] *Public Ledger*, June 18, 1857; *Mott v. Pennsylvania Railroad Company*, 30 Pa. St. Rep. 9, 16 (1858).
[192] *Ibid.*, p. 11; *Public Ledger*, June 17, 1857.

Judicial restraint of the executive, warned Staunton, was a dangerous adventure, calling for extreme caution, one which could vitiate the stability of law and unsettle the community. Attorney Meredith, a lawyer for the canal commissioners, pointed out that if the court declared the measure invalid there would be nothing to enjoin the governor upon since he would have nothing to act upon.[193]

Probably the most heavily emphasized argument of the canal commissioners was one which they put forth in their private capacities as "owners of real and personal property" and which was urged by Mott in a separate bill of equity filed as a loanholder of the state.[194] This was the contention that the works must be preserved in the interest of taxpayers and debtholders. The commonwealth, insisted Hirst, implicitly tendered to its creditors "a kind of mechanic's lien law" which made sale of the works unlawful. The anti-repudiation symbolism was effective, and when Meredith joined Hirst in the argument, his statement was reported by the *Ledger* to have "approached a solemnity rarely witnessed in courts." [195] The reply of the company attorneys was developed along the traditional lines of the sale theory: the works were a financial loss to the state, sale would provide added revenue and reduce the burden of taxation.[196]

But they did not stop with the financial issue. They introduced most of the rest of the sale ideology as well. Though Justice Lowrie reprimanded Staunton on one occasion for departing from the issue at hand, the lawyer managed to get in a good blow at that "standing army of office holders" which resided in the state and which was "eating out her vitals." [197] His colleague, G. T. Campbell, managed to point out that once business enterprise was "able to walk alone, then the necessity for the aid of the Commonwealth ceased," and that the state could now return "exclusively to its appropriate functions." [198] Mismanagement was "necessar-

[193] *Ibid.*, June 18, 19, 1857; *Mott* v. *Pennsylvania Railroad Company*, 30 Pa. St. Rep. 9, 16 (1858).
[194] *Ibid.*, 30 Pa. St. Rep. 9, 13 (1858).
[195] *Public Ledger*, June 18, 1857; *Pennsylvanian*, June 19, 1857.
[196] *Mott* v. *Pennsylvania Railroad Company*, 30 Pa. St. Rep. 9, 17 (1858); *Public Ledger*, June 18, 19, 1857.
[197] *Ibid.*, June 18, 1857.
[198] *Ibid.*, June 17, 1857.

ily incident" to the operation of enterprises by the state; businessmen were to be relied upon in such affairs.[199]

Mott also challenged the measure of 1857 in his capacity as a shareholder in the Pennsylvania Railroad Company. He contended that the purchase of the works by the company would involve a violation of its charter which as a stockholder he had a right to resist. In this connection he was joined momentarily by S. B. Cooper, Jacob Lower, and W. Perkins, commissioners of Allegheny County which held twenty thousand shares of stock in the Pennsylvania,[200] who petitioned to act with him as parties against the bill. President Thomson of the Pennsylvania denied that the commissioners represented the bondholders of the county for whose security the stock was issued, and presented petitions in favor of sale by certain of the bondholders including himself.[201] Within twenty-four hours, however, the commissioners mysteriously withdrew their petition and the issue of their status was left undecided.[202] Mott argued that the purchase of the works would amount to a diversion of corporate property from corporate purposes, involving an increase of loans beyond the amount of capital stock.[203] The railroad attorneys bitterly replied that Mott had but recently purchased three shares in the company and that he "came in to create discord where harmony existed." They insisted that the Pennsylvania belonged to a class of "public corporations" that were "not to be governed by the narrow and confined rules of private corporations." They were "not moneyed corporations such as banks and private companies." [204]

Upon the conclusion of this colorful argument, the court unanimously decided that the canal commissioners were wrong on all counts. Chief Justice Lewis, who delivered the opinion of the court, admitted that the justices had differed somewhat in the reasoning by which they denied Mott's plea as a dissenting stockholder,[205] but the denial itself was unanimous. On June 25, 1857,

[199] *Mott v. Pennsylvania Railroad Company*, 30 Pa. St. Rep. 9, 17 (1858).
[200] *Public Ledger*, June 18, 1857.
[201] *Ibid.*
[202] *Ibid.*, June 19, 1857.
[203] *Ibid.*, June 17, 1857.
[204] *Ibid.*, June 17, 18, 1857.
[205] *Mott v. Pennsylvania Railroad Company*, 30 Pa. St. Rep. 9, 23 (1858).

at the Merchant's Exchange in Philadelphia, the Main Line was sold to the Pennsylvania, and the company took possession on August 1. But the canal commissioners did not lose entirely. Another section of their argument in the Mott Case had been concerned with the clause in the sale measure of 1857 which released the Pennsylvania from all further state taxation if it paid an additional two and a half millions for the works. In this connection they were victorious, but that is a topic for later discussion.[206]

The commissioners did not give up easily. In 1858, after the measure disposing of the remainder of the works to the Sunbury and Erie had been enacted, they reported receiving "urgent" petitions requesting that the constitutionality of the bill be challenged.[207] They obtained an opinion from Attorney Charles Buckalew, concurred in by Hirst and Jeremiah Black, which held that the measure was unconstitutional on the ground that it violated the Sinking Fund Amendment which had been authorized by the electorate after the Mott Case had been argued. That amendment provided that all proceeds of the sale of the works must be applied to the payment of the state debt.[208] Buckalew declared that the measure of 1858 violated this mandate on four counts: (1) since the bill provided that upon a resale of the works one-fourth of the excess over the sale price was to be taken by the Sunbury and Erie, it did not provide for the direction of all proceeds toward the liquidation of the state debt; (2) since it required the Sunbury and Erie to subscribe five hundred thousand dollars in the stock of the Allegheny Valley Railroad Company, part of the value of the works was diverted to the use of a corporation; (3) since it provided that all demands against the state upon the lines of canal sold be paid by the purchaser, it included an application of proceeds in the price which was not administered through the Sinking Fund; (4) since it limited resale of the North Branch Canal to residents or property owners along the line, it lessened the price paid to the state and hence did not

---

[206] See *infra*, pp. 269 ff.
[207] *Legislative Documents, 1858*, p. 9.
[208] Cf. *supra*, pp. 277 ff.

permit a full application of proceeds to the purpose of debt liquidation.[209]

These objections were hairsplitting indeed. And it was perhaps for this reason, rather than because of the "indelicacy" of challenging the legislative and executive branches of the government, that the commissioners expressed "great reluctance" to bring them to the courts.[210] In any case the commissioners were on their last legs. Even when public ownership had elicited mass enthusiasm, they had always been looked upon as suspicious characters. But now that a new philosophy had emerged to blacken the entire principle of public enterprise, their guilt was clearly established. The anti-state doctrine which arose with the campaign to sell the public works in the forties, and which was actually introduced as legal argument in the Mott Case of the fifties, was rapidly transforming conceptions of the valid sphere of the government and its agents in economic life. Like a similar philosophy which arose during the same period to discredit mixed enterprise investment, that doctrine was teaching the people of Pennsylvania that a state policy whose legitimacy they had long accepted was actually a violation of the "first principles" of their democratic faith.[211]

[209] *Legislative Documents, 1858*, pp. 9–10.
[210] *Ibid.*, p. 10.
[211] Supra, pp. 166–67. The offices of the canal commissioners were abolished in January, 1859. *Pa. Laws, 1859*, p. 6.

PART THREE
THE STATE AS REGULATOR

V

SOCIAL REFORM AND VESTED RIGHTS

1. Slavery and Indentured Service

THE charter, mixed corporation, and public works policies we have thus far examined originated almost entirely after the Revolution. In connection with them the state had little precedent on which to build, there were sudden expansions and contractions of policy, and administrative tasks were overwhelming. The field of social legislation, where in most instances the state built upon a long tradition of colonial experience, has a somewhat quieter aspect. Yet there too, as a consequence of economic change and the rise of the vigorous humanitarian movements of the time, the record of state action is complex enough. In the labor field slavery and the slave trade were abolished, indentured service died away, and the emergence of a factory economy produced a revolution in the conditions of work for important sectors of the labor supply. It is true that during our period slave labor did not play an important part in the internal economy of the state, for it soon became clear that the economic tasks with which the state was to be concerned were unsuited to the employment of slaves.[1] By 1820 the number of slaves in Pennsylvania was only 211.[2] Nevertheless Philadelphia continued, for some time, to be the foremost port in the Union for the slave trade, and the efforts of the state to strike at that problem were, commercially, of some importance.[3]

The peculiar fact of Pennsylvania's Quaker background produced a heritage of experience and thought in the realm of social reform which served as a basis upon which many post-Revolutionary actions were taken. As early as 1688 the Quakers agitated

---

[1] For early views on the use of slave labor in Pennsylvania, see M. Carey, *Essays*, pp. 232–34; R. Wright, *The Negro in Pa.*, p. 2.
[2] *List of Inhabitants*, p. 3.
[3] Du Bois, *Suppression of Slave Trade*, pp. 162, 166. See also *idem.*, *Philadelphia Negro*, pp. 412–16; R. Wright, *The Negro in Pa.*, pp. 22–26; Turner, *Slavery in Pa.*, pp. 64–88.

against slaveholding;[4] they eventually abolished it among members of their own group, and in 1712 they petitioned the Assembly for its complete abolition throughout the colony.[5] During the Revolution the anti-slavery movement gained impetus. By 1775 the Society for the Relief of Free Negroes Unlawfully Held in Bondage had been formed.[6] Five years later the legislature enacted a measure decreeing that no child henceforth born of slave parents could be held in slavery for that reason.[7] The act of 1780, in addition to abolishing hereditary servitude, also abolished most of the prevailing legal discriminations against slaves. Owing to its ambiguous language, however, the enforcement of this measure was difficult. Even a master with the best intentions was never sure that he was following registration provisions correctly.[8]

In 1789 a society was incorporated which sought both to remedy this confusion and to take advantage of it to further emancipation. The Pennsylvania Society for Promoting the Abolition of Slavery had had a voluntary existence for some years, Franklin serving as its first president,[9] but with its incorporation its activities expanded.[10] The society listed its general objectives as follows: the conversion of public opinion in behalf of Negro freedom; the procurement of freedom for those Negroes held in slavery in violation of state law; and the improvement of the condition of Negroes by means of education and other humanitarian activities.[11] It was in connection with the second of these aims that the society tried to force emancipation on the basis of technicalities in existing law. The society complained that provisions to limit the slave trade were ineffective,[12] and it brought pressure upon the legislature to enact others more stringent. In 1788 a new law was passed which tightened the provisions of the measure

---

[4] Needles, *Pa. Society for Abolition of Slavery*, p. 12; Bettle, "Notices of Negro Slavery," *Memoirs of Hist. Soc. of Pa.*, I (1826), 365.

[5] *Ibid.*, p. 371.

[6] Needles, *Pa. Society for Abolition of Slavery*, p. 14; Pa. Society for Abolition of Slavery, *Constitution*, pp. 19–20.

[7] *Statutes at Large*, X, 67–73.

[8] Turner, "Abolition of Slavery in Pa.," *Pa. Mag. of Hist. and Biog.*, XXXVI (1912), 141–42. See also Pa. Society for Abolition of Slavery, *Constitution*, pp. 23–24.

[9] *Ibid.*, p. 11.

[10] Pa. Society for Abolition of Slavery, *Address*, p. 4.

[11] *Ibid.*

[12] *Ibid.*, p. 3.

previously adopted and also imposed a fine of one thousand pounds for engaging in the trade.¹³

Nothing illustrates better than the anti-slavery movement the link between the theory of political democracy and the theory of social reform. It was not accidental that the drive to abolish rights in slave property should accelerate during the Revolutionary period. The contrast was glaring between the constitution of 1776, with its flamboyant natural rights declarations, and the fact of Negro servitude. The Society for the Relief of Free Negroes was built upon the principle of that contrast, since it insisted that the new "laws and Constitutions" effected the freedom of many Negroes, though they were still kept in slavery.¹⁴ The act of 1780 also reveals the impact of the Revolutionary ideas. The legislature resolved "to extend a portion of that freedom to others, which hath been extended to us." ¹⁵

In 1794, under the auspices of the Society for Promoting the Abolition of Slavery, a national anti-slavery convention was held in Philadelphia. Guided by Benjamin Rush, this convention produced a declaration which summarized the leading ideas of the movement to abolish rights in slave property. They were: (1) that the continuance of slavery was inconsistent with the libertarian theories upon the basis of which the Revolution had been fought, (2) that slaveowning unfitted men for the tasks of citizenship in a free republic, (3) that the presence of slavery in the country discouraged the fight for democracy abroad, (4) that slavery violated the precepts of Christianity, and (5) that it produced an ever present threat of insurrection and domestic violence.¹⁶

These arguments already foreshadow the substance of reforming ideologies which were later to sweep the state in campaigns for various types of governmental action. But the anti-slavery movement did not achieve its purposes without opposition. The

¹³ *Statutes at Large*, XIII, 52–56.
¹⁴ Needles, *Pa. Society for Abolition of Slavery*, p. 14.
¹⁵ *Statutes at Large*, X, 67. For a similar relationship between the Revolutionary ideas and anti-slavery theory in Massachusetts, see Hartz, "Otis and Anti-Slavery Doctrine," *New England Quarterly*, XII (1939), 745–47.
¹⁶ *Celebration of Ninetieth Anniversary*, p. 12.

act of 1780 was opposed on the grounds (1) that it would tend to weaken other states which had not adopted a similar law by making the slaves there uneasy during the critical period of war, (2) that in a short time war would come to Pennsylvania itself and that the new freedoms granted the Negro might then lead to revolt within the state, and (3) that the Negroes were not yet fitted for the larger responsibilities which the measure of 1780 imposed upon them.[17]

It is important to observe that all of these arguments were concerned with the expediency rather than with the legitimacy of the 1780 measure. It was not contended that the restrictions and losses imposed upon the slaveholder were violations of property rights which the constitution of 1776 secured as strongly as any other. There was no evidence of a demand on the part of the masters for indemnification from the state. The slaveholders were, as a matter of fact, on the defensive throughout this period. Far from questioning the validity of governmental action on the ground that it violated property rights, opinion widely held that the law of 1780 "did not pursue the full development of natural rights set forth in our state constitution." [18] The judiciary was eventually asked to decide whether any slavery at all was constitutional. In 1802 a committee of the House remarked upon the constitutional question,[19] and some years later the Pennsylvania Society presented a case, which it carried to the High Court of Errors and Appeals, in which it contended that as a result of the Declaration of Rights in the constitution of 1790, slave-owning had become invalid. The society lost the case, however, the court holding that slavery had legally existed in Pennsylvania before the adoption of the constitution and that adoption had not changed its status.[20]

[17] Needles, *Pa. Society for Abolition of Slavery*, pp. 24, 25.
[18] Pa. Society for Abolition of Slavery, *Address*, p. 3.
[19] The committee declared: "Yet under the most solemn engagements to support this constitution, and under the immediate observation of every member of this House, numbers of our fellow men are held in bondage . . . . Is there nothing obligatory in the constitution of this State and of the United States?" *House Journal, 1802*, p. 361.
[20] Turner, "Abolition of Slavery in Pa.," *Pa. Mag. of Hist. and Biog.*, XXXVI (1912), 138 ff.

While the abolition of slavery was clearly conditioned by the natural rights philosophy of the Revolution and the democratic philosophy of the subsequent period, similar influences cannot be discovered on a large scale in connection with the disappearance of indentured service in Pennsylvania. Research has disclosed that some natural rights enthusiasm was mobilized behind a campaign to alleviate the conditions of indentured servants in New York, but in Pennsylvania the question appears to have been dealt with almost exclusively on a pragmatic plane. In 1785, to be sure, a measure was enacted by the Assembly which ameliorated the conditions of the servant upon arrival in Philadelphia. But this measure was so closely in line with previous enactments that it does not appear to have sprung in any appreciable measure from a new equalitarian sentiment regarding the servant trade. It consisted mainly of changes in the administration of existing provisions.[21]

The Revolution did, however, produce serious practical problems for the maintenance of the indentured service system. Many servants enlisted in the American and British armies in order to escape service. Conflicts arose between military officers and masters.[22] In 1776 the Council of Safety ordered that no indentured servants might enlist in the Revolutionary army without the consent of their masters and that all who had enlisted prior to that time must be discharged.[23] But recruiting officers frequently paid no attention to this measure, and there were the same difficulties in enforcing a similar enactment of the Supreme Executive Council in the following year.[24] In 1778 the Assembly ordered county treasurers to compensate masters for servants enlisted in any of the Pennsylvania regiments.[25]

This policy of indemnification is in striking contrast to the policy pursued with respect to Negro slavery, and it is important to ask whether it reflects a belief that the masters of servants

[21] Cf. W. Miller, "Effects of Revolution on Indentured Servitude," *Pa. Hist.*, VII (1940), 131–41.
[22] Geiser, *Redemptioners in Pa.*, p. 100; Herrick, *White Servitude in Pa.*, pp. 250–51.
[23] Pennsylvania, *Colonial Records*, X, 723–24.
[24] *Pa. Archives*, 2d, I, 42.
[25] *Statutes at Large*, IX, 216–17.

possessed property rights which a master of slaves did not. Since the equalitarian impetus of the Revolution appears to have exerted little effect upon attitudes toward indentured service, it may appear that such a belief existed. No final answer can be given to this question, but it would be erroneous to assume the prevalence of such a belief on the basis of the state's indemnification policy in connection with servant enlistments. For no legislative enactment authorizing the liberation of servants was involved in that case similar to the one which authorized the liberation of the children of slaves: recruitment of servants for Pennsylvania regiments was in clear defiance of law. It is fruitless to speculate about what attitudes might have prevailed had a law abolishing the servant trade been enacted.

But it is of some significance to observe that the state did, indirectly, strike a fatal blow at indentured service, and that with little consideration for the vested rights involved. That blow was the abolition of imprisonment for debt. The institution of debtor imprisonment was the legal rock upon which indentured service rested.[26] Since it was possible to imprison a servant for failure to discharge debts, merchants and importers had the entire coercive apparatus of the state behind them. Viewed from this angle, the decline of indentured service, which was reflected in a diminishing supply of servants from abroad after 1817,[27] also becomes part of the movement for social democracy, even though the influence of the democratic slogans is not marked in discussions concerning it. For the gradual betterment of the debtor's position, which I shall discuss below, was an integral part of that movement.

[26] "With the final abolition of imprisonment for debt the institution of indentured service received its legal death blow, and necessarily died out without any special enactment." Geiser, *Redemptioners in Pa.*, p. 42. See also Herrick, *White Servitude in Pa.*, p. 266.

[27] For an economic discussion of the decline of the servant trade, involving the retention of workers by other countries for industrial purposes, the growth of slavery in the South, and the development of northern labor, see W. Miller, "Effects of Revolution on Indentured Servitude," *Pa. Hist.*, VII (1940), 136, 140; also Herrick, *White Servitude in Pa.*, pp. 254–66.

2. Workers and the State

In the realm of labor policy the sharpest impact on the role of the state came from the organization of free workers in the changing Keystone economy. Sporadic organization and strikes during the post-Revolutionary period, struggle against early conspiracy judgments during the opening years of the nineteenth century,[28] eventually gave way to a full-blown labor awakening during the twenties. After a famous strike of journeymen carpenters in Philadelphia during the summer of 1827, a period of vigorous labor agitation began which lasted for about fifteen years. The membership of the labor unions during this time, the membership of the political parties that they organized, and the issues behind which they mobilized their strength, indicate that this period of labor organization bore, in John Commons' periodization, the characteristics of merchant rather than factory capitalism.[29] The distinction is important. For the labor unions of the first period were composed primarily of journeymen mechanics, not of factory workers. Factory workers were not well organized. And while in the forties and the fifties factory hands joined the union movement in increasing numbers,[30] the main strength of the movement throughout the pre-Civil War epoch continued to come from the journeymen trades.

Despite that fact, however, an important phase of legislative action affecting labor was concerned with the factory system. In order to understand why the comparatively unorganized factory workers should receive legislative attention, it is necessary to observe that the drive for factory legislation at this time was closely linked to the movement for public education. Owing to the increasing exploitation of child labor in Pennsylvania factories after 1830, it became clear to middle-class partisans of universal education that action would have to be taken toward controlling the factory system. Moreover, the education issue

---

[28] See Commons, *History of Labour*, I, 68 ff., 81, 118, 127, 138 ff.; Commons, *Documentary History of American Industrial Society*, III, 59 ff.; IV, 15 ff.
[29] Commons, *History of Labour*, I, 88–108.
[30] For a survey of labor organization during the later period, see Cale, *The Organization of Labor in Philadelphia, 1850–1870*.

served as a link to unite factory workers with journeymen unionists. For one of the main objectives of the organized journeymen, at least until the fifties, was the achievement of a system of universal education. Thus the factory workers, though poorly organized, found powerful supporters in both the union and middle-class elements of the community; it was this triple alliance which managed to compel the legislature, at a comparatively early time, to take action regarding the factory system.

As early as 1824 the problem of child labor in the new cotton and woolen factories drew legislative attention. In that year the House appointed a committee to consider the problem, and it reported a bill which made it unlawful for any textile manufacturer to employ minors between the ages of twelve and eighteen unless they could read and write or unless provision for their education was made by the manufacturer himself. Representative Richards, chairman of the committee, asserted: "There are now many thousand children employed in our manufactories, the nature of the employment is constant and unremitting from sunrise until night. . . ." Richards emphasized the importance of enacting factory legislation when the factory system was comparatively young and the evils apparent in the British system had not been reached. The bill of the Richards committee, however, was not enacted into law, and ten years more were to elapse before further legislative action was taken.[31]

In 1837 the Senate appointed a committee to investigate child labor in factories.[32] This committee, headed by Senator Peltz, held extensive hearings, calling before it workers, employers, foremen,

---

[31] Barnard, *Factory Legislation in Pa.*, pp. 2–3.

[32] The fact that child labor in factories was not governed by the apprentice system was put forth to justify the inquiry. "It may be asked, why confine this inquiry exclusively to manufactories, and not extend it to business of other kinds? The answer is, that in most occupations the apprenticing system prevails. In our factories, there is no such thing; no indenture is executed to secure to the child its trade; no provision is made for its education. This deficiency is peculiar to the factory system alone; and here is the point where legislative interposition seems to be necessary." *Senate Journal, 1837–38*, I, 325. The master-apprentice relationship was traditionally governed by state law. See *Dallas' Laws*, I, 540–42; IV, 475. Acts regulating apprentices were extended to redemptioners in 1820. *Pa. Laws, 1819–20*, p. 17. See also *Pa. Laws, 1838–39*, pp. 337–46. The last statute provided that a majority of the managers of the house of employment for the poor might, under certain conditions, bind poor children as apprentices. For critical discussions of

educators, and other persons who might shed light on factory conditions.³³ Its report revealed an unsavory state of affairs. It estimated that of the hands employed in cotton mills the proportions, as to age and sex, were roughly as follows: males, one-third; females, two-thirds; under the age of twelve years, one-fifth. It asserted that not more than one-third of all those under eighteen years of age employed in the mills could either read or write, and that the illiteracy of the others was due to "their early employment in factories, and to the total neglect of their education afterwards." It revealed that in some factories in the Philadelphia district working hours exceeded fourteen per day, and that children were compelled to work as long hours as adults.³⁴ The Peltz Committee reported a bill which provided that no child under ten years of age should be employed in factories, that all factory children not able to read and write should be given three months of schooling yearly, and that ten hours daily should be the maximum working time for all children under sixteen years.³⁵ Partially owing to the panic of 1837, however, this measure, like the Richards bill earlier, failed to pass.

In the forties a ten-hour movement got under way in Pennsylvania, as in other parts of the country,³⁶ and petitions again came to the legislature calling for action on the factory system.³⁷ In 1837 the Peltz Committee had reported that the majority of witnesses who came before it had agreed that ten hours a day was the maximum time any adult might work in a factory without ultimate injury to his health.³⁸ In 1848 both the Democratic and the Whig parties went on record as favoring a factory law.³⁹ A measure was passed which outlawed the labor of children under twelve years of age in cotton, woolen, silk, or flax factories, and

---

factory conditions in Pennsylvania during the thirties, see *Banner of the Constitution*, April 25, 1832, and other issues.

³³ *Senate Journal, 1837–38*, II, 278–359. See also Peltz, "Correspondence."
³⁴ *Senate Journal, 1837–38*, I, 322–27.
³⁵ *Ibid.*
³⁶ Otey, "Women and Child Wage-Earners in U.S.," p. 121; *House Journal, 1847*, I, 139–40; *1848*, I, 9, 38, 55, 101, 125, 158.
³⁷ See *ibid., 1848*, I, 38, 55, 101, 125; *1847*, I, 139–40.
³⁸ *Senate Journal, 1837–38*, I, 326.
³⁹ For the declarations of the parties, see Martin and Shenk, *Pa. History Told by Contemporaries*, pp. 487–88.

placed a ten-hour limit on the work of adults except by special contract.[40] Superficially the law seemed to go even further than the Peltz bill had gone in the regulation of factory conditions, but it was vitiated by the provision that a longer working day might be maintained by special contracts between employers and individual operatives. A group of manufacturers asserted that the measure of 1848 had been based upon a "greatly over-rated" conception of profits and upon a preoccupation with "the bright and sunny side of the picture" to the exclusion of depression periods. They declared that they would be compelled to take wholesale advantage of the provision permitting special contracts for longer hours.[41]

When the law of 1848 went into effect there were a series of strikes which shut down factories in Allegheny City, Pittsburgh, and Philadelphia.[42] There were rumors, the truth or falsity of which it is hard to establish, to the effect that the manufacturers had appointed a committee to search for a new location on the Ohio river in western Virginia, "not too remote from the coal region," where they might operate without ten-hour restrictions — "a sort of Western Lowell."[43] The strikes lasted through the summer, and, after some rioting, the mills opened during the latter part of August. For the most part a compromise was worked out whereby operatives worked only ten hours a day but were docked in wages for the reduction in time.[44] In the following year, after a call by Governor Johnston for legislative modification of

[40] *Pa. Laws, 1848*, pp. 278-79.

[41] *Pittsburgh Morning Post*, Aug. 4, 1848. The factory owners, though denouncing the hours provisions of the measure of 1848, voiced approval of its child labor provisions. They asserted that child labor had never been profitable, and that "the practice originated through the entreaties of indigent parents, whose wants were supplied by the earnings." *Ibid.*

[42] *Public Ledger*, July 6, 1848; *Pittsburgh Morning Post*, July 6, 1848; *Pennsylvanian*, Feb. 13, 1849.

[43] *United States Gazette*, quoted in *Pittsburgh Morning Post*, July 17, 1848; *Pittsburgh Morning Post*, July 22, 1848.

[44] Barnard, *Factory Legislation in Pa.*, p. 20. The condition of the factory operatives became serious, a committee was appointed to solicit donations for their assistance, and many workers' meetings were held. Political candidates appear on the whole to have steered clear of these meetings, but Democratic politicians seem to have revealed a greater sympathy for the workers than their Whig opponents. See *Pittsburgh Morning Post*, July 25, Aug. 11, Sept. 1, 1848; *Public Ledger*, Jan. 19, 1849; Barnard, *Factory Legislation in Pa.*, pp. 18-20.

the measure of 1848,[45] that law was repealed and a more stringent one enacted. The latter measure raised the child-labor age limit from twelve to thirteen years, and provided that all minors over that age could be employed for no more than nine months, the remaining three to be set aside for educational purposes.[46] This law was supplemented by another in 1855.[47]

None of the factory measures was well administered. In the act of 1849 parents and guardians were held responsible only for a violation of schooling provisions. The prosecution of violators was left up to anyone who wished to bring suit against them, the reward being half of the fifty-dollar fine set. The same reliance upon the initiative of private citizens for enforcement was also embodied in the law of 1855. It was grossly inadequate. After the initial excitement over their passage disappeared, the factory measures gradually became dead letters on the statute books. Many entrepreneurs subsequently set up factories unaware of the fact that the measures existed.[48] The political thought dealing with them was characterized by an appalling lack of administrative wisdom. A witness called before the Senate committee in 1837[49] recommended the formation of visiting committees for the purpose of checking up on employers. But such proposals, even by those who campaigned hardest for labor legislation, were rare.

If they were ready to support factory legislation, the journeymen mechanics were still mainly concerned with measures directly serving their own interest. At an early time they extracted from the legislature a series of laws which secured payment to workmen by giving them a lien on buildings for labor and materials provided in construction. Unknown to the common law, such measures were not part of the eighteenth-century background of labor regulations.[50] They originated in the nineteenth

---

[45] *Ibid.*, p. 20; *House Journal, 1849*, I, 41. For petitions calling for repeal of the proviso in the measure of 1848, see *Senate Journal, 1849*, I, 46, 53, 69, 73, 117, 118.
[46] *Pa. Laws, 1849*, pp. 671-72.
[47] *Ibid., 1855*, p. 472. See also *Pa. Archives*, 4th, VII, 517.
[48] Barnard, *Factory Legislation in Pa.*, p. 24. Cf. remarks of Governor Johnston, *Pa. Archives*, 4th, VII, 309.
[49] *Senate Journal, 1837-38*, II, 314.
[50] Cf. *Bouvier's Law Dictionary*, II, pp. 1978 ff.

century largely because of waves of real-estate speculation which swept the state and which frequently resulted in the employment of mechanics by operators who lacked funds to compensate them when construction jobs were completed. Peter A. Browne, in his excellent digest of lien legislation up to the year 1814,[51] describing the reckless building which got under way in the Philadelphia region at the outset of the century, asserted that the situation might have been "fatal" not only to the interests of the workers but to the cause of real-estate improvement itself, "had not legislative wisdom promptly rushed a remedy."[52] That remedy was a measure, enacted in 1803, which secured to mechanics and others payment for labor and materials in connection with buildings in the Philadelphia territory.[53] This measure was expanded in various ways during the next fifteen years.[54]

With the emergence of an organized labor movement in the late twenties, a new campaign of broader scope got under way for the passage of lien legislation.[55] One of the main reasons put forward for independent political action on the part of labor groups in Philadelphia was that, through such action, they could procure more comprehensive lien provisions.[56] The laborers pointed to the fact that liens were established for money-lenders, landholders, and tavern-keepers; they insisted that "none of these creditors *work* like the workman."[57] It was utopian to expect mechanics, many of them without formal education, to investigate the solvency of employers. Moreover, in trades where slack seasons occurred, laborers were expected to acquiesce in the postponement of wage payments; only a lien could secure that unfair advantage would not be taken of their confidence.[58] Beginning in 1831, as a result of the new agitation, a series of measures broadened the lien provisions to include a larger range of workers and a greater amount of property.[59] Moreover the ideas

---

[51] Browne, *Law of Pa. Securing Payment for Labor*.
[52] *Ibid.*, pp. iii–iv.
[53] *Pa. Laws, 1801–1803*, pp. 591–92.
[54] See *ibid., 1807–1808*, pp. 165–66; *1812–13*, p. 38; *1814–15*, pp. 46–47.
[55] Cf. *Mechanics Free Press*, Aug. 22, Nov. 14, 1829.
[56] *Ibid.*, Sept. 12, 1829.
[57] *Ibid.*, Dec. 20, 1829.   [58] *Ibid.*
[59] *Pa. Laws, 1830–31*, pp. 36–37. Cf. Sergeant, *Lien of Mechanics*.

advanced to justify lien legislation [60] were soon taken up by a movement, led in the legislature by Senator Robert Powell,[61] for the enactment of laws making workers privileged creditors in property assignments arising from bankruptcies. After numerous defeats,[62] this movement bore fruit in 1854 when the legislature gave mechanics first preference, up to one hundred dollars, in the property assignments of insolvent corporations.[63]

The mine workers carried on what was pretty much a separate agitation of their own. Miners were frequently victimized by expansionist booms which characterized the development of the coal regions.[64] The first boom got under way in the Schuylkill region in 1828 and left behind it a superabundance of small operators and workmen.[65] But the organization of miners did not take place on an important scale until the early forties.[66] In 1843 petitions came to the legislature from miners asking for the enactment of lien laws.[67] The House Committee on the Judiciary granted that miners had a right to legislative protection, but it refused to recognize the validity of extending the lien principle to them. It drew a distinction between workers on ordinary realty and workers in collieries. Construction workers enhanced the value of property and hence they had a right to a lien against it for payment; but miners contributed nothing to the value of mines, indeed their work detracted from the value of mining property. Nor could the lien principle be extended to the equipment or the personal property of the operators, for that would arrest operations in the coal fields.[68] On the basis of this reasoning, the miners' petitions were denied in 1843.

Six years later an intensified movement for the protection of

---

[60] See *House Journal, 1833–34*, II, 559; Price, *Limitations of Actions against Real Estate*, chap. XXXVI.

[61] Powell introduced measures of this kind in 1828, 1829, and 1830. *Mechanics Free Press*, Jan. 30, 1830.

[62] Cf. *House Journal, 1828–29*, II, 533–34.

[63] *Ibid., 1854*, p. 480.

[64] Cf. *Miner's Journal*, Jan. 27, 1849.

[65] Itter, "Early Labor Troubles in Schuylkill District," *Pa. Hist.*, I (1934), 28–37.

[66] Trachtenberg, *Legislation for Coal Miners in Pa.*, pp. 12–19.

[67] *Senate Journal, 1843*, I, 51, 94, 175, 184.

[68] *Ibid.*, I, 518.

workers with reference to wage payments was initiated in the mining area.⁶⁹ A large laborers' meeting held in Pottsville in January of that year declared that "the hour of compromise is past."⁷⁰ The miners were undoubtedly encouraged by the enactment of the factory law of 1848. Many of them went out on strike in May 1849.⁷¹ The upshot of this campaign was not the achievement of a lien provision for miners but an extension to them of the privileged-creditor concept. The legislature passed a law which provided that the wages of miners, mechanics, and laborers, not exceeding fifty dollars each, were to be paid first in all assignments of property resulting from bankruptcies in the mining of coal.⁷² Still unsatisfied, the miners continued their campaign for lien legislation, and after renewed agitation during the crisis of 1857,⁷³ they succeeded in obtaining a temporary lien measure⁷⁴ which in 1859 was established as permanent.⁷⁵ Notable as these successes were, however, there was one objective which, despite strong pressure, the miners failed to achieve during our period. This was state action against the hated store-order system of payment, always a bitter grievance among miners and one which was clearly responsible in part for the strikes of 1849.⁷⁶ Legislative success on this score had to await a subsequent stage in the organization of labor and in the growth of the economy.⁷⁷

3. *The Theory of Labor Legislation*

While the colonial tradition which had for two centuries accepted labor regulation as a function of the state served as a receptive background for the labor measures of our period, the

[69] Cf. *House Journal, 1849,* I, 716, 408.
[70] *Miner's Journal,* Jan. 27, 1849.
[71] *Ibid.,* May 5, 19, 1849.
[72] *Pa. Laws, 1849,* p. 337. The measure was limited to seven counties where most of the mines were located: Schuylkill, Berks, Washington, Centre, Somerset, Westmoreland, and Carbon.
[73] *Senate Journal, Extra Session, 1857,* p. 475.
[74] *Pa. Laws, 1858,* pp. 615–16.
[75] *Ibid., 1859,* pp. 318–19.
[76] *Miner's Journal,* Feb. 17, May 19, 1849; *Senate Journal, 1843,* I, 51, 94; Trachtenberg, *Legislation for Coal Miners in Pa.,* pp. 16–17, 14.
[77] Cf. *infra,* p. 319, note 16.

distinctive quality of the theory that rationalized them lay in its relation to the newer doctrines of political democracy. It is interesting that the classic anti-charter ideology was as vigorously developed in labor polemics as in any other aspect of the literature of the time. It is in such periodicals as the *Mechanics Free Press*, published in Philadelphia during the twenties and thirties, and in pamphlets such as Stephen Simpson's *Workingman's Manual*, that we find the campaign against "monopolies" and the defense of "individual enterprise" developed most forcefully. And the bias against governmental action, which appears so deceptively on the surface of the anti-charter dogma, was there in equal strength. Witness Simpson's tireless denunciation of "government, unjust, despotic, proud, all-grasping government." [78]

Was it inconsistent, then, for labor writers to campaign for governmental action in their own behalf? One is reminded at once of the way in which the anti-charter ideology fused with the theory of public ownership. But from a logical point of view, could that ideology merge so easily with a defense of labor legislation? Since the anti-charter doctrine insisted that charter grants represented a species of class legislation which impaired the sovereignty of the people, it could easily unite with a defense of state enterprise which represented the public as a whole. But was not labor legislation as clearly designed to favor a single group as any involved in corporate policy? Was it not too a kind of class legislation? It could easily be contended that the enactment of labor measures was necessary to counteract the disparities produced by the charter program.[79] But a more remarkable bridge was built between anti-charterism and pro-labor doctrine, which made the latter similar in some respects to the idea of public ownership. The laborers identified themselves with the only legitimate members of the community.[80] Hence they were able to argue that measures in their behalf were unsullied by class implications, served the mass interest, and were a logical corollary of anti-charter principles.

---

[78] *Workingman's Manual*, p. 9.
[79] *Mechanics Free Press*, June 21, Sept. 20, 1828; Nov. 14, 1829.
[80] *Ibid.*, May 31, 1828; June 21, Mar. 28, May 30, 1829.

This sounds like the sheerest propaganda. But it reflected in fact a genuine bias among organized laborers. As markets expanded and the factory system appeared, workers failed persistently to grasp the legitimacy of the functions that the new merchant, banking, and entrepreneurial groups were performing. Their thinking was wedded to an older period governed by a simple master-workman relation in which both employer and employee performed pretty much the same type of labor. The new groups of managers and middlemen, who were becoming increasingly remote from the actual productive process, appeared in their eyes as parasites. It is not surprising that the anti-bank theory of the workers was the most radical in the whole of Pennsylvania's literature of reform. They were impelled to elaborate, as a central tenet of their doctrine, a criticism of parasitic economic behavior. "According to the order of nature," wrote Simpson, "whose unalterable laws never can be violated with impunity; and which serve as the infallible criterion of justice no man is born for sloth, and none can be slothful without bringing the pain of punishment upon themselves, or upon society." [81]

The labor synthesis becomes clearer when we examine certain more specific points of the doctrine involved. Simpson was of course ready to agree with Adam Smith that the joint-stock company was undesirable,[82] but despite his fiery denunciations of government in that connection, he was unwilling to concur with the central premises of Smith's system. And, significantly enough, the reason he was unwilling to do so lay in his belief that Smith had failed to include in his system an adequate appreciation of natural law. This was in striking contrast to the views of Franklin or Webster who found in classical economics the logical and complete extension of the nature concept into the economic field. Simpson was preoccupied with the "natural justice" aspects of natural law, and that preoccupation led him to substitute Jefferson for Smith as his master in social thought.[83] For the workers, the Jeffersonian state of nature was not merely a place where men

---

[81] Simpson, *Workingman's Manual*, p. 56.
[82] *Ibid.*, p. 12 and *passim*.
[83] *Ibid.*, p. 47.

were free and equal politically; it was a place where certain economic equalities existed as well. "Laborers, servants, menials, slaves, awake!" declared a labor manifesto in 1828, "Know that the God of Nature has provided ample means for your comfortable subsistence — that it has been wrested from you by the usurping tyranny of man." [84] As for the "general contract" by which governments were created, it was evident that it called for "legislative protection" of the "interests of the labourer" as well as for periodical elections and popular sovereignty.[85]

One of the most important principles flowing from this interpretation of the nature concept was the principle that every person in the community had a right to a reasonable subsistence standard. This principle sharply contradicted the notion that the wages of labor should be determined by the uncontrolled play of supply and demand. Few complaints were stronger than the one raised against the idea that "labour is strictly a commodity, being as much an article of commerce as woolen, cotton or yarn." [86] It was in answer to this idea that Simpson put forth the "happiness of man" [87] as the principle by which wage scales should be determined.

The workers' criticism in this connection became more specific with the growth of factories and labor-saving machinery. Actually, because markets were constantly broadening, technological factors were not responsible in any but a transitory way for unemployment during this period. This fact was pointed out with reference to the textile manufacture by the Peltz Committee in the House.[88] But the fear of technological unemployment began to grow, particularly as machinery invaded old trades where long years of apprenticeship had been served and where unionism was comparatively strong. The notion developed that a worker had a vested right in his job, and hence an equal claim with the em-

[84] *Mechanics Free Press*, Aug. 23, 1828. See also resolution of factory workers in strikes of 1848, *Public Ledger*, July 6, 1848. For the use of natural law by labor in Massachusetts, see Hartz, "Seth Luther: Working Class Rebel," *New England Quarterly*, XIII (1940), 410 ff.
[85] *Mechanics Free Press*, Sept. 20, 1828. See also issues of Sept. 27, June 7, Apr. 3, 1828.
[86] *Ibid.*, May 30, 1829.
[87] *Workingman's Manual*, p. 46 ff.   [88] *Senate Journal*, 1837–38, I, 322–27.

ployer upon profits accruing from the new machinery. His claim was compared to that of the landholder upon the state when his land was appropriated for the construction of public works. "The art, trade, and mystery of a mechanic, for the attainment of which he has served five, seven, or nine years, and with which by personal industry he ought to be enabled to make a comfortable living, is as much his property, and calls as loudly for protection, and much more so in justice than does the landed property of the farmer, or the habitation of the citizen." [89] But the laborers were contending for more than the simple right to work. If their claim upon the profits of the new machinery was equal with that of the employer, certain implications naturally flowed from it regarding hours, working conditions, and wages as well. The effects of machinery "ought to be *diminished exertion and increased remuneration.*" [90] It was on this idea that much of the criticism of factory conditions was based.

The right-to-work idea was not a creation of this epoch. In French thought it reached back to the Revolutionary constitution of 1789 and it had been elaborated by such socialist thinkers as Fourier. But the workers were a property-conscious group, and it was a native heritage of thought to which they appealed. This is demonstrated to some extent by the way in which doctrines favoring the extension of the public school system and doctrines favoring factory legislation were blended. It would be hard to exaggerate the faith which the workers of this period placed in the achievement of free public education. Few doubted that it would by itself virtually effect a revolution in social conditions.[91]

[89] *Mechanics Free Press*, Mar. 28, 1829. See also *ibid.*, Sept. 26, 27, 1828, Apr. 18, 1829.

[90] *Ibid.*, Nov. 27, 1829. "Since the introduction into common use of scientific inventions and improvements has enabled a given quantity of manual labor to produce fifty, in some instances perhaps an hundred fold more of wealth than the same labor would have produced previous to their introduction; and since in consequence of them, all the markets in the world are overflowing with wealth of every description, insomuch that the demand for productive labor is rapidly decreasing, and productive employment growing every day more difficult to be obtained, we have a right to expect, from OUR REPRESENTATIVES, sufficient of such NEW INSTITUTIONS as will enable us to retain in our hands a due and equitable proportion of the products of our own labor. . . ." *Ibid.*, June 21, 1828.

[91] Cf. *ibid.*, Oct. 25, Nov. 21, 22, 1828; Aug. 28, July 25, July 18, Jan. 24, 1829. The legislative attitude is admirably revealed in a report by the House Committee

The educational movement was linked integrally to the prevailing democratic theory: education was indispensable to the survival of popular government, a public system was therefore another of man's "natural rights," and charity schools inflicted a "stigma" which was a clear violation of them.[92] In this way the educational argument from natural law merged with the economic expression of that idea to rationalize factory legislation. As far as child labor was concerned, governmental action involved not only the worker's natural right to his job or his claim upon the leisure and profits made possible by the new machinery, but it involved as well the larger issue of the continuation of a democratic political system. Witnesses called before the Senate committee of 1837–1838 emphasized this belief abundantly. One of them, a school teacher, declared that under existing conditions factory children would be unlikely to "discern, understand, and discharge the duties devolving on them as members of the Social Compact."[93]

The way in which the educational and factory questions were mingled is interestingly illustrated in *An Exposition of the System of Moral and of Mental Labor Established . . . at Dyottville*, a pamphlet published by Dr. T. W. Dyott some four years before the Peltz investigation was undertaken.[94] Dyott had built a glass factory in which he had provided teachers, residence halls, and doctors for the children whom he employed, combining work with education and thus producing "contented labor."[95] The education which he conferred upon his employees was not "of the highest class of scientific refinement," but such education would be harmful, since it would make the young workers dissatisfied with their lot. Dyott endeavored to cultivate their minds to "a certain practical point," and he presented an extensive argument to prove that such a scheme could be undertaken by private entrepreneurs without damaging losses.[96] This was a remarkable combination

---

on Education on manual labor academies launched by colleges at Gettysburg and Easton. See *House Journal, 1832–33*, II, 562 ff. See also *Pa. Archives*, 4th, VI, 126.

[92] Cf. Tyson, *Social and Moral Influences of the Revolution*, pp. 7, 27, 28; *Hazard's Register*, XIV (1834), 65; XVI (1835), 391; XIII (1834), 41–44, 97; XI (1833), 145; *Mechanics Free Press*, Dec. 12, 1829.

[93] *Senate Journal, 1837–38*, II, 314.

[94] Philadelphia, 1833.

[95] Dyott, *Labor at Dyottville*, p. 45.   [96] *Ibid.*, pp. 35–37.

of business paternalism, reform righteousness, and prevalent labor theories. But at bottom, as Dyott himself admitted, it was an effort to justify the introduction of the factory system against the criticisms that were being leveled against it.[97] Though it appears to have encouraged the legislature in its interest in the factory question,[98] Dyott's plan was, by the middle thirties, pretty much of an anachronism in Pennsylvania thought. For the reliance upon factory owners in the provision of education, which had also been part of the Richards proposal of 1824, was fast disappearing. The movement for universal education was taking the matter out of the hands of individuals and putting it into the hands of the state.[99]

It has been said that "laissez-faire notions of the wrong of state interference" produced a considerable hostility toward labor legislation during this period in Pennsylvania.[100] Yet the evidence reveals little of such philosophic thought. When in 1848 the factory owners issued their argument against the law abolishing child labor and limiting hours, they attacked the measure on various grounds but they did not once deny that its enactment was within the rightful sphere of governmental power. There were no assertions, such as appeared in the latter phases of the public works argument, that the measure was a "sin against first principles." Nor does it ever appear to have been challenged in the courts, despite the bitter antagonisms it evoked, as an unconstitutional invasion of individual rights either to property or to liberty of contract. The absence of the constitutional challenge as far as the 1848 measure is concerned cannot be attributed to the fact that that measure included a proviso permitting special contracts between employer and employee. For no legal chal-

---

[97] Dyott asserted that he was presenting a "*seminal* principle, which at once obviates all objections on the score of humanity, feeling, and policy, against the introduction and establishment of every variety of manufacturing industry." *Ibid.*, p. 37.

[98] A committee of the legislature, headed by John Sergeant, was appointed to investigate the Dyott establishment, and returned a favorable report which appears in *ibid.*, pp. 44–45.

[99] See Wickersham, *Education in Pa.*, pp. 290–338. Six years after his pamphlet had been published Dyott was sentenced to from one to seven years at hard labor in solitary confinement because of fraudulent financial dealings. *Highly Interesting Trial of Dyott.*

[100] Sumner, *Child Labor Legislation in U.S.*, p. 71.

lenges appear to have occurred, either, in connection with the measures of 1849 and 1855 which did not embody such a proviso. The *Post*, in urging a repeal of the clause, asserted that the constitutionality of such an action "cannot be doubted." [101] It maintained that the legislature had power to protect people against the consequences of their own acts. But to infer from these remarks that the constitutional issue was of great importance in popular discussion during the controversy of 1848 would be erroneous. All of the available evidence indicates that the labor regulations were pretty universally accepted, in line with the *Post's* reasoning, as within the legitimate area of governmental authority.

This fact becomes even clearer upon an examination of the report of the Peltz Committee in 1837. In recommending governmental action to limit child labor and working hours, the committee made it a point to answer various arguments which had been presented against such a measure. It denied that the measure would lessen the productivity of factories, it denied that it would seriously handicap Pennsylvania manufacturers in competition with manufacturers of other states, and it replied to other contentions of a similar kind.[102] But it did not feel called upon even to mention the question whether such action was within the rightful realm of state power, much less to enter into a defense of the measure in that connection. The absence of this consideration characterizes also the testimony of all witnesses who were called before the committee, and those witnesses came from various classes of the community.[103] The entire discussion, both in the hearings and in the report, proceeds upon the assumption that it was universally recognized that the state, if it so desired, might regulate hours and working conditions in factories.

The fact is that "laissez-faire notions" had little to do with the attitude of Pennsylvania toward factory legislation during this period. There was, it is true, considerable opposition to that legislation; there were a few instances, even, when "the spirit of

---

[101] See *Pittsburgh Morning Post*, July 6, 1848.
[102] *Senate Journal, 1837–38*, I, 322–27.
[103] *Ibid.*, II, 278–359.

our government" [104] was invoked against it, and in 1830 some Pennsylvania employers appear to have maintained that a national act by Congress shortening hours in factories would be "an infringement upon the rights of the people." [105] But even the latter contention, one which, in a subsequent era, would be taken as a commonplace, was rarely presented. When the pattern of thought is viewed as a whole, such utterances are of marginal significance.

The opposition relied almost entirely upon denials of the expediency and the practicability of factory control. Thus one of the most important considerations advanced against legislative action was the fear that it would retard the growth of manufactures.[106] It was contended that regulatory action would undo the work of the state's promotive policy in the manufacturing field. Such arguments, called by the Peltz Committee "the strongest objections" [107] leveled against the curtailment of hours, focused on the issue of competition with manufacturers in other states. Pennsylvania employers contended that if hours legislation was passed they would be unable to withstand the competition of New England where a twelve-hour day was common, or the competition of the South, where slave labor could be utilized.[108] Certain proprietors, testifying before the Peltz Committee in 1837, opposed state hours regulation, but declared that they were heartily in favor of regulation on a national scale, and recommended that Pennsylvania take the lead in securing it, even if an amendment to the Constitution should be necessary for that purpose.[109]

It is interesting that the demand of some employers for uni-

[104] *Harrisburg Reporter and Legislative Union*, Feb. 1, 1826, quoted in Barnard, *Factory Legislation in Pa.*, p. 4.
[105] *Mechanics Free Press*, Aug. 21, 1830.
[106] *Pittsburgh Morning Post*, July 6, 1848; *Senate Journal, 1837-38*, I, 322-27.
[107] *Ibid.*, II, 304-307.
[108] One of the resolutions passed by the factory owners in 1848 was: "That the extensive and enterprising competition in various States of the Union, in producing coarse cotton goods, has reduced the business to an estimated and small profit, and that, whilst other manufacturing establishments, both in the free and slave States are untrammeled in the hours of their labor, any attempts on the part of Pennsylvania ALONE to reduce the hours of labor would have a most destructive tendency on a great, growing and important branch of industry, conducive alike to the comfort and prosperity of our Commonwealth. *Pittsburgh Morning Post*, Aug. 4, 1848.
[109] *Senate Journal, 1837-38*, II, 324.

formity of labor practices throughout the country was paralleled by a similar demand for uniformity within the state, and that the latter sometimes led to a desire on the part of employers themselves for the use of governmental authority. Proprietors presenting this view argued that they were placed at a disadvantage by the enforcement by competitors of labor conditions harsher than those they enforced; one of them favored the appointment of a state superintendent of factories to secure a greater degree of standardization.[110] Opposition to hours legislation was also motivated by a fear that action by the state would result in a lowering of wages. The fact that parents of child workers did not ordinarily participate in the drive for shorter hours was attributed by some to a belief that this campaign would bring reduced earnings for children.[111] While it had no desire to soothe the feelings of parents who exploited children in factories, the Peltz Committee replied with vigor to the general contention that legislation would reduce earnings or output, arguing that better conditions would greatly enhance the productivity of workers.[112]

In seeking, then, to evaluate the part played by the newer democratic ideas in the struggle over labor legislation, the evidence seems plain that those ideas were utilized far more widely by the champions of legislation than by those who opposed it. Employer groups developed no philosophy comparable to the elaborate doctrine, based on natural law, social contract, and individual right, advanced by the labor movement. Nor should this seem odd. For two centuries regulatory action in the labor field had been accepted as a normal and legitimate function of the state. Why should the democratic principles require the liquidation of so ancient a tradition? It is not hard to understand why the expediency of a measure, rather than the right of the state to enact it, seemed much the most meaningful basis for opposition. Yet in the fields of mixed enterprise investment and public works the democratic ideas were discovered during the later period as weapons for undermining the legitimacy of state action. Why was not the same comprehensive discovery made by factory proprie-

[110] *Ibid.*, II, 304–307.
[111] *Ibid.*
[112] *Ibid.*, I, 322–27.

tors during the forties and fifties? Quite apart from relevant differences in the organization of economic interests in these instances which I shall later discuss,[113] two things must be remembered in answering this question. One is the fact that neither the mixed enterprise nor public works policies, emerging after the Revolution, was so deeply entrenched as the state function of labor regulation which extended back to the earliest years of the colonial era. Another is the fact that the oppressive character of factory measures was not nearly so great as the statute book might suggest. When employers discovered that those measures could be violated with comparative impunity, the need for revolutionary doctrinal creations to oppose them was bound to seem less pressing. Here, as elsewhere, much of the meaning of state policy and the ideas which surrounded it, is likely to be found in the record of its administration.

4. *The Control of Economic Practice: Licensing and Prohibition*

"It is the duty and interest of all governments," asserted a Pennsylvania statute of 1781, "to prevent fraud, and promote the interests of just and useful commerce." [114] The colonial tradition of licensing, inspection, and similar regulations was maintained steadily from the Revolution to the Civil War and was in certain instances appreciably expanded. Inspection policy was most heavily emphasized in connection with articles produced for export, since the reputation of Pennsylvania merchants in interstate commerce depended upon it.[115] A legislative committee laid down the following criteria for determining whether an article should be made subject to inspection: "If the article is either entirely or chiefly consumed at home, the expediency of requiring an inspection is in all cases doubtful. If it forms an important item of export, a well regulated inspection is productive of benefit, by preventing the exportation of inferior descriptions of the same article, and thus giving it a character in foreign markets." [116]

[113] See *infra*, p. 319.
[114] *Dallas' Laws*, I, 883–89.
[115] Cf. *House Journal, 1832–33*, II, 456. See also remarks of Justice Sergeant, *Adams v. Rogers*, 9 Watts 121, 122 (1839).
[116] *House Journal, 1832–33*, II, 456. See also *ibid., 1833–34*, II, 547.

THE CONTROL OF ECONOMIC PRACTICE   205

The inspection program included such articles as flour,[117] fish,[118] beef, pork, hogslard, flaxseed, butter, biscuits,[119] harness and leather,[120] tobacco,[121] shingles,[122] potash and pearlash,[123] staves, heading and lumber,[124] ground black-oak bark,[125] pickled fish,[126] spirituous liquors,[127] and gunpowder.[128] An act of 1835, which codified previous inspection measures, laid down for each commodity detailed regulations concerning packing, dimensions of containers, brand marks of dealers, and inspection methods and markings.[129] Administration of the inspection program appears

[117] *Dallas' Laws*, I, 883–89; II, 2–3; II, 226–28; II, 713–16; III, 774–75; IV, 224–25; *Pa. Laws, 1796–1801*, pp. 607–609; *1810–11*, p. 46; *1824–25*, pp. 213–16; *1830–31*, p. 47.

[118] *Dallas' Laws*, II, 491–92; *Pa. Laws, 1809–10*, pp. 128–31; *1817–18*, pp. 111–14; *1860*, pp. 287–90.

[119] *Dallas' Laws*, II, 671–76, 727–28; *Pa. Laws, 1803–1804*, pp. 5–7; *1813–14*, pp. 173–76; *1827–28*, pp. 117–18.

[120] *Ibid., 1843*, pp. 133–37.

[121] *Ibid., 1831–32*, pp. 58–59; *1833–34*, p. 179. See also *House Journal, 1830–31*, II, 864. There was some criticism of the tobacco inspection policy on the ground that it led tobacco exporters to use other ports than Philadelphia. *Ibid., 1833–34*, II, 555–56.

[122] *Dallas' Laws*, II, 738–40.

[123] *Ibid.*, II, 765–68; *Pa. Laws, 1826–27*, pp. 45–49.

[124] *Dallas' Laws*, II, 797–99; *Pa. Laws, 1801–1803*, p. 573.

[125] *Ibid., 1803–1804*, pp. 499–503; *1807–1808*, p. 160; *1811–12*, p. 248.

[126] *Ibid., 1860*, pp. 287–90.

[127] *Ibid., 1813–14*, pp. 100–104; *1814–15*, pp. 171–73. See also *House Journal, 1807–1808*, I, 258.

[128] *Dallas' Laws*, III, 764–69; *Pa. Laws, 1801–1803*, pp. 127–29.

[129] *Ibid., 1834–35*, pp. 384–424; *House Journal, 1833–34*, II, 750. In case of disagreement between owner and inspector, disinterested "triers" were to be appointed by any justice of the peace or alderman to determine the issue, and if a decision was rendered in favor of the owner, a penalty was levied on the inspector. In certain earlier inspection laws, if judgment of the inspector was sustained by the "triers," the owner had to pay a fee for each container judged not merchantable; if not, then the inspector had to pay all costs. Cf. *Dallas' Laws*, I, 883–89. In earlier inspection laws also enforcement of penal provisions was left, as in the case of labor legislation, to the initiative of private individuals. For example, in an early act regulating the inspection of butter intended for exportation, one-half of the penalty imposed for the use of kegs other than those prescribed by law or of less than the required weight went to the informer, and one-half to the inspector for state use. *Pa. Laws, 1803–1804*, pp. 5–7. Some court litigation arose in connection with the interpretation of certain of the inspection laws. Cf. *Garrigues v. Reynolds*, 6 Binney 330 (1814). A supplement to the general inspection law excepted from inspection flour or meal shipped on the Delaware and Susquehanna rivers and bound for a place out of the state, but within the country. For an interpretation of this supplement and the word "exportation," see *Commonwealth v. King*, 1 Wharton 448 (1836). A problem arose concerning goods shipped into Pennsylvania from other

in many cases to have been shoddy, particularly during the period before 1835 when a multiplicity of laws rendered requirements ambiguous.[130]

Inspection was only one aspect of a varied policy pattern, ramifying into remote corners of business procedure. Despite the criticism of wartime price-fixing measures by the Council of Censors in 1789, the price-fixing objective was reflected during the post-Revolutionary period in legislation governing the services of porters, carters, wagoners, draymen, and wood sawyers. And when such measures gradually fell into the dead-letter category, the same objective persisted in regulations governing certain of the newer corporate enterprises.[131] The enforcement by cities of safety measures affecting business activity,[132] the enactment of laws to strike at fraudulent practices which emerged with the growth of manufacturing,[133] the comprehensive reconstruction of licensing policy — all were parts of the continuous job of adapting an old regulatory function to new circumstances. Licensing governed a variety of businessmen, e.g., inn-keepers,[134] ped-

---

places but intended for exportation. Cf. *Pa. Laws, 1830–31*, p. 47. For an excellent presentation of the inspection program in Philadelphia, see *House Journal, 1845*, II, 483.

[130] *Pa. Archives*, 4th, VI, 197; *House Journal, 1803–1804*, p. 730.

[131] *Dallas' Laws*, II, 210–12; II, 654–70; IV, 153–54. The price-fixing objective was prominent in an inspection measure of 1815 which penalized wagoners for receiving money from any person "as an inducement for selling any whiskey or flour, under the market price of the day, and not make return thereof to the proper owner of such whiskey or flour." *Pa. Laws, 1814–15*, pp. 171–73. See also *infra.*, p. 291.

[132] *Dallas' Laws*, III, 771–72.

[133] *Pa. Laws, 1850*, pp. 450–52; *1853*, pp. 643–45. A measure of 1855 penalized the use of false stamps, labels, and trade marks for the purpose of deceit in trade. *Ibid., 1855*, p. 514.

[134] An act of 1786 "for the prevention of vice and immorality, and of unlawful gaming, and to restrain disorderly sports and dissipation," provided for the annual licensing of all keepers of inns, taverns, and public houses by the Supreme Executive Council, and for the revocation of licenses in case of violation of the regulations included in the act. The justices of the peace at their first annual meeting were given the discretionary power to determine the number of taverns which might be licensed for the following year, having "regard to the particular neighborhoods and situations, the most suitable for the accommodation of inhabitants and travellers." *Dallas' Laws*, II, 474–81. A law of 1830 prohibited the licensing of taverns beyond the actual requirements of public use, and provided that no license was to be granted unless the applicant was recommended as to honesty and temperance by at least twelve reputable citizens. The enforcement of these provisions was left with the

THE CONTROL OF ECONOMIC PRACTICE 207

dlers,[135] retailers of foreign goods, [136] liquor merchants,[137] brokers of various kinds, [138] wharfage pilots, [139] and auctioneers. [140] Motivated until the twenties by police purposes, licensing policy gradually was transformed into an important source of state revenue as well, and fees in certain cases were made proportionate to the sale volume of businesses.[141] Whether it was in connection with any of these policies, or in connection with the fixing of weight-and-measure standards which, because of federal inaction, the state was compelled to undertake,[142] the objectives of government were pervasive and they played a daily part in the activities of businessmen.

An examination of the argument produced by the liquor trade will help to illuminate attitudes toward the type of policy discussed above. Though that trade represented but one area in

---

guardians of the poor who were charged with reporting all violations. *Pa. Laws, 1829-30*, pp. 352-55. In 1834 additional licensing requirements were laid down, among which was one forbidding the extension of credit to anyone for the purchase of liquor. *Ibid., 1833-34*, pp. 117-23. See also *ibid., 1814-15*, p. 91; *1840-41*, pp. 121-22; *1859*, pp. 653-54.

[135] A measure of 1784 required peddlers or hawkers to obtain a yearly license from the president or vice-president of the Executive Council after the justices of the county court had certified their honesty. Bond was required. In order to encourage state industry, peddlers were forbidden to sell outstate products except at fixed intervals. Enforcement of these requirements was left to any individuals who cared to bring suit in cases of violation, their reward being one-half of the penalty involved. *Dallas' Laws*, II, 191-93. Subsequently the categories of persons who might be licensed as peddlers were sharply limited, and the licensing authority given to the Courts of Quarter Sessions. *Ibid.*, IV, 372-73; *Pa. Laws, 1829-30*, pp. 147-48; *1817-18*, pp. 302-303; *1829-30*, pp. 39-40.

[136] *Ibid., 1829-30*, pp. 387-92. Enforcement of this measure depended on county treasurers who were authorized to bring suit against delinquents. Their basis of information was made up of annual lists which constables were directed to provide to the courts. *Ibid.*

[137] *Ibid., 1829-30*, pp. 387-92.

[138] Stock brokers, exchange brokers, and bill brokers were made subject to annual licensing in 1841. *Ibid., 1841*, pp. 396-400. Eight years later merchandise and real estate brokers were brought under the licensing provisions. *Ibid., 1849*, pp. 570-77.

[139] *Dallas' Laws*, II, 606-28; III, 422-35; IV, 424-26; *Pa. Laws, 1801-1803*, pp. 542-67.

[140] *Dallas' Laws*, II, 55, note z.   [141] *Pa. Laws, 1829-30*, pp. 387-92.

[142] *Dallas' Laws*, II, 392-94, 582-83; *Pa. Laws, 1816-17*, pp. 92-93; *1817-18*, p. 182; *1818-19*, pp. 150-51; *1821-22*, pp. 139-40, 149-50; *1826-27*, pp. 41-42; *1847*, pp. 51-52; *1859*, p. 610. See also *Evans v. Myers*, 25 Pa. St. Rep. 114 (1855); *Pa. Archives*, 4th, VI, 330.

which the state's licensing program operated, the temperance movement of the time called forth a notable debate concerning the legitimate sphere of state action in economic life. With the outbreak of the Revolution, the supply of foreign liquor was cut off, and a boom got under way which quickly multiplied the number of distilleries in the state.[143] Concomitant with this expansion, however, there appeared a widening sentiment for more stringent regulatory action than licensing policy had hitherto afforded. Anthony Benezet maintained: (1) that the newly expanded distilling industry was utilizing grain that was badly needed by the army; (2) that the consumption of liquor reduced efficiency in production; and (3) that the liquor trade violated Christian precepts.[144] Benezet's first point was most compelling. The need for grain was felt with increasing severity, and in 1779 the assembly outlawed distilleries completely in most sections of the state.[145]

The ban was lifted after the Revolution, however, and until about 1840 the temperance forces concentrated their efforts once again upon making the licensing program more stringent. The religiosity of the temperance crusade is a familiar phenomenon of the time, and it is unnecessary to enter into a discussion of it here.[146] It is important to remark, however, upon the way in which Benezet's earlier fusion of the morality and the productivity arguments was now elaborated. It had been a common practice among certain employers to compensate workers partly in liquor. This practice was most popular among farmers, but it also prevailed in the industrial trades, largely on the assumption that liquor served as a stimulant to work.[147] With the specialization of industry, particularly with the increase of dangerous work in mining, it became clear that employers must not only give up this practice, but must try to keep liquor as far away from indus-

---

[143] Duffield, *Spirituous Liquors*, p. 22.

[144] Benezet, *Spirituous Liquors*.

[145] *Statutes at Large*, IX, 297–99.

[146] See Cherrington, *Evolution of Prohibition*, pp. 74–162. For an excellent discussion of the temperance movement in Pennsylvania, see Martin, "Temperance Movement," *Pa. Mag. of Hist. and Biog.*, XLIX (1925), 196 ff.

[147] Cf. Pa. Society for Discouraging Use of Spirits, *Third Report*, p. 10; Watson, *Use of Distilled Liquors*, pp. 10–15.

trial premises as possible.[148] The first trade association to take definite action in this regard appears to have been the Master Paper-Makers who in 1805 not only abolished the liquor "ration" but completely prohibited the use of liquor in mills.[149] Revelations of harsh conditions in factories in the thirties and forties coincided with a renewed emphasis upon the idea that laborers exposed "to heat and vapour in their daily work" escaped "most of the diseases which were considered the unavoidable consequence of their occupations" if they were freed from the alcoholic curse.[150] The result was that not only various employer groups, but organized labor as well,[151] came to the support of temperance crusaders. The crusaders were soon well-organized. Meeting on a state-wide basis in 1831,[152] organizing themselves into a permanent state association in 1834,[153] they began besieging the legislature for new laws [154] and the courts for more stringent enforcement of licensing provisions.[155]

The forties brought important developments in the anti-liquor movement. In the first place, industries had developed to a point where the employer interest made itself felt in the legislature apart from organized temperance societies. Operators of mines frequently petitioned the legislature for the enactment of laws creating partial or total temperance zones around their establishments. Thus, between 1846 and 1860, a series of measures were passed that forbade the sale of intoxicating liquor in quantities of less than thirty gallons to individuals within three miles of certain coal and iron mines in Armstrong, Clarion, Luzerne, and Carbon counties.[156] Beginning in 1846, also, local-option provisions were

[148] *Ibid.*, pp. 10–11.
[149] *Ibid.*, pp. 12–15; Duffield, *Spirituous Liquors*, 26.
[150] Pa. Society for Discouraging Use of Spirits, *Third Report*, p. 12. The society declared: "The vice of the operative reflects on the master," and it urged all employers to discharge workmen guilty of intemperance. *Ibid.*, p. 45. See also *Extracts from Rush's Inquiry into Ardent Spirits*, pp. 5–6; Philadelphia Medical Society, *Report of Committee on Ardent Spirits*.
[151] Cf. *Mechanics Free Press*, Mar. 28, 1829.
[152] Pa. Society for Discouraging Use of Ardent Spirits, *Third Report*, p. 16.
[153] Pa. Temperance Society, *Fifth Anniversary Report*, p. 6.
[154] *Ibid.*, pp. 4, 15.
[155] *Ibid.*; *Democratic Union*, Feb. 21, Mar. 9, 1844.
[156] See on this whole topic the excellent study of Martin, "Temperance Movement in Pa. Prior to the Civil War," *Pa. Mag. of Hist. and Biog.*, XLIX (1925),

obtained by various counties.[157] Yet action on an even larger scale was taking place in other parts of the Union, and the Pennsylvania reformers were inspired by it. Not long after the passage of the statewide prohibition act in Maine in 1851, they sought to force a similar measure through the Pennsylvania legislature.[158]

The clergy appear to have been widely organized behind the prohibition movement; one polemicist declared that "a body of certain clergy were in constant lobbying attendance at the legislature."[159] The clerical tinge of the prohibition drive became so pronounced, in fact, that some pro-liquor advocates asserted that the enactment of prohibition would restore theocracy in Pennsylvania.[160] Immigrants, particularly the German population, were by and large in opposition. Liquor dealers appear to have organized thoroughly for the first time when the movement for statewide prohibition got under way. Geographically, there was a rural-urban split: large cities normally favored the prohibition measure, while rural regions normally opposed it.[161] This was a somewhat curious alignment, for the traditional assumption in American political history is that it is the rural areas which push through morality legislation against the opposition of the urban areas, and certainly that has been the case in the modern history of prohibition. But the rural-urban alignment in Pennsylvania during the fifties was not without its economic logic. The shipment of grain in the form of liquor was much less expensive, and in an era when transportation facilities were often poor this was not an unimportant factor. Urban populations, on the other hand, paid higher prices for foodstuffs as a result of the demand for grain by distilleries.

The anti-liquor forces introduced a bill in the legislature which

---

212ff. Cf. *Pa. Laws, 1846*, p. 431; *1847*, pp. 430–31; *1851*, p. 548; *1852*, p. 587; *Miner's Journal*, May 19, 1848.

[157] *Pa. Laws, 1846*, pp. 431–32.

[158] Cf. G. Graham, *Speech before Temperance Circle*, p. 4. See also *Hunt's Merchants' Mag.*, XXX (1854), 416 ff., 703–709; State Prohibitory Committee, *Address*, p. 15; *Truth Vindicated*, p. 3; Price, *Speech on Sale of Liquors*.

[159] *Few Reasons Why "Maine Liquor Law" Should Not Be Passed in Pa.*

[160] Cf. Graf, *Temperance Question*; *Few Reasons Why "Maine Liquor Law" Should Not Be Passed in Pa.*, p. 7.

[161] *Harrisburg Morning Herald*, Sept. 23, 1854.

called for total prohibition along the following lines: the prohibition of the private manufacture and sale of liquor; the creation of governmental agencies for its purchase and sale for restricted purposes; the enforcement of the measure by state agents endowed with powers of search and seizure. In order to prevent the passage of this bill, an alternative measure was enacted that submitted the prohibition question to popular vote.[162] After weeks of passionate controversy, a plebiscite was held in 1854.[163] The temperance crusaders were defeated by 5,178 votes, and the back of the prohibition movement was broken.[164]

Before the prohibition struggle, little attention was paid to the argument that liquor interests represented an industry that the state could not restrict without seriously weakening its economic position. With the initiation of the prohibition campaign, however, this contention became "the most powerful argument against prohibition." [165] A Lancaster publicist drew a distinction between Pennsylvania and other states that had enacted or were about to enact laws suppressing the liquor traffic. He pointed out that Maine and several of the eastern states produced little more grain than they required for domestic consumption, while Pennsylvania produced a surplus which depended upon the distilling industry for its outlet. Since the maintenance of such an industry in other states involved a steady importation of grain and hence a "constant drain on their resources," the enactment of prohibition by their legislatures was less a matter of "extreme morality" than it was a matter of "policy and interest." But, by the same logic, the brewing industry should be fostered in Penn-

[162] *House Journal, 1854*, pp. 48 ff.
[163] *Ibid., 1855*, p. 23.
[164] State Prohibitory Committee, *Address*, pp. 3, 6, 9. See also *American Quarterly Temperance Magazine*, May 1833; *Permanent Temperance Documents*, p. 185. "The bulk of the liquor vote was given by Berks, Bucks, Lancaster, Lebanon, Lehigh, Montgomery, Northampton, Schuylkill, and York counties. In all of these the population is largely German, except in Schuylkill, where it is Irish and Catholic. . . . Nearly all our large towns and cities have voted for the law, while the vote against it, comes from the rural districts." State Prohibitory Committee, *Address*, p. 9. Cf. *Miner's Journal*, Dec. 2, 1854; Martin, "Temperance Movement in Pa. Prior to the Civil War," *Pa. Mag. of Hist. and Biog.*, XLIX (1925), 219.
[165] *Few Reasons Why "Maine Liquor Law" Should Not be Passed in Pa.*, p. 9. For a discussion of Pennsylvania investments in the liquor trade, see *Hunt's Merchants' Mag.*, XXII (1850), 333.

sylvania. It supplied not only a domestic but an outstate market as well: Philadelphia brewers had recently opened up a growing trade with the South; brewers in Pittsburgh were exporting liquors to the West. To cut off this trade at a time when Pennsylvania merchants were competing for the southern and western trade, and when legislative assistance in various ways had been given them in that competition, would be unreasonable. Moreover farmers in the interior relied upon distilleries as markets; freight rates were frequently so high as to prevent grain from reaching larger markets in any but manufactured form. The foreign demand for Pennsylvania grain was only at rare times sufficient to make up for the losses that prohibition would involve. Corn was the leading crop of the state, and corn was not shipped in great quantities to foreign countries. Farmers would have to turn to wheat, but the flour market was already glutted. Livestock would not be an adequate substitute because of the comparatively low prices it brought.[166]

The prohibition forces replied that the capital invested in the liquor trade was not only morally lost at the outset but resulted in heavy financial losses to the community owing to state care for the derelicts which intemperance produced.[167] They asserted, also, that the money put into the distilling industries could be employed profitably elsewhere,[168] and pointed to the earlier abolition of slavery as evidence that state prohibitory action need not involve heavy economic damage.[169]

A second bone of contention regarding the expediency of prohibition centered about the licensing system. There was a remarkable shift of positions here. While there had been some opposition to the earlier crusade of the temperance forces to streamline the licensing process, the defenders of the liquor interest, now faced with a militant sentiment in favor of prohibition, were glad to fall back on alternative proposals which called for a more stringent

[166] *Few Reasons Why "Maine Liquor Law" Should Not Be Passed in Pa.*, pp. 10-12.
[167] *Tavern Keepers versus the License System*, p. 7.
[168] Coombs, *Appeal to Voters of Pa.*, quoted in *Few Reasons Why "Maine Liquor Law" Should Not Be Passed in Pa.*, p. 9.
[169] *Ibid.*

licensing policy. The anti-liquor groups, on the other hand, now had nothing but contempt for their previous faith in licensing procedures. They discovered that licensing violated certain first principles which only prohibition could satisfy. Albert Barnes, in a widely quoted pamphlet, argued that since the licensing system implicitly sanctioned articles licensed, its use in the liquor field amounted to the "sustaining of evil by law." [170]

The prohibition movement, not only in Pennsylvania but in other states as well, brought forth serious considerations of governmental action from a legalistic point of view. Even before the movement got under way in Pennsylvania, the question of liquor control had come before the federal Supreme Court, and the decision rendered on it had been an important one in defining the sphere of state police power. The power to regulate or even to prohibit had been upheld. But the decision handed down in the *License Cases* in 1847 [171] had been a confused one, and it had dealt only with state power in regard to liquor in interstate traffic. The citation of Taney's opinion, a common practice, was not considered a sufficient answer to the question of legality either by the defenders or the antagonists of prohibition. Moreover the debate in Pennsylvania involved not only the prohibition idea as voted upon in the plebiscite but the measure which the temperance forces had introduced earlier. That measure, it will be remembered, called for the creation of governmental agencies for the purchase and sale of liquor and for state agents endowed with powers of search and seizure. The inclusion of these issues broadened the scope of argument concerning the limits of governmental power.

In the Senate Eli K. Price, a moderate temperance man who refused to accept prohibition, sought to distinguish between the creation of state liquor stores and the "matter of internal police"

---

[170] Barnes, *Throne of Iniquity*, p. 16. See also Price, *Position on Liquor Question*, p. 37.

[171] 5 Howard 504 (1847). Cf. remarks of Governor Pollock on these decisions as they affected the prohibition argument in Pennsylvania. *Pa. Archives*, 4th, VII, 783. See also State Prohibitory Committee, *Address*, p. 5; G. Graham, *Speech before Temperance Circle*, p. 19.

which had been settled by the Supreme Court. While state regulation was justified, entry into the liquor business was "a purpose for which . . . the government was never established." [172] The strength of this type of argument can best be understood if viewed against the background of the current disenchantment with public enterprise in both the mixed corporation and public works fields. There were more specific grounds for opposing the idea of a police force to implement prohibition. It was denounced as violating ancient and "sacred" rights of domicile as well as specific constitutional provisions against unreasonable searches and seizures.[173] Classic symbols were invoked — Magna Charta, the common law, "natural right," "English liberty." The *North American* declared that the idea was "tyrannical beyond any exercise of power known to any restricted government." [174]

Even more important than these arguments, however, was the fundamental contention that investments in the liquor trade represented inalienable property rights which could not be destroyed. This argument must not be confused with the one discussed earlier which held that prohibition was economically inexpedient. In an earlier period, conceivably, the discussion might have ended on the question of expediency. But now prohibition was an "interference with lawful business." [175] The liquor trade was "perfectly legitimate," being recognized as such by the revenue laws of the national government.[176] To destroy it would involve not only a violation of the great Anglo-American mandates of natural law,[177] but the express provision of the state constitution which guaranteed the right of "acquiring, possessing, and protecting property." [178] The fact that the opponents of prohibition had agreed to submit the issue to a popular vote put this argument in a somewhat anomalous position. For if the argument was valid,

---

[172] *Truth Vindicated*, p. 10.
[173] *Speeches in Senate on Liquor Law*, pp. 18, 19.
[174] Quoted in Price, *Position on Liquor Question*, p. 27.
[175] *Few Reasons Why "Maine Liquor Law" Should Not Be Passed in Pa.*, pp. 4–5. The writer maintained that reparations by the state would be necessary if the prohibition measure was enacted.
[176] *Ibid.*, pp. 4–5.
[177] *North American*, quoted in Price, *Position on Liquor Question*, p. 27.
[178] *Few Reasons Why "Maine Liquor Law" Should Not Be Passed in Pa.*, p. 12.

not even a popular vote could legitimize the prohibition measure. When it became clear that a strong sentiment was being mobilized in favor of the measure, the anti-prohibitionists fell back more heavily upon the anti-majoritarian implications of their position. The *North American* launched an attack upon the "blind recklessness of excited majorities." It asserted that the anti-prohibitionists would rely, if defeated, upon "the firmness of an upright and independent judiciary." [179]

The anti-prohibitionists pleaded for rights of liberty as well as property. They insisted that the "legitimate province of government" did not include the treatment of every vice to which human nature was heir,[180] that the abuse of an article was not sufficient ground for its abolition.[181] Behind the German opposition to prohibition was more than the threat to traditional habits of beer drinking or to agricultural interests. Some Germans were immigrants, come from abroad as a result of political reaction and imbued with a strong liberal spirit. They found a despotic quality in the prohibition idea which conflicted with some of their deepest feelings about government. This attitude was reflected in a pamphlet written in 1852 by Edward Graf, a German theologian, who bitterly attacked the prohibition measure as deriving from a "dangerous hierarchical assumption." [182] There was also the obvious argument that a prohibition law could not be successfully enforced.[183] Nor was the denunciation of the licensing system in which the temperance advocates now indulged designed to strengthen their case on this point. For if it had been found impossible to enforce a stringent licensing program, it hardly seemed likely that outright prohibition could be enforced more adequately.

If the opponents of prohibition were ready to move to the broad ground of philosophic and legal controversy, the defenders of the measure were equally willing to do so. But it is significant that

---

[179] *North American*, Mar. 9, 1854.
[180] *Ibid*.
[181] *Few Reasons Why "Maine Liquor Law" Should Not Be Passed in Pa.*, p. 12.
[182] Graf, *Temperance Question*, p. 13.
[183] See *Pennsylvanian*, Oct. 9, 1854; Price, *Position on Liquor Question*, p. 27; G. Graham, *Speech before Temperance Circle*, p. 19; *Miner's Journal*, Dec. 2, 1854.

when the validity of the proposal for government stores was challenged, that challenge did not evoke replies similar to the justifications of public enterprise in other fields. No doubt the explanation is two-fold: the basic difference in purpose which separated the utilization of the public enterprise principle in the liquor field from its utilization in a field such as the public works, where its objective was to promote rather than to restrict traffic; and the fact that the fifties were an epoch in which the entrepreneurial activities of the state were being discredited. Compelled thus to justify the government store idea on other grounds, the supporters of the original prohibition bill turned to meanings implicit in the licensing process. They argued that a licensed tavern was itself a "government agency," and that the ownership of liquor stores was a no less legitimate exertion of state authority than the licensing of them.[184] The conclusion which might logically be drawn from this argument is that every business controlled by the licensing system was also a business the government might enter in its own right.

But, above all, the liquor traffic did not fit into the category of lawful businesses. The point, Senator Kunkel insisted, was not whether the sale of liquor had once been recognized by national or state governments as a legal occupation. The prohibition bill definitely made it a crime; hence criminal penalties were justifiable.[185] Moreover the property rights involved were not inalienable. Here much was made of the precedent established by the earlier abolition of slavery. "They did not hesitate in that case to disregard the rights of property," declared Senator Kunkel, "and we need not be more scrupulous in regard to property in liquors, employed to destroy the lives of men." [186] The champions of the liquor interests asserted that no property rights were violated by the law of 1780 abolishing slavery, since it provided only for the ending of hereditary slavery and did not emancipate existing slaves. In fact, however, the vested rights of the slave-

---

[184] *Truth Vindicated*, p. 12.

[185] Quoted in Price, *Position on Liquor Question*, pp. 17–18. In his *Appeal to the Voters of Pennsylvania*, Coombs emphasized the same distinction. Quoted in *Few Reasons Why "Maine Liquor Law" Should Not Be Passed in Pa.*, p. 4.

[186] Quoted in Price, *Position on Liquor Question*, pp. 17–18.

holder were as surely damaged by a measure which provided that the children of his slaves were free as by a measure which provided for complete emancipation.[187]

In a broader doctrinal sense the defense of state power by the prohibitionists was remarkably well developed. To be sure, Albert Barnes appealed to the decisions of the courts.[188] But his theory, like that of Coombs, was built upon an original application of democratic concepts. Society has a right to protect itself. This right is derived inherently from the fact of social organization; without it society could not survive. The right of self-protection extended to "everything where injury or wrong would be done." But the principles of prohibition did not logically imply, as its opponents charged, that government must take action to abolish every human sin. A distinction must be drawn, as Blackstone had done, between an occupation which involved public harm and one which involved only private harm. The latter may be left untouched, but the former must be rooted out. For the "private interest" must be "sacrificed" to the "public good." It did not matter how lucrative the business was, how much capital was invested, or how seriously individuals suffered economic loss. It was Kent, one of the strongest legal defenders of individual rights, who had laid down the principle that the state had the power to prohibit uses of property that were socially dangerous. That power involved the right to destroy property outright or to render it valueless.[189]

Out of the prohibition struggle there thus emerged two grand philosophies: one opposing state power, the other defending it. As it happened, the defense of state action sustained a serious defeat. But this was not simply because prohibition was blocked in 1854. Actually the prohibitionists had whipped up such a powerful antagonism to the liquor trade [190] that in the following year the legislature was compelled to enact a licensing measure of unprecedented severity.[191] The real fiasco of prohibition theory is

---

[187] Cf. *ibid.*, p. 19; *Few Reasons Why "Maine Liquor Law" Should Not Be Passed in Pa.*, p. 10.
[188] Barnes, *Throne of Iniquity*, p. 5.   [189] *Ibid.*, pp. 5, 7, 8, 11.
[190] Cf. *House Journal, 1855*, p. 23.
[191] *Tavern Keepers versus the License System*.

to be found in the way in which the new licensing measure was opposed: it was opposed by the same kind of doctrine which had been marshaled against complete prohibition. The law was assailed, with all the relevant philosophic apparatus, as an invasion of inviolable property rights, as a transgression of the mandates of democratic principle.[192] And the House Judiciary Committee, when the measure was enacted, was compelled to justify licensing in the same high-flown democratic language, speaking of the "inherent right" of "civil society," discoursing on the nature of "social or public relations," citing legal cases from *Brown v. Maryland* onward. It had not before been imperative to justify in this way the licensing function of the state, an authority long accepted and well established. The House committee declared that the rightfulness of the licensing power was an issue which it hardly seemed "necessary to discuss," but confronted with the new doctrinal opposition, it realized that this was no longer true.[193]

What had happened was that the grandiose democratic ideas invoked to stave off prohibition had spilled over into the issue of licensing. The extremity of the prohibitionist crusade had evoked a reaction which now cast philosophic doubt upon a policy whose legitimacy had before been accepted even by the pro-liquor groups. For the prohibition ideologists this was an ironic kind of retribution. Given the precedents of the abolition of the liquor trade during the Revolution and the abolition of hereditary slavery afterwards, the legalistic assault upon prohibition during the fifties was sufficiently dubious. But to confront now a similar attack upon the simple idea of licensing restrictions was a hard experience. Moreover that attack, like the case against prohibition out of which it grew, was bound to gain inspiration from the great anti-state doctrines fashioned during the same period to eliminate mixed enterprise and public works. In 1858 one legislator branded the new licensing measure as a "patriarchal" policy at war with democratic precepts, and insisted that the liquor industry was "the only kind of business with which our State

[192] Price, *Speech on Sale of Liquors*, p. 6. See also Boucher, *Pittsburgh and Her People*, I, 528–29; *Pennsylvanian*, April 25, 1854.
[193] *House Journal, 1855*, p. 247; *1857*, p. 416.

now meddles." [194] He was obviously thinking of the recent departure of the state from the area of public investment and enterprise. In other fields the state continued to meddle as before, even in certain instances increased its meddling. But the liquor trade, because of the reaction elicited by the prohibitionists, had now become one of the special wards of the guardians of freedom. Unwittingly the most radical champions of public authority in Pennsylvania had opened a breach in that implicit acceptance of the legitimacy of state power which hung over from the colonial era.

5. *Debtor and Creditor*

The drive for social reform, reshaping the role of the state in many ways, made some of its most significant headway in the realm of debtor-creditor policy. Here it sought to rescue the debtor from hardships produced by the booms and recessions which characterized the expansion of the economy. The colonial attitude toward the debtor-creditor relationship could not survive the increasingly complex, uncertain, and depersonalized financial life of the nineteenth century. But this economic change cannot of itself explain the shape that debtor-creditor legislation took. It was deeply conditioned also by the emergence to political consciousness and power of debtor groups relatively inarticulate during the earlier era. The result was that the theory of reform in this field reflected a mingling of the ideologies produced by both business development and the advancing democratic movement.

One of the most spectacular of the campaigns involved was the drive to abolish imprisonment for debt which swept virtually every state in the nation during the decades before the Civil War. The idea of debtor imprisonment had been introduced into the law of Pennsylvania as early as 1705. Debtors were liable to confinement for the smallest sums; colonial legislation allowed magistrates' cognizance, without appeal, for debts below forty shillings.[195]

[194] *Legislative Record, 1858*, p. 325.
[195] *Dallas' Laws*, I, 72–73. See also *Farmers' and Mechanics' Bank v. Smith*, 3 Serg. and Rawle 63, 70 (1817).

The Revolutionary constitution of 1776 provided that imprisonment must not continue in cases where no strong presumption of fraud existed and where all assets had been delivered up to creditors.[196] However, this provision did not represent a great advance over alleviating measures taken during the colonial epoch. The Convention of 1790 retained it, except for a slight change in wording.[197] A growing sentiment in favor of reforming the institution of imprisonment for debt, if not in favor of its outright abolition, was reflected regularly in gubernatorial messages during the last decade of the eighteenth century and during the first two decades of the nineteenth.[198] In 1792 the legislature enacted a measure which provided that seven cents a day for the food of destitute prisoners should be paid by creditors who had jailed them, and that all prisoners should be discharged whose creditors refused to make the necessary payments.[199] The same principle was extended in the "Bread Act" of 1814 where the sum charged to the creditor was raised to twenty cents daily and where it was provided that imprisonment should continue for no longer than thirty days for debts under the amount of fifteen dollars.[200] The increase in debtor imprisonment attendant upon the depression of 1819 [201] led to a measure in that year which abolished female imprisonment entirely.[202]

During the twenties and the thirties a full-fledged movement against imprisonment for debt appeared in the state. Behind it were a body of humanitarian reformers who linked it generally to a larger campaign for prison reform. Almost as important a group as the humanitarians were the newly awakened laboring classes. As F. T. Carlton has demonstrated,[203] the workers represented a significant bloc in the movement for the abolition of debtor imprisonment throughout the country. But in Pennsylvania, where the union movement was especially strong, the cam-

[196] *Constitutions of Pa.*, p. 244. [197] *Ibid.*, p. 207.
[198] *Pa. Archives*, 4th, IV, 213, 338, 749, 780.
[199] *Statutes At Large*, XIV, 269.
[200] *Pa. Laws, 1813–14*, pp. 221–22.
[201] *Senate Journal, 1819–20*, p. 221.
[202] *Pa. Laws, 1818–19*, p. 57. See also *Niles Register*, XV (1818–19), 470.
[203] Carlton, "Abolition of Imprisonment for Debt," *Yale Review*, XVII (1908–09), 339–45.

paign of the laborers was of more than ordinary significance. Their position on the debtor-creditor relation was characterized by a peculiar dualism. They campaigned for the strictest legal enforcement of contract obligations in connection with lien laws and similar measures, but in the matter of debtor imprisonment, and stay laws as well, they fought for a loosening of the legal sanctions. In the one case they were creditors; in the other, they were likely to be debtors.

The groups opposing abolition of imprisonment for debt hardly dared to carry on a publicity campaign for their position, but they exerted effective pressure upon the legislature. One of them was comprised of lawyers who profited from fees involved in plaintiff action and discharge. The Prison Discipline Society, a Boston organization which led the campaign for prison reform throughout the country, asserted that nine-tenths of the lawyers were opposed to any modification of the laws in regard to imprisonment for debt.[204] A second group included the transporters of indentured servants; as has been indicated in a previous section,[205] their trade largely rested on coercive authority derived from the institution of debtor imprisonment. Small money-lenders and pawnbrokers also profited from the institution. The state had enacted legislation exempting from execution articles of absolute household necessity, but the fact that a person might nevertheless be imprisoned for a small debt frequently frustrated that legislation. In order to stave off imprisonment, the debtor turned to pawnbrokers and money-lenders and offered household articles as security.[206] Finally, magistrates who derived fees from the handling of debtor imprisonment cases were often aligned against the abolition of the institution.[207]

The sheer ineffectiveness of imprisonment as a means of collecting debts was a factor which condemned it in the public mind. The following table, dealing with the three years from 1827 to 1830, is an adequate illustration of imprisonment practices. These figures reveal that in 2,683 cases out of a total 3,001 the reason

[204] Prison Discipline Society, *Eighth Annual Report*, p. 24.
[205] Cf. *supra*, pp. 185 ff.
[206] *House Journal, 1832–33*, II, 635.
[207] *Public Ledger*, Jan. 9, 1844.

Table 5
DISCHARGES OF IMPRISONED DEBTORS IN PHILADELPHIA
1827–30

Causes of Discharge [208]	Amount of Debt									
	Under $5	6 to 10	11 to 20	21 to 30	31 to 40	41 to 50	51 to 100	101 to 500	501 to 1,000	Total
1. By Bread Act, the creditor failing in weekly payment.	154	104	65	21	14	11	15	9	2	395
2. By Thirty Day Act for the relief of poor debtors under fifteen dollars.	84	37	16	...	...	...	...	...	...	137
3. Cases bonded for the benefit of the insolvent laws.	402	253	202	80	47	51	53	22	3	1,113
4. By committing magistrate or the plaintiff.	201	266	141	77	43	39	82	71	58	1,038
5. By payment of debt and costs.	181	63	32	15	10	8	7	...	2	318
	1,082	723	456	193	114	109	137	102	65	3,001

for discharge was other than the payment of debt. As a device for collection, imprisonment failed in over 89 per cent of the cases. The tragi-comic fact of the smallness of the sums involved also helped to condemn debtor imprisonment. During the three years analyzed above there were no fewer than 1,805 cases of imprisonment for debts under ten dollars. Such cases amounted to almost 80 per cent of the total number. Of these cases liberation was achieved in only 244 by the payment of debt. The *Philadelphia Gazette* in 1831 devoted almost a whole broadside of one of its issues, while the legislature was in session, to the cases of imprisonment for debt in Philadelphia during the previous few months. In not one of the cases did the sum for which the debtor was committed to prison exceed one dollar.[209]

---

[208] Prison Discipline Society, *Sixth Annual Report*, p. 46.
[209] Cited, *ibid*.

While the reformers seized upon facts of this sort, they relied also upon certain general concepts. From what has been said of reform theory in other connections, it is not hard to understand the way in which its principles were applied here. Imprisonment for debt violated the basic natural right of a man to personal liberty. It was useless to contend that imprisonment followed as a consequence of failure to meet legitimate contract obligations, for a man could not, according to the dictates of natural law, enter into a contract which involved the disposal of his freedom.[210] The close parallel in this regard between debtor imprisonment and indentured service is clear. There were similar principles behind both institutions, and it was logical that blows directed against the former should also weaken the latter. But there was, nevertheless, an essential difference between them: imprisonment deprived the individual of the right to work and made him unproductive, while indentured service involved the performance of productive labor.

Thus more than natural liberty was involved in the criticism of imprisonment. It was pointed out that the community suffered an "absolute loss" in productive energies as a result of the confinement of debtors.[211] This view was bound up, as the temperance ideas had been, with an emerging economic morality preached by such writers as Freedley. If the accumulation of wealth had become a social duty, imprisonment clearly violated fundamental norms. Thus the ideology of business came to the support of the ideology of democracy to condemn debtor imprisonment. This was, as I have already suggested, a logical combination. In terms of the newer economic environment, debtor

[210] *Mechanics Free Press*, Dec. 25, 1830. Simpson wrote: "The relation of debtor and creditor, therefore, being purely factitious, wholly unknown to man in a state of nature, . . . where paper credits are not current, we must consider it as a creature of law, whose properties are decided, not by justice, but by power. . . . It is obvious, that if the principle of equity in the distribution of property prevailed, there could exist no motive to monopoly and capital to resort to the expedients of CREDIT. . . . The relation of debtor and creditor, therefore, is produced by the rapacity of capital to accumulate, and on the side of the borrower, by the *necessities* and *temptations* of poverty, superinduced by wrong principles, in the distribution of labour." Simpson, *Workingman's Manual*, pp. 188, 89. See also *ibid.*, pp. 190–91.

[211] *Mechanics Free Press*, Dec. 25, 1830. Cf. Hartz, "Seth Luther: Working-Class Rebel," *New England Quarterly*, XIII (1940), 414.

imprisonment was as anachronistic as slavery or indentured service. What the situation required was an effective bankruptcy law rather than the continuation of eighteenth-century techniques in the debtor-creditor relation. In the thinking of an older time, failure to pay debt might possibly point to criminality on the part of the debtor, but in a newer environment, where the debtor-creditor relation was governed increasingly by impersonal credit fluctuations, such a connection could by no means be automatically inferred.

The impact of this economic change was reflected in repeated charges that debtor imprisonment did not sufficiently distinguish between crime and misfortune, that it involved, as a Philadelphia mass meeting in 1830 put it, a "strange mixture of civil and criminal law." [212] It was freely granted that penal sanctions for fraud must be continued. But in most cases imprisonment for debt was "nothing more nor less than punishment for poverty." [213] It was argued, finally, that debtor imprisonment was unconstitutional. The fact that no jury trial was necessary before imprisonment was held to violate the constitutional provision which guaranteed the jury privilege. It was also contended that the Declaration of Rights of the constitution, which secured the general personal freedom of the citizens of the state, was violated by imprisonment for debt.[214] These arguments, however, were tortured ones, since the constitutions of 1776 and 1790 implicitly recognized the validity of debtor imprisonment in certain cases.

The mounting intensity of the campaign against debtor imprisonment produced decisive legislative action in 1832. In that year a House committee was dispatched to examine conditions in the Arch Street prison in Philadelphia, and its revelations were sufficiently lurid to jolt the complacency even of a conservative legislature.[215] The fact that alleviating measures enacted in Massachusetts and New York had produced generally good results appears to have exerted considerable influence upon the

[212] *Ibid.*, May 23, 1829. See also *House Journal, 1834–35*, II, 212 ff.
[213] *Mechanics Free Press*, May 23, 1829.
[214] Prison Discipline Society, *Fifth Annual Report*, p. 379. For a legislative discussion of the constitutional question, see *House Journal, 1834–35*, II, 253.
[215] *Ibid., 1832*, II, 633–42.

proposal the committee presented.²¹⁶ That proposal involved the complete abolition of debtor imprisonment for sums less than $5.33. It was enacted into law.²¹⁷ Almost at once there were petitions for its repeal,²¹⁸ but, as Representative Wallace pointed out, those petitions came, with one exception, exclusively from the city of Philadelphia where money-lenders, lawyers, and others in the opposition were grouped. In 1834 a House committee again examined the problem of debtor imprisonment, and its report upheld the action that had been taken two years earlier.²¹⁹ The measure was not repealed, and agitation immediately began for the abolition of debtor imprisonment entirely.

In 1842, that objective was achieved.²²⁰ But the opposition it encountered, even at this late date, is striking. Immediately after debtor imprisonment was totally abolished, the legislature was preoccupied with another struggle over whether it should be reinstituted. The movement for reinstitution, reported the Philadelphia *Public Ledger* in 1844, had behind it "a zeal that renders its success by no means improbable." ²²¹ The fight in the legislature gained added meaning because of the recent repeal by Congress of the national bankruptcy act, which had been looked to by many as a possible solution to the insolvency problem. A state insolvency measure of 1836 permitted debtors to be discharged after complying with its provisions, and there now remained no way in which debtors could be held. This fact was made much of by those who favored the repeal of the measure of 1842 abolishing imprisonment for debt; but those who favored its continuance found in it the main reason for their position.²²² The law of 1842 was also criticized on the ground that, because it involved contracts made before its passage, it violated the contract clause of the national Constitution and the clause forbidding the enactment of ex post facto measures. It was hotly denied, however, that the imprisonment power was part of any contract. "Such an

---

²¹⁶ *Ibid., 1832*, II, 640.
²¹⁷ *Pa. Laws, 1832–33*, pp. 480–81.
²¹⁸ *House Journal, 1833–34*, I, 348, 365, 391, 418, 437, 452, 506.
²¹⁹ *Ibid.*, II, 657.
²²⁰ *Pa. Laws, 1842*, pp. 339–49. See also *Niles Register*, LXII (1842), 322.
²²¹ *Public Ledger*, Jan. 9, 1844. ²²² *Ibid.*

idea," declared the *Ledger*, "never enters into the original contract; it is an after-thought, suggested by disappointed avarice and enforced by heartless cruelty." [223]

The colonial basis upon which the institution of debtor imprisonment rested was part of a larger body of pre-Revolutionary legislation dealing with the problem of insolvency. Beginning in 1730 the Pennsylvania Assembly enacted a series of measures that involved two fundamental principles: persons in debt for sums under a certain limit might deliver up to creditors all personal and real assets and thereby be discharged from imprisonment; and certain essential household and occupational articles might be exempted from creditor action. Persons discharged under these measures could not be recommitted to prison for debts contracted before their discharge, but all property acquired after that time was made subject to new executions for old debts.[224] Insolvency legislation during the period from the Revolution to the Civil War was concerned mainly with the modification or the expansion of these basic ideas. Taken as a whole, two motives are discernible in it: a steady effort to better the legal position of the debtor, and a pragmatic attempt to rationalize a large body of practice that had grown up over more than a century and that was faced with the task of adjusting itself to economic change. The debtor-creditor problem, as a legislative committee in 1834 declared, was "one of the most difficult tasks in legislation." [225]

[223] *Ibid.*
[224] Cf. *Dallas' Laws*, I, 256–68. For an admirable discussion of colonial insolvency legislation, see *House Journal, 1834–35*, II, 249–51.
[225] *Ibid.*, II, 245. The relief of insolvency was not always a matter of general law. Many special acts granted relief in individual cases. Cf. *Dallas' Laws*, II, 712. For changes in the statewide insolvency provisions before 1814, see *ibid.*, II, 488–90, 780–82; III, 181–82, 472–73, 237–39; *Pa. Laws, 1806–1807*, pp. 167–68; *Dallas' Laws*, IV, 269–76. These measures extended the colonial insolvency provisions in various interstitial ways, such as liberalizing residence qualifications and expanding the area exempted from execution. Problems were presented in interstate relations in connection with insolvency measures. The courts of Pennsylvania consistently followed a rule of reciprocity in regard to discharges granted under laws of other states. "It would be highly mischievous, as well as incongruous, that when a debtor has been discharged from his imprisonment by the laws of his own state, a fellow citizen shall follow him to other parts of the union, and there arrest him again by new process." *Jeffries* v. *Thompson*, 2 Yeates 482, 483 (1799). See also *Miller* v. *Hall*, 1 Dallas 229 (1788); *James* v. *Alden*, 1 Dallas 188 (1786); *Donaldson* v. *Chambers*, 2 Dallas 100

The constitutional limitations on imprisonment for debt which accompanied the economic disruption and political equalitarianism of the Revolutionary and post-Revolutionary periods were paralleled by legislative actions liberalizing previous insolvency measures. In 1785 a genuine bankruptcy act was passed whose provisions extended to all merchants, scriveners, bankers, brokers, or factors.[226] Under this measure the debtor could not, after a settlement had been made, be sued subsequently for past debts. The act expired after seven years. Effort was immediately made to reintroduce the bankruptcy principle, however, and this agitation was related to restrictions on imprisonment for debt which were being introduced at the same time. The social theory in both cases was similar: the emphasis on the distinction between legitimate debt and crime,[227] the argument that existing legislation, because it did not permit a man to recover after insolvency, deprived "Agriculture, Commerce, and Manufactures" of the productivity of debtors.[228]

But the campaign in behalf of the bankruptcy principle could not, by its nature, utilize the democratic and humanitarian symbolism in so spectacular a way as could the campaign against imprisonment for debt. Consequently the theory in defense of the bankruptcy principle reveals more sharply than the other the impact of new business practices upon attitudes toward the debtor-creditor relation. The increasingly speculative character of business was brought forth to justify the idea that creditors must "abide by the misfortunes of men."[229] E. V. Wiston, himself an insolvent debtor, declared in 1803 that that idea was at the basis of corporation practices in both the purchase and sale of stocks. Investors were frequently compelled to sell stocks at a

---

(1788); *Hilliard and Pippit* v. *Greenleaf*, 2 Yeates 533 (1799); *Fisher* v. *Hyde*, 3 Yeates 256 (1801); *Smith* v. *Brown*, 3 Binney 201 (1810); *Boggs* v. *Teackle*, 5 Binney 332 (1812); *Walsh* v. *Nourse*, 5 Binney 381 (1813); *Commonwealth* ex rel. *Dusar* v. *Riddle*, 1 Serg. and Rawle 311 (1815).

[226] *Dallas' Laws*, II, 268–381. "To come under this law, there must be a trading, a debt contracted, and an act of bankruptcy, all posterior to its date." *Joy* v. *Cossart*, 1 Yeates 50, 54 (1791). Cf. remarks concerning this measure by Sergeant, *Poulson's Daily Advertiser*, Jan. 25, 1822.

[227] Cf. Wiston, *Letters on Insolvency*, pp. 9, 10.

[228] *Ibid.*, p. 7.

[229] *Ibid.*, p. 9.

lower price than that at which they were purchased, and it was unthinkable that they should have a recourse to the courts for an indemnification of their loss on the part of the corporation concerned.[230]

It was denied that severe legal penalties for insolvency discouraged reckless engagements in credit. In 1810 an anonymous pamphleteer in Philadelphia declared that the most disastrous deals were negotiated by the debtor immediately before insolvency, and that the motive behind them was usually a last-stand effort to salvage his business in order to avoid the drastic penalties of insolvency legislation. Fear of this legislation, therefore, encouraged rather than discouraged the improvident assumption of debt. The creditor, on the other hand, realizing the stringent character of insolvency penalties, frequently reckoned that credit would not be applied for unless obligations could be met. This often resulted in an over-liberal credit policy. To relax insolvency provisions would be to introduce an opposite psychology in both cases. Moreover, existing legislation was unfair to many creditors themselves. By imprisoning a man or in some way obtaining preference in payment, one creditor could seriously damage the position of others in relation to the debtor. Provisions for an equal distribution of assets among creditors were needed.[231]

These arguments were put forward against the background of a general disillusion with the state and national bankruptcy laws that had already been tried.[232] Various new proposals were suggested. Owing to pressure from Philadelphia, the legislature in 1812 enacted for that city a measure that resembled in many ways the bankruptcy statute enacted in 1785.[233] As a legislative

[230] *Ibid.*, p. 9. "One who contracts a debt, or incurs a liability to another, knowing his inability to pay . . . ought to be regarded as an offender of little less criminality than one who commits a larceny of the same amount; and ought to be punished accordingly. But the case is widely different, when a debtor is disabled from paying by reason of a fire, or shipwreck, or other accidental circumstance." *House Journal, 1834–35*, II, 252.

[231] *Debtor and Creditor.* For a discussion of preferences in assignments, see *McClurg* v. *Lecky*, 3 Penrose and Watts 83 (1831). In 1843 the preference system was abolished except in connection with the wages of labor. *Pa. Laws, 1843*, pp. 273–74. See also *Leas' Appeal*, 9 Pa. St. Rep. 504 (1848).

[232] See Warren, *Bankruptcy in U.S. History*, pp. 3–45; M. Carey, *Excerpta*, VII.

[233] *Pa. Laws, 1811–12*, pp. 114–27.

committee said, this law "was considered rather as an experiment which it was thought expedient to make a trial of, than as forming a complete and final system for the relief of insolvents." [234] Its provisions were abused, fraud was the result,[235] and it was repealed within ten months after passage. The legal decisions handed down in connection with it, however, had lasting repercussions upon the attitude of Pennsylvanians toward the debtor-creditor problem. In an opinion delivered by Chief Justice Tilghman the state Supreme Court, in line with its policy of a liberal interpretation of the contract clause of the federal Constitution, upheld the measure of 1812 as not impairing the obligation of contracts.[236] The state's power was sustained despite the fact that the chief justice expressly recognized the measure to be a bankruptcy statute. This decision was reversed, however, by the federal Supreme Court in a brief opinion written by Marshall.[237] The limitations thus imposed upon the state in the realm of bankruptcy legislation conditioned its action throughout the period before the Civil War.[238]

The economic emergency of the Revolutionary and post-Revolutionary periods also produced, in Pennsylvania as elsewhere, those stay laws that were in large part originally responsible for the inclusion of the contract clause in the Constitution in 1787.[239] In Pennsylvania, however, they were not extreme. In 1781 the Revolutionary tender laws were repealed, and a measure enacted that ordered the courts to grant a stay of execution on the principal of all rents and annuities contracted before 1777, though legal action was still permitted for the collection of interest in gold and

---

[234] *House Journal, 1812–13*, p. 61.

[235] *United States Gazette*, Sept. 24, 1812; *House Journal, 1812–13*, p. 61.

[236] *Farmers' and Mechanics' Bank* v. *Smith*, 3 Serg. and Rawle 63 (1817).

[237] *Farmers' and Mechanics' Bank of Pennsylvania* v. *Smith*, 6 Wheaton 131, 134 (1821).

[238] Cf. remarks of House Committee on the Administration of Justice, *House Journal, 1834–35*, II, 245. "In addition to the inherent difficulties of the subject . . . we have some to encounter growing out of our political constitutions and federal relations. It may be sufficient merely to mention at present the constitutional objections, which are supposed to exist to the passage of bankrupt or insolvent laws by the State Legislature, while the General Government which possesses the power declines to exercise it." *Ibid.* See also *Pa. Archives*, 4th, VII, 812.

[239] B. F. Wright, *Contract Clause of the Constitution*, pp. 3–26.

silver.[240] Similar measures were enacted in 1784, 1804, and 1806.[241] None of the last appears to have been challenged before the courts.

After the War of 1812 the need for a codification of insolvency legislation became increasingly clear. To achieve this a new law was passed in 1814.[242] But this measure did not appreciably change the status of the debtor, nor can it be said to have effectually cleared up legal confusion. Comprehensive digests of insolvency legislation and court adjudications under it were not available until the surveys of Edward D. Graham of Philadelphia appeared in 1822 and 1827.[243] Graham recommended various interstitial changes in legal practices in insolvency proceedings, some of which were eventually included in law.[244] If public opinion, as Graham asserted, was largely ignorant of the specific provisions of insolvency legislation,[245] it was nevertheless a fact, as a House committee investigating the judicial system reported in 1834,[246] that there was widespread dissatisfaction with the operation of debtor-creditor measures. This committee recommended a series of changes,[247] and two years later the last general measure on insolvency was enacted by the legislature.[248] When the national bankruptcy act was passed in 1841 the question arose whether state insolvency laws were thus superseded. The Philadelphia Court of Common Pleas determined that they were not, that an individual could take advantage of the provisions of either state or national laws as he pleased.[249] The early repeal of the national act, however, prevented the jurisdictional problem from becoming significant.

[240] *Dallas' Laws*, I, 902–907.
[241] *Ibid.*, II, 236; *Pa. Laws, 1803–1804*, pp. 383–400; *1805–1806*, pp. 558–59.
[242] *Ibid., 1813–14*, pp. 216–22.
[243] E. Graham, *Insolvent Laws of Pa.*; *View of Insolvent Laws of Pa.* For the difficulties produced by the complexity and disorganization of the insolvency measures, see *House Journal, 1812–13*, p. 293. See also *ibid., 1822–23*, pp. 50, 93, 580; *Insolvent Register*.
[244] *View of Insolvent Laws of Pa.*, pp. 1–4.
[245] *Ibid.*, p. 3.   [246] *House Journal, 1834–35*, II, 245.
[247] *Ibid.*, II, 251–54. For a general survey of insolvency legislation passed in Pennsylvania, see *Moncure v. Hanson*, 15 Pa. St. Rep. 385, 389 (1850). See also *Wolfram v. Strickhouser*, 1 Watts and Serg. 379, 381 (1841).
[248] *Pa. Laws, 1835–36*, pp. 729–41; *House Journal, 1835–36*, II, 348 ff.
[249] *Hunt's Merchants' Mag.*, VI (1842), 355.

Although it did not attempt to reintroduce bankruptcy legislation, the state nevertheless continued its policy of enacting stay laws during depression periods. Senator Raguet, in his report on the effects of the financial crisis of 1819, listed first the ruinous sacrifices of landed and personal property which were taking place at sheriffs' sales throughout the state. Farms and houses were selling at less than a third or less than a fourth of their former value; some farmers were reported to have migrated westward as a result. Household goods, farming stock, and essential implements were similarly being sold at prices far below cost.[250] The situation was made worse by the fact that banks, which were being held responsible for the depression, were in many instances purchasing property sold under their own judgments and mortgages.[251] Early in 1820 the legislature enacted a measure that provided for the appraisement of all real and personal property taken in execution and the granting of a stay of one year unless the property brought two-thirds of its appraisal value at auction.[252] The provisions of this law were subsequently extended for an additional year,[253] but a new provision was made that the defendant could not use the property involved unless he paid semiannual interest to the plaintiff on the judgment against it.

As had been the case in connection with the stay laws of 1804 and 1806, no important constitutional question of the state's power appears to have arisen as a result of the measures of 1820 and 1821. It is true that in the case of *Peddle* v. *Hollinshead*,[254] adjudicated two years after the last law had been enacted, Justice Duncan of the Supreme Court emphasized that the previous legislation conferred upon the debtor no vested right in the continuance of its provisions beyond the time deemed desirable by the legislature. But this holding implicitly recognized the validity of the action; it did not cast doubt upon the state's power to take it. Nor does state power appear to have been seriously challenged in 1836, when similar conditions existed and when a similar measure was passed. In the forties, however, the validity of such action

[250] *Senate Journal, 1819–20*, p. 221.
[251] *Ibid.*, p. 234.
[252] *Pa. Laws, 1819–20*, pp. 188–91.
[253] *Ibid., 1820–21*, pp. 138–39.
[254] 9 Serg. and Rawle 277 (1823).

began to be questioned. The Harrisburg *Democratic Union*, speaking for the "commercial community in general," emphasized the necessity of having judges "in good old Pennsylvania determined to shake off repudiation in every form." [255]

The *Union* was referring specifically to a measure enacted in 1842, patterned pretty much after the stay law of 1820. This measure was invalidated by the District Court of Allegheny County on the ground that it impaired the obligation of contracts.[256] But the judgment of the District Court was reversed by the state Supreme Court in an opinion written by Chief Justice Gibson.[257] Gibson distinguished between the Pennsylvania measure and one held unconstitutional by the federal Supreme Court in the case of *McCracken* v. *Hayward*.[258] The latter, an Illinois statute, had provided for a perpetual suspension of judgment on property. Gibson held that the Pennsylvania measure, which provided only for a stay of one year, was more reasonable and hence within the state's power. He referred to previous stay laws in Pennsylvania "whose validity had not been contested." [259]

It was evident, however, that the stay principle was meeting increased opposition both in popular thought and in the courts. A measure passed in 1857 was challenged on the ground that it operated retrospectively. The Supreme Court upheld it, however, by interpreting its provisions in such a way as to make it inapplicable to judgments already in process before its enactment.[260] Nevertheless Justice Woodward, who wrote the opinion of the court, insisted that if the measure had had a retrospective application, it would be clearly void. Such a measure would involve "taking away a right of property without compensation." If it could be enacted, both federal and state constitutions would become "a dead letter," and civil rights would "have no security but the legislative will." [261] In 1861, dealing with a measure of that year, Woodward handed down the first decision invalidating

---

[255] *Democratic Union*, Apr. 23, 1845. See also *Pa. Archives*, 4th, VI, 347.
[256] *Democratic Union*, Apr. 23, 1845. See also *Niles Register*, July 30, 1842.
[257] *Chadwick* v. *Moore*, 8 Watts and Serg. 49 (1844).
[258] 2 Howard 608 (1844).
[259] *Chadwick* v. *Moore*, 8 Watts and Serg. 49, 52 (1844).
[260] *Chaffee* v. *Michaels*, 31 Pa. St. Rep. 282 (1858). [261] *Ibid.*, p. 284.

a stay law in the history of the state.[262] The measure granted a stay of execution on all judgments or debts arising from contracts in which stay privileges had specifically been waived by the debtor. In Woodward's mind, such a measure clearly fitted his previous description of pernicious legislation: the waiver was part of the original contract; the legislation was not remedial but a direct impairment of contract obligations such as the constitution forbade.[263]

An integral part of the movement to improve the status of the debtor was a succession of laws exempting various articles from execution. The legislature of 1812 which received Groves's report for the repeal of the Philadelphia bankruptcy act also received a report from a committee headed by Representative Miner, which lamented the fact that the only assets exempted from execution by law were military arms.[264] Since debtors at that time were still liable to imprisonment for very small sums, the effect of such limited exemptions was harsh. Moreover, a family dependent upon the wife for support could be impoverished by judgments against her property in the name of the husband.[265] Arguing that the "necessity of government arises from the disposition of the strong to tyrannize over the weak," the Miner Committee recommended the exemption from execution of certain basic household articles and craftsmen's tools, though it "doubted" whether such a law would not be an invalid interference with the rights of the creditor if it were given any but a prospective application. The committee recognized its proposal to be an "experiment," [266] but the principles that it developed became established in legislation. Before 1849 various exemption measures listed specifically articles that might be exempted, but

---

[262] *Billmeyer* v. *Evans and Rodenbaugh*, 40 Pa. St. Rep. 324 (1861). It is notable that several of the Pennsylvania stay laws upheld were unlimited in duration, and that the court did not feel called upon to cite emergency conditions as a justification for the validation. Cf. *Chadwick* v. *Moore*, 8 Watts and Serg. 49, 52 (1844).

[263] *Billmeyer* v. *Evans and Rodenbaugh*, 40 Pa. St. Rep. 324, 326–28 (1861).

[264] *House Journal, 1812–13*, p. 344. For earlier legislative expressions of a similar attitude, see *ibid., 1804–1805*, p. 489.

[265] *Ibid., 1812–13*, p. 344.

[266] *Ibid.*, p. 345.

in that year a law was enacted giving the debtor himself the right to designate exempt property.[267] None of the exemption acts was invalidated by the courts as embodying an unconstitutional extension of state power, though in certain cases they appear to have been viewed with disfavor by judges and were interpreted strictly.[268]

Related to this type of legislative action was another which sought to improve the position of the tenant. Some four years before the Revolution, the Assembly passed a law providing for the sale of goods distrained for rent.[269] This law remained on the statute books, without alteration, throughout the entire post-Revolutionary period and the depression years which followed the panic of 1819. In 1828, however, its provisions were modified so that certain basic articles were exempted from the lien action of the landlord.[270] The argument that centered about this measure, particularly in the Philadelphia area, was as bitter as any evoked in the debtor-creditor field. The working class groups in favor of it denied that a distinction existed between common debts and rent sufficiently clear-cut to justify a favored position for the landlord.[271] Landlords charged that the measure was an unconstitutional invasion of property rights, though no case appears to have arisen in the courts on this question. Rents rose in Philadelphia after the enactment of 1828; landlords required greater security from tenants. There was talk of a legislative ceiling on rents.[272] The controversy was ended, however, and landlord-tenant relations were stabilized, by a modification of the law in 1830.[273]

[267] For a list of special acts exempting tradesmen's tools from 1814–46, see *Richie* v. *McCauley*, 4 Pa. St. Rep. 471 (1846). The decisions in this case held that the term "necessary tools of a tradesman" did not include a regular business establishment employing a large capital. See also *Pa. Laws, 1820–21*, p. 146; *Richie* v. *McCauley*, 4 Pa. St. Rep. 471, 473 (1846); *Knabb* v. *Drake*, 23 Pa. St. Rep. 489 (1854).

[268] Cf. *Brant's Appeal*, 20 Pa. St. Rep. 141, 143 (1852); *Case* v. *Dunmore*, 23 Pa. St. Rep. 93, 94 (1854).

[269] *Dallas' Laws*, I, 612–19.

[270] *Pa. Archives*, 4th, V, 847.

[271] Cf. *Mechanics Free Press*, Nov. 21, 28, 1829; Jan. 23, 30, 1830.

[272] *Ibid.*

[273] *Pa. Laws, 1829–30*, p. 187.

The fight of the landlords in this instance, like the fight of other groups against specific aspects of social legislation, did not threaten the continuance of state power as a whole. By 1860 the reform policy of government had carved a winding path through the economy, but there was no indication that its work was coming to an end. In a few cases, to be sure, as in the regulation of the liquor trade and the enactment of stay laws, state authority was sharply challenged toward the close of our period on the ground of principle. But compared to the violent attacks which led during the same decades to the complete termination of mixed enterprise and public works policy, these challenges were unimportant. The social responsibility of government remained one of the key premises of politico-economic thought.

VI

ISSUES IN CORPORATE CONTROL

1. *Duration, Repeal, and Alteration of Charters*

The promotional aspect of charter policy examined earlier was but one phase of a dual role which the state had with reference to the corporate system: once charters were granted the state shifted from the role of promoter to the role of regulator, except as it supplemented corporate privileges in special acts and as it served as partial owner in mixed corporations. Strictly speaking, it is erroneous to interpret this development as a shift, since many of the most important corporate regulations were imposed in charter acts themselves; promotional and regulatory aims were thus mingled in them. While the authority of the state to include regulatory provisions in charter grants was virtually limitless, accounting for that plasticity of the corporate device which impressed the Packer Committee of 1837, the power of the state to revoke or alter charters already granted was challenged at an early time. The latter question appeared in 1779 when the charter of the Pennsylvania College was summarily altered by the Revolutionary legislature; [1] and in 1785, when the state charter granted to the Bank of North America was repealed, it attained a prominent position in public debate. No clause had been included in the bank's charter authorizing its subsequent repeal by the legislature, nor had any time limit upon its duration been set. Despite the revocation act of 1785, the bank continued to operate, owing to its national charter and to state charters that had been obtained from Massachusetts and Rhode Island. There was confusion concerning the legal effect of the Pennsylvania repealing act, a movement got under way for its annulment, and in 1787 the charter of the bank was renewed. The act of 1787, however, limited the duration of the charter grant to fourteen years.[2]

---

[1] *Statutes at Large*, IX, 26–27, 175–76; Brunhouse, *Counter-Revolution in Pa.*, pp. 77–79, 152–54.
[2] *Statutes at Large*, XII, 57, 413; Lewis, *Bank of North America*, pp. 72–73; Konkle, *Thomas Willing and First American Financial System*, pp. 108 ff.

The controversy over the repeal of the charter of the Bank of North America was an integral part of the larger controversy over the utility of banking corporations which that charter evoked.[3] The argument of the prominent defenders of the bank — Robert Morris, James Wilson, Thomas Paine and Pelatiah Webster — was remarkable for its anticipation of contract theory later to be used by Marshall. Though the distinction between an ordinary legislative measure and one granting corporate privileges was most thoroughly explored by Paine, all of the pro-bank theorists insisted that charter legislation carried contract obligations for the state which made arbitrary revocation illegitimate. Since no contract clause, either state or national, was as yet available to provide a constitutional basis for this point of view, higher law interpretations were relied upon.[4] Both Paine and Webster suggested a recourse to the courts for the directors of the bank, Webster recommending that they build a case on the Declaration of Rights of the constitution of 1776, but the disorganized political situation at the time impelled the directors to confine their argument to the legislature.[5]

Contending that the contract interpretation would afford "a great invitation to fraud," the advocates of repeal insisted on the supremacy of public welfare as a standard of legislative action. They denied that the bank charter was a contract on the ground that the state had received no consideration for granting it and, pointing out that the constitution could be altered, they declared that the legislature could not grant "charters more sacred and more permanent that the government itself."[6] The controversy did not result in an established doctrinal victory for either side. The renewal of the charter of the bank might be interpreted as a victory for the anti-revocation theorists, but since there were definite alterations in the charter as renewed this victory was not a victory for the contract principle which they had presented.

[3] See H. Miller, *Banking Theories in U.S. before 1860*, pp. 49–50.
[4] Paine, *Works*, I, 331–70; J. Wilson, *Selected Political Essays*, pp. 125–49; Webster, *Political Essays*, p. 456; Davis, *Earlier American Corporations*, II, 311 ff; B. F. Wright, *Contract Clause of Constitution*, pp. 16 ff.
[5] Lewis, *Bank of North America*, pp. 54 ff.
[6] M. Carey, *Annulling the Charter of the Bank of North America*, pp. 13 ff, 123.

Early in the second decade of the nineteenth century the practice of including reservation and time-limit provisions in corporate charters became general. The first reservation clause to appear in the banking field, one which served as a general pattern for subsequent legislation, was Section 18 of the famous Banking Act of 1814 which provided for a forfeiture of charters if banks created under it failed to comply with various regulations, the most important of which was the provision for the payment of all liabilities, including notes issued, in specie on demand. The duration of charters granted by the act was limited to eleven years.[7] Though duration limits were ordinarily not included in turnpike, bridge, canal, and railroad charters, and were omitted in some water and gas company charters, reservation clauses began to appear around 1812 in charters of these types.[8] After 1830, in railroad charters, a very broad assertion of the revocation power was included, with the procedure for revocation outlined in detail — through *scire facias* issued by the Supreme Court, upon the direction of the governor or the legislature.[9]

Moreover, the duration of charters in the transportation and utility fields was affected by three specific provisions which they often included. The first of these was a provision for the termination of corporate privileges unless the projected undertaking was completed within a specified period of time.[10] The second was a provision for the establishment of a fund from profits above a certain percentage limit, which was to be used to redeem corporation stock within a certain period in order to make the utility free to the public.[11] Finally, provisions were frequently included granting authority to the state or local governments to purchase the work in question after a certain length of time, either at an appraised value or upon payment of the cost of construction and a certain rate of interest upon it.[12]

[7] *Pa. Laws, 1813–14*, pp. 154–73.
[8] See *ibid., 1812–13*, pp. 239–45; *1849*, pp. 10–17, 79–87; *1855*, pp. 217–19; *1857*, pp. 77–83. [9] *Ibid., 1832–33*, pp. 134–43; *1846*, pp. 179–81, 312–26.
[10] *Dallas' Laws*, III, 607–17, 360–71; *Pa. Laws, 1815–16*, pp. 42–46; *1822–23*, pp. 249–56; *1849*, pp. 79–87; *1855*, pp. 217–19.
[11] *Dallas' Laws*, IV, 216–224, 247–60; *Pa. Laws, 1810–11*, pp. 226–39.
[12] *Dallas' Laws*, II, 330–32; *Pa. Laws, 1810–11*, pp. 119–34; *1811–12*, pp. 178–80; *1812–13*, pp. 239–45; *1828–29*, pp. 270–80; *1830–31*, pp. 145–56; *1848*, pp. 544–45.

In the manufacturing field, though limited reservation clauses appeared prior to 1825,[13] broader provisions began to appear after that time, usually positing bluntly the power of the legislature "to revoke, alter, or annul the charter hereby granted, at any time they may think proper."[14] Duration limits in manufacturing charters varied from ten to thirty years; a twenty-year period was most common and was adopted in the General Manufacturing Act of 1849.[15] In the insurance field the reservation principle appeared as early as 1809 and was applied throughout the period prior to the Civil War.[16] The increased preoccupation of the legislature with reservation and time-limit provisions which began to appear in the third decade of the nineteenth century was partially a product of the decision of the federal Supreme Court in the Dartmouth College Case of 1819.[17] Article IX, Section 17 of the state constitution of 1790 included a provision to the effect that no "law impairing contracts" might be passed, identical with the contract clause of the federal Constitution save for the word "obligations" which was not included in the state clause.[18] After the Bank of North America controversy, however, the revocation issue did not again attain an important place in public discussion until the chartering of the Second Bank in 1835. One of the remarkable achievements of Biddle in that year was the extraction of a state charter that, contrary to established policy, did not contain a reservation clause of any kind. This omission infuriated the leaders of the reaction against the bank, since it made them practically helpless in a legal sense. The issue became one of the central concerns of the constitutional convention which convened in Harrisburg two years later.

A resolution was introduced there calling for a committee to

---

[13] See for example the charter of the Monongahela Manufacturing Society, *Pa. Laws, 1811–12*, pp. 240–44.

[14] *Ibid., 1825–26*, pp. 213–16. Cf. *ibid., 1838–39*, pp. 231–35; *1835–36*, pp. 337–39.

[15] *Ibid., 1819–20*, pp. 146–49; *1825–26*, pp. 198–201; *1818–19*, pp. 69–71; *1815–16*, pp. 114–117; *1814–15*, pp. 33–36; *1844*, pp. 349–52; *1813–14*, pp. 288–91; *1849*, pp. 563–69.

[16] *Ibid., 1808–1809*, pp. 65–71. Cf. *ibid., 1811–12*, pp. 86–87; *1839–40*, p. 11; *1840–41*, pp. 91–92.

[17] *Dartmouth College v. Woodward*, 4 Wheaton 518 (1819).

[18] *Constitutions of Pa.*, p. 208.

inquire into the possibility of a revocation of the Second Bank charter by the convention itself. Clauses were enacted providing for the limitation of the life of bank charters to twenty years and for the revocation and alteration of such charters by the legislature when necessary on the condition that no injustice would thereby be done to the stockholders involved. The vote on these provisions was 86 to 29. A resolution, introduced by Meredith of Philadelphia, was passed to the effect "that it is the sense of this Convention, that a charter duly granted by act of Assembly, to a bank . . . is, when accepted, a contract with the parties to whom the grant is made." Amounting to nothing more than a restatement of the Dartmouth College principle, this resolution nevertheless encountered heavy opposition; the vote in its favor was 59 to 41.[19]

In 1855 the legislature enacted a general reservation clause for all charters to be granted subsequently.[20] Two years later this enactment was fortified by a special constitutional amendment, which read as follows: "The legislature shall have the power to alter, revoke, or annul any charter of incorporation hereafter conferred by or under any special or general law whenever in their opinion it may be injurious to the citizens of the commonwealth, in such manner, however, that no injustice shall be done to the corporators." The amendment received an overwhelmingly affirmative vote.[21]

It would be a mistake to assume that the power of outright charter revocation was widely used. It is true that the charters of ten banks created by the Banking Act of 1814 were revoked during the business recession that followed it.[22] And there were instances of revocation in the transportation field also.[23] But on the whole the nullification of charters was a rare practice. In the banking field, where the Banking Acts of 1824 and 1850 continued the policy of making revocation a penalty for the suspension of specie payments, the idea was notoriously hollow. In 1837

[19] *Convention Journal*, I, 804 ff.
[20] Pa. Laws, *1855*, pp. 423–24.
[21] *Constitutions of Pa.*, p. 146.
[22] *House Journal, 1821–22*, p. 344.
[23] See *ibid., 1832–33*, II, 757 ff.

Table 6
POPULAR VOTE ON THE RESERVATION AMENDMENT
1857

	For	Against		For	Against
Adams	2,519	502	Lancaster	4,981	32
Allegheny	5,264	439	Lawrence	707	172
Armstrong	33	27	Lebanon	1,255	66
Beaver	1,606	25	Lehigh	437	470
Bedford	2,424	114	Luzerne	3,796	585
Berks	7,414	747	Lycoming	1,689	49
Blair	418	44	M'Kean	(no returns)	
Bradford	1,168	37	Mercer	883	357
Bucks	2,673	501	Mifflin	1,236	100
Butler	789	135	Monroe	92	56
Cambria	950	171	Montgomery	4,706	859
Carbon	476	11	Montour	592	37
Centre	1,145	91	Northampton	2,332	58
Chester	8,472	282	Northumberland	1,545	26
Clarion	1,401	368	Perry	2,229	113
Clearfield	239	205	Philadelphia	7,987	161
Clinton	556	49	Pike	426	17
Columbia	2,134	63	Potter	384	....
Crawford	1,582	168	Schuylkill	4,262	291
Cumberland	3,722	1,274	Snyder	691	201
Dauphin	2,150	508	Somerset	983	42
Delaware	2,075	206	Sullivan	238	22
Elk	26	247	Susquehanna	2,439	231
Erie	922	20	Tioga	2,369	102
Fayette	1,103	157	Union	505	15
Forrest	10	2	Venango	1,010	35
Franklin	5,238	125	Warren	317	103
Fulton	234	169	Washington	1,034	663
Greene	363	188	Wayne	1,436	11
Huntingdon	1,338	65	Westmoreland	8,974	442
Indiana	612	206	Wyoming	300	4
Jefferson	475	740	York	2,630	863
Juniata	1,209	213			
			Total	118,605	14,332*

* The totals of these columns should be 123,205 and 14,282.

the legislature refused to validate suspension, but not a single bank charter was revoked. Noteholders whom the law of 1824 authorized to bring revocation action against banks simply did not do so, despite the fact that at the most recent state elections the majority of Pennsylvanians favored Democrats who were vigorous in their anti-bank protestations. The case was, as Governor Ritner aptly put it, "a remarkable instance of the virtual repeal of a general law of the land by the expressive, but silent action of public necessity, by which even the fierceness of party zeal had been restrained." [24] During the panic of 1857 the same thing happened, but less silently. The legislature frankly withdrew that part of the act of 1850 which made charter revocation a penalty for suspension.[25] Revocation was an unfamiliar action for legislators. When in 1859 a proposal was presented in the legislature to revoke the charter of the Pennsylvania Railroad Company, confusion and inaction was the result. One member could find only "two or three attempts" at revocation previously made by the legislature, and asked "what the result would be if it was decided that the Pennsylvania Railroad had forfeited its charter." [26]

The fact that the power of revocation was rarely utilized, however, does not mean that reservation policy failed to enhance the state's authority over the corporate system. In matters short of revocation, in connection with a great variety of control provisions which we shall examine below, the legislature assumed a power of striking breadth. This power was fortified not only by reservation policy but by a consistent judicial practice of strictly construing the terms of charter grants. The policy of strict construction was the reflection of a larger attitude of judicial self-abnegation, enunciated by Justice Shippen as early as 1799 and championed by such outstanding judges as Tilghman, Gibson, and Black,[27] which characterized the Pennsylvania judiciary in its approach to legislative power. Thus two years prior to the Dartmouth College decision the state Supreme Court interpreted the contract clauses of the state and federal constitutions in restricted

---

[24] *Pa. Archives*, 4th, VI, 362. Cf. *ibid.*, VI, 763.
[25] Hutcheson, "Philadelphia and Panic of 1837," *Pa. Hist.*, III (1936), 188.
[26] *Legislative Record, 1859*, p. 447.
[27] See *Respublica* v. *Duquet*, 2 Yeates 493, 501 (1799); *Moore* v. *Houston*, 3 Serg. and Rawle 169, 196 (1817); *Sharpless et al.* v. *Mayor of Philadelphia*, 21 Pa. St. Rep., 147, 164 (1853).

fashion. "I presume," declared Chief Justice Tilghman, "it will hardly be contended that the words, *impairing the obligations of contracts*, are to be understood in their greatest extent. If they are, the consequences are alarming."[28] Marshall's decision of 1819 overruled this view, but while the Pennsylvania court held thereafter that a charter was a contract and that any material change in its provisions was constitutionally forbidden,[29] it adhered consistently to the strict construction practice. "All acts of incorporation and acts extending the privileges of incorporated bodies, are to be taken most strongly against the companies," Chief Justice Black declared. "Whatever is not expressly and unequivocally granted in such acts is taken to have been withheld."[30]

2. *The Dartmouth College Doctrine: The Case of the Second Bank*

An aspect of unreality characterizes the great debate over the revocation power that took place in the Convention of 1837. For the issues around which it centered had for the most part been irrevocably decided. The passions evoked by Meredith's resolution declaring a charter to be a contract seem remarkably gratuitous. For almost twenty years that principle had been established in state and federal law, and what the forty-one members of the convention who voted against it could accomplish in a legal sense it is hard to know. What the supporters of the resolution could accomplish is equally baffling. Had any of them desired a relaxation of the strictness with which the state judiciary interpreted charter grants or a keener judicial surveillance of legislative action, they could scarcely have hoped to achieve these objectives by introducing a resolution which affirmed merely the elementary principle of contract and which, as was obvious at the

---

[28] *Farmers' and Mechanics' Bank* v. *Smith*, 3 Serg. and Rawle 63, 70, 71 (1817).
[29] Cf. remarks of Chief Justice Gibson in *Monongahela Navigation Co.* v. *Coon*, 6 Pa. St. Rep. 379, 381–82 (1847); of Justice Bell in *Commonwealth* v. *The Easton Bank*, 10 Pa. St. Rep. 442, 449 (1849); also *Commonwealth* ex rel. *Claghorn* v. *Cullen*, 13 Pa. St. Rep. 133, 139 (1850); *Gray* v. *The Monongahela Navigation Co.*, 2 Watts and Serg. 156 (1841).
[30] *Packer* v. *Sunbury and Erie Railroad Company*, 19 Pa. St. Rep. 211, 218 (1852).

time, could pass only by a limited majority. Moreover the legislative policy of including time-limit and reservation clauses in business charters antedated even the Dartmouth College decision; the omission in the Second Bank charter was a rare exception, not the rule. The provisions adopted by the convention in this regard did little more than restate a principle which was already almost universally operative.

The truth is that the debate over state power in the convention, one which transformed the Dartmouth College issue from a precise legal question into a vigorous clash of popular ideologies, cannot be understood save as an immediate and undisciplined reaction to the charter of the Second Bank. The belief that the convention could itself repeal that charter was held by a minority led by the radical Charles Brown of Philadelphia County. They confronted obvious arguments: that the convention could no more violate the contract clause of the federal Constitution than could the legislature; that the powers of the convention were limited to amending the constitution and did not extend to ordinary matters of legislative policy.[31] In strict theoretical terms, however, the assumption of the revocation power by the convention was a logical corollary of much of the traditional anti-charter doctrine, particularly as presented by Ingersoll, and it is interesting that he failed to support Brown and his followers here. For if, as he argued, the chartering of corporations was a granting away of sovereignty by a legislature not authorized to do so,[32] it would seem that a constituent convention would provide the logical machinery for a restitution to the people of the sovereignty that had thus been impaired.

This was, in substance, Brown's argument. There must, he insisted, be a "recuperative power" in every free government, and it was the natural function of constituent conventions to exercise it. It could not be exercised by the legislative branch, for it was, in the first instance, the unwise actions of that branch which made recuperation periodically necessary. To deny the existence of re-

[31] *Convention Proceedings*, V, 542–44, 567.
[32] Cf. *supra*, pp. 73 ff. "I disclaim," Ingersoll said in the Convention of 1837, "all power of this convention to act directly on banks." *Convention Proceedings*, XIV, 5.

cuperative power would lead to the conclusion — branded by Brown as absurd on its face — that the power to change the form of government was inferior to the power to alter its policy.[33] When Brown's argument encountered the reply that the constituent convention was no more accurate a reflection of the sovereign will than the legislature, one of his supporters challenged the anti-revocation forces to submit the question of the repeal of the Second Bank charter to a statewide plebiscite so as to register more accurately the sovereign opinion.[34] This challenge was effective, since a plebiscite on the bank in the emotionally charged atmosphere of 1837 was pure anathema to its defenders.

There were various denials of the principle of contract. A partial denial was presented by Ingersoll who fashioned a category of "political corporations," companies which, though created for commercial purposes, resembled municipal corporations and shared the prerogatives of "sovereignty" sufficiently to justify revocation of their charters at legislative will.[35] He was vague about which corporations were embraced by the political category, at one point including both transportation and banking corporations, at another point insisting only on the latter.[36] In connection with banks Ingersoll attempted to reconcile his position with Marshallian precedents. He argued that Marshall had not explicitly applied the contract principle to bank charters, that this had been done only by Story in his concurring opinion in the Dartmouth College Case, and by "unauthorized" legal commentators, and that Marshall had himself recognized the "political" character of banks in *McCulloch* v. *Maryland*.[37]

Ingersoll's argument was weak, and a few contributions to it by Thomas Earle failed to enhance its strength. On a superficial plane there was, to counter it, the established practice of bonus payments to the state by banks for charters, a practice superlatively exemplified in the case of the Second Bank and one which,

[33] *Ibid.*, V, 505–506. For a different view of the powers of constituent conventions presented by Brown in connection with Meredith's contract resolution, see *ibid.*, V, 521.
[34] *Ibid.*, IX, 152–53.
[35] *Ibid.*, XIV, 14 ff. For replies to this argument, see *ibid.*, V, 539.
[36] *Ibid.*, XIV, 14, 15.
[37] *Ibid.*, XIV, 6, 14, 28–29, 31, 35.

in Porter's words, was evidence of contract "usually to be found in the dealings of individuals." [38] Ingersoll dodged the bonus issue badly, admitting in one instance that "perhaps" bonuses should be refunded upon charter revocation, branching off into an irrelevant attack upon the bonus system in general, and finally expressing only "doubt" that bonus payments involved contract obligations.[39] Moreover it was tortured reasoning to contend that Marshall had excluded bank charters from the Dartmouth College doctrine, especially in light of such cases as *Bank of the United States* v. *Planter's Bank of Georgia* and *Briscoe* v. *Bank of Kentucky*. In the first of these cases Marshall had explicitly held that a state assumed the role of a "private citizen" in relation to the transactions of banks that it chartered, even though it was a partial owner of their stock.[40]

Most revocation theory went beyond Ingersoll to a more forthright denial of the Dartmouth College doctrine, occasionally citing as evidence that charter rights might be validly impaired the action of the Revolutionary Radicals against the Pennsylvania College and the Proprietaries' Property.[41] Though because of the liberal contract-clause interpretations of the state Supreme Court it was possible to argue that true judicial wisdom resided in Harrisburg and not in Washington,[42] a more radical denial of Marshallian doctrine meant an inevitable collision with the whole principle of judicial supremacy. The human fallibility of judges, their record of disagreement on vital issues, the political and economic influences which shaped decisions — all were emphasized by the revocation theorists, as was the classic refutation of *Marbury* v. *Madison* by Chief Justice Gibson of the state court.[43] "The supreme court may decide the question over and over again,

---

[38] *Ibid.*, V, 534, 538.

[39] *Ibid.*, XIV, 5, 23, 24.

[40] 9 Wheaton 905, 906 (1824). For the citation of this precedent in the convention in reply to Ingersoll, see *Convention Proceedings*, V, 539.

[41] *Ibid.*, IX, 129; XIV, 18. For Porter's reply to this citation of precedent, see *ibid.*, V, 542-43.

[42] *Ibid.*, XIV, 5, 25, 44.

[43] *Ibid.*, V, 571-74; XIV, 33, 38, 39-41; *Eakin* v. *Raub*, 12 Serg. and Rawle 330 (1825). Ingersoll declared: "Constitutional are as much political principles, as judges are men." *Ibid.*, XIV, 42.

in any way they choose," declared Earle, "and it will not affect the question." [44]

Certain larger conceptions were also at hand to undermine Marshallian theory. The doctrinal route from natural law to popular sovereignty to periodical elections was, as a result of the rotation-in-office controversy and others, already well traveled. To say with Jefferson and Paine that the earth belonged to the living was to reiterate a principle of which the conservatives, at least, were thoroughly tired, and to cite Blackstone on the exclusively civil character of the right of inheritance was merely to enrich the argument with a dash of legalism appropriate to its atmosphere.[45] After that it was not hard to proceed to the good Lockean contention that, even if charter enactments were contracts, only the contracting generation could be bound by them.[46] It was on the basis of this reasoning that Woodward brushed aside all reservation clauses as gratuitous assertions of a "necessary and essential" principle of popular sovereignty implicit in every charter.[47]

But for the anti-revocation theorists, too, the higher law was not wanting in uses to which it could be put. It is interesting to speculate about how much more appealing their case would have been had they been able to present it only a few years later when the anti-repudiation doctrine began to grow after the breakdown of state credit. The austere references of that ideology to the sacredness of public-loan obligations were admirably designed to enhance the attractiveness of contract morality as applied to the state.[48] It is not accidental, perhaps, that Porter who as governor became the acknowledged father of anti-repudiation doctrine was one of the strongest defenders of the Dartmouth College theory

---

[44] *Ibid.*, V, 573.

[45] *Ibid.*, IX, 126, 130, 132.

[46] *Ibid.*, V, 518–19, 573; IX, 148. Porter insisted in reply on the corporate continuity of the popular sovereign: "the people remain the same. . . ." *Ibid.*, V, 552. See also remarks of Keim of Berks County, *ibid.*, V, 610. This point had been elaborately developed by Paine earlier. *Works*, I, 336 ff.

[47] Woodward argued that "if it is immoral to revoke a charter without a reservation, it is equally so to revoke one that contains an express reservation." *Convention Proceedings*, IX, 149.

[48] See *supra*, p. 19.

in the convention. Yet even then the opponents of revocation did not have to rely exclusively upon the weight of the Marshallian precedents, though they warned the convention against breaking through "a settled course of adjudication." [49] Expanding their defense of charter rights to embrace all property rights, they agreed with Meredith that it had a "far higher sanction" than anything to be derived from a mere "ordinance of men" and they made lavish use of concepts such as "the first moral lesson" and the "law of our nature." [50]

Their opponents replied by citing Taney's strict construction decision in the Charles River Bridge Case, by contending that if the state could endow corporations with eminent domain privileges to invade the property of others it could on the same principle invade any rights accruing from charter grounds, an argument which neatly supplemented the criticism of the corporate use of eminent domain in the traditional anti-charter theory.[51] Every suspension of specie payments, moreover, was branded as a violation of contract obligations by the banks themselves, reasoning which was not without its persuasive effect in the panic environment of 1837. When the anti-revocation theorists sought to answer this argument by insisting that suspension, as Biddle said, had been dictated by considerations of general financial expediency, they unwittingly opened the floodgates for an acceptance of virtually the whole of the pro-revocation case.[52] For right, not expediency, was the essence of the Dartmouth College principle. They were immediately confronted with the reply that if corporations could violate contract obligations on the ground of expediency the state, assuming that its charters were contracts, could surely do the same, having in mind "the good of the people of the whole Commonwealth." [53]

An additional word is necessary concerning the role of the judicial power in the twistings and turnings of this debate. Anti-

[49] *Convention Proceedings*, V, 566–67.
[50] *Ibid.*, V, 515–17; IX, 137, 172. In a bid for agrarian support it was strongly argued that the security of land titles would be shaken by the adoption of the principle implicit in revocation provisions. *Ibid.*, V, 563; IX, 170, 179; XIV, 6.
[51] *Ibid.*, XIV, 16, 20, 46; V, 579, 587.
[52] *Ibid.*, V, 506; IX, 170. See Gallatin, *Writings*, II, 559.
[53] *Ibid.*, IX, 128.

revocation theorists insisted that the judiciary should determine when charter revocations were justified because of corporation malpractices,[54] a contention which became important in connection with Meredith's contract resolution which restricted itself to charters "duly granted." It was immediately asked whether lobby pressure to procure charters was sufficient to exclude a franchise from the meaning of Meredith's resolution, a query acutely relevant in light of the Second Bank experience.[55] Because the age failed to provide any coherent justification of pressure-group activity, Meredith had no way of answering this embarrassing question, and attempted to dodge it by a confused and wordy reply.[56] Pro-revocation theorists followed up their argument by pointing to *Fletcher* v. *Peck* [57] where Marshall himself had emphasized the insuperable difficulties in the way of establishing fraud in the legislature by judicial process, insisting that the judiciary was incompetent to deal with the termination or alteration of charters.[58] The notion that a judicial writ was needed in this respect, declared Ingersoll, was an unjustified importation from Britain where courts served as agents of royal prerogative, an idea "at war with the American system." [59] Action on charters was exclusively and properly a matter of legislative judgment.

This defense of the legislative power by the pro-revocation theorists is liable to be misleading. For in their role as anti-charter ideologists, they were presenting simultaneously a vigorous attack on the legislative power, one which in the Convention of 1837 actually led to constitutional restrictions on the legislative chartering prerogative.[60] In the latter instance Ingersoll did not hesitate to invoke Marshall's higher law theory of legislative limitations.[61] Yet this dualism, seized upon by Merrill among their opponents as a "great inconsistency" and a "strange position," [62] was logi-

[54] *Ibid.*, V, 567; IX, 180.
[55] *Ibid.*, V, 575.
[56] *Ibid.*, V, 582.
[57] 6 Cranch 87 (1810).
[58] *Convention Proceedings*, XIV, 5; V, 564.
[59] *Ibid.*, XIV, 28, 30. Cf. *supra*, p. 73.
[60] Cf. *supra*, pp. 73 ff.
[61] *Convention Proceedings*, XIV, 11.
[62] *Ibid.*, IX, 152, 153; for Brown's reply to Merrill, see *ibid.*, V, 600.

cally dictated by their larger anti-corporation view. If that view condemned the ease with which the legislature granted franchises, it had to defend complete freedom for the legislature in revoking them. This defense, however, never came close to offsetting the enormous damage to legislative prestige wrought by the persistent excoriation of charter enactments.

Apart from its different outlook on the legislative power, however, it is clear that the pro-revocation theory was logically allied with the traditional anti-charter doctrine. A subtle evidence of this linkage is to be found in the fact that the Dartmouth College principle, when it was blown up into a popular ideology to attack the pro-revocation theory, produced as a logical by-product an attack also upon the anti-charter doctrine. It attacked that doctrine in classic fashion — by corrupting the integrity of its concepts. When it identified the corporation and the state with two individuals in a relation of business contract, it served to clothe the corporation with a kind of personal individuality — a symbolic effect which, as I have demonstrated before, nullified the distinction between individual and corporate enterprise which was at the heart of the anti-charter theory. If Porter could insist that corporate dealings were indistinguishable from the dealings of "individuals," Forward could say that "there was no difference in the matter whether applied to A and B, or the commonwealth on one side, and any citizen, on the other." [63] If there were two roles that the corporation could never assume in the anti-charter doctrine, they were the roles of individual and citizen. The doctrine thrived precisely on the notion that the corporation was the hated oppressor of both.

The state, too, emerged in the role of a contracting individual. As early as 1785 Paine, realizing that this symbolic effect was inherent in the application of contract morality to charter grants, flatly stated that the state stood as a "private citizen." [64] In 1837 Meredith likened the state-corporation relationship to a contract

[63] *Ibid.*, IX, 137.
[64] *Works*, I, 334. For the use of Paine in this connection by the Dartmouth College theorists, see *Convention Proceedings*, V, 556, 560; for an attack on Paine's position, *ibid.*, XIV, 11. Marshall later used the same language. See *supra*, p. 246.

"between two private individuals." Yet it is important to emphasize that there was nothing in the prevailing Lockean theory of social contract to justify such a view, despite the fact that Paine tried cleverly to suggest that there was, and Ingersoll was warranted in his counter-argument in 1837 that it was essential to distinguish between a "state and an individual." [65] A social contract could forge a civil society or a "will of the people," a fiduciary relation might exist between this society and its governmental agents, but these were utterly different things from contracts entered into by governmental agents with selected, more or less wealthy, minorities. Here we see that the traditional anti-charter doctrine could no more tolerate the state in the role of individual than it could the corporation. For that theory, itself relying heavily upon Lockean doctrine, insisted that a charter grant was an express violation of the social contract, a betrayal by governmental agents of the popular trust, and an impairment of popular sovereignty.[66] To contend that contract theory paralyzed the state once such illegitimate privileges had been granted was to fly in the face of the whole logic of the anti-charter doctrine.

It is not difficult to see the similarity between the above effects of the Dartmouth College doctrine as a political ideology and certain phases of the theory of the forties and fifties which, denying the legitimacy of public investment and enterprise, also undermined the anti-charter doctrine. The individualization of the corporation, with a consequent nullification of the distinction between individual and corporate enterprise, and the measurement of the state by the code of business entrepreneurs, both were characteristic of the later theory. The Dartmouth College ideology even anticipated that peculiar glorification of the business leader at the expense of the politician so characteristic of the later doctrine. In 1837 Ingersoll bitterly denounced the anti-revocation theorists for pronouncing "an encomium . . . upon the directors of all the banks of Pennsylvania, contrasting their highly extolled virtues with the much contemned vices of politicians courting the people." [67] These similarities do not appear entirely

---

[65] *Ibid.*, V, p. 516; XIV, 6.   [66] Cf. *supra*, pp. 69 ff.
[67] *Convention Proceedings*, XIV, 50, 51; *ibid.*, V, 566, IX, 164.

accidental when we realize that both the earlier and the later theory had two motives in common: the defense of the private corporation and the elimination of governmental interference with it.

Implicit in the pro-revocation and anti-revocation theories, though scarcely elaborated in a conscious way, were actually two different conceptions of political life, embodying two conceptions of economic policy, one of stability, the other of change. The Dartmouth College ideology, with its emphasis upon previously acquired property rights and its grave respect for the organic growth of the law, betrayed an ideal political world of measured change, limited shifts. On the other hand, the democratic dogma that was mobilized against it, with its changing popular sovereign, its rotating offices, and its worship of the immediate mass will, reflected a version of political life as a fluid, contingent affair. The policy conception implicit in the latter view came to the surface in one of the rambling speeches of Thomas Earle: "Each generation should act for itself. If one generation was free to say we will have banks and other corporations, the following generation might say we will have no banks, and no corporations. One generation might have turnpikes, and another railroads, if they thought them better. Let each generation, as it comes upon the stage, manage its own affairs, in its own way. Each generation is more competent to regulate its internal policy, than a preceding generation." [68]

This statement carried out with heroic logic the implications for economic policy of ascendant democratic attitudes. But how well could it satisfy the requirements of business enterprise? The answer is obvious. The developing exploitation of the corporate device was itself a sure indication that business enterprise was moving into a new era of long-range planning which called for an increasingly stable legal and political environment. In many little ways the Dartmouth College theorists gave expression to this growing economic urgency, and the business depression which coincided with the Convention of 1837 admirably inspired them

[68] *Ibid.*, V, 574.

to do so. They tried to hush up the entire revocation issue on the ground that its open discussion would destroy business "confidence" at a crucial moment. On the same ground they effectively repressed a proposed committee of inquiry into the Second Bank.[69] One of their most telling arguments against the inclusion of a reservation clause in the constitution as well as against the limitation of the legislative power to recharter corporations was that such action would create damaging uncertainty among corporation managers. This would not only drive capital out of the state and eliminate Pennsylvania's leading position in the financial world,[70] but it would vitiate, so Scott of Philadelphia argued, Pennsylvania's increasingly fruitful policy of chartering corporations jointly with other states, a policy already responsible for bridges over the Delaware, the Chesapeake and Delaware Canal Company, and the Chesapeake and Ohio. Other states would surely not "bind themselves" while Pennsylvania, with a reservation clause in its constitution, was "left free to play fast and loose." [71]

While this argument clearly had meaning as a broad view of proper economic policy, in the specific context of the revocation issue fears such as Scott's were fantastic. Reservation policy had established itself twenty years earlier and 1837 was no time to insist that it would lead to economic ruin. Scott and his colleagues were rightly charged with seeking to "go backward" to a pre-reservation period which antedated the state's greatest corporate development.[72] Yet had not the pro-revocation theorists themselves gone backward in opening up an argument that had already been settled in law and in policy? We are confronted again with the curious artificiality of much of the entire controversy, an example of the historic lateness which often characterizes some of the most fruitful elaborations of social thought.

[69] *Ibid.*, V, 576–77; cf. *ibid.*, 585.
[70] Cf. *ibid.*, V, 507, 563, 607; IX, 143, 154, 174.
[71] *Ibid.*, IX, 171. Cf. *ibid.*, IX, 173.
[72] *Ibid.*, IX, 109, 159, 171.

3. Regulatory Policy

A complete examination of regulatory policy in the corporate field, with its myriad and changing provisions, would require a separate book. Yet some view of that policy, especially as it appeared in charter enactments, impresses us with the breadth of the new regulatory responsibilities which the state assumed with the growth of the corporate system. All charters included provisions governing in detail the size of the directorate, the powers it wielded, its term of office, and the method by which it was selected.[73] An unsophisticated popular theory of banking, which frequently found a personal villain where an economic circumstance prevailed, placed undue emphasis upon penalties for bank directors as a solution to the monetary problem. During every financial crisis the cry for heavier penalties arose. Yet there was little progress in thought on this subject beyond the first bank charter of 1793 which made directors personally liable for any indebtedness authorized in excess of charter limits.[74] The idea of personal liability was adapted in various ways: by making directors responsible for the declaration of dividends that impaired capital stock,[75] a practice that was also common in the manufacturing and insurance fields; [76] by making them liable for "fraudulent insolvency"; and by progressively expanding the legal content of this concept.[77]

Efforts to prevent a concentration of power in corporations preoccupied the legislature from the outset. Monopolistic practices were especially feared in the banking field, and a number of special measures were taken to strike at them there. Rotation of directors was often made mandatory in banks, and public offi-

---

[73] Burdine, "Regulation of Industry in Pa., 1776–1860," p. 161.

[74] *Dallas' Laws*, III, 323–35.

[75] *Pa. Laws, 1803–1804*, pp. 235–50; Burdine, "Regulation of Industry in Pa., 1776–1860," p. 182.

[76] *Pa. Laws, 1815–16*, pp. 23–25. For Whitestown Manufacturing Company, see *ibid.*; in the York County Manufacturing Company personal liability was imposed for indebtedness beyond 50 per cent of capital stock. *Pa. Laws, 1819–20*, p. 148. See also *ibid.*, *1838–39*, pp. 231–35; *1844*, pp. 537–40.

[77] Cf. charter of Lehigh County Bank, *Pa. Laws, 1844*, pp. 412–17, and the procedure relating to fraudulent insolvency in the Banking Act of 1850, *ibid.*, *1850*, pp. 477–95.

cials were frequently excluded from membership in bank directorates.[78] Charter provisions limited the number of days on which stock subscriptions might be made, the number of shares for which single individuals or associations might subscribe, and the locality from which subscriptions might be received.[79] After 1810, in order to ward off excessive foreign control, it became an established practice to forbid the transfer of bank stock to anyone who was not a citizen of the country.[80] Another reliance for the dispersion of corporate power, the scaled voting system, was adopted in the first bank charter granted by the state.[81] It was criticized as depriving large stockholders of equal rights and as discriminating against banking capitalists, since it was not so severely imposed in other fields. It was defended as a "limitation on the power of capital over mind," as a necessary protection for small stockholders, and as especially important in banks which were "essentially different" from other corporations because of the larger power they ordinarily wielded in the community.[82]

It is clear, however, that the loose use of proxy privileges lightened to some extent the burden which scaled voting imposed. Proxy voting, which was permitted in most charters as a matter of practical necessity, soon began to evoke criticism as a technique for power concentration. It was charged with being at war with "the genius and principles of our government," with maintaining in control of banks officers who were not the free choice of stockholders, with encouraging fraud upon stockholders and the public, and with erecting a barrier against the free investigation of corporate management.[83] A general law of 1820, which did not, however, apply to banking corporations where proxy voting was under heaviest attack, sought to regulate but not to abolish the

---

[78] Burdine, "Regulation of Industry in Pa.," p. 183.
[79] Cf. *Dallas' Laws*, III, 323–35; *Pa. Laws, 1813–14*, pp. 154–73; *ibid., 1850*, pp. 477–95. For the selling of bank stock at public auction, see the act incorporating the Merchants' and Manufacturers' Bank of Pittsburgh, *ibid., 1832–33*, pp. 102–106.
[80] This provision first appears in a measure of 1810 extending the charter of the Bank of Pennsylvania. *Ibid., 1809–10*, pp. 27–28. See also *ibid., 1813–14*, pp. 281–82. The Banking Act of 1850, however, does not mention this matter.
[81] *Dallas' Laws*, III, 323–35.
[82] *Pa. Archives*, 4th, VII, 707 ff.
[83] *Ibid.*, VI, 129, 192, 618.

proxy system.[84] Despite repeated gubernatorial pleas for the abolition of the system,[85] the legislature refused to tamper with it in any basic way. The House Judiciary Committee during the thirties hinted that the Dartmouth College doctrine cast doubt upon the power of the state to abolish proxy privileges expressly granted in charters. Pointing out that proxies had originally been permitted because stock investments were to "be obtained from persons residing so great a distance from the scene of operations" that they could not "attend personally at the elections" of directors, the committee also emphasized that the abolition of the proxy system would discourage investments of outstate and foreign capital in Pennsylvania corporations.[86]

Stockholder liability was a hotly contested issue. Early charters made little reference to the matter, and the establishment of limited-liability privileges in law was vigorously criticized on the ground that they had never been "expressly declared by the people." The argument against "privileging a few to be exempt from the liabilities common to all the rest" [87] was an integral part of the classic anti-charter doctrine, and by invoking the whole apparatus of democratic theory, it was able to offset to some extent the contract moralizing of the Dartmouth College ideologists. More stringent liability provisions, on the other hand, were assailed as penalties upon the small stockholder, as the prelude to new fraudulent practices in the corporate field, and as techniques for the discouragement of outstate investment in Pennsylvania enterprises.[88]

These arguments might have prevailed, had the belief not emerged that tighter liability rules in the banking field would serve as a barrier against monetary fluctuations. Beginning in the thirties the legislature, spurred on by the encouragement of Governors Porter and Shunk,[89] defined stockholder liability in bank charters more rigorously than before, and the Banking Act

[84] *Pa. Laws, 1819–20*, pp. 169–70.
[85] *Pa. Archives*, 4th, VI, 129, 192, 618.
[86] *House Journal, 1833–34*, II, 721–22. Cf. *ibid., 1828–29*, II, 616.
[87] *Doylestown Democrat*, Sept. 29, 1847; *Convention Proceedings*, XIV, 11; Harrisburg *Democratic Union*, Mar. 8, 1845, Feb. 24, 1844.
[88] *Ibid.*, Feb. 22, 1845.
[89] *Pa. Archives*, 4th, VII, 66, 131, 185.

of 1850 made these regulations general.⁹⁰ Individual liability was introduced into the manufacturing and mining fields by the General Act of 1853, though pressure subsequently led to a confinement of this provision to debts due to miners, quarrymen, and other laborers, and for such supplies as machinery, materials, and country produce.⁹¹ In the insurance field stockholders were ordinarily made liable only to the extent of the amount invested in capital stock or the amount remaining unpaid on shares of capital stock held. Members of mutual companies generally were liable for a proportionate share of the losses sustained by the company, although this liability was more expressly defined in certain acts than in others.⁹² Transportation and other public-utility corporations, apparently because of a desire to encourage investment in them, were wholly exempt from express individual liability provisions.

Significant as organizational forms were, the established sphere of regulatory power extended far beyond them into the realm of corporate policy. Owing to the absence of uniform legislation among the states, lack of experience with complex monetary problems, and the speculative spirit of the age, policy regulation in the banking field presented the most serious difficulties.⁹³ Its development, as Governor Porter once said, reflected "a succession of plausible theories," ⁹⁴ though they were concerned not with the legitimate sphere of governmental action but with practical measures to be taken within an acknowledged breadth of state authority. During the first two decades of the nineteenth century, unincorporated banks, products of a speculative fever in the interior counties, led to four successive prohibitory measures, penalizing not only the banks but the acceptors of their notes as well.⁹⁵ An-

---

⁹⁰ *Pa. Laws, 1833–34*, pp. 8–10; *1844*, pp. 412–17; *1850*, pp. 477–95; *Pa. Archives*, 4th, VII, 715.
⁹¹ *Pa. Laws, 1853*, pp. 637–38; *1854*, pp. 215–16.
⁹² See *ibid., 1806–1807*, pp. 80–86; *1833–34*, pp. 109–113; *1838–39*, pp. 30–31; *1810–11*, pp. 240–47; *1829–30*, pp. 81–85; *1846*, p. 71.
⁹³ D. Dewey, *State Banking before Civil War*, passim.
⁹⁴ *Pa. Archives*, 4th, VI, 840.
⁹⁵ *Pa. Laws, 1808–1809*, pp. 35–36; *ibid., 1816–17*, pp. 138–42; *1827–28*, pp. 323–25; *1829–30*, p. 48. See also *ibid., 1840–41*, pp. 357–58.

other knotty problem concerned penalties for the suspension of specie payments by duly incorporated establishments. It is interesting that the earliest banking acts made no provision for the payment of notes in specie and did not require banks to maintain a specie reserve of any kind.[96] Beginning with the Banking Act of 1814, specie suspension became a malpractice for which charter revocation was the formal if usually unimposed penalty. Yet it was not until the enactment of the Free Banking Act of 1860 that the maintenance of specie reserves was required by law.[97]

Liabilities of banks were always limited in proportion to capital stock, and the trading and investment activities of banks, especially in connection with real property, also fell under statute regulation.[98] Detailed regulations were set down for dividend issues, especially for issues during the suspension of specie payments when any division of profits evoked popular protest.[99] A maximum interest rate of 6 per cent was set for loans, and prior to the closing years of our period banks were often required to issue a stated proportion of loans to persons in specified occupations; farmers, mechanics, and manufacturers were often favored.[100] Until 1842 banks were also customarily required to loan specified sums to the state.[101]

The desire of the state to encourage investment in public utilities led to a regulatory policy there in certain respects more lenient than elsewhere. Broad permission was granted, particularly to railroad companies after 1840, to borrow money, issue bonds and preferred stock, undertake refunding operations, and aid weaker companies through the purchase of stock, the loan of money, or the endorsement of bonds.[102] As far as service and

[96] See remarks of Justice Read in *Bank of Pennsylvania* v. *Spangler*, 32 Pa. St. Rep. 474, 476–77 (1859).
[97] *Pa. Laws, 1860*, pp. 459–71.
[98] Burdine, "Regulation of Industry in Pa., 1776–1860," pp. 184–85.
[99] *Pa. Laws, 1822–23*, pp. 127–40; *Pa. Archives*, 4th, VI, 619.
[100] Burdine, "Regulation of Industry in Pa., 1776–1860," p. 186, fn. 33. Cf. *Pa. Laws, 1808–1809*, pp. 43–51; *1823–24*, pp. 59–75.
[101] Cf. *Dallas' Laws*, III, 323–35; *Pa. Laws, 1803–1804*, pp. 235–50; *1822–23*, pp. 127–40; *1840–41*, pp. 307–20.
[102] *Ibid., 1850*, pp. 129–31; *1852*, pp. 79–80; *1857*, pp. 13–14.

earnings were concerned, however, utility corporations operated under detailed regulations. Transportation corporations were subject to penalties for failing to keep works "in good and perfect order and repair"; water companies in times of scarcity were often compelled to ration supplies, giving preference to domestic over manufacturing purposes; telegraph companies were prohibited from engaging in service discrimination.[103] Charters frequently included provision for a redemption or contingent fund to be made up of earnings above a certain rate, or for the payment of such earnings directly into the state treasury. Special funds were sometimes required for the maintenance of utilities in good repair.[104] The detailed regulation of rates, moreover, was always conceived as a function of the state in the public-utility field. This was not a common conception elsewhere, though that it was not completely ruled out in other fields is demonstrated by the striking example of the charter of the Philadelphia Ice Company, granted in 1837, which set down stipulations for the fixing of "reasonable" prices at periodical intervals.[105]

Transportation charters traditionally set maximum rates or laid down provisions governing the promulgation of rates by corporate managers. In certain cases, especially in early acts, provision was made for the raising or the reduction of rates according to the percentage of net earnings. Usually in such cases tolls could be raised to guarantee an income of 6 per cent on capital and had to be reduced when income exceeded 12, 15, or 25 per cent.[106] In other instances toll increases were flatly limited to a certain percentage, and in still others, by virtue of charter clauses reserving legislative authority to alter rates, the legislature was relied upon as a continuous agency of discretionary control.[107]

Rate measures also included provisions exempting certain

[103] *Ibid.*, *1832–33*, pp. 32–43; *1849*, pp. 263–67; Burdine, "Regulation of Industry in Pa., 1776–1860," p. 232.

[104] *Dallas' Laws*, III, 133–43; *Pa. Laws, 1849*, pp. 263–67; Burdine, "Regulation of Industry in Pa., 1776–1860," p. 231.

[105] *Pa. Laws, 1836–37*, p. 356.

[106] *Dallas' Laws*, III, 607–17; IV, 322–24; *Pa. Laws, 1828–29*, pp. 201–12; *1845*, pp. 284–85.

[107] See *ibid.*, *1806–1807*, pp. 45–48; Burdine, "Regulation of Industry in Pa., 1776–1860," pp. 229–30.

classes of individuals from rate payment. Farmers traveling within the limits of their land, individuals traveling to certain religious or civic functions, and paupers freed from ordinary tax payments, were customarily exempted from the payment of turnpike tolls.[108] By virtue of charter requirements gas companies were often compelled to supply gas light to municipal corporations at reduced rates. Managers of gas and water companies were usually permitted to set their own rates for the public at large within the limits of the terms "uniform" and "reasonable." [109] But in the case of railroad companies, where mile rates were set for freight and passengers, the state did not hesitate to lay down different rates for the eastern and western transportation of freight.[110] Ferry rates were usually under the control of the courts of quarter sessions,[111] as distinguished from other utility rates which were a legislative responsibility. Telegraph companies appear to have been the only utilities which were not subjected to rate regulation.

Controls in the insurance field were not so highly developed as in banking. Insurance corporations were based either on the mutual or joint-stock principle, though individual charters often permitted a combination of the principles and this combination was recognized by the General Insurance Act of 1856.[112] Though early insurance charters failed to limit the types of risks in which business might be done, such limitation began to appear after 1810 and was systematized by the act of 1856.[113] Investment controls were emphasized, though limitations appear to have been most stringent in this connection during the early period. Since early insurance charters established the policy of permitting investment in the stock of other Pennsylvania corporations,[114] the area of permissible investment naturally expanded with the growth of the corporate system in the state. A general legislative

---

[108] *Ibid.*, p. 230, fn. 37.
[109] *Pa. Laws, 1848*, pp. 213–18; *1852*, pp. 155–61; *1822–23*, pp. 25–29.
[110] *Ibid., 1825–26*, pp. 216–26.
[111] *Ibid., 1806–1807*, pp. 19–20; *1857*, pp. 17–18.
[112] *Ibid., 1856*, pp. 211–17.
[113] Burdine, "Regulation of Industry in Pa., 1776–1860," pp. 201–202; *Pa. Laws, 1856*, pp. 211–17.
[114] *Dallas' Laws*, III, 489–94.

tendency to relax early investment restrictions had its culmination in the general act of 1856 which permitted companies to invest in respondential or bottomry bonds, ground rents, bonds and mortgages on real estate, public stocks or loans, and securities of other types.[115] It was customary, however, to limit real-estate holdings and to provide for their liquidation within a definite period of time. The problem of foreign corporations was taken more seriously in this field than in any other throughout the entire period. Business with corporations of other nations was prohibited as early as 1810, and agents of outstate corporations were hemmed in by complex licensing, reportorial, and taxing provisions.[116]

In the manufacturing and mining fields regulations were laid down in usual detail. The types of business in which companies might engage were sharply limited.[117] Occasionally in the mining field production minimums were set by law, charter revocation being the penalty for failure to meet them. The Pennsylvania Coke and Iron Company, chartered during the legislative session of 1831–1832, was compelled, for example, to manufacture within three years five hundred tons of iron using only bituminous coal or anthracite in the process.[118] Real property holdings were closely restricted.[119] Ordinarily authorization to borrow money, and to issue bonds and preferred stock, was not granted in manufacturing and mining charters but had to be obtained by supplementary act. Such acts did not appear in any considerable number until after 1840, and they embraced a series of specific regulations concerning interest rates, the sale of bonds below par, and dividend issues.[120] Moreover, as indicated in an earlier chapter, manufacturing and mining establishments also operated under an expanding set of labor regulations. The General Manufacturing Law of 1849 and its supplements fortunately systematized a mass of this policy.

---

[115] *Pa. Laws, 1856*, pp. 211–17.
[116] *Ibid., 1809–10*, pp. 81–82; *1826–27*, pp. 239–40; *1849*, pp. 216–17; *1851*, pp. 353–54; cf. *1857*, pp. 318–19.
[117] Burdine, "Regulation of Industry in Pa., 1776–1860," p. 161.
[118] *Pa. Laws, 1831–32*, pp. 106–11; *1834–35*, pp. 231–32.
[119] Burdine, "Regulation of Industry in Pa., 1776–1860," p. 161.
[120] *Pa. Laws, 1841*, pp. 114–15; *1854*, pp. 163–64; *1855*, pp. 9–10.

Corporate taxation, including special levies on the tonnage of certain railroad corporations, was one of the most significant of state policies. The Banking Act of 1814 imposed a 6 per cent tax on dividends accruing from corporation stock which it authorized, and this tax was later increased to 8 per cent and in certain cases to 11 per cent.[121] During the thirties the movement to increase dividend levies in the banking field gained strength from the drive for public education, and Governor Wolf declared that there was no property which "with a greater regard to justice" could be taxed for "beneficial or useful purposes" than profits arising from the "transactions of moneyed institutions."[122] Prior to 1840 taxation of stocks and dividends in other fields embraced a variety of individual charter provisions, but in that year, owing largely to the grim condition of the public credit, it was systematized. A measure was enacted taxing all capital stock, but since the levies it imposed were scaled according to the dividends the stock produced, this measure was hardly distinguishable from a direct tax on dividends such as prevailed in the banking field.[123] Like the bank tax it soon became a significant source of public revenue, and a supplementary law of 1844 made corporation officers individually liable for tax payments if its provisions were not complied with.[124]

4. The Approach To Enforcement

It would be naive to assume that the policy pattern, as we find it formally and impressively enunciated in statute books, was in operational fact always imposed upon the corporate system. In all too many instances the significance of statute records is confined to the theoretical sphere. The failure of general regulatory measures to emerge to prominence until the late forties meant that over most of our period control policy involved a welter of variety and inconsistency which not even the finest administrative system could have enforced. In the banking field, especially, evasions of law were widespread. In 1823 a House committee

---

[121] *Ibid.*, *1813–14*, pp. 154–73; *1823–24*, pp. 59–75; *1834–35*, p. 99.
[122] *Pa. Archives*, 4th, VI, 195 ff. Cf. *ibid.*, VI, 301.
[123] Snyder, *Taxation in Pa.*, p. 63.
[124] *Pa. Laws, 1844*, pp. 486–503.

reported that all measures against unincorporated banking were "daily violated with impunity." [125] In 1836 Governor Wolf announced that proxy controls were being "entirely disregarded or shamefully evaded." [126] In 1839 Governor Porter declared that laws prohibiting dividend issues during time of specie suspension were being "contemptuously trampled on" and that the situation was "revolting." [127] In 1850 Governor Johnston reported that the laws regulating the denomination of notes were being "practically disregarded." [128] In 1855 the auditor-general complained of widespread "neglect or failure" in the payment of dividend taxes.[129]

The growth of administrative wisdom was slow. Excessive reliance was placed upon reportorial techniques over the entire period. The Banking Act of 1814 required of all banks created under it annual reports on capital stock, debts due, funds deposited, notes in circulation, cash on hand, and dividends declared.[130] Subsequent measures expanded these requirements, partially as a result of the intensification of regulations concerning debts and insolvency.[131] In the transportation field it was not until 1823 that turnpike reporting was regularized,[132] and annual statements were not uniformly required of railroad corporations until 1859.[133] The General Manufacturing Law of 1849 together with certain supplementary measures systematized reporting procedures in manufacturing and mining, imposing an annual-report requirement similar to that prevailing in the banking field.[134] Though insurance companies, unlike other corporations, were not compelled to file annual reports with the state, they were required to publish financial statements each year.[135] In most cases the auditor-general was placed in charge of reports filed with the

[125] *House Journal, 1822–23*, p. 622. Cf. *ibid., 1811–12*, pp. 591–92.
[126] *Pa. Archives*, 4th, VI, 130.
[127] *Ibid.*, VI, 620.
[128] *Ibid.*, VII, 392.
[129] *Senate Journal, 1855*, p. 4.
[130] *Pa. Laws, 1813–14*, pp. 154–73.
[131] *Ibid., 1832–33*, pp. 102–106; *1845*, pp. 433–37; *1850*, pp. 477–95.
[132] *Ibid., 1822–23*, pp. 282–83.
[133] *Ibid., 1859*, p. 358.
[134] See *ibid., 1853*, pp. 637–38.
[135] Burdine, "Regulation of Industry in Pa., 1776–1860," p. 212.

state, though in some instances the secretary of the commonwealth was given this duty.

Striking breakdowns of the reporting system were common. Speaking in 1859 the auditor-general lamented widespread failure on the part of railroad companies to comply with reportorial requirements, pointing out, somewhat gratuitously, that this "indicates a very great disinclination on their part to give information respecting their affairs." [136] In the following year, again in connection with railroad companies, he reported that "in many instances the blanks are so imperfectly filled up as to render the information they contain of little practical value," though he held out some hope — the basis for which he did not state — that the value of providing correct answers might become "more apparent" to companies in the future.[137] In 1858 eighteen insurance companies were listed in official documents as not complying with publicity requirements.[138] In 1857 the auditor-general reported that the publication of notices concerning penalties prescribed for failure to comply with reportorial measures had "been tried without much success." [139] Nor is this surprising. In 1855 in reply to a request by the Senate for information about whether suits had been instituted against manufacturing and mining companies failing to file annual reports, the auditor-general replied that no action had been taken.[140] He spoke vaguely in 1861 of the need for "some legislative remedy." [141]

Yet it would be unjust to blame this situation on the auditor-general's office. The casual fashion in which the legislature stacked obligations upon that official was shocking. In addition to auditing ordinary state finances, he was required to serve as state director in certain mixed enterprises, appoint directors for others, investigate a chaotic system of public works expenditures, execute economic measures from licensing to corporate reporting, and perform miscellaneous tasks assigned from time to time.[142] All of this was to be done on an annual budget which as late as

---

[136] *Legislative Documents, 1859*, p. 454.
[137] *Ibid.*, 1860, p. 548.
[138] *Ibid.*, 1858, p. 677.
[139] *Ibid.*, 1857, pp. 785 ff.
[140] *Ibid.*, 1855, p. 605.
[141] *Ibid.*, 1861, p. 454.
[142] Cf. *Senate Journal, 1855*, p. 4.

1856 amounted to less than fifteen hundred dollars, over one third of which was spent on postage and telegraphic dispatches.[143] It is small wonder that E. Banks, auditor-general in 1856, flatly told the legislature that a check-up on the reporting of mining and manufacturing corporations "would require more time and labor than could be devoted to that object without neglecting the current business of the office . . . ."[144]

Moreover the legislature frequently made demands, not only upon the auditor-general but upon other administrative officers as well, that were clearly impossible of fulfillment. No industrial censuses were taken in Pennsylvania prior to the Civil War, and there was no way in which the number of companies failing to comply with reportorial requirements could be accurately known. Charter records provided, of course, no adequate guide to the situation, since the percentage of failures and false starts was always high. When the speaker of the Senate forwarded a resolution to the state treasurer calling for information relative to loans floated by transportation corporations, the latter simply replied that "the information desired is not in my possession, nor have I the means to ascertain same."[145] Similarly, when asked about suits against corporations breaking reportorial laws, the auditor-general pointed out that he did not even have the "necessary means" to "ascertain the names and locality of the companies . . . ."[146] Such information as was obtained in these matters was almost entirely of the hit or miss variety, being provided sometimes merely by interested private citizens.[147]

Yet it should not be assumed that the legislature was inordinately fond of delegating regulatory responsibilities to executive officials. The heavy reliance it placed upon its own investigating committees is testimony to the fact that in the regulatory field, as elsewhere, it was reluctant to part with authority. Though the right of committees to investigate corporate operations was often expressly reserved in charters, as for example in the Banking Act

---

[143] *Legislative Documents, 1856*, p. 575.
[144] *Ibid., 1855*, p. 605.
[145] *Senate Journal, 1854*, p. 641.
[146] *Legislative Documents, 1855*, p. 605.
[147] *Ibid., 1858*, p. 677.

of 1814, such reservations were usually vague. This encouraged flare-ups in which corporate directors challenged the power to investigate, especially in the banking field where charters permitted certain accounts to remain secret.[148] It often led, moreover, to hesitant action by the committees themselves, especially in light of the fact that the complexity of corporate business not infrequently exceeded the technical knowledge of committee members or the time available to attain it. A banking committee of 1837 admitted its "own incompetency" to deal with the subject.[149] Committees occasionally fell back upon reportorial techniques, in which case they were no more successful than the auditor-general. One committee complained that replies to its queries were "unintelligible," [150] another that companies "failed to return answers." [151] Punitive action in these cases was not even suggested.

Even had the committee technique been improved, it is clear that it was inherently incapable of satisfying regulatory needs. Not only was it sporadic in operation, largely dependent upon the immediate mood of public opinion for its motivation, but the legislature to which it reported was far too large a body for the initiation of punitive action in specific cases. The situation called for a supervisory instrument so continuous and experienced in its activity that it could not be easily hoodwinked by the corporate interests with which it dealt; it called for some type of administrative commission. Yet the failure of the commission idea to achieve strength is one of the most striking characteristics of administrative thought in the corporate field throughout our period. The need for more continuous regulation was, to be sure, clearly recognized, especially in connection with banks. But as late as the fifties most proposals for satisfying this need looked either toward the formation of standing legislative committees [152] or toward the imposition of greater responsibilities upon the over-

[148] Cf. *House Journal, 1815–16,* p. 158; *1821–22,* p. 586; *1823–24,* pp. 784–86; *1828–29,* II, 561, 563; *1837–38,* II, 846 ff.
[149] *Ibid.,* II, 847.
[150] *Ibid., 1822–23,* p. 544.
[151] *Ibid., 1837–38,* II, 847.
[152] See remarks of George Tucker, *Hunt's Merchants' Mag.,* XXXVIII (1858), 148 ff.

worked auditor-general. The latter solution was adopted in the banking field by the Free Banking Act of 1860.[153]

It is to Governor Porter's credit that he recommended the creation of a permanent banking commission of three members to be endowed with considerable authority,[154] but his proposal had little support. Governor Shunk, who certainly could not be accused of harboring pro-bank views, opposed the idea on the curious ground that it would "induce a dangerous reliance upon the vigilance of such officers," suggesting as a substitute the hackneyed idea of extending individual stockholder liability.[155]

5. The Inalienable State Power: The Case of the Pennsylvania Railroad

There is little doubt that for corporate interests the weakness of the state administrative system mitigated in considerable measure the apparent breadth of the regulatory power. Yet it was inevitable that new ideas should be produced to compensate for the limitations which reservation and strict-construction policy placed upon the effect of the Dartmouth College principle. If the main controversy over that principle appeared in the thirties in connection with the Second Bank, it was logical that the great controversy which crystallized the new ideas should appear in the fifties in connection with the Pennsylvania Railroad Company: beginning in the forties railroads supplanted banks as the source of the deepest tensions between state and corporate power.

The new controversy was a complex affair, with roots entangled not only in regulatory policy but in charter, mixed corporation, public works, and state finance policies as well. Though the ideas it produced had serious implications for the whole of the legislative power over the corporate system, it centered immediately about the taxation of railroad tonnage. The Pennsylvania Railroad and the Harrisburg and Lancaster Railroad which it leased, bore the brunt of tonnage tax policy. The tax was originally imposed in the Pennsylvania's charter of 1846 as a

[153] See *supra*, pp. 48–49.
[154] *Pa. Archives*, 4th, VI, 616.
[155] *Ibid.*, VII, 69.

guarantee to the state against losses which might be sustained as a result of competition between the new railroad and the public works. Pressure for its imposition came primarily from the western and southwestern counties of the state which not only feared the impending defeat of the Baltimore and Ohio which was implicit in the charter of the Pennsylvania but feared also a rise in taxation as a result of the damaging impact of that company on the public transportation system.[156] The promoters of the company had no affection for the tax in 1846, but they were so anxious to frustrate the ambitions of Baltimore that they even utilized the tax idea themselves as a polemical weapon for breaking opposition in the west. Some modification of the tax as it affected coal and lumber interests was made prior to a historic struggle during the latter fifties for its total abolition.[157]

In this struggle the alignment of interests was practically identical with that involved in the original controversy over the charter of the Pennsylvania Railroad. Certain new considerations were present, however, which served to intensify the traditional antagonism between Philadelphia and Pittsburgh. One of these was the discriminatory rate schedule that the Pennsylvania had introduced with respect to the western trade. The other was the fact that while Philadelphia retained her stock interest in the Pennsylvania, Allegheny County lost hers during the panic of 1857, a consideration which distinctly decreased concern in the west for the Pennsylvania's rate of earnings.[158] After a number of unsuccessful efforts, the company won its first victory in the legislature on the tonnage-tax issue in 1857 when a bill was enacted for the sale of the public works. That measure contained the proviso that, should the Pennsylvania purchase the works for nine million dollars, the company would be released forever not only from the tonnage tax but from all state taxation on capital stock, bonds, dividends, and other property. This exemption was held unconstitutional by the Supreme Court in the same case in

---

[156] Cf. *supra*, p. 52.
[157] Sipes, *Pennsylvania Railroad*, p. 13; *Legislative Record, 1857*, pp. 3, 88. Cf. *ibid., 1861*, pp. 386, 598; Scharf and Westcott, *History of Philadelphia*, III, 2192.
[158] Cf. *ibid.*, p. 502.

which the court upheld the constitutionality of the general sale principle.[159]

Failing here, the company maintained that the tonnage tax was a violation of the federal Constitution and refused to make further payments to the state. By 1861 it was in arrears to the amount of $661,158 and a strong effort got under way in the legislature to revoke the company's charter in retaliation.[160] The matter was permitted to rest with the attorney-general, however, and after some litigation in which the company failed to establish its constitutional argument, the tax was finally repealed in 1861. The repealing measure provided that the sum of the back tonnage tax was to be invested by the Pennsylvania in the completion of eleven other railroads in the state. Some of the most important of these roads, such as the Chartiers Valley and Pittsburgh and Connelsville roads, were the pet projects of the western counties, and the aid thus served to weaken opposition in that region.[161] The Pennsylvania was also compelled to pay an additional sum to the state for release from the tax. And finally, as a further concession to the west, the company was required to reduce its local rates by the full amount of the tax.[162]

Debate about the expediency of the tax can be rapidly summarized. The company and its associated interests in the east wheeled out the usual competitive dogmas and pointed to the usual threats in Maryland and New York. In connection with the fact that the tonnage tax was imposed not for customary revenue purposes but in order to maintain the financial position of the public works,[163] they pursued two lines of argument. Prior to the sale of the works they contended that the Pennsylvania Railroad was not in fact competing deleteriously with the state line. An increase of state receipts on the Columbia Railroad,

---

[159] *Mott* v. *Pennsylvania Railroad Company*, 30 Pa. St. Rep. 9, 27 (1858).
[160] *Legislative Documents, 1861*, p. 807.
[161] *Legislative Record, 1861*, pp. 383, 502 ff, 647.
[162] *Ibid.*, p. 598. Cf. Stanton Davis, *Pa. Politics, 1860–1863*, pp. 198 ff.
[163] See Pennsylvania Railroad Company, *Eighth Annual Report, pp.* 7–8. The company emphasized the fact that the tonnage tax could not be placed in the same class as bonuses paid for charters. — *Ibid.*, p. 7. For an opposite view, cf. *Legislative Record, 1859*, p. 448.

owing largely to the business thrown upon that road by the Pennsylvania, was adduced again and again as evidence that the private line was actually operating for the enrichment of the state.[164] After the sale of the works they contended that the original reason for imposing the tax had disappeared and that since the state had no longer any interest to protect, the tax ought forthwith to be abolished.[165]

They argued, moreover, that the company's discriminatory rate schedule was traceable to the tonnage tax because of competition with untaxed roads in the Central States.[166] In connection with this argument, glowing promises of reduced local rates and immediate economic development in the west were held out in return for repeal. The lights of New York and Baltimore would soon be lit with gas from the bituminous coal of Allegheny, their bakeries would soon be using the flour of Westmoreland. Moreover, economic boom would produce new taxable wealth which would more than compensate for losses in tonnage-tax revenue; an untaxed Pennsylvania Railroad would do for the western counties what the untaxed Reading Railroad had done for the Schuylkill area.[167] Concerning the east, little need be said. Why was Philadelphia losing out to New York in the commercial field? The true reason lay in the fact that the Pennsylvania Railroad was taxed while the New York and Erie was not.[168] All this was quite apart from the ruinous impact of a mileage tax which doubly penalized producers distant from their markets, which was not in fact a tax upon a railroad company but a tax upon the whole producing and consuming public.[169]

[164] Pennsylvania Railroad Company, *Eighth Annual Report*, p. 91. Cf. *Legislative Record*, *1858*, p. 214; *Will the Interest of Pa. be Advanced by Tonnage Tax?* p. 25.
[165] *Legislative Record*, *1858*, p. 153; *1859*, p. 450; Stokes, *Letter on Tonnage Tax*, p. 11; *Public Ledger*, June 18, 1857.
[166] *Legislative Record*, *1858*, p. 319. Stokes, *Letter on Tonnage Tax*, pp. 24–25; *Will the Interest of Pa. be Advanced by Tonnage Tax?* pp. 19–20.
[167] *Legislative Record*, *1858*, p. 215; *Will the Interest of Pa. be Advanced by Tonnage Tax?* pp. 20, 27, 29.
[168] *Legislative Record*, *1858*, pp. 153, 213; *1861*, p. 527; *Will the Interest of Pa. be Advanced by Tonnage Tax?* p. 24.
[169] *Legislative Record*, *1861*, p. 527; *ibid.*, *1857*, No. 91, p. 1; *1858*, p. 213; Stokes, *Letter on Tonnage Tax*, pp. 17–20; *Will the Interest of Pa. be Advanced by Tonnage Tax?* pp. 27, 28.

The western counties were not easily impressed. Pittsburgh, until the very end, was intransigent. The Board of Trade of Philadelphia sent a committee to the Board of Trade of Pittsburgh to enlighten their western compatriots in 1858, but the two groups appear to have parted on terms of undiminished hostility.[170] The fact that a tax was a burden on the business of a company, declared the opponents of repeal, could not justify its repeal; on that theory all taxes would have to be withdrawn.[171] Moreover the prevalent scale of earnings of the Pennsylvania showed that rates in the western areas were not as low as they could be, and "until those charges have first been brought down to the lowest paying standard" the notion that an abolition of the tax would result in rate reductions was a chimera.[172] Indeed all of the evidence pointed to the fact that the Pennsylvania's rate schedule, instead of being a necessary product of the tax, was in reality a crude technique for striking back at the western counties because of their opposition to repeal; red-blooded Pittsburghers would not easily be intimidated by such an act of commercial war.[173]

The patterns of argument are familiar enough. What gave this controversy its main significance from our point of view were certain larger ideas which it served to crystallize. One of the vaguest of these was a blend of nineteenth-century optimism and free-trade theory. Senator A. K. McClure of Franklin asked his colleagues to remember that they lived in "the noon-tide of the nineteenth century." [174] There was much discussion of "the principle of unrestrained commerce," of laws of trade which were "absolute and selfish," and of the "intelligence of the age." [175] If the process of education was not a quick one, the prophets of the new era were at any rate satisfied that it proceeded with certainty. "Enlightened public opinion," wrote Mayor Roberts Vaux of

[170] *Report to Pittsburgh Board of Trade, passim.*
[171] *Legislative Record, 1858*, p. 319; *1859*, p. 481.
[172] *Ibid., 1858*, p. 319.
[173] *Report to Pittsburgh Board of Trade*, p. 14; *Legislative Record, 1861*, p. 500.
[174] *Ibid.*, pp. 526, 527, 598. Cf. Stanton Davis, *Pa. Politics, 1860–1863*, p. 194.
[175] Stokes, *Letter on Tonnage Tax*, p. 10; Pennsylvania Railroad Company, *Eighth Annual Report*, p. 9; *Legislative Record, 1858*, p. 213.

Philadelphia in a letter to the legislature of 1858, "is slowly but surely accepting as a fundamental truth, that restrictions on the exchange of values are detrimental . . . ."[176]

William A. Stokes of Westmoreland County was the most elaborate of the anti-tax philosophers. In a pamphlet published in 1859,[177] he began his analysis with an account of the savage. The distinctive mark of the savage was solitude. The distinctive mark of civilization was an increase of social intercourse. Since the tonnage tax was a restriction on commercial intercourse, it was a "barbarous contrivance of taxing civilization." There were, moreover, certain "universally received principles of social economy" which were also relevant. These condemned all "taxes on trade, obstruction of intercourse, discouragement to industry, intrusion by government into private interest, legislative meddling in individual enterprise . . . ." They were based on the concept of the "independent man" who was "always the most powerful, because each person being the best judge of his own interests, untrammelled effort must be most effective." The tonnage tax was thus an "artificial political intervention."[178]

False anthropology and crude Benthamism do not mix persuasively. The glorification of the "independent man" was a curious conclusion for a theory which had begun by finding the mark of savagery in atomistic solitude. But the defenders of the tonnage tax were in no mood to favor the Stokesian philosophy with philosophic criticism. They denied that it rose to the "dignity of an argument." "And all this talk about fettering trade," declared Senator Franklin Bound of Northumberland in 1861, "is a transparent humbug — a miserable pretext on which to justify a great wrong."[179] Moreover the Pittsburgh interests had their own version of "the regular laws of trade." According to this version it was not the state but the Pennsylvania Railroad itself which was their worst violator. Would not the regular laws, given Pittsburgh's geography and resources, naturally make that city the primary market center for the West-East trade? Was it not

[176] *Ibid.*
[177] Stokes, *Letter on Tonnage Tax.*
[178] *Ibid.*, pp. 5–6, 17, 28–29, and *passim.*
[179] *Legislative Record, 1861*, p. 501.

their frustration, by the Pennsylvania's artificial and discriminatory rate schedule, which accounted for Pittsburgh's growing commercial stagnation and the emergence of rival interests in Cleveland, Chicago, and Cincinnati? [180]

Even at best there were limits to what the Stokesian philosophy could accomplish. Given the nature of this struggle, and the magnitude of the interests involved, it is not surprising that it should move to the constitutional level. Exactly when this shift took place it is hard to say. Certainly there is no evidence to indicate that the protagonists of the Pennsylvania Railroad, when they were offering the tonnage tax as an olive branch to the western counties in 1846, believed any part of it to be a violation of constitutional provisions. By 1857, however, a corps of lawyers were at Harrisburg seeking to convince the legislators of the state that the tonnage tax violated Article I, Section 8 of the federal Constitution which endowed the national government with power over interstate commerce, and Article I, Section 10 which forbade states to levy duties or imposts.[181] This argument could apply only to the tax as it affected outstate commerce, and it was because of its reliance upon it that the company was willing in 1858 to pay to the state a sum of revenue based upon local shipments.[182] In 1859 Messrs. Cuyler, Meredith, and Crittenden, Philadelphia attorneys, published an opinion in which they denied the constitutionality of the tonnage tax, declaring that the case against it was so overwhelming that "we cannot believe that the Legislature of Pennsylvania will persist in the effort to exact the payment of this tax." How it happened that an argument so obvious and conclusive had but recently come to prominence, when the tonnage tax had been analyzed from virtually every angle as far back as 1846, they were at a loss to state. All they could say was that the true nature of the tax was "probably overlooked originally." [183]

[180] *Report to Pittsburgh Board of Trade*, p. 5: "Pittsburgh once transacted a considerable produce business, which gave promise of a vast increase. The discrimination against us in railroad charges not only checked the increase but has driven to western points most of that which we formerly had. See *Legislative Record, 1858*, p. 313.
[181] *Ibid.*, *1857*, No. 77, p. 5. *Report to Pittsburgh Board of Trade*, p. 2.
[182] *Legislative Documents, 1859*, p. 1,031. [183] *Ibid.*, p. 1,036.

Their opinion was remarkably brief, much shorter for example than the opinions of Binney and Meredith in the investment controversy of 1846, ostensibly because the power of their argument made lengthy discussion unnecessary. They insisted upon a distinction between tonnage-tax and ordinary toll impositions, arguing that the tax was not provided as a payment for services rendered in the transportation of property or for expenditures made in providing transportation facilities. In connection with the issue of the commerce power they cited a varied list of cases, reaching from *Gibbons* v. *Ogden* through *Brown* v. *Maryland* to the *Passenger Cases*, in which state power had been both upheld and nullified.[183a] Apparently they tried merely to prove, in a most general way, that legal sanction had been given to the supremacy of national power in the field of interstate commerce. They briefly invoked the memory of interstate commercial wars under the Articles of Confederation and the passion for their elimination which had characterized the framers of 1787. They concluded with references to the national welfare and to the supremacy of the federal Constitution: "Pennsylvania has hitherto gloried in the fact that she has never wilfully violated that compact." [184]

Interesting questions arise. If this was a powerful case, why did the company devote so much of its effort to pressing it in the legislative halls at Harrisburg? Litigation, to be sure, was expensive, but hardly as expensive as the maintenance of lobby pressure. And the most that could be gained in the legislature was a repeal of the tax, whereas the courts could obliterate it forever. Why, also, did Cuyler, Meredith, and Crittenden utilize precious sentences, in the course of their brief opinion, to emphasize the importance of abolishing the tax outside the courts on the basis of its blatant unconstitutionality? The pursuit of unconstitutional policies by misguided legislators was a lamentable thing, but it had happened before. It is hard not to believe that the answers to these questions are traceable to an inner realization from the outset, on the part of the company and its attorneys,

---

[183a] 9 Wheaton 1 (1824); 12 Wheaton 419 (1827); 7 Howard 283 (1849).
[184] *Ibid.*, pp. 1,032–34.

THE INALIENABLE STATE POWER 275

that their case was weak. It was, to be sure, persuasive in the Philadelphia region where the will to believe was strong to begin with; in 1857 all save two of the legislators from that region appear to have been convinced.[185] But elsewhere the argument was greeted with limited interest. By 1858, according to the committee of the Pittsburgh Board of Trade which conferred with representatives of the Philadelphia Board on the tonnage tax, the Philadelphians themselves were ready to admit that the constitutional argument was untenable.[186] And in 1859, after a verdict of the Court of Common Pleas of Dauphin had gone against the company,[187] its counsel dropped a writ of error from the United States Supreme Court and negotiated a temporary deal with the attorney-general for the repayment of the tax.[188]

What was the trouble with the constitutional argument? It introduced, in the first place, a most glaring contradiction in the theory of the company's publicists. On the expediency plane, as I have already revealed, their case was built largely around the contention that the whole burden of the tonnage tax including that part of it nominally imposed on outstate shipping was borne by *local* freights. It was only because of this contention that they could argue that the elimination of the tax would eliminate also a discriminatory rate schedule and would initiate a new era of prosperity in the western counties. It was not easy, in light of this reasoning, to argue at the same time that the tax was in fact a tax on *outstate* freights and hence unconstitutional owing to the exclusive power of the federal government in interstate commerce. The two arguments were placed alongside one another time and again by the defenders of the tax as evidence of the "sophistry" of the company's whole polemic.[189] Moreover, since 1846 the company had lived by a tireless invocation of the sym-

[185] *Legislative Record, 1859,* p. 481; *1857,* No. 78, p. 5.

[186] *Report to Pittsburgh Board of Trade,* p. 2. In 1859 Mr. Neall of the House declared himself to be "one of the few who believed the tonnage tax to be unconstitutional." *Legislative Record, 1859,* p. 447.

[187] April term, 1859. *Legislative Documents, 1861,* p. 807.

[188] The company agreed to pay down one hundred thousand dollars and to make monthly payments of fifty thousand dollars thereafter. *Ibid.,* pp. 807–808. See also Stanton Davis, *Pa. Politics, 1860–1863,* pp. 192–93.

[189] *Report to Pittsburgh Board of Trade,* p. 10. Cf. *Legislative Record, 1861,* pp. 669, 377.

bolism of state competition; recalcitrant western counties had been given large doses of this ideology and even now they were being told that they ought to acquiesce in the repeal of the tonnage tax if only because Keystone patriotism demanded the defeat of the New York and Maryland railroads in the Central states.[190] Suddenly to become alarmed over interstate rivalries which had taken place under the Articles of Confederation, to argue that "selfishness is not in accordance with the spirit of the age," to announce that railroads were "national" in scope,[191] and to glorify the supremacy of federal power, was bound to have a profoundly incongruous effect. Pittsburgh had learned from Philadelphia all that it needed for a reply to that sort of reasoning.

The case of the railroad attorneys was challenged, moreover, in a purely legal sense. Attorneys Quiggle, Godwin, and M'Clintock argued that the taxation by a state of one of her own railroads could not be called a duty or an impost in the sense in which those words were used in Article I of the federal Constitution. Shipping on the Pennsylvania Railroad could not be classified as imports or exports within the meaning of that provision. The tax was a cost of the railroad included in its rate schedule as a compensation for the use of the road and as a return for the capital invested in it. Moreover it was a rule of law that the powers of the state over its own corporate "creatures" should be interpreted liberally.[192] Technically the latter point was weak. If the federal Constitution was in fact violated, as the Pennsylvania's attorneys pointed out, nothing express or implied in the charter could lend sanction to such violation.[193]

But in the intensity of popular debate this obvious fact was quickly lost sight of, and on top of the normal power of the state over its corporate creations there was piled a number of curious versions of contract doctrine. It was argued that since the charter of the Pennsylvania Railroad company which originally imposed

[190] *Ibid., 1858*, p. 214; Stokes, *Letter on Tonnage Tax*, p. 384; *Will the Interest of Pa. be Advanced by Tonnage Tax?* p. 27.
[191] Quoted in *Report to Pittsburgh Board of Trade*, p. 10.
[192] *Ibid.*, p. 19.
[193] *Legislative Documents, 1859*, pp. 1,032–34.

the tonnage tax was in the nature of a "compact or agreement," the company had no right to ask for a release from the tax.[194] Moreover every instance in which the company had acquiesced in a modification of the tax or evinced an acceptance of it served to fortify the original contract. A petition from the Board of Trade and Merchants' Exchange of Pittsburgh put the issue as follows:

> That the acceptance of the charter with its conditions constitutes a contract.
> That the acceptance of each successive modification, solicited by the company, was a confirmation of its provisions, and especially, the modification which changed the tax from five mills to a continuous one of three mills.
> That the purchasing of the main line, after the decision of the Supreme Court . . . was a new ratification of the contract.[195]

Nor was this all that could be done with a principle that had been used to good effect in sheltering corporate power. It was argued that the state had an implied contract with its own creditors not to abolish the tax. The proceeds of the public works had been pledged "in good faith" to the public creditors; as an integral part of those proceeds the increasing tonnage-tax revenue ought "most sacredly" to be preserved and applied to the liquidation of the state debt.[196] After 1857, moreover, with the embodiment of a portion of the state's sensitive financial conscience in the constitution, it was possible to argue that the repeal of the tonnage tax was far more unconstitutional than its imposition. The tax must go to the sinking fund established for the proceeds of the public works, insisted the redoubtable Senator Bound — "It is so fixed by the Constitution."[197]

Simultaneously with its half-hearted attempt to destroy the tonnage tax by invoking the federal commerce power the Pennsylvania Railroad sought to achieve the same objective through the utilization of the contract clause. The latter effort began in 1857

---

[194] *Legislative Record, 1861*, p. 500. Cf. *Report to Pittsburgh Board of Trade*, p. 14.
[195] *Legislative Record, 1858*, p. 319. Cf. *Report to Pittsburgh Board of Trade*, p. 17.
[196] *Legislative Record, 1858*, p. 319; *1861*, p. 384.
[197] *Ibid.*, p. 374. Cf. *ibid.*, p. 501.

when the company extracted from the legislature that remarkable bill for the sale of the Main Line of the public works which exempted it forever not only from tonnage taxation but from all state levies on capital stock, bonds, dividends, and other property as well. Tax exemption grants were not unknown in the state prior to this time: a general measure of 1838 exempted religious and educational corporations from state taxation, and special measures had occasionally given such exemption to banking and utility corporations. But earlier exemptions in the business field had been of limited scope and they had been construed with great strictness by the state judiciary.[198] In terms of revenue foregone and the breadth of the exemption area the grant to the Pennsylvania Railroad in 1857 was unprecedented. It was challenged in the legislature as an unconstitutional impairment of state power.[199] But fear that the company might not purchase the works unless the tax-exemption provision was included in the sale bill, as well as considerable lobby pressure, led to the victory of the exemption proviso. Taken in conjunction with the sale measure, it amounted to nothing less than a gigantic fraud upon the state. All tax revenues from the road were clearly on the secular increase, but taking the tonnage tax alone at its 1856 figure of $280,739 the exemption was serious enough.

The exemption provision came before the court when the canal commissioners challenged the validity of the entire sale measure of 1857 and applied for an injunction to restrain Governor Pollock from executing its provisions.[200] In an earlier chapter I analyzed this case in so far as it was concerned with the rejected argument that the state could not constitutionally part with the public works,[201] and it is unnecessary to enter into a discussion of that controversy here. The sale argument, however, was not wholly irrelevant to the exemption phase of the case. The conten-

---

[198] For litigation under tax exemption measures, see *The New York and Erie Railroad Co.* v. *Sabin*, 26 Pa. St. Rep. 242 (1856); *Bank of Pennsylvania* v. *The Commonwealth*, 19 Pa. St. Rep. 144 (1852); *Academy of Fine Arts* v. *Philadelphia County*, 22 Pa. St. Rep. 496 (1854).

[199] *Legislative Record, 1857*, No. 9, p. 1. Cf. *ibid.*, No. 93, p. 1; No. 77, p. 6; No. 91, pp. 1, 3. Cf. also *1859*, p. 480.

[200] *Mott* v. *Pennsylvania Railroad Company*, 30 Pa. St. Rep. 9 (1858).

[201] See *supra, chap.* IV, pp. 175 ff.

tion that the works were pledged to the state's creditors embraced the familiar popular argument that the tonnage tax was similarly pledged and could therefore not be abolished by legislative act.[202] But the major portion of the argument against the exemption provision was developed along different lines. Issues were involved here of a kind that the question of sale power *per se* could not produce.

The first of these was the contention, presented by Hirst on behalf of the canal commissioners, that the idea of total and permanent exemption violated principles of equality in taxation that amounted to "a theory of . . . Republican Government." This violation was made doubly striking by the fact that the exemption privilege had been granted to a corporation at a time when the corporate system was acquiring rapidly increasing proportions of the wealth of the state. "If this system be once established," warned Hirst, "we shall see scores of petty corporations knocking at the halls of our Legislature for similar enactments. It is instituting a class in this Commonwealth with privileges above all others . . . ."[203] A second line of argument went deeper. The legislature, it was urged, had no constitutional right to impair the power of succeeding legislatures by granting away forever a portion of the taxing authority. That authority was in the nature of a trust, held on behalf of the popular sovereign, and could never be alienated. But its trust characteristics did not derive from the peculiar nature of the taxing power, even though that power might be the "highest" conferred upon the legislature. It derived from the larger fact that the whole of legislative authority was held in trust for the people. Any contract to obliterate any part of it must thus be void: "The Legislature cannot make any contract which is against the power conferred by the Constitution."[204]

Counsel for Governor Pollock and the Pennsylvania Railroad Company argued that the justification for the tonnage tax had disappeared with the decision to sell the public works.[205] But

[202] *Public Ledger*, June 18, 1857. Cf. *Pennsylvanian*, June 19, 1857.
[203] *Public Ledger*, June 17, 1857.
[204] *Ibid.* Cf. *Pennsylvanian*, June 28, 1857; *Mott v. Pennsylvania Railroad Company*, 30 Pa. St. Rep. 9, 18 (1858). [205] *Public Ledger*, June 18, 1857.

since exemption from a much broader area of taxation was involved here, this argument had limited relevance. They contended also that judgment concerning the validity of the exemption contract must be postponed until subsequent legislatures sought to impose taxation in violation of it: "To anticipate the decision would be to impair the authority of deliberate decisions." [206] If the phrasing of this argument was vague, its strategic import was clear. For to postpone a decision on the exemption measure would provide time for the acquisition of third-party rights under its operation, and would thus bring the measure more securely within the confines of federal Supreme Court sanction. Since Marshall's famous decision in *New Jersey* v. *Wilson* [207] the federal court had persistently invoked the contract clause to protect state tax-exemption grants, especially when third-party rights had vested under them.[208] Cases such as *State Bank of Ohio* v. *Knoop* [209] and *Dodge* v. *Woolsey* [210] could be cited by the railroad attorneys as precedents supporting the tax-exemption concept *per se*, but it was clear that these cases would be even more important once the measure of 1857 had gone into effect.

But even as far as state precedent was concerned the company's case had strength. It is true that the Pennsylvania judiciary had traditionally insisted that tax-exemption grants "must be evinced by terms so explicit as to leave no doubt" [211] of legislative intention. But the grant of 1857 was plain beyond question; a specific price had been set for the purchase of the favor. A line of cases, moreover, fortified the company's contention that the taxing power was very broadly granted and that discretion in its use lay with the legislature.[212] Only five years earlier, in the famous case of *Sharpless* v. *The Mayor of Philadelphia*, the court had elaborated this principle to its fullest extent in sustaining legislative authorization of local mixed corporation invest-

[206] *Ibid.*
[207] 7 Cranch 164 (1812).
[208] B. F. Wright, *Contract Clause of the Constitution*, pp. 35-38.
[209] 16 Howard 369 (1853).
[210] 18 Howard 331 (1856).
[211] *The New York and Erie Railroad Co.* v. *Sabin*, 26 Pa. St. Rep. 242, 245 (1856).
[212] *Mott* v. *Pennsylvania Railroad Company*, 30 Pa. St. Rep. 9, 20 (1858). *North American and United States Gazette*, June 17, 1857.

ment.²¹³ Railroad attorneys had also supported the principle there, but interestingly enough for a wholly different objective as regards the economic sphere of the state. There they had contended for an unlimited power of taxation in order that that power might be put to the positive use of financing railroad corporations; in the Mott Case they were arguing for unlimited power in order that the users of the power might themselves destroy it.

The decision that held invalid the exemption provision was unanimous, Chief Justice Black writing the opinion of the court, Justices Knox and Lowrie concurring. The combination of the exemption and the sale measures, exclaimed Black, amounted to "one of the most magnificent exhibitions of a 'mock auction' that the world has ever witnessed!" ²¹⁴ All of the opinions in the case sharply dismissed the company's plea for a postponement of judgment on the exemption contract, and sought by rhetorical warnings to head off a decision on the issue by the federal Supreme Court.²¹⁵ All of them, moreover, accepted Hirst's argument on the equity principle in taxation, thus reversing the position which the court had taken in the Sharpless Case. The Chief Justice developed the equity argument in an original way, emphasizing not only the increasing proportions of the total wealth held by corporate bodies but the peculiar reliance of railroad corporations upon tax-supported protection. The intensity of the sectional passions which railroad routes evoked meant, he argued, that the roads would remain at "the mercy of popular outbreaks" were it not for the protecting arm of the law.²¹⁶ It was, however, in the matter of legislative discretion that the opinion of the court stood in most striking contrast with the Sharpless decision. Instead of an austere tone of self-limitation, there was now a vigorous assertion of judicial prerogative. "It is a question of constitutional authority," said the Chief Justice,

---

²¹³ Cf. *supra*, pp. 113 ff.

²¹⁴ *Mott* v. *Pennsylvania Railroad Company*, 30 Pa. St. Rep. 9, 26 (1858). For Justice Knox's view, see *ibid.*, p. 41.

²¹⁵ *Ibid.*, p. 39. See also *ibid.*, pp. 29, 32, 36. Cf. argument of Attorney Hirst, *Pennsylvanian*, June 17, 1857; also *Mott* v. *Pennsylvania Railroad Company*, 30 Pa. St. Rep. 9, 18 (1858).

²¹⁶ *Ibid.*, p. 29.

"and not a case of confidence at all. Limitations of power established by written constitutions have their origin in a distrust of the infirmity of man. That distrust is fully justified by the history of the rise and fall of nations." [217]

In dealing with the issue of permanent alienability the court caught up the limited suggestions of counsel and expanded them into a political theory. Lowrie's opinion, by far the most philosophic of the three, was concerned almost exclusively with the alienability proposition, with virtually no reliance upon technical matters of precedent. The key to his effort here, as well as to that of his colleagues, lay in the fact that he steadfastly refused to deal with the alienability issue solely on taxation grounds. The justices viewed it as an issue whose logic embraced the fate of the entire governmental authority. "If one portion of the legislative power may be sold," declared the Chief Justice, "another may be disposed of in the same way. If the power to raise revenue may be sold today, the power to punish for crimes may be sold tomorrow, and the power to pass laws for the redress of civil rights, may be sold the next day. If the legislative power may be sold, the executive and judicial powers may be put in the market with equal propriety." [218] Here was a vision alongside which Hirst's fears of repeated tax-exemption grants seemed comparatively mild.

Hirst had, to be sure, emphasized the fact that the taxing authority was but a portion of the larger legislative power; his argument concerning the delegated character of the taxing authority had, indeed, been based upon that relation. And the court unanimously agreed. "In the nature of things," declared Justice Lowrie, "it is impossible to imply an authority in governmental agents to diminish the governmental power that is naturally inherent in the people that constitute them." [219] But the court went so far beyond Hirst in considering the case from the standpoint of the totality of state power that it could not rest content with the well-worn concept of legislative bodies holding power on trust.

[217] *Ibid.*, p. 27. For Justice Knox's view in this regard, see *ibid.*, pp. 37–38.
[218] *Ibid.*, p. 27.
[219] *Ibid.*, p. 35.

Other ideas were added to that one, and they brought the court curiously close to the dogma of the prohibition theorists of the time. Those theorists, of course, had not been confronted with any such question as the impairment of a delegated power by the trustees who held it. But they had been confronted with the question of society's inherent authority to abolish an evil which was conceived to threaten its welfare; they had developed a theory, therefore, which had revolved around the imperative duty of social self-preservation. As the court viewed the alienability proposition, the issue it involved was a similar one: Did society have a right to "commit suicide" by the impairment of its most vital functions? Was there a self-preservation imperative which prevented it from doing so?

It was necessary, in the first place, to prove that government was essential to the life of society. Though this would seem to be an easier task than to prove that universal teetotaling was socially essential, a technical purist might find certain difficulties facing it in the Mott Case which proof of the other proposition did not encounter. For the delegated character of state power so heavily relied upon in that case proceeded from the Lockean premise that the popular sovereign was wholly distinct from government and could if necessary survive without it. In terms of that premise the destruction of governmental functions did not mean the destruction of society. But this philosophic problem troubled no one on the bench. Lowrie, who most closely resembled such thinkers as Barnes and Coombs, was not apparently conscious of its existence. Within the space of a paragraph he was able to say on the one hand that the "people's power is not parted with by the institution of government" and on the other that "there can be no society without government." [220] The confusion is perhaps of more than superficial significance, for it was reflected as well in the larger rationalization of state power that the court produced. The implication of many of the remarks it made was a power rationalization based on a purely survivalist ethic, but the heavy influence of the Lockean dogma prevented such a rationalization from clearly emerging. Instead there was

[220] *Ibid.*

talk of "inherent and inalienable" rights of society which somehow corresponded with Lockean rights of individuals,[221] and the chief justice contributed the idea that government "has no more right to commit political suicide than an individual has to destroy the life given by his Creator." [222]

Varying conclusions were drawn from the court's opinion. The Board of Trade and the Merchants' Exchange of Pittsburgh declared that the decision "confirms the right" of the legislature to continue the tonnage tax,[223] while William Stokes argued, by means of a logic which he did not clearly explain, that the nullification of the exemption provision placed an "implied moral obligation" on the legislature to abolish the tax "to the extent of their power." [224] But with reference to the alienability principle there appears to have been virtually no disagreement: the decision of the court was quickly acquiesced in even by the supporters of the Pennsylvania Railroad. The Philadelphia *Ledger*, whose editorials in the fifties were normally decisive in their opposition to state action in economic life, declared that the decision in the Mott Case was "founded on such strong reasons of public policy that it seems singular that any legislature should attempt, in the face of them, to render the government powerless, or assume that it may bind the action of subsequent Legislatures by surrendering a right as clearly belonging to those who succeed as to itself." [225]

A vigorous affirmation of state power, wrapped in high-flown philosophy, was a queer package for the Pennsylvania Railroad to receive when it was seeking desperately to whittle down the sphere of government. But the great ideological investment made by the company and its friends in the tonnage-tax struggle had not been wasted. The free-trade theory of McClure, the anthropology and the individualism of Stokes, the incantations concerning national power of Cuyler and Meredith, all combined to inject into discussions of corporate business the most significant

[221] *Ibid.*
[222] *Ibid.*, p. 27.
[223] *Legislative Record, 1858*, p. 319.
[224] Stokes, *Letter on Tonnage Tax*, p. 11.
[225] *Public Ledger*, June 24, 1857. See also *Harrisburg Telegraph*, July 1, 1857; *Legislative Record, 1861*, pp. 500, 378.

anti-state theme since the appearance of the Dartmouth College doctrine. Challenging governmental power on the plane of political theory and law, the new publicists surrounded the issue of corporate control with a doctrinal atmosphere very much the same as the one which exerted so corrosive an effect upon the idea of public investment during the years immediately preceding the Civil War.

PART FOUR

THE MYTH OF LAISSEZ FAIRE

VII

ECONOMIC POLICY
AND DEMOCRATIC THOUGHT

1. *The Policy Pattern*

IN FACE of the evidence it would be hard to contend that the objectives of economic policy cherished by the state from the Revolution to the Civil War were either limited or unimportant. They ramified into virtually every phase of business activity, were the constant preoccupations of politicians and entrepreneurs, and they evoked interest struggles of the first magnitude. Government assumed the job of shaping decisively the contours of economic life. The business charter program which appeared shortly after the Revolution, giving birth to the corporate system, was a promotional technique profounder in its impact than any the colonial period had witnessed. Its evolution, like that of other policies, was conditioned by a set of changing group alignments. Concerned primarily with banking and transportation prior to the 1830's, it was enmeshed in regional rivalries for commercial pre-eminence and credit facilities. With the increasing flow of capital into industrial fields after 1825, it became the focal point of a vigorous contest between the individual entrepreneur and the industrialist seeking corporate privileges. Effective as the former was in slowing down the extension of the charter program to such businesses as mining and manufacturing, the program as a whole experienced rapid secular growth, expanding markedly during the boom periods of the second and fifth decades of the nineteenth century.

"The use of the mixed enterprise under the corporate form in which the government owns part of the stock and private investors own the remainder," writes one recent student, "has been relatively rare in the United States." [1] Considering the remarkable growth of the mixed corporation in Pennsylvania and else-

---

[1] Guest, in Eldridge, *Collective Enterprise*, p. 449.

where during our period,[2] I think we are justified in challenging such a view. To be sure, some of the techniques of public-private partnership which emerged after the Revolution in Pennsylvania to broaden the state's economic function were sporadic developments, closely in line with established promotional practice: loan policies for farmers and industrial entrepreneurs, interest guarantees on corporate loans, and bounties. But the mixed enterprise program overshadowed all such policies combined and, embracing both profit and control objectives, it had more than simply a promotional significance. Originating in the banking field in the late eighteenth century, it flourished with increasing strength for half a century, eventually being extended to transportation and embracing various types of enterprise there. In 1844 over one hundred and fifty mixed-corporations were currently listed in the official records of Pennsylvania, with public investments ranging from a few shares of stock to several thousand.[3] It is hard to view such a policy as an incidental phase of state action worthy of only marginal notice.

Nor is it easy to regard as incidental the role of the state as entrepreneur exclusively in its own right. Throughout our period the disposal of public lands was a kind of entrepreneurial venture, but it was a passive program, directed always toward a point of saturation.[4] It was with the inception of the public works in the 1820's, where a process of steady expansion and increasing investment was premised at the outset, that the entrepreneurial function of the state assumed major proportions. The most powerful group behind the initiation of the works was the mercantile group of Philadelphia which, seeing the inability of both the private and the mixed corporation to meet transport objectives, sought some way to salvage its position relative to the merchants

---

[2] A comprehensive study of the theory and administration of the mixed corporation in various American states prior to the Civil War is an important job remaining to be done in politico-economic history. Cf. on mixed enterprise outside of Pennsylvania, Virginia, *Journal of the House of Delegates, 1855–56*, pp. 6, 82; Wallace, *History of South Carolina*, II, 406; Violette, *History of Missouri*, pp. 235 ff.

[3] *House Journal, 1844*, II, 28–46.

[4] For the evolution of land policy, see *House Journal, 1803*, p. 452; *1807–8*, II, 95; *1812–13*, p. 99; *1816–17*, pp. 256, 374; *1833–34*, II, 162.

of New York and Baltimore in competition for the trade of the West. If the works system failed in its cherished aim of competing successfully with the Erie Canal, the immensity of the effort it involved can scarcely be denied. It was a system which lasted steadily until the close of our period, which became the pivotal factor in state finance, and which in its time consumed more wordage in official records than any other single phase of state policy.

Meanwhile public regulatory policy was acquiring new content. It is often overlooked that the expansion of the corporate system not only encouraged the growth of business enterprise but brought it increasingly under a set of new controls.[5] The appearance of the Dartmouth College principle in 1819 did not affect the established practice of providing elaborate regulations in original charter acts. And even as far as subsequent regulations were concerned, the inclusion of reservation clauses in charters and the pursuit of a strict construction policy by the state judiciary limited severely the effect of the anti-state barrier erected by Marshall. Nor was it only in connection with the forms of corporate organization — with such problems as directorates, voting, and stockholder liability — that statute regulations were extensive. The governance of corporate policy was provided for in equal detail. Indeed it is in the myriad regulations laid down with reference to trading, rates, service, and production, that the immensity of the new control responsibilities assumed by the state with the growth of the corporate system is most apparent.

Neither were regulations absent in areas of enterprise outside the confines of charter policy. The reaction against the price-fixing measures of the Revolution did not spell the end of the old colonial pattern of control; many of the earlier policies such as licensing and inspection were expanded. But far more important than these were the new variations of colonial practice wrought by economic change, the achievement of political rights by labor and debtor groups, and the emergence of the famous reform movements of the period. The abolition of hereditary slavery

---

[5] On this point see Handlin, "Origins of the American Business Corporation," *Jour. of Econ. Hist.*, V. (1945), pp. 17 ff.

without indemnification in 1785 gave a new meaning to the state's prohibitory function and served as precedent during the 1850's for a crusade to abolish the liquor trade which was almost successful. The growth of labor unionism and a public education movement in the nineteenth century led to measures in 1848, 1849, and 1855 limiting child labor and placing hour limits upon adult labor, and to a large variety of lien laws and privileged-creditor measures protecting the interests of miners and mechanics. The latter provisions were part of a wider movement which altered the debtor-creditor relationship against the background of the uncertain financial life of the period, which improved the position of the debtor, and which gave to the state, as in stay laws and exemption measures, an emergency relief function during depression periods.

Far from being limited, the objectives of the state in the economic field were usually so broad that they were beyond its administrative power to achieve. Here lies one of the central clues to an understanding of the pattern of government action. In certain respects the reasons for administrative failure were imbedded deep in the economic and political history of the time. Produced by an expanding commercial capitalism, important sectors of policy were hopelessly involved in a bitter intra-state sectional competition. In a state split up to begin with by unusual geographic and group factors, this involvement persistently frustrated the pursuit of coherent plans. No one can study the undisciplined granting of charters, the disorganized allotment of mixed corporation investments in the transportation area, the helter-skelter growth of local, disconnected lines in the public works program, without perceiving the damaging impact of the sectional factor and the political trading which it involved. The party system was hopelessly inadequate to the task of unifying policy on a state-wide plane. Organizationally decentralized, it was itself largely at the mercy of sectional and pressure-group forces — as was demonstrated by the high degree of regularity with which issues of economic policy from public investment to labor legislation cut across party lines. To interpret accurately the sweep of economic policy in party terms, to label one party as interventionist and another as "laissez-faire," is simply impossible. Nor could much be expected from the governor toward the maintenance of an over-all state purpose, though the plea for a more coherent articulation of economic policy was a perennial aspect of gubernatorial messages. The governor's power was limited at the outset by the looseness of party organization. From 1790 to 1837 he was constantly assailed by legislative jealousies; with the reduction of his prerogatives by the Constitutional Convention of 1837 he became more feckless than before. It was the legislature which had the master hand during this epoch, and it was there that competing sectional and group interests were enthroned.

Quite apart from these interests, however, the breadth of legislative authority had pernicious results. Reluctant to delegate tasks to executive officers, the legislature devoted great quantities of time to issues of detail with which it was manifestly unsuited to deal. The refusal of the legislature to enact general laws of incorporation until the close of our period led to the growth of a wilderness of unsystematic charter provisions. The over-retention of legislative power in the public works area led to an uncertainty which corroded the morale of the works administration, to a chaotic treatment of the claims question, to unnecessary obsolescence because of failure to appropriate essential funds for repairs. In mixed enterprise policy a similar lack of system was the result, with the rights of the state being forgotten as often as they were remembered. Above all reliance upon investigating committees of the legislature for the implementation of regulatory policy was a serious administrative mistake. Limited in time and knowledge, easily hoodwinked by private interests, especially in the corporate field, such committees were ineffective.

What was needed, given the great scope of economic policy, was a stable and expert administrative system. It did not develop. The evidence of this period provides a striking confirmation of the importance of the growth of modern administrative science, and it is unfortunate that the lessons which it offers have remained almost wholly uninvestigated.[6] When the history of

[6] A pioneer effort in this field is L. White, "Origin of Utility Commissions in

American public administration is written and contemporary administrative progress is evaluated in the perspective of the past,[7] the record of state experience during our period will, I think, emerge as of central relevance. At its worst the policy of Pennsylvania ignored the administrative question, as in the case of repeated failures to provide for state directorships in mixed corporations; or it relied upon the action of interested individuals for policy enforcement, as in the case of the factory laws of 1848 and 1849 which soon became dead-letter statutes. Despite the growth of administrative obligations, there was a pervasive inability to think in terms beyond a routine executive setup. An overworked auditor-general, with limited staff and appropriation, was compelled to shoulder tasks covering virtually every phase of economic policy. Only in the public works area, where the pressure of necessity could not be avoided, did a comprehensive administrative machinery appear. But one has only to observe the sad history of the canal board, distrusted from the outset, never given authority sufficient to its task, victimized by legislative factions and administrative inferiors alike, and finally thrown into the political arena, to perceive that the mistakes there were manifold.

Yet it is necessary to interpret the shortcomings of the state in correct perspective. Its earlier history had not prepared it for administrative tasks of the scope of those which suddenly emerged during the period we are considering. Nothing in the economic policy of the colonial era could compare in magnitude with the public works program; nothing in its regulatory policy could compare with the immense variety of specific controls involved in corporate regulation. Moreover the uncertainty of the economic and technological environment of this period would have posed innumerable difficulties for even the best established and most expert administrative service. In the public investment area the state was pioneering enterprises distinctly in advance of

---

Mass.," *Jour of Pol. Econ.*, XXIX (1921), pp. 177 ff. See also Caldwell, *Administrative Theories of Hamilton and Jefferson.*

[7] In this connection Professor Leonard D. White's forthcoming studies in the development of administration should help to fill an important gap in our historical knowledge.

private effort; we can scarcely blame the state if the canals which it built were soon made obsolescent by the emergence of the railroad age. The record of public administration can be fairly evaluated, indeed, only when it is set alongside the record of private enterprise. If many of the public investments were lost, what is to be said of the estimated one hundred million dollars sunk simultaneously by private capital in mineral industry failures alone? [8] If there were public administrative breakdowns, what is to be said of the devastating succession of monetary debacles which marked periods in the economic history of the age? If there was public corruption, what is to be said of the fictitious stock, false promises, and worthless shinplasters which accumulated in the wake of private action? We must not fall into the error of gazing at only one side of the coin.

Yet there was a sense in which private enterprise could survive its failures whereas public administration could not. No one can study the last two decades of our period without observing the remarkable series of attacks which converged on state policy from many directions beginning in the forties. Outstanding in the regulatory field were the campaigns of liquor and agrarian interests against the licensing and prohibitory functions of the state and the attack of the Pennsylvania Railroad and its allied interests upon the policy of corporate taxation. More damaging in their results, however, were the movements against public enterprise, spurred on by state bankruptcy and administrative failure. Much as the western areas opposed the manner in which the public works were sold, much as the canal commissioners insisted upon the illegality of the sale, nothing after 1857 could block the liquidation process. The flurry of local mixed enterprise investment which followed the basic sale of state stockholdings in 1843 was momentary. If the propertied and sectional interests opposing the movement failed before the Supreme Court in 1853, they soon pushed through amendments which abolished not only the policy of investment but the program of corporate loans and interest guarantees which had been associated with it.

[8] This is the estimate of Tyson, *Commerce of Philadelphia*, p. 11.

This sudden curtailment of public spending, public lending, and public enterprise radically altered the scope of economic policy. It was during this period, when the state was on the brink of the Civil War, that the most historic change in the governmental economic function began to take place. Nor did this go unobserved. In his annual message of 1859 Governor Packer, recommending the abolition of the canal board after the Sunbury and Erie purchase, remarked as if with some astonishment that "a most interesting era has been reached in the history of the Commonwealth." Speaking of the epochal reduction in executive responsibilities produced by the termination of public investment and enterprise, as well as by the gradual disposal of public lands which was now virtually complete, he declared: *"From these and other causes, governmental action has become greatly simplified, and the nature of the subjects of its operations has changed in a degree no less remarkable."* [9]

But the later period must be studied not only in light of those sectors of economic policy that were liquidated but also in light of those that were not. The attacks on regulatory and taxation policy produced limited damage. To be sure the Pennsylvania Railroad succeeded in obtaining an abolition of tonnage-tax burdens in 1861 but only at the price of more stringent rate regulation and other impositions. It failed in its effort to emancipate itself completely from state taxation and that failure evoked from the Supreme Court a doctrine of inalienable state power which actually strengthened the regulatory function. Moreover the electorate in 1857, at precisely the moment when it authorized constitutional amendments abolishing public investment, authorized also an amendment which gave definitive sanction to the state's policy of reserving the right to alter and revoke corporate privileges. In the promotional area, also, significant policies persisted. The charter program not only survived but experienced a rapid expansion during the last two decades of our period: over half the charters granted by the legislature from 1790 to 1860 were granted during those decades.

The growth of charter policy is of peculiar importance. For

[9] *Pa. Archives*, 4th, VIII, 98 (italics mine).

the expansion of the corporate system was closely related to that contraction of public investment and enterprise which so radically slashed the sphere of the state in economic life. The rate of charter grants is not an adequate index of the growth of corporate strength, but it is undeniable that the late period witnessed the emergence of a corporate development, spearheaded by the Pennsylvania Railroad Company in the transportation field, which was unprecedented in terms of capitalization, promotional techniques, and experienced management. Historically this development appears to have been a prerequisite for the departure of the state from the investment area. Though not in the banking field, where sufficient amounts of private capital had been available from the outset, public enterprise in the transportation field had been undertaken at a time when the tasks involved glaringly exceeded the capacity of an undeveloped corporate system. It seems highly unlikely, in light of the intensification of regional commercial rivalries, that the state would have been permitted to terminate investment policy had corporate enterprise been as inadequate to the achievement of transportation objectives as when that policy had been initiated.

2. *The Theory of State Action*

The rule that is not infrequently carried to a study of the political thought of our period is the rule of governmental inaction in economic life — theories of action we note as exceptional. Yet in many instances precisely the opposite orientation is necessary if we are to appreciate in its wholeness the doctrine which justified the economic policy of the age. Much of that policy was not explicitly rationalized because its legitimacy was taken for granted in terms of the earlier mercantilist tradition of the colonial period. Even explicit applications of the newer democratic theory, however, are liable to be deceptive unless they are related to the whole setting of popular thought in which they evolved. There is no better instance of this difficulty than the anti-charter doctrine of the period which, invoking major democratic symbols and thriving vigorously in the equalitarian atmosphere of Pennsylvania politics, might suggest in isolation that democratic thought was inherently hostile to state economic policy. Yet when studied in its doctrinal context, the anti-charter theory takes on an entirely different meaning, a portion of which appears in its relation to the ideology of public enterprise. Instead of finding that the two doctrines clashed, we discover that they coalesced again and again in the thinking of the period.

There was a basis in policy for this doctrinal alliance. To preserve state investments in mixed enterprise banks, it was necessary at the turn of the eighteenth century to attack the chartering of private banks which might compete against them. But it was not until the emergence of the public works movement in the 1820's that the fullest possible fusion of the anti-charter and state enterprise theories was made. In certain respects, it is true, the fusion of the theories at this time was a curious distortion of economic fact. For in the transportation field public investment was initiated not as a rival but as a supplement to the charter program. Yet it is not hard to understand why the public works theorists of the twenties, given their desire to exploit every polemical device available and given the immensity of the benefit they posited as resulting from their program, should utilize the anti-charter doctrine to insist that the corporate system could not be trusted with the great objectives they sought to achieve. Once the works were built, moreover, the anti-charter theme acquired greater reality. The defense of the public system involved a task similar to that which had appeared in connection with mixed enterprise banks: the negation of requests for the chartering of private companies which were its potential competitors. Finally, during the forties and fifties, in the bitter debate over the sale of the works to business corporations, the defenders of state enterprise built most of their case around the anti-charter ideas on which they had traditionally relied.

It is futile to believe that in the popular controversies with which I have been concerned in this study a respect for doctrinal consistency is meticulously preserved. Yet the truth is that the fusion of the anti-charter and public enterprise ideologies was not doctrinally inconsistent. For the anti-charter theory did not, as a superficial interpretation might have it, assail all economic policy. It assailed only the discriminatory character of charter grants, and this, as even the Keating Committee of 1834 had to admit, carried with it an implicit justification of state action on behalf of the whole community. But the argument was not only one in which public action emerged as the legitimate alternative to the illegitimate action of specially privileged corporations. It was also one in which many charter privileges were assailed as invading spheres which from the outset constituted the legitimate province of government, and this was one of the meanings of the persistent cry that charter grants impaired popular sovereignty. When the House Committee on Corporations insisted that charters should be granted only in instances where the inadvisability of state enterprise had been proved, it was expressing the logic of the anti-charter ideas. Only in light of those ideas can the relationship between public enterprise and democratic theory be understood.

It was in the principle of public profit that the positive character of the democratic theory of state enterprise showed itself perhaps most clearly. In the mixed enterprise field, where the principle appeared in the late eighteenth century and where mixed bank dividends soon became an important source of state revenue, there was a sound basis in economic fact for its elaboration. When it was expanded by the public works propagandists of the 1820's, however, it is obvious that such a basis did not exist. The experience of both the private and the mixed corporation in the transportation field was sufficient to demonstrate this. Yet if it was factually hollow, the vision of public profit fitted neatly into other aspects of social thought. It supplemented that strong anti-tax bias which, as Mathew Carey himself lamented, traditionally governed the thinking of the state. And since it was better that profits should accrue to the people than to the chartered aristocrat, it blended also with the anti-corporate phase of public ownership doctrine. What emerged from such public works theorists as Carey and Lehman was the idea of a positive profit-making state — a state in which taxes were abolished, poorhouses obsolete, governmental institutions supported by public works revenue, and public schools universal. The dream of great wealth which motivated land speculator and mining investor captured the imagination of the state itself. The concept of profit led to the concept of public service, and the state became a gigantic entrepreneur whose gains were to be publicly shared.

Despite the importance of the anti-corporate and public profit themes, the theory of public enterprise could not fail to reflect the promotional pressures which were in fact primarily responsible for the inception of state investment in the transportation field. It was heavily involved in the competitive ideology produced by the intercity race for commercial pre-eminence — eloquently elaborated in Philadelphia by such figures as Breck and Tyson. Yet there was an inevitable paradox here. For while public investment theorists could insist upon the competitive principle where other communities were concerned, they were compelled to insist on precisely the opposite principle where sections embraced by the government from which they sought funds were concerned. When they were fighting for the public works in the twenties the merchants of Philadelphia could preach the gospel of economic war in connection with Baltimore or New York; but confronted with sections in the north and south of Pennsylvania which did not identify their interests with those of Philadelphia, they had to preach also the gospel of regional economic brotherhood. Nor were the alliances of mercantile and railroad interests which pressed for local investment in the forties and fifties freed of this necessity: in county and city politics, as Wharton and Pettit discovered in 1846, there were also recalcitrant sections whose feelings had to be soothed. The theory that emerged to soothe them had to make transportation investment a thoroughly public task.

Nor could this be accomplished in serious degree by the sentimental argument presented by Loring and others that transport facilities were linked to the honor and prestige of the community. It was necessary to prove in economic terms that public investment was the key to an all-inclusive prosperity. The importance of this necessity is fully appreciated when we perceive that investment often confronted, in addition to sectional opposition, horizontal antagonisms of group and class, as exemplified in the opposition of wagoning interests to the works scheme of the twenties and propertied interests to the railroad investment of the forties and fifties. The elaboration of the idea of economic interdependency to meet such varied conflicts gave to public investment doctrine an over-all economic significance which lifted it out of the limited context of transportation and banking. Innumerable theorists were at hand, from Lehman to Read, to prove that investment primed the pump of the entire economy, and this conception was implicit in arguments like Sullivan's which held that investment would be self-liquidating on the basis of enhanced tax revenue. It was also implicit in the theory, developed by Raguet's Senate Committee in 1819 and expanded by public works theorists of the following period, which viewed investment as a substitute for less productive forms of poor relief. The evidence shows plainly that investment theory was not preoccupied with the ambitions of a single group but always conceived its objective as the enhancement of the welfare of the whole economy.

Surely it is only in light of this conception that the deficit spending theory of the period can be understood. For that theory, as it evolved from the report of the House Committee on Ways and Means in 1832 to the report of the state treasurer in 1841, could scarcely content itself with emphasizing the value of spending for a single sector of the community. The expanding debt which it sought to justify loomed as a burden upon the entire state. The shift from the earlier vision of profits to the new defense of deficits was doctrinally not so difficult as might appear. To move from the one to the other it was necessary only to cease interpreting profit as the accumulation of surpluses in the treasury and interpret it rather as the accumulation of strength in the economy. Once this was done, other major tenets of the new doctrine emerged automatically — its sharp distinction between public and private financial morality, its insistence that spending was the responsibility of a democratic state to its people. Nothing is to be gained from identifying this crude ideology of spending with modern Keynesian theories of public investment. But surely, in light of its elaboration, we may be permitted to question the italics of one recent writer who expresses a view not uncommonly held: "Two opposing philosophies with respect to public finance exist in high governmental circles today. The first, which may be called the *traditional* view, is that a continuously unbalanced budget and rapidly rising public debt imperil the financial stability of the nation. The second, or *new* conception, is that a huge public debt is a national asset rather than a liability and that continuous deficit spending is essential to the economic prosperity of the nation." [10]

A broad view of the community's taxing power was necessarily implicit in the theory of public investment. Given the intensity of Pennsylvania's anti-tax bias and the strength of the public profit theme, it is not hard to understand why this view remained buried on the level of assumption for a long time. To be sure, it was adumbrated by Wharton and Sergeant in Philadelphia in 1846 when they replied to Binney and other opponents of municipal investment. But it was not until the famous Sharpless Case of 1853, sustaining the constitutionality of the local subscription program, that the taxation principle found a fully explicit elaboration. Though the argument in that case was involved in technical questions of the distribution of state and local authority, the root challenge to the taxing power presented there — the inequity charge — was a challenge to the entire public enterprise tradition as it had evolved on both state and local levels since the eighteenth century. This was clearly recognized in the argument of Read and Dallas defending public investment and in the opinion of Chief Justice Black. When they denied the charge of inequity by establishing the public character of the investment function, they traveled familiar ground. But when they established the corollary principle that no right of private property was sufficiently absolute to interfere with the taxation which the investment function involved, they brought to the surface an aspect of investment theory that had previously been only an implicit assumption. With Black's eloquent defense of the discretionary power of the legislature to tax, the theory of public spending and public enterprise became a conscious whole.

[10] Moulton, *New Philosophy of Public Debt*, p. 1.

Embracing ideas of anti-corporationism, public profit, deficit spending, state services, economic promotionalism, pump-priming, and a broad taxing power, the theory of spending and enterprise was not a simple pattern of thought. One thing, however, is clear: underlying all of its phases was the belief in a positive role for the state in economic life.

The theory of economic regulation had a more extensive colonial ancestry than the theory of public enterprise, but, like the other, it did not hesitate to exploit democratic doctrine. Though the inclusion of restrictions in charter grants proceeded from a state power over corporate forms traditionally acknowledged since the earliest history of the corporation, the principle of the right of the state to alter and revoke charters had to utilize, as the controversy over the Bank of North America made obvious as early as 1785, the whole force of democratic theory. To be sure the Dartmouth College dictum appeared to limit this principle, and the Meredith resolution affirming it passed in the Convention of 1837. But it passed by a comparatively small margin, and the mass of theory opposing it can scarcely be dismissed as uninfluential. That theory expressed the ethos of reservation policy developed to limit the contract principle and it even expressed the spirit of many of the specific corporate regulations themselves. Whether it found expression in Brown's theory of recuperative power or in Ingersoll's doctrine of the political corporation, the defense of state authority traced back to the democratic concept of the popular community.

Life alongside the Dartmouth College doctrine was bound to be an uneasy one for that concept. The success with which the anti-charter theory used it to attack the very idea of a business corporation, the fashion in which the theory of public enterprise used it to discredit corporate competition, both give hints of this. It is not hard to understand why Ingersoll and others should insist that the majesty of the concepts of sovereignty and the popular will was violated by the notion that the community could be reduced to a common footing of contract with businessmen. In popular thought the concept of the community did not have, as

Earle suggested in his theory of a continuous revision of economic policy, the static character essential to the logic of the Marshallian contract. It depended for its meaning upon a mass opinion which was never fixed, and it had little respect for the judgments of dead generations. Paine on popular sovereignty did not get along easily with Paine on charter contracts. This was why Woodward, utilizing the concept of popular sovereignty, could insist that a state power of control was necessarily implied in every charter enactment.

Moreover a similar view appeared in the course of judicial decision despite the acceptance by the courts of the Dartmouth College doctrine. It is true that the idea of community welfare involved here was not comprehensively developed until the Mott Case of 1857 in which the state Supreme Court developed its theory of inalienable state power. But the primacy of community interest had always been implicit in the strict construction of charter grants, a policy which the Pennsylvania courts pursued with unusual consistency throughout our period. The fight of the Pennsylvania Railroad for the principle of permanent alienability of state power may be viewed as a last-ditch effort to revitalize the contract clause for the protection of corporate interests after it had been debilitated by strict construction and reservation policy. In abstract terms the alienability principle had implications which were grave; given the increasing power of the corporate system in the halls of the legislature, it could theoretically have furnished a method for the achievement of an unprecedented breadth of corporate freedom. But it is hard in fact to believe that a victory for the Pennsylvania Railroad in 1857 would have provided a precedent for that wholesale deterioration of state power which the court envisaged in the Mott Case. Even had the state judiciary sanctioned the widening impairment of state power by means of the contracting-away process, the national Supreme Court, despite its record of tax-exemption protection, would eventually have stopped it. Its elaboration of the theory of inalienable state power in a whole series of cases after the Civil War shows that the alienability reliance under the contract clause was not one which the corporate system could have utilized with long-range effect. Yet for Pennsylvania's theory of state power the breadth with which Black and Lowrie viewed the issue in 1857 represented a significant contribution. They lifted aspects of that theory to the rank of a philosophy when they argued that there were powers which under no circumstances the legislature could part with and that these powers flowed not only from the idea of delegated government but from the sheer needs of community survival.

The concept of public interest also flourished in regulatory theory not directly concerned with corporate control. Here, where democratic ideas fused with the reform enthusiasms of the age, it is striking to observe the extent to which common ideas underlay ideologies produced by separate campaigns for legislation. One of these ideas was the belief that the state had a responsibility for securing conditions essential to the survival of free government. It is often remarked that American thought in our period was colored by a sense of the country's democratic mission, but it is not always recognized that this feeling could serve as a defense for state action in the economic sphere. Yet the relationship is evident. The abolition of vested rights in slave property was necessary because slave-owning unfitted men for life in a free community and discouraged the fight for representative government abroad, child-labor legislation was necessary because education was a prerequisite to the continuance of democracy, restrictions on the alcohol trade were necessary because intemperance corrupted a free citizenry. Save perhaps for temperance theorists like Barnes and Coombs, who also mingled their doctrine with a kind of social survivalism which went beyond the purely democratic theme, no one thoroughly explored, it is true, the implications of this line of argument. But it was one of the things which gave a militant cast to regulatory doctrine.

Another version of the public interest idea, influenced to some extent by attitudes engendered by business development, called for regulatory action on the ground that the economic productivity of the community must be preserved. Here again the appearance of the same idea in different reform campaigns cannot be ignored. There was a demand for new debtor-creditor statutes, emergency relief measures during depression periods, hours legislation in factories, and temperance legislation, in order that the productivity of the poor, the overworked, and the intemperate might be rescued for society. Whether developed by Wiston in connection with bankruptcy legislation or by Coombs in connection with liquor prohibition, this type of argument reflected a growing ideology of work and thrift. It is interesting that in the temperance field clergymen and mining operators united to advance it. Strikingly utilitarian in cast compared with the democratic theories mentioned above, it shared the ideal of enhanced economic strength that inspired the theory of public spending.

Regulatory doctrine was also fortified by the idea of individual right drawn from the natural law base of the democratic theory. While this idea found classic expression in the anti-charter doctrine's defense of "individual enterprise" against the corporate system and hence implicitly justified all corporate regulation, it was most consciously utilized in regulatory theory outside the scope of the corporate issue. There its main function was to justify an expanding pattern of legislation on behalf of underprivileged economic groups. A whole series of rights arose, fathered by the Revolutionary doctrines, which it became the duty of the state to secure. Negroes had a right to freedom, debtors had a right to measures in their behalf, factory children had a right to education, all laborers had a right to fair working conditions. In case after case the concept of natural right was advanced with faith in its magic power, but it was the labor movement which explored its meaning most fully. Proceeding from a state of nature in which property was commonly held, Stephen Simpson and his colleagues found higher law justification for principles which ranged from the right to a job to the right to shorter hours. It is often pointed out that the individualism of the democratic theory served to fortify property rights, but it is also worth remembering that the same individualism could be utilized, as here, to call for regulatory or even prohibitory legislation.

The doctrine of economic regulation viewed the state in various roles: as champion of the community against the corporation, as the provider of conditions required by democratic survival, as the guarantor of increased production, as the defender of human rights. Like the theory of public spending and enterprise, it discovered that there was more than a single route to the concept of positive government.

It is apparent that the theory of economic policy reflected a synthesis of two major traditions: the ancient acceptance of state action which reached back to the seventeenth century of Thomas Budd, and the newer tradition of democratic thought. Though these traditions have not infrequently been interpreted as antithetical, the conclusion is inescapable that during the decades that followed the Revolution, as during the Revolutionary period itself, they formed a dominant synthesis in Pennsylvania thought. The carry-over of the colonial tradition was clearly reflected in the goal of heightened productivity shared by investment and regulatory doctrine, but its force was more pervasive than this. It was part of the unexpressed doctrinal environment in which the whole problem of state action was projected, the explanation of why, prior to the closing years of our period, the legitimacy of economic policy as a state function was rarely challenged even by its opponents. Yet it was the democratic theory, and above all the concept of the popular community that it provided, which gave to the theory of economic policy its color and vitality. It was the intensely equalitarian character of that concept which found expression in the anti-corporate bias of the doctrines of public enterprise and corporate regulation. It was the Lockean fashion in which that concept made of government a utilitarian instrument of the people which appeared in the service themes of public profit and deficit spending. It was the involvement of that concept with the prevalent sense of the historic importance of the democratic experiment which appeared in much of regulatory doctrine. At once the most ubiquitous and the most poorly understood idea in the political thought of the age, usually expressing itself in the simple cliché of "the people," this idea was the main instrument by which the democratic theory embodied its broad and neglected conception of state responsibility in the economic field.

Equally relevant, as I have said, is the limited extent to which the theory of state action was *challenged* in terms of the democratic concepts over most of the period. To be sure policy measures did not go unassailed prior to the forties and fifties, but the attack upon them was couched almost exclusively in terms of their practicability or expediency. The theory of public enterprise emerged in the 1780's, but no one appears to have perceived a conflict between that theory and the Revolutionary doctrines or the doctrines of democracy that followed them. Not even when the theory was advanced to restrain the ambitions of private capitalists, when it assailed the corporate system and discouraged the chartering of corporate rivals to public institutions, did the argument develop that the theory conflicted with any democratic or constitutional norm. The interests which sought to incorporate the Bank of Philadelphia in 1803 did not go to the courts or appeal to the founders when confronted with the argument that a new bank would jeopardize the investment of the state in the Bank of Pennsylvania; instead they appealed to the public profit idea themselves, offered to pay the state a large bonus if their charter was granted. Nor did the theory of public transportation enterprise encounter any democratic challenge. Widely as the public works theorists of the twenties utilized the democratic slogans, their opponents spoke only in terms of sectional interest and expense.

Save for an early reaction against the extreme price-fixing measures of the Revolution and for the Dartmouth College theory, the democratic legitimacy of the regulatory idea also encountered pervasive acceptance. There was opposition, but again it was opposition on the plane of expediency. Arguments were leveled against the abolition of hereditary slave property rights in 1785, but none of them suggested that the measure violated democratic norms. Nor did such a suggestion appear in the arguments generated by the pattern of licensing, inspection, and taxation controls carried over from the colonial era. Despite the Dartmouth College argument against revocation and alteration of charters, the assumption of expanding regulatory responsibilities in charter enactments was not assailed as beyond the legitimate sphere of the state. None of the factory measures of the period were challenged before the courts: in 1837 the Peltz Committee, systematically refuting arguments against hours legislation, failed even to notice a democratic or constitutional challenge, and as late as 1848 the textile factory proprietors, issuing a manifesto against the recently enacted hours law, could think of nothing to say but that competition with other regions was severe and that their profits had been overrated. If, as we are sometimes told, the emergence of democratic ideas automatically corroded the idea of state action, why did the opponents of investment and regulatory policy fail in so many instances to utilize them?

But this was not an enduring condition. Intensified attacks on important sectors of economic policy during the forties and fifties, the inception of that "most interesting era" of which Governor Packer spoke in 1859, were indications of the fact that over the last years of our period the doctrine of positive government was beginning to fall upon evil times. A counter doctrine was emerging and was giving an unprecedented tone to politico-economic discussion.

3. The Attack on the State

From the outset the theory of state action had contained serious contradictions. The concept of the popular community that it utilized had a deceptive strength. It lacked realism. Whether it found expression in the symbols of "sovereignty" or the "people" or any of the other magic words on which it relied, it defended a unified and infallible popular will with which the facts of political life could not possibly square. Representatives of party, section, and interest group could never be better than traitors to the transcendent ideal which it posed, could never, judged by its standards, be more than "politicians," instruments of "local corruption," and "borers." Thus the main concept which rationalized policy served, by a kind of self-annihilating logic, to discredit the only agents by which policy could be initiated or implemented. One of the most interesting criticisms leveled against Brown's theory of recuperative power was the charge that constitutent conventions distorted the Will of the People as badly as the legislatures whose damage he intended them to repair. When the popular will is so wonderful that not even a constituent convention can serve as its acknowledged organ, the men who are chosen to give it expression are rogues before they begin. Norms of policy that recognize nothing but the interplay of interest pressures are inadequate; but norms that scarcely recognize them at all lead directly to a disillusionment with the political process.

This disillusionment was enhanced, moreover, by other contributions of the democratic theory. The administrative failures of the state were not traceable entirely to its inexperience and to the uncertain economic environment which it confronted. They were partially traceable also to the prevalent belief in an amateur intelligence in government, a fundamental aspect of the democratic faith and one bound to be disastrous in a setting where administrative competence was imperative. In the broadest sense it was this belief that rationalized the reluctance of the legislature to delegate technical responsibilites, the enforcement of political rotation in administrative services, and the extension of the elective process which, in the case of the canal board, ended all hope for the redemption of the most important administrative body of the era. Eventually, as Governor Bigler's pleas in the fifties show, there was some change of heart. But it came too late to be effective. Long before the fifties the practical results of the unrealism of the democratic ideals had helped to solidify contempt for the men who were chosen to implement them.

If the administrative record of private enterprise was also bad, nevertheless the prestige of the business entrepreneur was rising while that of the politician was in decline. The expansion of the popular philosophy of economic self-interest nourished alike by the ideologies of boom and depression, and the sheer growth of business enterprise with the results that for all of its waste it was achieving, both lifted the businessman in symbolic rank. The entrepreneur whose virtues Freedley depicted in the fifties was a man of heroic stature.

It is when viewed against this setting of ideas that the philosophy produced by the anti-governmental movements of the late period can be best appreciated. For without some preparation in earlier attitudes it is doubtful whether that philosophy could have flowered so remarkably in so short a time. It is fair to discuss it as a single unit. For though the doctrinal attacks on various state policies evolved separately, the great extent to which they resembled one another is obvious. It is unimportant whether William A. Stokes in the field of corporate control had heard of Edward McPherson in the field of public works, or whether either was acquainted with the efforts of Thomas Williams in the field of mixed enterprise investment. One hailed from Westmoreland, another from Dauphin, and another from Allegheny, but they drew in remarkable fashion upon a single well of inspiration. The work of all was needed. For the idea which they sought to make dominant — the idea that state economic policy was a violation of first principles — contradicted clearly, as the chief justice said in 1857, the tradition of the past.

Natural law is always a source from which truth more compelling than experience can be gleaned, and it is not surprising that the new theorists relied upon it. Its function became pathetically obvious in the Sharpless Case where the anti-investment attorneys, confronted with strong opposition based on precedent, tried feverishly to lift debate to the higher law plane. Yet if its function was less obvious in other instances, as for example in the crusades against prohibition and public works, its elaboration was less precise, involving little more than a flood of clichés in which concepts of nature, religion, and science mingled riotously. Usually the dogma of fundamental law had not only a political but also an economic aspect, well exemplified in austere references by Stokes and Williams to the iron laws of economic life. One might speculate about the impact here of classical economic theory, but the implications of the doctrine were so sparsely explored that a more likely influence appears to have been the growth in complexity of business enterprise itself which, as in the writings of Tyson and Freedley, induced a new popular respect for the rules of business activity.

Though they evolved in this heady atmosphere of abstraction, the more specific themes of the anti-governmental doctrine stand out clearly enough. One of them was a polar idea which embraced both a vigorous individualism and a defense of community welfare. On one hand it was pointed out, with occasional references to the Declaration of Rights of the state constitution, that individual rights to property and freedom were violated by such policies as taxation and regulation and the competition of public with private enterprises. On the other hand it was argued that the liberation of individuals from such restrictions would, because of energies flowing from personal self-interest, lead to maximum economic productivity for the entire community. This contention, admirably summarized in the individualism of Stokes, is a measure of the distance that was being traveled from earlier investment and regulatory doctrine in which state policy was justified precisely on the ground of heightened productivity.

It was in this connection that the contrasting symbolic roles of politician and businessman, fashioned slowly over the earlier period, were jerked into focus against state economic policy. There was a code of business wisdom which the Stokesian individual had mastered, and his glory lay in its secret. Nor was there ground for hope that public administrators could eventually attain to its understanding. A determinism rooted in the nature of political institutions, as McPherson and Campbell pointed out in the public works area, placed the business mystery forever beyond the intelligence of government. In the mixed enterprise field Mr. Justice Kennedy came close to recognizing that determinism as a principle of public law. Given its existence one could only rejoice, as the *Harrisburg Telegraph* rejoiced, that capitalists were actually available to operate in place of the state. There were, to be sure, a few iconoclasts like Roumfort who pointed to the corruption that had characterized the growth of corporate enterprise, but their heresy had little effect. The revulsion against corporate mismanagement produced by the panic of 1857 was curiously forgotten when public and private action were being compared. In that year Democrats could brand corporation officials as "fat and lazy" and simultaneously defend the anti-investment amendments as applying "the same sound practical rules to the financial affairs of the state, that our business men do to theirs." [11]

The hope that governmental agents might transform themselves into businessmen contrasts strikingly with the theory of public spending in its classic phase which had cherished the principle that the state and the individual must be governed by different codes of action. It is scarcely surprising that this principle collapsed with the onset of state and local financial debacles: as early as 1844 William B. Reed of Philadelphia was pleading for the repudiation of "the pestilent dogma which distinguishes public from private morality." [12] Much of the intensity of the whole anti-state doctrine derived from the atmosphere of crisis, if not of hysteria, which financial breakdowns provided. In certain cases, the anti-repudiation symbolism was utilized to defend the maintenance of state policy. In the Sharpless Case it was argued that a decision invalidating mixed enterprise investment would impair the credit of the state; in the Mott Case the canal commissioners maintained that the public works were pledged to state creditors and could not be sold; tonnage-tax policy was also defended on the ground of creditor obligations. But in popular thought these lines of argument were weak compared with those which held that state policy must be terminated precisely because its investment phases had led to the financial shame depicted so bitingly by Sidney Smith, a sentiment which dominated the enactment of the anti-investment amendments of 1857.

Those amendments embodied an acute distrust of the legislative power, a bias which coincided with an increasing faith in the judiciary as a barrier against legislative action. From the outset, owing to the obvious dominion there of sectional, pressure-group, and party procedures, the legislature did not fare well in light of the strong political idealism of the period. In the Convention of 1837, called expressly to reduce the preroga-

[11] *Pennsylvanian*, Aug. 25, 1857.
[12] *Model Administration*, p. 17.

tives of the executive, the legislative power was usually friendless: if it was assailed by the Dartmouth College polemicists as a revoker of charters, it was assailed by their opponents as a granter of them. During the late period theorists everywhere rediscovered the idea of judicial surveillance. Opponents of mixed enterprise investment, armed with higher law if not with precedent; the Pennsylvania Railroad, having suddenly discovered the federal commerce clause in its quest for barriers against tonnage taxation; even liquor interests, frightened by the threat of a plebiscite favorable to prohibition — all looked toward the courts. Confronted with this movement, the judiciary for a long while refused to alter its traditional philosophy of legislative trust. But in the Mott Case of 1857 it gave in.[13] When it repudiated there the doctrine of legislative discretion enunciated only four years earlier in the Sharpless Case, it echoed the constitutional pessimism which Senator Buckalew had eloquently elaborated in defense of the anti-investment amendments. The legislative power, long in discredit, was now definitively branded as unsafe.

The anti-state doctrine was a remarkable creation. Formulated with a keen sense of polemical strategy, striking the theory of state action at some of its weakest points, it nevertheless had a positive quality as well. In place of the elaborate philosophy of state participation it offered the people of Pennsylvania a novel philosophy of its own. In this new world of doctrine, where a peculiar blend of political and economic higher law charged the atmosphere with righteousness, businessmen were heroes and politicians were villains, a balanced budget was the mark of state morality, and the menace of communism was, as in the Sharpless Case, ground for constitutional argument. It was an excellent set of symbols for the task at hand: the substitution of the concept of negative for the concept of positive government.

---

[13] It is interesting that the reversal of the Court's position should have been occasioned neither by the legal attack on mixed enterprise nor by the attempt to utilize the federal commerce clause against railroad taxation, but by the effort of the opponents of the Pennsylvania Railroad to invalidate the grant to it of permanent tax exemption. In the specific context of the latter issue the idea of judicial supremacy enunciated by the Court may actually be viewed as a fortification of the legislative power. But in the long run the vigorous assertion of the Court's

Few would deny that this philosophy comes closer to fitting the "laissez-faire" label than any other encountered in the present study. It is instructive to compare it with the anti-charter doctrine fashioned during the earlier period. Superficially the two ideologies appear to have much in common: a reliance upon natural law, a kind of economic individualism, even a devotion to the idea of a harmonious competition of interests, though the last was of minor importance in the anti-charter doctrine. In fact, however, the two theories were as profoundly antagonistic as any to be found in the pre-Civil War history of the state. Heavily involved in the theory of public enterprise and corporate regulation, the anti-charter principles could not fail to clash with the later attack upon state policy, an antagonism that flared with remarkable clarity in the controversy over the sale of the public works to corporations. Almost everywhere that the later philosophy appeared it was impelled to strike at the anti-charter doctrine, and it did so, deceptively enough, by utilizing some of the same symbols which that doctrine had made part of the political legend of the state. For the drift of virtually its entire criticism of state policy was to rationalize precisely what the anti-charter theory had been created to attack — the business corporation. The growth of the theory of McPherson and Stokes was the historic evidence of the decline of the theory of Ingersoll and Brown.

That the purport of the anti-governmental theory was to rationalize the corporate system is apparent in the nature of the three main struggles from which it flowed — the struggles against mixed enterprise, public works, and corporate taxation policies. Since unincorporated enterprise was not involved in any of these policies, their curtailment or elimination could mean only one thing — greater independence for the corporation. The independent man whom Stokes worshiped was the Pennsylvania Railroad Company; the businessmen whom the *Telegraph* glorified were the operators of that corporation; the entrepreneurs whose liberty McPherson cherished were companies frustrated

---

prerogative in the Mott Case contributed to the building of a skepticism of legislative action which was subsequently to attain prominence in judicial thought. In this conection, see *infra*, p. 319.

in their search for charters because they would compete with the public works. These latter-day heroes were precisely the villains of the anti-charter ideologists. In the anti-charter scheme they were aristocrats, their companies were monopolies, they oppressed the individual, and they violated whatever economic laws might exist. Perceiving that the later theory served to rationalize the corporate system, we are able to understand why it was in fact the Dartmouth College doctrine, transformed from a legal principle into a popular ideology by the Second Bank controversy, which foreshadowed it during the earlier period. Similarly defending the corporation against state interference, that ideology was impelled, by a logic inherent in its motivation, to anticipate the categories of the later doctrine. It mobilized democratic individualism in behalf of the corporation, it contrasted corporate operators favorably with politicians, and it cherished the judiciary as a barrier against legislative power. Clashing with important factors in the doctrinal environment in which it appeared, it did not come into its own until the closing years of our period.

It is not hard to see that its growth during those years was closely associated with the new strength which corporate enterprise was then attaining and which, as I suggested earlier, was a prerequisite for the departure of the state from the investment area. The fact that the Pennsylvania Railroad accepted the tonnage tax in the forties and discovered that it was illegal in the fifties was not, as its attorneys implied, due to a heightening of philosophic perception. It was due to an increase in economic power and political influence which gave the company a position in relation to the state entirely different from the position it had when it sought its original charter from the legislature. In the investment field, indeed certain exponents of the new politico-economic faith admitted, with remarkable candor, that the recent growth of corporate enterprise had inspired their understanding of it. McPherson in journalism, Johnson in politics, Campbell in law, all measured the proper breadth of state policy by the extent of corporate growth, frankly stating that what had once been legitimate for the state had ceased to be so with the emergence of more powerful corporate enterprises.

Yet the relationship between corporate growth and the anti-state doctrine was an intricate one. The new ideology cannot be explained as the product of a devious and self-conscious conspiracy on the part of rising corporate interests, although it is true that the propaganda released by the Pennsylvania Railroad against public ownership and corporate control offers a real hint of such strategy. Actually in one important area — the area of mixed enterprise investment — corporate interests were the main opponents of the new philosophy. It was Read and Dallas, railroad attorneys, who in the Sharpless Case presented the most elaborate argument of the time against it. There was nothing mysterious about this. Corporate businesses simply wanted to maintain the flow of public aid. But it is important to observe that the case against them relied heavily upon their own strength and their own capacity. When the ideologists fighting mixed corporation investment spoke grandly of the powers of private enterprise, they were showering with praise the very interests who were aligned against them. It was an essential irony. Mixed enterprise investment had been initiated because of the weakness of the private corporation, and unless it could be demonstrated that this weakness had disappeared there would hardly be adequate ground for terminating it. Thus the anti-state doctrine in the mixed enterprise field was as integrally related to corporate growth as elsewhere. If its victory was a specific political defeat for cash-hungry corporate interests — scarcely a reflection on their strategic ability when one considers the state-wide financial hysteria they had to contend with — those interests had the satisfaction at any rate of knowing that the new philosophy was virtually the same as the one which they themselves were pressing in the areas of public works and corporate control. Invoking great democratic symbols, the whole drift of its meaning was to rationalize the freedom of the business corporation from state interference.

Yet this analysis does not exhaust the complexity of the relationship between corporate growth and the anti-state doctrine which it inspired. Even in the fields of public works and corporate control, not all of the corporate enterprises whose freedom was championed by the new theory were technically private corporations. Some of the most important among them were mixed corporations, offshoots of the local investment drive. The Pennsylvania Railroad and the Sunbury and Erie, two companies which purchased most of the public works, were mixed corporations with provisions in their board membership for directors chosen by local governments. Strictly speaking, then, the termination of public ownership and the reduction of corporate taxation were fully as much victories for the mixed as for the private corporation. It is extremely interesting that the crusaders against these policies, when they spoke of the heroes of business and the villains of government, completely ignored the public elements in many of the very enterprises which they were so valiantly defending. But this was hardly a piece of conscious doctrinal manipulation. In actual fact the effectiveness of public directors in shaping the policy of mixed corporations had become so limited that to classify the management of these enterprises as private management seemed proper enough.[14] This was quite apart from the additional fact that the permanent abolition of mixed enterprise policy during the same period made it obvious that in the future the enterprises whose freedom would be enhanced by the curtailment of public ownership and control would be exclusively private in character. From many points of view the later period was a transitional period in corporate growth,[15] and the complexity of its ideological repercussions is traceable to this fact. Though they oversimplified the issue, those theorists who frankly pinned their anti-state philosophy to the expansion of corporate power saw deeply into the character of the doctrinal transformation which was then taking place. The new theory was integrally associated with that remarkable upheaving of corporate enterprise of which McPherson spoke so eloquently.

Perceiving that the anti-governmental ideology was thus related to the movement of corporate development, we are better able to understand why it flourished with most richness and effect

---

[14] *Supra*, p. 99.
[15] Cf. Dodd, *Lectures on the Growth of Corporate Structure*, p. 6; Cochran and Miller, *Age of Enterprise*, pp. 70 ff.

in its attack upon public enterprise. Public enterprise appeared only in banking and transportation, economic fields in which the corporate system had attained its major power during our period. If in the industrial field stringent labor laws were enacted without being challenged before the courts and without encountering a mass of anti-state philosophy, it is perhaps relevant to observe that corporate enterprise had not yet achieved a comparable power there. Surely the resources available to the largest textile factory in the state to repel the labor legislation of 1848 were picayune compared with those available to the Pennsylvania Railroad to attack tonnage taxation. A glance at a subsequent era, when corporate enterprise had become powerful in the industrial field, will show that such labor legislation was ruthlessly assailed in the legislature, was condemned in the press, was brought before the courts and invalidated by them, on the basis of the anti-governmental concepts which I have been describing. Witness the famous opinion of Mr. Justice Gordon in the Godcharles Case of 1886 which served as a landmark on the road to that "laissez-faire" constitutional law so familiar to students of the latter nineteenth century.[16]

Thus the mature development of the anti-state doctrine is not to be found even during the closing years of our period. It is to be found after the Civil War, when the corporate system, invading all areas of business activity, achieved supremacy in the economic life of Pennsylvania and the nation. During that period of American business history, aptly described as the age of the "corporate revolution,"[17] business units of unprecedented strength confronted not only the traditional intervention of the state but also the intervention of an expanding national govern-

---

[16] *Godcharles* v. *Wigeman*, 113 Pa. St. Rep. 431 (1886). The measure involved here was one against store-order payments. For a denunciation of the measure as an invalid exercise of governmental power, see *Philadelphia Record*, Oct. 5, 1886; *Pittsburgh Despatch*, Oct. 5, 1886; *Pittsburgh Commercial Gazette*, Oct. 5, 1886. For a defense of the measure as being in line with earlier and accepted principles of labor legislation in the state, see *Pittsburgh Daily Post*, Oct. 5, 1886; Wilkes-Barre *Evening Leader*, Oct. 8, 1886. For an excellent discussion of the case as path-breaking in the development of "laissez-faire" constitutional law, see Twiss, *Lawyers and the Constitution*, pp. 127–29.

[17] Cf. Fainsod and Gordon, *Government and the American Economy*, pp. 7 ff.; Berle and Means, *Modern Corporation and Private Property*, pp. 13 ff.

ment.[18] In the course of the struggles thus unleashed the anti-state symbols were lifted to a rank of doctrinal importance higher than anything the Pennsylvania publicists of the forties and fifties could have hoped for. Freedley's defense of business competition flowered into the Darwinian survivalism of Sumner.[19] Williams's legal hysteria over the communist menace blossomed into the memorable argument of Choate.[20] Field arose to fight the battles of McPherson.[21] Concept for concept, in a remarkable way, the ideas fashioned by the anti-state theorists toward the close of our period found historic fulfillment in the subsequent age. While the original theory of state action receded into a half-remembered past, those ideas advanced with messianic vigor, worked themselves into popular thought, and became the platitudes of righteous men.[22]

Is it unreasonable to suggest that this ideological movement may itself have had something to do with creating that vague and fallacious "laissez-faire" conception of the earlier period which continues to flavor much of American historical thinking? History has its strategic uses. An image of the past can be worth a score of arguments based on the present. Surely it is not irrelevant to observe that certain members of the Pennsylvania House, when they demanded immediate liquidation of public works in 1854, chose to become historians as well as philosophers. Not only did they contend that the "separation of politics from trade" was essential to democracy, but they also spoke fondly of a period both "original" and "pure" in the past when that principle had prevailed — a period which testified to the vigor of their own imaginations but which had never in fact existed.[23]

[18] Cf. Hacker, *Triumph of American Capitalism*, pp. 374 ff.
[19] Sumner, *Social Classes; idem, Challenge of Facts, passim.* See also Hofstadter, *Social Darwinism, passim.*
[20] *Pollock v. Farmers' Loan and Trust Co.*, 157 U. S. 429, 531–32 (1895).
[21] See Swisher, *Stephen J. Field*, pp. 363 ff.; Lerner, "Supreme Court and American Capitalism," *Yale Law Journ.*, XLII (1933), 692 ff.
[22] On this whole topic see Gabriel, *American Democratic Thought*, pp. 143–60.
[23] *Supra*, pp. 166–67.

APPENDICES

APPENDICES

I.

REPORT ON AUCTION OF STATE MIXED-ENTERPRISE HOLDINGS, 1843 *

A. STOCKS SOLD

At Philadelphia, June 13

Company	Number of Shares Sold	Proceeds
Bank of Philadelphia	3,666	$243,506.75
Danville and Pottsville Railroad Co.	10	10.00
Cumberland Valley Railroad Co.	100	275.00
Schuylkill Bridge Co. (Pottstown)	60	1,110.00
Schuylkill Bridge Co. (Matson's Ford)	120	660.00
Bank of Pennsylvania	2,148	161,936.50
Union Canal Co.	10	10.00
Pennsylvania and Ohio Canal Co.	500	12,505.00
Chesapeake and Delaware Canal Co.	500	2,500.00
Springhouse, etc. Turnpike Co.	500	3,800.00
Schuylkill Navigation Co.	1,000	39,140.00
Ridge Road Turnpike Co.	500	812.50
		466,265.75

At Harrisburg, June 19

Company	Number of Shares Sold	Proceeds
Columbia Bank and Bridge Co.	90	3,318.00
Wrightsville, York, and Gettysburg Railroad Co.	400	1,124.25
Codorus Navigation Co.	600	1,031.50
Harrisburg Bridge Co.	20	140.00
Waynesburg, Greencastle, and Mercersburg Turnpike Co.	250	373.75
Berks and Dauphin Turnpike Co.	580	6,936.25
Lancaster and Elizabethtown Turnpike Co.	100	2,971.25
Centre and Kishacoquillis Turnpike Co.	400	637.50
Susquehanna and York Borough Turnpike Co.	50	1,050.00
York and Gettysburg Turnpike Co.	400	4,123.75
New Holland Turnpike Co.	116	1,195.50
Hanover and Carlisle Turnpike Co.	100	490.00
Bellefonte and Phillipsburg Turnpike Co.	770	1,000.00
Harrisburg and Millerstown Turnpike Co.	800	1,283.75

* *House Journal, 1844*, II, 28–46.

AUCTION OF STATE MIXED-ENTERPRISE HOLDINGS, 1843
(cont'd)

Company	Number of Shares Sold	Proceeds
Middletown and Harrisburg Turnpike Co.	280	3,530.00
Bellefonte, Aaronsburg, and Youngmanstown Turnpike Co.	15	32.50
Bald Eagle and Nittany Valley Turnpike Co.	64	128.00
Mouth of Juniata Bridge Co.	10	10.00
York Haven and Harrisburg Turnpike Co.	408	408.00
Bank of Pennsylvania	15	2,290.00
		32,074.00

At Northumberland, June 24

Northumberland Bridge Co.	5	5.00
Lewisburg Bridge Co.	400	6,095.00
Danville Bridge Co.	5	10.00
Milton Bridge Co.	5	27.50
Centre Turnpike Co.	60	273.75
Derrstown and Youngmanstown Turnpike Co.	153	768.25
Lewisburg and Jersey Shore Turnpike Co.	128	143.37
Towanda Bridge Co.	100	1,058.74
Susquehanna and Tioga Turnpike Co.	28	28.00
Phillipsburg and Susquehanna Turnpike Co.	10	11.25
Columbia Bank and Bridge Co.	25	1,042.50
Bank of Pennsylvania	70	10,930.00
Nescopeck Bridge Co.	5	6.87
		20,400.25

At Wilkes-Barre, June 29

Wilkes-Barre Bridge Co.	430	11,120.00
Easton and Wilkes-Barre Turnpike Company	250	1,517.85
Milford and Owega Turnpike Company	10	10.00
Belmont and Ochguga Turnpike Company	100	109.50
Carbondale and Lackawanna Turnpike Co.	19	19.00
Leonea and Harmony Turnpike Co.	96	96.00
Belmont and Easton Turnpike Co.	5	5.75
Philadelphia and Great Bend Turnpike Co.	20	52.50
Bank of Pennsylvania	21	3,316.25
Towanda Bridge Co.	5	66.25
Columbia Bank and Bridge Co.	5	202.50
Danville Bridge Co.	5	30.00
Bank of Philadelphia	5	400.00
Susquehanna and Lehigh Turnpike Co.	100	800.00
		17,745.60

AUCTION OF STATE MIXED-ENTERPRISE HOLDINGS, 1843
(*cont'd*)

At Pittsburgh, September 6

Company	Number of Shares Sold	Proceeds
Allegheny Bridge Co.	1,600	53,194.75
Monongahela Bridge Co.	2,000	31,266.25
Big Beaver Bridge Co.	600	11,937.50
Conemaugh Bridge Co.	100	1,937.50
Loyalhanna Bridge Co.	100	540.50
Raubstown Bridge Co.	171	1,643.75
Williamsport Bridge Co.	300	2,912.50
Monongahela Navigation Co.	300	587.50
Greensburg and Pittsburgh Turnpike Co.	1,780	3,383.75
Pittsburgh and Steubenville Turnpike Co.	320	443.75
Mt. Pleasant and Somerset Turnpike Co.	300	300.00
Somerset and Bedford Turnpike Co.	672	672.00
Washington and Pittsburgh Turnpike Co.	855	1,051.30
Pittsburgh Farmers and Mechanics Turnpike Co.	224	255.00
Bedford and Hollidaysburg Turnpike Co.	160	161.25
French Creek Bridge Co.	300	517.50
Franklin and Allegheny Bridge Co.	10	12.50
Erie and Waterford Turnpike Co.	10	320.00
Bank of Pennsylvania	300	45,025.00
Cumberland Valley R.R. Co.	100	100.00
Bank of Philadelphia	52	3,640.00
Columbia Bank and Bridge Co.	118	4,750.25
Pennsylvania and Ohio Canal Co.	360	9,025.00
		173,677.55

At Philadelphia, October 24

Company	Number of Shares Sold	Proceeds
Bank of Philadelphia	1,510	117,182.50
Bank of Pennsylvania	2,196	384,256.00
Columbia Bank and Bridge Co.	662	28,090.25
Harrisburg Bridge Co.	4,480	22,836.25
Northumberland Bridge Co.	2,395	2,395.00
Danville Bridge Co.	590	3,097.50
Nescopeck Bridge Co.	275	980.00
Milton Bridge Co.	87	652.50
Mouth of Juniata Bridge Co.	490	514.50
Towanda Bridge Co.	395	4,368.75
Franklin and Allegheny Bridge Co.	1,245	1,438.12
French Creek Bridge Co.	50	56.25

AUCTION OF STATE MIXED-ENTERPRISE HOLDINGS, 1843
(cont'd)

Company	Number of Shares Sold	Proceeds
Pennsylvania and Ohio Canal Co.	640	18,085.00
Monongahela Navigation Co.	2,200	6,660.00
Cumberland Valley Railroad	100	175.00
Belmont and Easton Turnpike Co.	350	700.00
Philadelphia and Great Bend Turnpike Co.	350	50.00
Chambersburg and Bedford Turnpike Co.	1,550	2,650.00
Phillipsburg and Susquehanna Turnpike Co.	330	371.25
Bellefonte, Aaronsburg and Youngmanstown Turnpike Co.	547	3,087.87
Centre Turnpike Co.	1,540	6,588.75
Milford and Oswega Turnpike Co.	1,230	1,230.00
Sterling and Newfoundland Turnpike Co.	64	64.00
Lackawanna and Lackawaxen Turnpike Co.	48	48.00
Waterford and Erie Turnpike Co.	90	2,810.00
Union Canal Co.	1,240	1,240.00
		609,567.50

Recapitulation

June sales at	Philadelphia	466,265.75
	Harrisburg	32,074.00
	Northumberland	20,400.25
	Wilkes-Barre	17,745.60
September sale at Pittsburgh		173,677.55
October sale at Philadelphia		609,567.50
Total		$1,319,730.65

B. STOCKS NOT SOLD

Canal and Navigation Company Stocks

	Number of Shares	Value
Bristol Tow Boat Co.	320	$ 8,000.00
Delaware and Schuylkill Canal Co.	1,500	75,000.00
Bald Eagle and Spring Creek Navigation	1,500	59,778.66

Railroad Company Stocks

Danville and Pottsville Railroad Co.	2,885	174,778.90
Cumberland Valley Railroad Co.	1,700	70,000.00
Franklin Railroad Co.	2,000	100,000.00

AUCTION OF STATE MIXED-ENTERPRISE HOLDINGS, 1843
(cont'd)

Turnpike Company Stocks

Company	Number of Shares	Value
Downingtown and Ephrata	640	64,000.00
Brandywine, Philadelphia and New London	50	2,500.00
Perkiomen and Reading	1,360	68,000.00
Harrisburg, Carlisle and Chambersburg	2,124	106,200.00
Chambersburg and Bedford	2,760	138,000.00
Gap and Newport	512	25,600.00
Morgantown, Churchtown and Blue Bal	180	9,000.00
Little Conestoga	200	10,000.00
Millerstown and Lewistown	717	35,850.00
Lewistown and Huntingdon	930	46,500.00
Milesburg and Smethport	1,610	32,200.00
Snow Shoe and Perkersville	200	5,000.00
Lycoming, Potter and M'Kean	400	20,000.00
Cayuga and Susquehanna	300	6,000.00
Bridgewater and Wilkes-Barre	516	25,800.00
Clifford and Wilkes-Barre	154	7,700.00
Stoystown and Greensburg	3,823	128,217.00
Huntingdon, Cambria and Indiana	3,477	173,850.00
Pittsburgh and New Alexandria	967	48,350.00
New Alexandria and Conemaugh	320	16,000.00
Pittsburgh and Butler	947	23,675.00
Butler and Mercer	882	22,050.00
Raubstown and Mount Pleasant	300	15,000.00
Mount Pleasant and Somerset	360	33,000.00
Armstrong and Indiana	360	9,000.00
Indiana and Ebensburg	560	14,000.00
Washington and Williamsport	329	16,450.00
Butler and Kittanning	200	5,000.00
Mount Pleasant and Pittsburgh	240	6,000.00
Somerset and Conemaugh	360	9,000.00
Somerset and Cumberland	320	8,000.00
Ligonier and Johnstown	160	8,000.00
Armstrong and Clearfield	224	5,600.00
Browningtown, Harrisville and Franklin	80	4,000.00
Butler and Freeport	200	4,000.00
Luthersburg and Punxsutawney	160	4,000.00
Birmingham and Elizabethtown	160	4,000.00
Susquehanna and Watersford	560	136,250.00
Mercer and Meadville	1,010	25,250.00

AUCTION OF STATE MIXED-ENTERPRISE HOLDINGS, 1843
(cont'd)

Company	Number of Shares	Value
Anderson's Ferry, Waterford and New Haven	100	10,000.00
Abington and Waterford	200	5,000.00
Warren and Ridgeway	280	7,000.00
Warren and New York State Line	40	2,000.00
Titusville and Union Mills	96	2,400.00
Warren and Franklin	160	4,000.00
Sugar Grove and Union	80	2,000.00
Carbondale and Lackawanna	5	250.00
Susquehanna and Tioga	300	30,000.00
Bethany and Dingman's Choice	160	8,000.00
Stoystown and Bedford	2,151	107,550.00
		$1,986,797.56

II.

MESSAGE OF GOVERNOR PORTER TO THE LEGISLATURE ON THE PUBLIC CREDITORS AND MIXED-ENTERPRISE BANKING, 1842 *

Gentlemen:

I cannot reconcile it to my sense of duty to permit this occasion to pass without renewing, in the most earnest manner, the appeal already made to the Legislature in behalf of the public creditors, and especially of those who have labored on our improvements and furnished materials for their repair and construction. Prostrated as the public credit in a great degree is, and overwhelmed as the business, energies and enterprise of the community are, it is undoubtedly an unpropitious time to impose additional burthens on the people, and is an ungracious duty to recommend or to sanction it. But the alternative admits of no qualification. We must act in conformity to the dictates of stern and unwelcome duty on the one hand, or disregard and set them at naught on the other. We must seek and desire the commendation of the honest and honorable, or we must earn and bear their contempt and derision. If we falter in this dilemma, we cannot escape one or the other of these judgments in the eyes of the world. I do hope and trust you will make adequate provision for all the public creditors — either by increased taxation, or some other available means. The burthen may be onerous,

* Pa. Archives, 4th, VI, 904–907.

but it can only be temporary. With the resources, vigor and enterprize of Pennsylvania, the present pecuniary embarrassment can only be of short duration. Let us then struggle manfully against it, in the hope of speedy relief.

The burthens borne in behalf of the State are light in comparison to those imposed for county, township, borough and other purposes. All the taxes paid by the people of Pennsylvania for all purposes amount per annum to the sum of four millions of dollars, as nearly as can be ascertained. Of this vast sum only seven hundred thousand dollars is levied and paid for the use of the State. It is therefore manifest that whatever may be the gross amount of taxes paid by the community, but a small portion is applied to the uses of the State Treasury, and on this score there is but little just ground to complain. Three per cent. on the assessed value of the real and personal property in Pennsylvania, assessed as it necessarily is far below its value, amounts to upwards of forty-two millions of dollars; a sum sufficient to pay off our public debt and leave a surplus of five or six millions in the Treasury. And yet, such is the general apathy or aversion to enter into an examination of a subject of this kind, that there are some to be found who seem at times almost disposed to doubt the ability of Pennsylvania to pay her debts.

I can scarcely find language strong enough to convey to you in a suitable manner, my ideas of the importance of a faithful adherence on the part of the State, to its solemn engagements. I have dwelt on this subject in my communications to every Legislature that has assembled since the duties of the Executive have been entrusted to my care. Allow me, therefore, most respectfully to ask your attention to my annual message on this subject.

So far as respects what are usually denominated the "Domestic Creditors," I sought in my annual message at your assembling, to place their claims on the true grounds. I have yet to hear the first word against the justice of their demands, or the extreme hardship of their case. They are our own citizens, who on the faith of the public, have devoted their money, their means, the sweat of their brows, to the public service, and have thus far been denied recompense. Nay, some of them have expended the last dollar they can command — have contracted large debts to enable them to prosecute their work — have just demands on the State amply sufficient to meet all their liabilities and to supply them with the means of recommencing business for their support, and yet are compelled to see the whole of their property under execution, and be themselves dragged to the very door of the jail. Is not this crying injustice? Is it not a disgrace to the State that thus beggars its own citizens, and then suffers them to be sacrificed for debts contracted on behalf of the State itself? How can any honest man who has the power to correct such evils, stand by and witness this state of things, without the blush of shame on his face? For myself, I should feel ill at ease if I left untried a single expedient to afford relief.

I can add little to the details of my former recommendations, or to the means of discharging these debts. It is for the Legislature now to act upon them. I will however suggest, that the State possesses a fund which might be applied to the payment of these debts, if other resources fail; and although it may not be at present available, it may ultimately become so, at least to a considerable extent. I refer to the stock held by the Commonwealth in the Bank of Pennsylvania, the Philadelphia Bank, and the Farmers' and Mechanics' Bank.

For these stocks the State paid $2,108,700. What they may ultimately be worth, I know not. My opinion of this investment has been communicated to the Legislature time and again, and it would be useless to reiterate it now. But I must be allowed, before closing the subject, to express my opinion, formed on the most thorough conviction, that unless the interest of individuals be enlisted in this matter, the State will never realize a dollar from it. It seems to me, therefore, that it would be advisable to transfer these stocks to trustees, or make some other disposition of them to supply the claims of the domestic creditors. If anything better can be done, it will afford me great pleasure to co-operate with you; but if not, the provision suggested might possibly save a remnant which might be applied to the debts long due to a class of just and meritorious creditors, who are most assuredly entitled at the hands of the Legislature, to the speediest relief which its wisdom can devise, and the means of the Commonwealth will possibly afford.

DAVID R. PORTER

Executive Chamber, Harrisburg, June 10, 1842.

III.

REPORT OF THE AUDITOR-GENERAL ON ADMINISTRATIVE ABUSES IN THE REPAIR OF THE JUNIATA BRANCH OF THE STATE WORKS IN 1838 *

(The following reasons were given for the suspension of accounts:)
Because, Time is charged for work which was not performed.

Because, Teams are charged in the names of persons who had no teams on the work, and in some instances the amount of which is receipted, without the knowledge or consent of the person in whose name the account was kept.

Because, Teams were charged at full and high prices, and the drivers' time charged in a separate account.

* *House Journal, 1840*, I, 234 ff.

Because, Foremen were partners in teams, one keeping time principally by bill, the other by check-roll, oftentimes not in the owner's name.

Because, Public teams and hands were freely devoted to the use of private individuals and political partizans, their time being continued on the check-roll.

Because, A large amount of money is charged for getting on hands — while others were discharged for opinions' sake.

Because, Improper time was added to the check-rolls, at the will of those having charge to cover the expenses of bringing hands from a distance, and a large amount retained by bill for the same thing, rendering it impossible to ascertain what amount has been charged for this item, or what number of days work ought to be deducted.

Because, Time is continued for hands and teams after they had left the work.

Because, Articles never purchased for, or used on the work, are charged in the accounts.

Because, Many persons were induced to receipt for money, which they never received, and to which they had no claims.

Because, Bribery was attempted for the purpose of procuring the public funds.

Because, Public property was converted to private use.

Because, Lumber and other articles were purchased to be delivered on the line at a given place, and fixed price as rendered per bill, and the contractor permitted to charge the Commonwealth with the daily pay of the teams employed to deliver it, and at least in one instance, two dollars per day was charged more than the teamster received, notwithstanding they were principally paid out of the contractor's store.

Because, Foremen and other hands bought materials, provisions and tools, settled accounts, sold property, or converted it to their own use, and had control of the boarding houses.

Because, Horse feed is charged to the Commonwealth, in addition to full pay for time.

Because, Officers and hands received pay, and had expenses paid while travelling in different parts of the state, vicinity of the work, or in attending elections.

Because, Many persons were hired at high prices, who were neither foremen, mechanics, nor even laboring men.

Because, Foremen and others, while in the public service, bought and slaughtered cattle, using the state teams and hands for that purpose, and supplying the line with meat by the pound at a high price.

Because, Public officers having sold public property, now refuse to render an account, or even a bill of sale.

Because, Materials, provision, &c., were not at all times procured at as low prices as they were offered at.

Because, Provisions (at least flour), fell in price after the "break," while the charge is continued at the most advanced price to the Commonwealth.

Because, One of the supervisors charged for three yoke of oxen for months, at $12 per day, exclusive of the driver, when it appears he had but two yoke, for weeks in succession, but one yoke of oxen on the work, and because $6.25 per day is charged by the same person for a two horse team, including the driver, which team and driver were employed in private use, a great part of the time.

Because, The blank check-rolls furnished by the state, upon which accounts were kept, were mutilated. The heading and certificate below being cut off, and others attached by wafers or otherwise, capable of easy separation and leaving it uncertain how many were attached, when sworn to, whether teams at $6, or $8, were not substituted for hands at ninety-five cents per day, or whether one individual may not have signed for others.

Because, A large amount of whiskey is charged to the Commonwealth.

Because, The disbursing officer could not, or would not correct the accounts returned by him, and

Because, I could not designate the true, from the false vouchers; or ascertain the amount "fairly expended" on that branch as directed by the resolution.

IV.

CLAIMS AND AWARDS FOR DAMAGES UNDER THE BOARD OF APPRAISERS OF THE PUBLIC WORKS, 1840 *

	Amount Claimed	Amount Awarded
Columbia and Philadelphia Railroad	$24,787.32	$ 3,890.00
Western Division	2,400.00	350.00
North Branch Division	3,778.70	850.00
Juniata Division	2,400.00	400.00
Susquehanna Division	470.00	350.00
Portage Railroad	1,017.50	57.50
Beaver Division	3,730.00	100.00
Erie Extension	15,170.22	7,250.00
West Branch Division	12,838.75	1,738.25
French Creek Division	250.00	50.00
	$66,842.49	$15,035.75

* *House Journal, 1840,* II, 462–63.

V.

PAYMENTS UNDER ACT OF 1838 AUTHORIZING BOUNTIES FOR SILK PRODUCTION *

1839	$ 568.44
1840	2,010.89
1841	4,418.55
1842	6,716.77
1843	3,425.76
1844	62.71
1845	18.00

* Statistics taken from the annual reports of the auditor-general.

TABLE OF LEGAL CASES

(Except for Federal cases, which are indicated by asterisks, all cases relate to Pennsylvania Courts.)

Academy of Fine Arts v. *Philadelphia County*, 22 Pennsylvania State Reports 496 (1854).

Adams v. *Rogers*, 9 Watts 121 (1839).

Bank of Pennsylvania v. *Commonwealth*, 19 Pennsylvania State Reports 144 (1852).

Bank of Pennsylvania v. *Spangler*, 32 Pennsylvania State Reports 474 (1859).

Bank of the United States v. *The Planters' Bank of Georgia*, 9 Wheaton 905 (1824).*

Billmeyer v. *Evans and Rodenbaugh*, 40 Pennsylvania State Reports 324 (1861).

Boggs v. *Teackle*, 5 Binney 332 (1812).

Brant's Appeal, 20 Pennsylvania State Reports 141 (1852).

Briscoe v. *Bank of Kentucky*, 11 Peters 257 (1837).*

Brown v. *Maryland*, 12 Wheaton 419 (1827).*

Case of the Philadelphia and Trenton Railroad Co., 6 Wharton 25 (1840).

Case v. *Dunmore*, 23 Pennsylvania State Reports 93 (1854).

Chadwick v. *Moore*, 8 Watts and Sergeant 49 (1844).

Chaffee v. *Michaels*, 31 Pennsylvania State Reports 282 (1858).

City of Pittsburg v. *Scott*, 1 Pennsylvania State Reports 309 (1845).

Commonwealth v. *Bank of Pennsylvania in Equity*, 3 Watts and Sergeant 173 (1842).

Commonwealth v. *The Easton Bank*, 10 Pennsylvania State Reports 442 (1849).

Commonwealth v. *King*, 1 Wharton 448 (1836).

Commonwealth ex rel. *Claghorn* v. *Cullen*, 13 Pennsylvania State Reports 133 (1850).

Commonwealth ex rel. *Dusar* v. *Riddle*, 1 Sergeant and Rawle 311 (1815).

Commonwealth ex rel. *Thomas* v. *Commissioners of Allegheny County*, 32 Pennsylvania State Reports 218 (1858).

County of Lawrence v. *Northwestern Railroad Company*, 32 Pennsylvania State Reports 144 (1858).

TABLE OF LEGAL CASES 335

Dartmouth College v. *Woodward*, 4 Wheaton 518 (1819).*
Dodge v. *Woolsey*, 18 Howard 331 (1856).*
Donaldson v. *Chambers*, 2 Dallas 100 (1788).*
Eakin v. *Raub*, 12 Sergeant and Rawle 330 (1825).
Evans v. *Myers*, 25 Pennsylvania State Reports 114 (1855).
Farmers' and Mechanics' Bank v. *Smith*, 3 Sergeant and Rawle 63 (1817).
Farmers' and Mechanics' Bank of Pennsylvania v. *Smith*, 6 Wheaton 131 (1821).*
Fisher v. *Hyde*, 3 Yeates 256 (1801).
Fletcher v. *Peck*, 6 Cranch 87 (1810).*
Garrigues v. *Reynolds*, 6 Binney 330 (1814).
Gibbons v. *Ogden*, 9 Wheaton 1 (1824).*
Godcharles v. *Wigeman*, 113 Pennsylvania State Report 431 (1886).
Gray v. *The Monongahela Navigation Company*, 2 Watts and Sergeant 156 (1841).
Harvey v. *Lloyd*, 3 Pennsylvania State Reports 331 (1846).
Harvey v. *Thomas*, 10 Watts 63 (1840).
Hays v. *Risher*, 32 Pennsylvania State Reports 169 (1858).
Hilliard and Pippit v. *Greenleaf*, 2 Yeates 533 (1799).
James v. *Alden*, 1 Dallas 188 (1786).*
Jeffries v. *Thompson*, 2 Yeates 482 (1799).
Joy v. *Cossart*, 1 Yeates 50 (1791).
Knabb v. *Drake*, 23 Pennsylvania State Reports 489 (1854).
Leas' Appeal, 9 Pennsylvania State Reports 504 (1848).
License Cases, 5 Howard 504 (1847).*
McClurg v. *Lecky*, 3 Penrose and Watts 83 (1831).
McCracken v. *Hayward*, 2 Howard 608 (1844).*
Miller v. *Hall*, 1 Dallas 229 (1788).*
Moncure v. *Hanson*, 15 Pennsylvania State Reports 385 (1850).
Monongahela Navigation Company v. *Coon*, 6 Pennsylvania State Reports 379 (1847).
Moore v. *Houston*, 3 Sergeant and Rawle 169 (1817).
Mott v. *Pennsylvania Railroad Company*, 30 Pennsylvania State Reports 9 (1858).
New Jersey v. *Wilson*, 7 Cranch 164 (1812).*
The New York and Erie Railroad Company v. *Sabin*, 26 Pennsylvania State Reports 242 (1856).

Packer v. *Sunbury and Erie Railroad Company*, 19 Pennsylvania State Reports 211 (1852).

Passenger Cases, 7 Howard 283 (1849).*

Peddle v. *Hollinshead*, 9 Sergeant and Rawle 277 (1823).

Pennsylvania Railroad Company v. *The City of Philadelphia*, 47 Pennsylvania State Reports 189 (1864).

Pollock v. *Farmers' Loan and Trust Company*, 157 U.S. 429 (1895).*

Respublica v. *Duquet*, 2 Yeates 493 (1799).

Richie v. *McCauley*, 4 Pennsylvania State Reports 471 (1846).

Schuylkill Navigation Company v. *Thomas*, 13 Sergeant and Rawle 431 (1825).

Sharpless et al. v. *The Mayor of Philadelphia*, 21 Pennsylvania State Reports 147 (1853).

Smith v. *Brown*, 3 Binney 201 (1810).

State Bank of Ohio v. *Knoop*, 16 Howard 369 (1853).*

Stiles v. *Jones*, 3 Yeates 491 (1801).

Walsh v. *Nourse*, 5 Binney 381 (1813).

Washington and Pittsburgh Turnpike Company v. *Cullen and Crane*, 8 Sergeant and Rawle 517 (1822).

Wheeler v. *Philadelphia*, 77 Pennsylvania State Reports 338 (1875).

Wolfram v. *Strickhouser*, 1 Watts and Sergeant 379 (1841).

BIBLIOGRAPHY

Akagi, Roy H. "The Pennsylvania Constitution of 1838," *Pennsylvania Magazine of History and Biography*, XLVIII (1924), 301–33.

Allegheny Valley Railroad. *Report of the President and Managers.* Pittsburgh, 1854.

American Quarterly Temperance Magazine. May, 1833.

Armor, William C. *Lives of the Governors of Pennsylvania.* Norwich, Connecticut, 1874.

[Armroyd, George.] *Connected View of the Whole Internal Navigation of the United States.* Philadelphia, 1826.

Ashmead, Henry G. *History of the Delaware County National Bank.* Chester, Pennsylvania: Press of the Chester Times, 1914.

Banner of the Constitution. Condy Raguet, ed., Washington and Philadelphia, 1829–32.

Barnard, J. Lynn. *Factory Legislation in Pennsylvania: Its History and Administration.* Philadelphia: Published for the University, 1907.

Barnes, Albert. *The Throne of Iniquity; or, Sustaining Evil by Law.* Philadelphia, 1852.

Bartlett, Marguerite G. *The Chief Phases of Pennsylvania Politics in the Jacksonian Period.* Allentown, Pennsylvania: H. R. Haas and Company, 1919.

Bell, Whitfield J. "Social History of Pennsylvania, 1760–1790," *Pennsylvania Magazine of History and Biography*, LVII (1938), 281–306.

Benezet, Anthony. *Remarks on the Nature and Bad Effects of Spirituous Liquors.* Philadelphia, 1778.

Berle, Adolf A., Jr., and Gardiner C. Means. *The Modern Corporation and Private Property.* New York: The Macmillan Company, 1933.

Bettle, Edward. "Notices of Negro Slavery as Connected with Pennsylvania," *Memoirs of the Historical Society of Pennsylvania*, I (1826), 349–88.

Biddle, Nicholas. *Correspondence of . . . Dealing with National Affairs, 1807–1844.* Edited by Reginald C. McGrane. Boston and New York: Houghton Mifflin Company, 1919.

Bidwell, Percy W., and John I. Falconer. *History of Agriculture in the Northern United States.* Washington, D. C.: Carnegie Institution of Washington, 1925.

Binney, Charles C. *The Life of Horace Binney.* Philadelphia: J. B. Lippincott Company, 1903.

Binney, Horace. *Opinion Upon the Right of the City Councils to Subscribe for Stock in the Pennsylvania Railroad Company.* Philadelphia, 1846.

Bishop, Alvord L. "The State Works of Pennsylvania," *Transactions of the Connecticut Academy of Arts and Sciences,* XIII (1907), 149–297.

Blandi, Joseph G. *Maryland Business Corporations, 1783–1852.* Baltimore: Johns Hopkins Press, 1934.

Bogen, Jules I. *The Anthracite Railroads; A Study in American Railroad Enterprise.* New York: The Ronald Press Company, 1927.

Boucher, John Newton. *A Century and a Half of Pittsburg and Her People.* New York: Lewis Publishing Company, 1908.

Boudin, Louis B. *Government by Judiciary.* New York: W. Godwin, Inc., 1932.

Bourne, Edward G. *The History of the Surplus Revenue of 1837.* New York: G. P. Putnam's Sons, 1885.

Bouvier's Law Dictionary and Concise Encyclopedia. 8th edition, 3d revision. Kansas City, Missouri: Vernon Law Company, 1914.

Bowen, Eli. *The Pictorial Sketch-Book of Pennsylvania.* [1st ed.], Philadelphia, 1852.

Bradsby, Henry C. *History of Bradford County, Pennsylvania.* Chicago: S. B. Nelson and Company, 1891.

Breck, Samuel. *Sketch of the Internal Improvements Already Made by Pennsylvania.* . . . Philadelphia, 1818.

Brenckman, Fred. *History of Carbon County.* Harrisburg: J. J. Nungesser, 1913.

Brigance, William N. *Jeremiah Sullivan Black, a Defender of the Constitution and the Ten Commandments.* Philadelphia: University of Pennsylvania Press, 1934.

Brown Brothers and Company. *Experiences of a Century.* Philadelphia: Private Printing, 1919.

Browne, Peter A. *A Summary of the Law of Pennsylvania, Securing to Mechanics and Others Payment for their Labor.* . . . Philadelphia, 1814.

Brunhouse, Robert L. *The Counter-Revolution in Pennsylvania, 1776–1790.* Harrisburg: Pennsylvania Historical Commission, 1942.

Budd, Thomas. *Good Order Established in Pennsylvania and New Jersey.* Cleveland: The Burrows Brothers Company, 1902. First published in 1685. (Here reprinted with introduction and notes by Frederick J. Shepard.)

Bull, Marcus. *Statement of the Origin and Subsequent History of the Mining Operations of the North American Coal Company.* n.p., n.d.

Burdine, J. Alton. *Governmental Regulation of Industry in Pennsylvania, 1776–1860.* Unpublished Ph.D. Thesis, Harvard University, 1939.

Caldwell, Joshua W. *Studies in the Constitutional History of Tennessee.* 2d ed. Cincinnati: The Robert Clarke Company, 1907.

Caldwell, Lynton K. *The Administrative Theories of Hamilton and Jefferson.* Chicago: University of Chicago Press, 1944.

Cale, Edgar. *The Organization of Labor in Philadelphia, 1850–1870.* Philadelphia: University of Pennsylvania Press, 1940.

Callender, Guy S. "The Early Transportation and Banking Enterprises of the States in Relation to the Growth of Corporations," *Quarterly Journal of Economics*, XVII (1902/03), 111–62.

Canals of Pennsylvania. Excerpt from Part IV of the Report of the Secretary of Internal Affairs of Pennsylvania. Harrisburg, 1900.

Carey, Henry C. *Essay on the Rate of Wages.* Philadelphia, 1835.

———. *Principles of Social Science.* Philadelphia, 1858–1859.

Carey, Mathew. *Brief View of the System of Internal Improvement of the State of Pennsylvania.* Philadelphia, 1831.

———, ed. *Debates and Proceedings of the General Assembly of Pennsylvania on . . . the Law Annulling the Charter of the Bank.* Philadelphia, 1786.

———. *Excerpta.* (Volumes of Pamphlets in the Library Company of Philadelphia.)

———. *Internal Improvement*, Nos. I and II. (Miscellaneous Pamphlets, Widener Library, Harvard University)

———. *Mathew Carey Autobiography.* Brooklyn, New York: E. L. Schwaab, 1942.

———. *Miscellaneous Essays.* Philadelphia, 1830.

Carlton, Frank. "Abolition of Imprisonment for Debt in the United States," *Yale Review*, XVII (1908/09), 339–44.

Catterall, Ralph C. H. *The Second Bank of the United States.* Chicago: The University of Chicago Press, 1903.

Chapman, John M. and Ray B. Westerfield. *Branch Banking.* New York: Harper and Brothers, 1942.

Cherrington, Ernest H. *The Evolution of Prohibition in the United States.* Westerville, Ohio: The American Issue Press, 1920.

Clark, Joseph S., Jr. "The Railroad Struggle for Pittsburgh. Forty-three Years of Philadelphia-Baltimore Rivalry, 1838–1871," *Pennsylvania Magazine of History and Biography*, XLVIII (1924), 1–37.

Clark, Victor S. *History of Manufactures in the United States, 1607–1860.* Washington, D. C.: Carnegie Institution of Washington, 1916.

Cleveland, Frederick A., and Fred W. Powell. *Railroad Finance.* New York: D. Appleton and Company, 1912.

———. *Railroad Promotion and Capitalization in the United States.* New York: Longmans, Green and Company, 1909.

Cochran, Thomas C., and William Miller. *Age of Enterprise.* New York: The Macmillan Company, 1942.

Commons, John R., et al. *History of Labour in the United States.* New York: The Macmillan Company, 1918–1935.

———. ed. *A Documentary History of American Industrial Society.* Cleveland: The A. H. Clark Company, 1910–11.

Commonwealth v. the President, Directors and Company of the Bank of Pennsylvania. Harrisburg, 1842.

Comparative Calculations and Remarks on Internal Improvements by Roads, Canals and River Navigation. Philadelphia, 1821.

Constitutions of Pennsylvania. Harrisburg: Legislative Reference Bureau, 1926.

[Cook, Joel.] *The Philadelphia National Bank. A Century's Record, 1803–1903.* Philadelphia: Philadelphia National Bank, 1903.

Corn Exchange Association of Philadelphia. *Second Annual Report.* Philadelphia, 1856.

Correspondence between the Lehigh Coal and Navigation Company and the Beaver Meadow Railroad and Coal Company. n.p., 1835.

Crall, F. Frank. "A Half-Century of Rivalry between Pittsburgh and Wheeling," *Western Pennsylvania Historical Magazine,* XIII (1930), 237–55.

Crumrine, Boyd, ed. *History of Washington County, Pennsylvania.* Philadelphia: L. H. Everts and Company, 1882.

Daily Keystone and People's Journal (Harrisburg). 1841–1845.

Dallas, A. J., comp. *Laws of the General Assembly of the Commonwealth of Pennsylvania.* Philadelphia, 1797–1801.

Davis, Joseph S. *Essays in the Earlier History of American Corporations.* Cambridge: Harvard University Press, 1917.

Davis, Stanton Ling. *Pennsylvania Politics, 1860–1863.* Cleveland: The Bookstore, Western Reserve University, 1935.

Day, Sherman. *Historical Collections of the State of Pennsylvania.* Philadelphia, 1843.

Debtor and Creditor. Philadelphia, 1810.

Democratic Union (Harrisburg). 1843–1845.

Dewey, Davis R. *Financial History of the United States.* New York: Longmans, Green and Company, 1909.

——————. *State Banking before the Civil War.* Washington, D. C.: Government Printing Office, 1910.

Dewey, John. *Freedom and Culture.* New York: G. P. Putnam's Sons, 1939.

[Dickinson, John.] *Late Regulations Respecting the British Colonies.* ... Philadelphia, 1765.

——————. *Letters from a Farmer in Pennsylvania.* New York: The Outlook Company, 1903. (First published in 1768.)

Dickinson, John. *Writings.* (Paul L. Ford, Ed.) Memoirs of the Historical Society of Pennsylvania, XIV (1895).

Dodd, Edwin M. *Lectures on the Growth of the Corporate Structure in the United States, with Special Reference to Governmental Regulations.* Cleveland: Cleveland Bar Association, 1938.

Doe, John. *A Letter to John Jones, John Smith and James Black, Esq., on the Subject of the Right and Power of the City of Philadelphia to Subscribe for Stock in the Pennsylvania Railroad Company.* Philadelphia, 1846.

Dorfman, Joseph. *The Economic Mind in American Civilization, 1606–1865.* New York: The Viking Press, 1946.

Doylestown Democrat. 1846–1847.

Duane, William, William B. Hood, and Leonard Myers. *A Digest of the Acts of Assembly Relating to the City of Philadelphia ... and of the Ordinances of the Said City.* Philadelphia, 1865.

DuBois, W. E. Burghardt. *The Philadelphia Negro.* Philadelphia: Published for the University, 1899.

——————. *The Suppression of the African Slave-Trade in the United States of America, 1638–1870.* New York: Longmans, Green and Company, 1896.

Duffield, George. *Samson Shorn, and his Locks Renewed, or the History of Spirituous Liquors in Pennsylvania.* Philadelphia, 1855.

Dunaway, Wayland F. *History of Pennsylvania.* New York: Prentice-Hall, Inc., 1935.

Durrenberger, Joseph A. *Turnpikes.* Valdosta, Ga.: Southern Stationery and Printing Company, 1931.

Dyott, Thomas W. *An Exposition of the System of Moral and of Mental Labor Established at the Glass Factory of Dyottville.* ... Philadelphia, 1833.

East, Robert A. *Business Enterprise in the American Revolutionary Era.* New York: Columbia University Press, 1938.

Edwards, George W. *The Evolution of Finance Capitalism*. New York: Longmans, Green and Company, 1938.

Eiselen, Malcolm R. *The Rise of Pennsylvania Protectionism*. . . . Philadelphia: University of Pennsylvania Press, 1932.

Eldridge, Seba. *The Development of Collective Enterprise*. Lawrence: University of Kansas Press, 1943.

Extract Relative to the Importance of the Lehigh Navigation to the Commonwealth. Harrisburg, 1835.

Extracts from Dr. Benjamin Rush's Inquiry into the Effects of Ardent Spirits. Philadelphia, 1818.

Facts and Arguments respecting the Great Utility of an Extensive Plan of Inland Navigation in America. Philadelphia, 1805.

Fainsod, Merle, and Lincoln Gordon. *Government and the American Economy*. New York: W. W. Norton and Company, 1941.

The Federalist (Henry Cabot Lodge edition). New York: G. P. Putnam's Sons, 1889.

Fellow Citizens of Pennsylvania. (Pamphlet Volume 742 in the Pennsylvania State Library, Harrisburg.)

Ferguson, Russell J. *Early Western Pennsylvania Politics*. Pittsburgh: University of Pittsburgh Press, 1938.

A Few Reasons Why a "Maine Liquor Law" Should Not Be Passed in the State of Pennsylvania. Lancaster, 1852.

Fowler, John A. *History of Insurance in Philadelphia for Two Centuries*. Philadelphia: Review Publishing and Printing Company, 1888.

Freedley, Edwin T. *Philadelphia and Its Manufactures*. Philadelphia, 1859.

——————. *Practical Treatise on Business*. 2d ed. Philadelphia, 1852.

Gabriel, Ralph H. *The Course of American Democratic Thought: An Intellectual History since 1815*. New York: The Ronald Press Company, 1940.

Gallatin, Albert. *The Writings of Albert Gallatin*. Edited by Henry Adams. Philadelphia, 1879.

Geary, Theophane, sister. *A History of Third Parties in Pennsylvania, 1840–1860*. Washington, D. C.: The Catholic University of America, 1938.

Geiser, Karl F. *Redemptioners and Indentured Servants in the Colony and Commonwealth of Pennsylvania*. New Haven, Conn.: The Tuttle, Morehouse and Taylor Company, 1901.

Gibbons, Charles. *Speech of, in the Senate, February 16, 1846*. Philadelphia, 1846.

BIBLIOGRAPHY

Giesecke, Albert A. *American Commercial Legislation before 1789.* Philadelphia: University of Pennsylvania, 1910.

Graf, Edward. *The Temperance Question Answered on Principles of Morals and Religion.* Philadelphia, 1852.

Graham, Edward E. *Sketch of the Insolvent Laws of Pennsylvania.* Philadelphia, 1822.

Graham, George. *Speech Delivered before the Excelsior Temperance Circle of Honor.* Philadelphia, 1853.

Hacker, Louis M. *The Triumph of American Capitalism; the Development of Forces in American History to the End of the Nineteenth Century.* New York: Simon and Schuster, 1940.

Hammond, John W. *Tabular View of the Financial Affairs of Pennsylvania.* . . . Philadelphia, 1844.

Handlin, Oscar, and Mary F. Handlin. "Origins of the American Business Corporation," *Journal of Economic History*, V (1945), 1-23.

Harrisburg Morning Herald. 1854.

Harrisburg Telegraph. 1857.

Hartz, Louis. "Laissez-Faire Thought in Pennsylvania, 1776-1860," *The Tasks of Economic History* (supplemental issue of *The Journal of Economic History*), III (1943), 66-77.

―――――. "Otis and Anti-Slavery Doctrine," *New England Quarterly*, XII (1939), 745-47.

―――――. "Seth Luther: Working Class Rebel," *New England Quarterly*, XIII (1940), 401-18.

Hazard's Register. Volumes I-XVI (1828-1835).

Herrick, Cheesman A. *White Servitude in Pennsylvania: Indentured and Redemption Labor in Colony and Commonwealth.* Philadelphia: J. J. McVey, 1926.

The Highly Interesting and Important Trial of Dr. T. W. Dyott, the Banker, for Fraudulent Insolvency. Philadelphia, 1839.

History of Allegheny County, Pennsylvania. Chicago: A. Warner and Company, 1889.

Holdsworth, John T. *Financing an Empire; History of Banking in Pennsylvania.* Chicago: The S. J. Clarke Publishing Company, 1928.

House Journals. See Pennsylvania. House of Representatives. *Journals.*

Huebner, Solomon. "The Development and Present Status of Marine Insurance in the United States," *Annals of the American Academy of Political and Social Sciences*, XXVI (1905), 421-52.

Hunt's Merchants' Magazine. Volumes VI-XXXVIII (1849-1858).

Hutcheson, Austin E. "Philadelphia and the Panic of 1837," *Pennsylvania History*, III (1936), 182–94.

The Insolvent Register for the Last Five Years. Philadelphia, 1830.

Internal Improvements. Rail Roads, Canals, Bridges. . . . Philadelphia, 1825.

Itter, William A. "Early Labor Troubles in the Schuylkill Anthracite District," *Pennsylvania History*, I (1934), 28–37.

Jenkins, Howard M., ed. *Pennsylvania, Colonial and Federal; a History, 1608–1903.* Philadelphia: Pennsylvania Historical Publishing Association, 1903.

John, J. J. "The Centre Turnpike Road," Historical Society of Schuylkill County, *Publications*, II (1907–10), 501–33.

Johnson, Edgar A. J. *American Economic Thought in the Seventeenth Century.* London: P. S. King and Son, Ltd., 1932.

Johnson, Emory R., et al. *History of Domestic and Foreign Commerce of the United States.* Washington, D. C.: Carnegie Institution of Washington, 1915.

Jones, Chester L. *Economic History of the Anthracite-Tidewater Canals.* Philadelphia: Published for the University, 1908.

Kaplan, Abraham D. H. *Henry Charles Carey: Study in American Economic Thought.* Baltimore: The Johns Hopkins Press, 1931.

Klein, Philip S. *Pennsylvania Politics, 1817–1832.* Philadelphia: Lamberton Fund, Historical Society of Pennsylvania, 1940.

Knox, John J. *A History of Banking in the United States.* Rev. ed., New York: B. Rhodes and Company, 1903.

Konkle, Barton A. *Joseph Hopkinson, 1770–1842, Jurist-Scholar-Inspirer of the Arts, Author of Hail Columbia.* Philadelphia: University of Pennsylvania Press, 1931.

——————. *The Life and Speeches of Thomas Williams, Orator, Statesman, and Jurist, 1806–1872, a Founder of the Whig and Republican Parties.* Philadelphia: Campion and Company, 1905.

——————. *The Life of Chief Justice Ellis Lewis, 1798–1871, of the First Elective Supreme Court of Pennsylvania.* Philadelphia: Campion and Company, 1907.

——————. *Thomas Willing and the First American Financial System.* Philadelphia: University of Pennsylvania Press, 1937.

Legal Intelligencer (Philadelphia). September 9, 1858.

Legislative Documents. (The binder's title for Pennsylvania, *Miscellaneous Documents read in the Legislature.*)

Legislative Record. See Pennsylvania, *Legislative Record.*

Lehigh Coal and Navigation Company. *Report of the Board of Managers.* . . . Philadelphia, 1834.

Lehigh Company, To the Committee on Corporations of the Senate. (Reply of the Lehigh Company.) Harrisburg, n.d.

Lerner, Max. "The Supreme Court and American Capitalism," *Yale Law Journal,* XLII (1933), 668–701.

Lewis, Lawrence. *A History of the Bank of North America.* Philadelphia: J. B. Lippincott and Company, 1882.

List of the Taxable Inhabitants, Deaf, Dumb, Blind Persons, and Slaves in the Several Counties of the Commonwealth of Pennsylvania. Harrisburg, 1843.

McClure, Alexander K. *Old Time Notes of Pennsylvania.* Philadelphia: The J. C. Winston Company, 1905.

McGrane, Reginald C. *Foreign Bondholders and American State Debts.* New York: The Macmillan Company, 1935.

—————. *The Panic of 1837.* Chicago: The University of Chicago Press, 1924.

McIlwain, Charles H. *The American Revolution.* New York: The Macmillan Company, 1923.

McKnight, William J. *A Pioneer Outline History of Northwestern Pennsylvania.* . . . Philadelphia: J. B. Lippincott Company, 1905.

McPherson, Edward. *Letters of a Pennsylvanian on the State Canals.* Harrisburg, 1858.

—————. *Sale of the Main Line. Letters on . . . the Sale of the Main Line of Public Improvements,* by a Citizen of Adams County. Philadelphia, 1857.

Martin, Asa Earl. "Lotteries in Pennsylvania Prior to 1833," *Pennsylvania Magazine of History and Biography,* XLVII (1923), 307–27; XLVIII (1924), 66–93.

—————. "The Temperance Movement in Pennsylvania Prior to the Civil War," *Pennsylvania Magazine of History and Biography,* XLIX (1925), 195–230.

—————, and Hiram Herr Shenk. *Pennsylvania History Told by Contemporaries.* New York: The Macmillan Company, 1925.

Mechanics Free Press (Philadelphia). 1828–1830.

Meigs, William M. *The Life of Charles Jared Ingersoll.* Philadelphia: J. B. Lippincott Company, 1897.

Miller, Harry E. *Banking Theories in the United States before 1860.* Cambridge: Harvard University Press, 1927.

Miller, William. "The Effects of the American Revolution on Indentured Servitude," *Pennsylvania History*, VII (1940), 131–41.

———. "A Note on the History of Business Corporations in Pennsylvania, 1800–1860," *Quarterly Journal of Economics*, LV (1940/41), 150–60.

Miner's Journal (Pottsville). 1825–1854.

"Minutes of the Grand Committee of the Whole Convention," in *Minutes of the Convention of the Commonwealth of Pennsylvania, 1789*. Philadelphia, 1789.

Montgomery, Morton L. *History of Berks County*. Philadelphia: Everts, Peck & Richards, 1886.

Moulton, Harold G. *The New Philosophy of Public Debt*. Washington, D. C.: The Brookings Institute, 1943.

Mueller, Henry R. *Whig Party in Pennsylvania*. New York: Columbia University Press, 1922.

Muhlenberg, William A. *Remarks of Mr. Muhlenberg of Berks County on Free Banking*. 1851.

Myers, ———. *Remarks of Mr. Myers of Berks County on the System of Free Banking*. Harrisburg, 1848.

Needles, Edward. *An Historical Memoir of the Pennsylvania Society for Promoting the Abolition of Slavery. . . .* Philadelphia, 1848.

Niles Register (Philadelphia). 1817–1843.

Norristown Register and Montgomery County Democrat. 1844.

North American (Philadelphia). 1843–1857.

North American and United States Gazette (Philadelphia). 1857.

Otey, Elizabeth L. *Report on Condition of Women and Child Wage-Earners in the United States*. (61 Congress, 2 Session, Senate Document No. 645, serial nos. 5685–5703), Washington, 1910.

Oviatt, F. C. "Historical Study of Fire Insurance in the United States," *Annals of the American Academy of Political and Social Science*, XXVI (1905), 335–58.

Paine, Thomas. *Works*. Philadelphia, 1797.

Peltz, A. M. "Correspondence." (Autograph Collection in Pennsylvania Historical Society.)

Pennsylvania, *Journal of the Convention of the State of Pennsylvania, 1837–1838*. 2 v. Harrisburg, 1837–1838.

———. *Laws*. 1802–1860. See also Dallas, A. J., *Laws*.

———. *Legislative Record*, 1856–1861.

———. *Message of the Governor in Relation to the Permanent Loan*. Harrisburg, 1839.

———————. *Minutes of the Provincial Council . . . from the Organization to the Termination of the Proprietary Government.* Philadelphia, 1851–52. (Usually known as *Colonial Records.*)

———————. *Miscellaneous Documents read in the Legislature,* 1852–61. See *Legislative Documents.*

———————. *Pennsylvania Archives.* Fourth Series. 6 volumes. Philadelphia and Harrisburg, 1852–1902.

———————. *Proceedings and Debates of the Convention of the Commonwealth of Pennsylvania, 1837–38.* 14 volumes, Harrisburg, 1837–1839.

———————. *Statutes at Large . . . from 1682 to 1809.* 17 volumes. Compiled by James T. Mitchell and Henry Flanders. Harrisburg: C. M. Busch . . . , 1896–1915.

———————. Auditor-General's Office. *Reports.* 1825–1860.

———————. House of Representatives. *Journals.* 1800–1858.

———————. House of Representatives Committee on Banks. *Report . . . Relative to Banks and Savings Institutions.* Harrisburg, 1856.

———————. Secretary of Internal Affairs. *Report on the Canals of Pennsylvania.* Harrisburg, 1900.

———————. Senate. *Journals.* 1819–1857.

———————. Senate Committee on Coal Trade. *Report . . . upon the Subject of the Coal Trade.* Harrisburg, 1834.

———————. Senate Committee on Resolutions Relative to Foreign Corporations. *Report.* Harrisburg, 1825.

Pennsylvania Railroad Company. *Annual Reports,* 1846–1860.

Pennsylvania Society for Discouraging the Use of Ardent Spirits. *Third Anniversary Report of the Managers.* Philadelphia, 1832.

Pennsylvania Society for Promoting the Abolition of Slavery. *An Address . . . on the Origin, Purposes, and Utility of their Institution.* Philadelphia, 1819.

———————. *Celebration of the Ninetieth Anniversary of the Organization.* Philadelphia, 1866.

———————. *Constitution.* Philadelphia, 1820.

Pennsylvania Society for the Promotion of Internal Improvements. *Address of Acting Committee.* Philadelphia, 1826.

———————. *First Annual Report.* Philadelphia, 1826.

Pennsylvania State Temperance Society. [*Fifth*] *Anniversary Report of the Managers.* . . . Philadelphia, 1834.

Pennsylvanian (Philadelphia). 1847–1857.

Permanent Temperance Documents. (In the Library Company of Philadelphia.)

Persons, Warren M. *Government Experimentation in Business.* New York: J. Wiley and Sons, 1934.

Phelan, James. *History of Tennessee; the Making of a State.* Boston: Houghton, Mifflin and Company, 1888.

Philadelphia. Board of Trade. *Report of the Delegates to the Warren Convention.* Philadelphia, 1833.

──────. Board of Trade Committee on Inland Transportation. *Report.* Philadelphia, 1856.

──────. Committee of Seven. *Address . . . to the Citizens of Philadelphia . . .* [on the Pennsylvania Rail Road]. Philadelphia, 1846.

──────. Committee on Railroads. *Report.* Philadelphia, 1854.

──────. Common Council. *Report of the Special Committee . . . in Relation to the Sunbury and Erie Railroad.* Philadelphia, 1854.

Philadelphia Medical Society. *Report of the Committee . . . with Regard to the Use of Ardent Spirits.* Philadelphia, 1829.

Philadelphia *Press,* 1857.

Philadelphia Record. 1886.

Pittsburgh. Board of Trade Committee. *Report to Board of Trade.* Pittsburgh, 1858.

Pittsburgh Commercial Gazette. 1886.

Pittsburgh Daily Gazette. 1846–1848.

Pittsburgh *Daily Post.* 1886.

Pittsburgh Dispatch. 1886.

Pittsburgh *Morning Post.* 1848.

Plummer, Wilbur C. *Road Policy of Pennsylvania.* Philadelphia: University of Pennsylvania, 1925.

Poulson's American Daily Advertiser (Philadelphia). 1822–1826.

Price, Eli K. *Of the Limitation of Actions, and of Liens, against Real Estate, in Pennsylvania.* Philadelphia, 1857.

──────. *Position . . . on the Liquor Question Defined by the Facts.* Philadelphia, 1854.

──────. *Speech . . . on the Bill to Restrain the Sale of Intoxicating Liquors.* Philadelphia, 1855.

Prison Discipline Society. *Annual Reports of the Board of Managers.* Vols. V–VIII. Boston, 1830–1833.

Proceedings . . . in Relation to the Great Pennsylvania Railroad. Philadelphia, 1846.

Proceedings of a Convention of Delegates Elected by the Citizens of the Different Districts Interested in the Connexion of the Susquehanna and Lehigh Rivers. Luzerne, 1832.

Proceedings of a Meeting of the Stockholders of the Bank of the United States. Philadelphia, 1838.

Proceedings Relative to Calling the Conventions of 1776 and 1790. Harrisburg, 1825.

Public Ledger (Philadelphia). 1853–1857.

Publicola, *pseud*. *Thirteen Essays on the Policy of Manufacturing in this Country*. Philadelphia, 1830.

Raguet, Condy. *Principles of Free Trade*. Philadelphia, 1835.

Read, John M. *Argument . . . in Favor of the Constitutionality of the Subscription by the City of Philadelphia to the Capital Stock of Hempfield, and Philadelphia, Easton, and Water Gap Railroad Companies, July 25, 1853*. Philadelphia, 1853.

———. *Opinion of . . . against the Right of the City Councils to Subscribe for Stock in the Pennsylvania Railroad Company*. Philadelphia, 1846.

Reed, William B. *The Model Administration. An Oration Delivered before the Whig Citizens of Philadelphia*. Philadelphia, 1844.

Report of a Committee Appointed to Investigate the Evils of Lotteries in the Commonwealth of Pennsylvania and to Suggest a Remedy for the Same. Philadelphia, 1837.

Report to Pittsburgh Board of Trade. See Pittsburgh, Board of Trade Committee.

Rezneck, Samuel. "Depression and American Opinion, 1857–1859," *Journal of Economic History*, II (1942), 1–23.

———. "The Rise and Early Development of Industrial Consciousness in the United States, 1760–1850," *Journal of Economic and Business History*, IV (1931/32), 784–811.

Ringwalt, John L. *Development of Transportation Systems in the United States*. Philadelphia: J. L. Ringwalt, 1888.

Rowe, Kenneth W. *Mathew Carey: A Study in American Economic Development*. Baltimore: Johns Hopkins Press, 1933.

Schalck, Adolf W., and David C. Henning. *History of Schuylkill County, Pennsylvania*. n.p., State Historical Association, 1907.

Scharf, J. Thomas, and Thompson Westcott. *History of Philadelphia, 1609–1884*. Philadelphia: L. H. Everts and Company, 1884.

Schlesinger, Arthur M., Jr. *The Age of Jackson*. Boston: Little, Brown and Company, 1945.

Schotter, Howard W. *The Growth and Development of the Pennsylvania Railroad Company* . . . Philadelphia: Press of Allen, Lane and Scott, 1927.

Selsam, John P. *The Pennsylvania Constitution of 1776: A Study in Revolutionary Democracy.* Philadelphia: University of Pennsylvania Press, 1936.

Senate Journals. See Pennsylvania. Senate. *Journals.*

Sergeant, Henry J. *Treatise on the Lien of Mechanics and Material Men in Pennsylvania.* Philadelphia, 1839.

Shelling, Richard J. "Philadelphia and the Agitation in 1825 for the Pennsylvania Canal," *Pennsylvania Magazine of History and Biography,* LXII (1938), 175–204.

Simons, Algie M. *Social Forces in American History.* New York: The Macmillan Company, 1911.

Simpson, Stephen. *Biography of Stephen Girard.* Philadelphia, 1832.

—————. *Workingman's Manual.* Philadelphia, 1831.

Sipes, William B. *The Pennsylvania Railroad.* . . . Philadelphia, 1875.

Smith, W. Roy. "Sectionalism in Pennsylvania During the Revolution," *Political Science Quarterly,* XXIV (1909), 208–35.

Smith, William. *Historical Account of the Rise, Progress and Present State of Canal Navigation in Pennsylvania.* Philadelphia, 1805.

Snyder, William P. *Compendium and Brief History of Taxation in Pennsylvania.* Harrisburg: Harrisburg Publishing Company, 1906.

Speeches in the Senate on the Prohibitory Liquor Law. Philadelphia, 1854.

State Central Prohibitory Committee. *Address . . . to the Legislature of Pennsylvania.* Philadelphia, 1854.

Stokes, William A. *Letter . . . to Honorable John Creswell, Jr., Speaker of the Senate of Pennsylvania on the Subject of the Tonnage Tax.* . . . Philadelphia, 1859.

Strickland, William. *Reports on Canals, Railways, Roads, and Other Subjects Made to the Pennsylvania Society for the Promotion of Internal Improvement.* Philadelphia, 1826.

Sullivan, John L. *Suggestions on the Canal Policy of Pennsylvania in Reference to the Effects of the Inland Navigation of the Adjoining States on the Commerce of Philadelphia.* Philadelphia, 1824.

Sumner, Helen L., and Ella A. Merritt. *Child Labor Legislation in the United States.* Washington, D. C.: Government Printing Office, 1915.

Sumner, William Graham. *The Challenge of Facts, and Other Essays.* ed. by Albert G. Keller. New Haven: Yale University Press, 1914.

———. *What Social Classes Owe to Each Other.* New York: Harper and Brothers, 1903.

Sunbury and Erie Railroad Company. *Report of the President and Board of Managers.* Philadelphia, 1853.

Swisher, Carl B. *Stephen J. Field, Craftsman of the Law.* Washington: The Brookings Institution, 1930.

Tanner, Henry S. *Description of the Canals and Railroads of the United States.* New York, 1840.

Tavern Keepers versus the License System. Philadelphia, 1855.

Taylor, George. *Effect of Incorporated Coal Companies upon the Anthracite Coal Trade of Pennsylvania.* Pottsville, 1833.

Teilhac, Ernest. *Pioneers of American Economic Thought in the Nineteenth Century* (Translated by E. A. J. Johnson). New York: The Macmillan Company, 1936.

Trachtenberg, Alexander. *History of Legislation for the Protection of Coal Miners in Pennsylvania, 1824–1915.* New York: International Publishers, 1942.

Trotter, Alexander. *Observations of the Financial Position and Credit of Such of the States of the North American Union as have Contracted Public Debts.* London, 1839.

Truth Vindicated: Senator Price and the Executive Committee. Philadelphia, 1854.

Turner, Edward R. "The Abolition of Slavery in Pennsylvania," *Pennsylvania Magazine of History and Biography,* XXXVI (1912), 129–42.

———. *Slavery in Pennsylvania.* Baltimore: The Lord Baltimore Press, 1911.

Twiss, Benjamin R. *Lawyers and the Constitution: How Laissez-Faire Came to the Supreme Court.* Princeton: Princeton University Press, 1942.

Tyson, Job R. *A Brief Survey of the Great Extent and Evil Tendencies of the Lottery System, as Existing in the United States.* Philadelphia, 1833.

———. *Lecture . . . before the Athenian Institute and Mercantile Library Company, on the Social and Moral Influences of the American Revolution.* Philadelphia, 1838.

———. *Letters on the Resources and Commerce of Philadelphia.* Philadelphia, 1852.

United States Gazette (Philadelphia). 1812–1825.

Van Vleck, George W. *Panic of 1857.* New York: Columbia University Press, 1943.

View of the Insolvent Laws of Pennsylvania. 2d ed. Philadelphia, 1827.

Violette, Eugene M. *A History of Missouri.* Boston: D. C. Heath and Company, 1918.

Virginia. *Journal of the House of Delegates, 1855–56.* Richmond, 1855–56.

Warren, Charles. *Bankruptcy in United States History.* Cambridge: Harvard University Press, 1935.

Watson, John. *Observations on the Customary Use of Distilled Liquors.* Philadelphia, 1810.

Webster, Pelatiah. *Political Essays on the Nature and Operation of Money, Public Finances, and Other Subjects.* Philadelphia, 1791.

Wetzel, William A. *Benjamin Franklin as an Economist.* Baltimore: The Johns Hopkins Press, 1895.

Wharton, Thomas I. *Letter to Robert Toland and Isaac Elliott, Esquires, on the Subject of the Right and Power of the City of Philadelphia to Subscribe for Stock in the Pennsylvania Railroad Company.* Philadelphia, 1846.

Whig Anti-Subscription Council Ticket. (Pamphlet Volume 742 in Pennsylvania State Library, Harrisburg.)

White, Josiah. *Circular.* Harrisburg, 1832.

————, and Erskine Hazard. *To the Members of the Legislature.* Harrisburg, n.d.

White, Leonard D. "Origin of Utility Commissions in Massachusetts," *Journal of Political Economy,* XXIX (1921), 177–97.

Wickersham, James P. *History of Education in Pennsylvania.* ... Lancaster: Inquirer Publishing Company, 1886.

Wilkes-Barre Leader. October 8, 1886.

Will the Interest of Pennsylvania be Advanced by the Tonnage Tax? n.p., n.d.

Williams, Thomas. *Argument on the Validity of Acts of Assembly Authorizing Subscriptions by Municipal Corporations to the Stock of Railroad Companies.* Philadelphia, 1853.

Wilson, James. *Selected Political Essays,* edited by Randolph G. Adams. New York: A. A. Knopf, 1930.

Wilson, William Bender. *History of the Pennsylvania Railroad.* Philadelphia: H. T. Coates and Company, 1899.

Wiston, E. V. *Letters on Insolvency.* Philadelphia, 1803.

Worthington, Thomas K. *Historical Sketch of the Finances of Pennsylvania.* Baltimore: American Economic Association, 1887.

Wright, Benjamin F. *American Interpretations of Natural Law.* Cambridge: Harvard University Press, 1931.

———. *The Contract Clause of the Constitution.* Cambridge: Harvard University Press, 1938.

———, ed. *A Source Book of American Political Theory.* New York: The Macmillan Company, 1929.

Wright, Richard R. *The Negro in Pennsylvania; a Study in Economic History.* Philadelphia: A. M. E. Book Concern, printers, 1912.

INDEX

INDEX

Abolition, 182, 183, 185, 212, 216, 291, 308
  See also Slavery
Adams County, 43, 97, 125, 134, 163, 167, 241
Administration, 33, 103, 142, 146, 148–60, 161, 164, 169, 170, 175, 181, 191, 204, 205, 262, 263, 266, 267, 292–95, 310, 312
Agricultural interests, 15, 17, 56, 57, 215
  See also Farmers and farms
Alienability
  See Inalienable state power
Allegheny (Pa.), 88, 106, 190
Allegheny County, 45, 88, 93, 97, 106, 123, 125, 163, 178, 232, 241, 268, 311
Allegheny mountains, 9, 22, 145, 149, 162
Allegheny Portage Railroad, 146, 149, 157
Allegheny Valley Railroad, 179
American Insurance Company of Philadelphia, 68
"American system," 15, 77
Anti-bank group, 49, 196, 242
Anti-charter doctrine, 64, 69–79, 120–22, 126, 140, 141, 171–75, 195, 244, 248–51, 256, 297–99, 303, 306, 315, 316
  See also Charter and charter policy
Anti-Democratic opposition, 21, 63, 140
Anti-executive prejudice, 148, 151
Anti-governmental movement, 74, 169, 311, 312, 315, 318
Anti-investment group, 114, 117–21, 125, 126, 311, 313
  See also Investments
Anti-Masonic party, 22
Anti-repudiation, 44, 177, 313
Anti-slavery movement
  See Abolition
Anti-state doctrine, 180, 218, 285, 291, 313, 314, 317, 319, 320
Anti-subscription movement, 105, 107–109, 111–13, 115, 120, 122, 123, 128
  See also Investments
Anti-tax bias, 55, 272, 299, 302
  See also Taxation
Appraisers, Board of, 159–60
Armstrong County, 125, 163, 209, 241
Assignment, 99–100

Attorney-general, 176, 269
Auditor-general, 33, 83, 92, 96, 102, 263–67, 294

Baltimore, 9, 10, 11, 42, 107, 116, 129, 133, 136, 141, 268, 291, 300
Baltimore and Ohio Railroad, 10, 11, 43, 44, 46, 53, 268
Baltimore and Susquehanna Railroad, 42, 44
Bank of North America, 68, 78, 90, 236, 237, 239, 303
Bank of Pennsylvania, 47, 48, 55, 56, 82, 90, 96–100, 103, 104, 255, 308
Bank of Philadelphia, 47, 48, 82, 90, 96, 97, 98, 100, 103, 104, 308
Bank of the United States (Second), 16, 18, 22–24, 28, 46, 47, 50, 55, 63, 64, 74, 78, 97, 99, 120, 239, 240, 243–53, 267, 316
Bank of the United States v. *Planter's Bank of Georgia*, 246
Bank stock held by state, 82, 83, 85, 87, 90, 104
Banking, 21, 40, 41, 49, 50, 53, 55, 58, 66, 74, 89, 92, 101, 196, 245, 248, 252, 254–58, 266, 267, 289, 290, 297, 301, 319
  See also Free banking
  branch, 47, 48
  private, 67, 263, 298
  sectionalism in, 46, 49
Banking Act of 1814, 48, 50, 63–65, 67, 238, 240, 258, 262, 263, 265
Banking Act of 1824, 240
Banking Act of 1850, 240, 254–57
Bankruptcy, 17, 193, 194, 227–29, 254, 263
  legislation, 222, 224–27, 230, 231, 233, 306
Banks, chartering of, 53, 55, 71, 90, 240, 246
Banks, E., 265
Barnes, Albert, 213, 217, 283, 305
Beaver County, 74, 125, 163, 241
Beaver River, 162
Bedford County, 10, 44, 56, 125, 133, 134, 163, 241
Benezet, Anthony, 208

358   INDEX

Bentham, Jeremy, 13, 273
Berks County, 8, 45, 70, 125, 133, 134, 163, 194, 211, 241
Biddle, Nicholas, 28, 50, 64, 131, 140, 239, 248
Biddle, Thomas, 26, 132
Bigler, Governor, 52, 66, 86, 93, 114, 152, 155, 161, 165, 173, 310
Billmeyer v. *Evans and Rodenbaugh*, 233
Binney, Horace, 105, 108–13, 274, 302
Black, Chief Justice, 88, 114, 122, 123, 179, 242, 243, 281, 302, 305
Blackstone, William, 118, 217, 247
Blair County, 125, 241
Bonus practice, 55, 56, 64, 245, 246, 269
Booms and boom psychology, 17, 18, 20, 31, 63, 78, 95, 193, 208, 219, 289, 310
  See also Depressions and recessions; Panics
Boston (Mass.), 7, 12, 107, 221
Boston and Albany Railroad, 10, 108
Bound, Franklin, 272, 277
Bounties, 290
Bradford County, 125, 163, 241
Breck, Samuel, 11, 131, 300
Brewing industry, 211, 212
Brewster, B. N., 117–21, 126
Bridges and bridge companies, 44, 45, 51, 84–87, 92, 97, 100, 102, 104, 130, 238, 253
Briscoe v. *Bank of Kentucky*, 246
Brokers, 207, 227
Brown, Charles, 244, 245, 303, 309, 315
Brown v. *Maryland*, 218, 274
Browne, Peter A., 192
Buchanan, James, 22
Buckalew, Charles R., 126, 179, 314
Bucks County, 45, 125, 163, 211, 241
Budd, Thomas, 4, 6, 307
Bull, Marcus, 61, 75
Business, development, 23, 219, 305
  See also Entrepreneurs; Private enterprise
  practice, 30–33, 223, 312, 327
Businessmen, 20, 21, 206, 207, 251, 314, 315
  See also Entrepreneurs
Butler County, 125, 163, 241

Cambria County, 125, 136, 163, 241
Campbell, G. T., 177, 312, 316
Canal and navigation companies, 85, 87, 92, 94, 104

  See also Canals
Canal Commissioners, Board of, 133, 145, 147, 150–53, 155, 156, 158, 159, 162, 169, 176–80, 278, 279, 294–96, 310, 313
Canal convention, 132–34, 139
Canals, 11, 14, 44, 58, 120, 130–34, 138, 141, 145, 148, 149, 238, 295
Carbon County, 125, 163, 194, 209, 241
Carbondale (Pa.), 61
Carey, Henry C., 15
Carey, Mathew, 12, 15, 16, 25, 131, 133, 134, 299
Carlton, F. A., 220
Centre County, 88, 125, 163, 194, 241
Chadwick v. *Moore*, 232
Chaffee v. *Michaels*, 232
Chambers, George, 75
Charles River Bridge Case, 248
Charlestown Silver Lead Mining Company, 66
Charters and charter policy, 27, 39–49, 51, 52, 55–59, 62, 63, 65–67, 72, 74, 83, 130, 167, 168, 172, 181, 195, 236–43, 267, 289, 292, 293, 296, 297, 303, 304, 308
  See also Corporations and corporate system; General Insurance Act; General Manufacturing Act
Chartiers and Allegheny Valley Railroad, 88, 269
Chesapeake and Delaware Canal Company, 253
Chesapeake and Ohio Canal, 253
Chester County, 8, 45, 74, 125, 133, 163, 241
Chew, Benjamin, 131
Child labor, 187–89, 191, 199–201, 203, 292, 305, 306
Choate, Joseph H., 320
Claims disputes, 159, 160, 293
Clarion County, 125, 163, 209, 241
Clarke, James, 104
Clearfield County, 44, 125, 163, 241
Clergy, 210, 306
Clinton County, 125, 163, 241
Coal and coal trade, 21, 40, 58–62, 193, 194, 209, 268
Coke, Edward, 118
Colonial era, 4–9, 18, 39, 129, 130, 181, 194, 204, 219, 220, 226, 289, 291, 294, 297, 303, 307
Columbia (Pa.), 145, 149

INDEX 359

Columbia County, 30, 125, 163, 241
Columbia Railroad, 52, 53, 145–48, 269
Commons, John R., 187
Commonwealth ex rel *Thomas* v. *Commissioners of Allegheny County*, 123
Confederation, Articles of, 274, 276
Connelsville (Pa.), 46, 93
Constituent conventions, powers of, 244, 245, 310
Constitution, federal, 4, 21, 70, 225, 229, 239, 244, 269, 273, 274, 276
Constitutional amendments, the anti-investment and reservation (1857), 82, 84, 85, 89, 123–27, 240, 241, 295, 296
Constitutional Convention of 1790, 8, 22, 71, 220
Constitutional Convention of 1837–38, 18, 22–25, 27, 29–31, 42, 45, 49, 72, 74, 239, 240, 243, 244, 248, 252, 293, 313
Constitutions, state, 7, 9, 18, 23, 25, 71, 115, 183, 220, 224, 237, 239
  See also Constitutional amendments
Contract clause (of federal Constitution), 225, 229, 233, 239, 242, 244–46, 277, 280, 303, 304
Cooper, S. B., 178
Cope, Thomas, 9
Corporations and corporate system, 3, Chap. II, 110, 120, 126, 129, 139, 140, 161, 172, 174, 238, 252, 255, 289, 293, 294, 297, 305, 307, 308, 311–13, 315–19
  See also Charters and charter policy; General Insurance Act; General Manufacturing Act.
Cotton and cotton manufacturing, 40, 136, 188, 189
Coudersport (Pa.), 87
County commissioners, 56, 57, 86, 117
Court of Common Pleas (Philadelphia), 230
Courts of Quarter Sessions, 207, 260
Cox, Joshua F., 77
Crawford County, 88, 125, 163, 241
Creditors, 103, 219–35, 247, 313
  See also Debtors
Cumberland (Pa.), 43
Cumberland County, 10, 97, 125, 133, 134, 163, 241
Cumberland Valley Railroad, 46
Cunningham, Thomas, 45

Dallas, Alexander, 116, 119, 302, 317
Danville and Pottsville Railroad, 108
Dartmouth College Case, 70, 102, 239, 240, 242–53, 256, 267, 285, 291, 303, 304, 308, 314, 316
Darwin, Charles, 320
Dauphin County, 125, 163, 241, 275, 311
Debt, imprisonment for, 186, 219–22, 224–27
  public, 138, 143–45, 175, 277, 301
Debtors, 186, 219–35, 291, 292, 305, 306
  See also Creditors
Declaration of Rights, 71, 80, 184, 224, 237, 312
Delaware and Hudson Coal Company, 61
Delaware County, 125, 163, 241
Delaware Extension, 162
Delaware River, 205, 253
Democratic party, 21–25, 62–65, 77, 78, 93, 103, 106, 140, 165, 189, 190, 242, 313
Depressions and recessions, 17, 23, 99, 190, 220, 252, 292, 306
  See also Booms and boom psychology; Panics
De Witt, Benjamin, 12
Dickinson, John, 5, 6
Directors, conflict between public and private, 96–100, 102, 294, 318
  corporate, 102, 254, 266, 291
Distilleries, 208, 210, 212
Dividends, 90–92, 98, 102, 108, 138, 258, 261–63, 299
Dodge v. *Woolsey*, 280
Doran, Joseph M., 29, 32
Duane, William J., 132
Duncan, Judge Thomas, 132, 231
Dunlop, James, 45
Dyott, T. W., 199, 200

Earle, Thomas, 30–32, 49, 245, 247, 252, 304
Easton (Pa.), 48, 129, 199
Education, 4, 6, 138, 182, 187, 188, 191, 192, 198–200, 262, 292, 299, 305, 306
  See also School system
Eiselen, Malcolm, 24
Elk County, 125, 163, 241
Emancipation
  See Abolition
Eminent-domain privileges, 70, 72, 76, 248

Employers, 202, 203, 209
Engineering Department, 156, 157
Entrepreneur,
  private, 32, 56, 57, 70, 59–61, 66, 69, 70, 79, 81, 120, 121, 127, 168, 173, 195, 196, 272, 289, 306, 310, 311, 315
    See also Businessmen; Private enterprise
  state as, 131, 168, 175, 216, 290, 298–300
    See also Public enterprise
Enterprise restricted by public ownership, 167, 168, 250
Equalitarianism, 9, 24, 25, 76, 77, 81, 186, 227, 228, 279, 297, 307
Erie Canal, 10, 108, 131, 135, 162, 291
Erie County, 125, 163, 241

Factory, legislation, 188, 189–91, 194–204, 294, 306, 309, 319
  owners, 200, 203, 204
  system, 181, 189, 196, 197, 199, 200
Farmers and farms, 55, 135, 136, 139, 208, 212, 231, 258, 260
  See also Agricultural interests
Farmers' and Mechanics' Bank, 82, 103, 104
Farmers' and Mechanics' Bank of Penn. v. Smith, 229
Fayette County, 125, 163, 241
Federalists, 7, 21, 24, 25, 77, 140
Field, Justice Stephen F., 320
Flax manufacturing, 40, 189
Fletcher v. Peck, 249
Flour, 205, 212
Forrest County, 125, 241
Forward, Walter, 72, 250
Fourier, Charles, 198
Franklin, Benjamin, 5, 15, 39, 80, 182, 196
Franklin County, 10, 75, 125, 133, 134, 163, 241, 271
Fraud, 95, 96, 146, 157, 204, 206, 229
Free banking, 49, 50, 68
Free Banking Act of 1860, 41, 49, 258, 267
Free trade, 5, 6, 15, 39, 271ff, 284
  See also Laissez faire; Protectionism
Freedley, Edwin T., 16, 20, 31, 32, 223, 310, 312, 320
Fulton County, 125, 241

Gallatin, Albert, 16
Gas companies, 238, 260
  lighting, 108
General Insurance Act of 1856, 260–61
General Manufacturing Act of 1849, 40, 41, 239, 261, 263
German elements, 22, 210, 211, 215
Germanville Glass Manufacturing Company, 57
Gettysburg (Pa.), 199
Gibbons v. Ogden, 274
Gibson, Chief Justice, 232, 242, 246
Girard, Stephen, 9, 21
Girard Bank, 55, 99, 120
Glass manufacturing, 40, 199
Godcharles Case, 319
Godwin, William, 276
Gordon, Justice, 319
Government stores, 216
Graf, Edward, 215
Graft, 120, 130, 155, 169
Graham, Edward D., 230
Grain, 208, 210–12
Great Britain, 6, 50, 60, 73, 119, 130, 138, 145, 188, 249
Greene County, 125, 163, 241
Greensburg (Pa.), 114

Hamilton, Alexander, 73
Handy, George, 64
Harrisburg (Pa.), 43, 44, 48, 64, 111, 112, 132, 148, 149, 169
Harrisburg and Lancaster Railroad, 66, 267
Hayhurst, Ezra S., 30
Hempfield Railroad, 11, 13, 114, 116
Hiester, Governor, 95
Higher law, 247, 249
  See also Natural law, Natural rights
Hirst, Attorney, 176, 177, 179, 279, 281, 282
Hobbes, Thomas, 118
Hollidaysburg (Pa.), 149
Hopkinson, Joseph, 24, 25, 27
House Committee of Education, 198
House Committee on Corporations, 299
House Committee on Roads and Inland Navigation, 86, 94
House Committee on Ways and Means, 101, 137, 143, 175, 301
House Judiciary Committee, 193, 218
Huntingdon County, 44, 87, 125, 136, 163, 241

INDEX

Immigrants, 210, 215
Inalienable state power, 267–85, 296, 304, 305
Incorporation
  See Corporations and corporate system
Indentured servants, 181, 185, 186, 221, 223, 224
Indiana County, 125, 163, 241
Individualism, 174, 200, 203, 284, 306, 312, 315
  See also Laissez faire
Ingersoll, Charles J., 16, 45, 70, 72–74, 132, 244–46, 249, 251, 303, 315
Innkeepers, 135, 206
Insolvency
  See Bankruptcy
Inspection, 4, 204–206, 291, 308
Insurance, 40, 41, 50, 51, 66, 68, 239, 254, 257, 260, 263, 264
  See also General Insurance Act
Interest rates, 258, 261, 290, 295
Intestate laws, 70
Investment, private, 84, 93, 97, 99, 104, 135, 141, 255
  public, 117–21, 126, 203, 204, 251, 280, 281, 292, 298, 300–302, 312–14
  restrictions set by state, 260, 261
Investments, by municipalities, 87–89, 92, 93, 95–97, 104–19, 122, 295, 300, 302
  by state, 82–90, 92, 94, 95, 97, 103, 104, 124, 167, 274, 290, 307
  See also Liquidation of state investment
Irish elements, 211
Iron and coal interests, 15, 40, 56, 136, 209
Iron manufacturing, 56, 58

Jackson, Andrew, 21, 23, 24, 29, 64
Jefferson, Thomas, 5, 24, 77, 196, 247
Jefferson County, 125, 163, 241
Johnson, A. B., 168, 316
Johnston, Governor, 40, 153, 190, 263
Johnstown (Pa.), 149
Journeymen, 187, 188, 191
Judiciary, role of, 215, 248, 249, 314

Keating Committee, 147, 148, 299
Keim, George M., 70, 247
Kennedy, Justice, 100, 312
Kent, Chancellor James, 118, 217

Keynes, John Maynard, 301
Kiskeminitas River, 133
Klein, Philip, 24, 25
Know-Nothing party, 105
Knox, Justice, 281

Labor, hours of, 189, 198, 200, 202, 292, 306, 309
  legislation
  See Factory, legislation; Child labor
Labor movement, 21, 137, 187, 192, 194, 196, 203, 220, 291, 292, 306
  See also Strikes
Laborers, 106, 137, 192, 194, 198, 209, 220, 234, 306
  See also Journeymen
Laissez faire, 5, 79, 81, 123, 175, 200, 201, 293, 315, 319, 320
  See also Free trade
Lake Erie, 10, 133
Lancaster County, 8, 45, 48, 125, 129, 133, 134, 136, 163, 211, 241
Land, speculation in, 17
  values, 136, 139
Landlord, 234, 235
Landowners, 95, 106, 107, 192, 198
Lateral Railroad Act of 1832, 70
Lawrence County, 125, 241
Lebanon County, 125, 133, 134, 163, 211, 241
Lebanon Valley Railroad, 53
Lehigh Coal and Navigation Company, 59–62, 75, 172
Lehigh County, 125, 133, 134, 163, 211, 241
Lehigh County Bank, 254
Lehigh River, 59
Lehman, William, 131, 299, 301
Lewis, Justice, 122, 178
License Cases, 213
Licensing, 139, 150, 204, 206, 208, 212, 213, 215–18, 261, 264, 291, 295, 308,
  See also Liquor trade
Liens and lien legislation, 191–94, 221, 234, 292
Liquidation of state investments, 53, 82–86, 89, 90, 97, 103, 104, 118, 146, 161–75, 180, 295, 320
  See also Investments, by state
Liquor trade, 7, 205, 207, 208, 210–14, 216–19, 235, 292, 295, 305
  See also Licensing; Prohibition
Loan office, 55–57, 290

INDEX

Loans, state, 55, 64, 98, 99, 150, 296
Lobbying, 27, 28, 43, 64, 72, 78, 164, 165, 210, 249, 274, 278
Local government investment
See Investments, by municipalities
Lockean doctrine, 25, 30, 80, 118, 247, 251, 283, 284, 307
Log-rolling, 45, 151, 292
Lower, Jacob, 178
Lowrie, Justice, 12, 122, 123, 177, 281–283, 305
Lowry, M. B., 78
Lumber, 40, 136, 205, 268
Luzerne County, 27, 94, 125, 163, 209, 241
Lycoming County, 94, 125, 163, 241

McClure, A. K., 93, 271, 284
McCulloch v. *Maryland*, 245
McCracken v. *Hayward*, 232
M'Dermett, William, 56
McDuffie, George, 16
McKean County, 44, 125, 163, 241
McPherson, Edward, 167–169, 174, 311, 312, 315, 316, 318, 320
"Main Line" (of public works), 134, 145, 148, 149, 156, 162, 163, 164, 166, 170, 172, 175, 176, 179
See also Public works
Man, Job, 99, 104
Management, separate from ownership, 58, 196
Manual labor academies, 199
Manufacturing, 6, 7, 15, 40, 56, 57, 64, 67, 106, 136, 190, 201, 202, 208, 239, 254, 257, 258, 261, 263–65, 289
Marble and marble quarrying, 40, 136
Marbury v. *Madison*, 246
Marshall, Christopher, 8
Marshall, John, 118, 229, 237, 243, 245–50, 280, 291, 304
Maryland, 10, 42, 43, 46, 133, 269, 276
Massachusetts, 224, 236
Mauch Chunk (Pa.), 61
Mechanics, 177, 192–94, 258, 292
Mercantilism, 4, 297
Mercer County, 125, 163, 241
Merchants, 8–11, 14, 95, 106, 186, 196, 212, 227, 290, 300
Merchants' and Manufacturers' Bank of Pittsburgh, 255
Merchants' Exchange, Philadelphia, 179

Meredith, Attorney, 177, 240, 243, 248–250, 273, 274, 284, 303
Mifflin County, 125, 163, 241
Milnes, William, 61, 62
Miner Committee, 233
Miners and mining, 40, 41, 57–60, 62, 70, 193, 194, 208, 209, 257, 261, 263–265, 289, 292, 306
Minersville (Pa.), 61
Mixed enterprise (state and private ownership), 34, 53, 82–130, 140, 166, 171, 180, 181, 203, 204, 214, 218, 235, 236, 264, 267, 280, 281, 289, 290, 292–95, 298, 299, 313–15, 317, 318
Money-lenders, 192, 221, 225
Monongahela Manufacturing Society, 239
Monongahela Navigation Company, 46, 85
Monopoly, 8, 58, 60, 72, 80, 139, 148, 171, 195, 254
Monroe County, 125, 163, 241
Montgomery County, 45, 97, 125, 134, 136, 163, 211, 241
Montour County, 125, 241
Morris, Robert, 23, 237
Mott, Henry S., 176–78
Mott Case, 179, 186, 280, 283, 284, 304, 313, 314
Mutual insurance companies, 257

Natural law, 5, 31, 69, 79, 80, 118, 121, 126, 196, 197, 203, 247, 306, 311, 315
See also Natural right; Higher law
Natural right, 5, 7, 183–85, 199, 214, 223, 306
Neal, Joseph C., 21
Negroes, 182, 184, 185, 306
New Jersey v. *Wilson*, 280
New Orleans (La.), 136, 141
New York (city), 7, 10, 12, 13, 14, 50, 107, 129, 136, 141, 162, 270, 291, 300
New York (state), 49, 123, 131, 185, 224, 269, 276
New York and Erie Railroad, 10, 13, 270
Norristown (Pa.), 97, 166
North American Coal Company, 61, 75
North Branch Canal, 179
Northampton County, 125, 133, 134, 163, 211, 241
Northern Liberties (Pa.), 97, 112

Northumberland County, 94, 125, 163, 241, 272
Northwestern Railroad Company, 58, 96

Ober, Benjamin, 101
Ohio and Pennsylvania Railroad, 88
Ohio River, 12, 13, 134, 162, 190
Out-of-state ("foreign"), control of banks, 255
   corporations, 44, 50, 51, 72, 261

Packer, S. J., 42, 60, 165, 296, 309
Packer Committee of 1834, 80, 82, 236
Paine, Thomas, 237, 247, 251, 304
Paley, William, 116
Panics, 18, 20, 55, 58, 90, 93, 189, 231, 234, 242, 312
   See also Booms and boom psychology; Depressions and recessions
Parkersburg (W. Va.), 11
Parties, political, 21–23, 26, 27, 33, 56, 62–64, 72, 77, 106, 124, 140, 165, 187, 190, 242, 292, 293, 309, 313
Partnerships, control of, 110
   limited, 60, 66
Passenger Cases, 274
Peddle v. *Hollinshead*, 231
Peltz Committee, 188–90, 197, 199, 202, 203, 309
Pennsylvania Coke and Iron Company, 261
Pennsylvania College, 236, 246
Pennsylvania Railroad, 10, 11, 12, 13, 27, 43, 44, 52, 53, 64, 88, 92, 93, 97, 105, 107–16, 119, 121, 161, 164, 165, 168, 171, 172, 176, 178, 179, 242, 267–85, 295–97, 304, 314, 316–19
Pennsylvania Railroad Iron Manufacturing Company, 57
Pennsylvania Society for Promoting the Abolition of Slavery, 182, 184
Pennsylvania Society for Promoting the Improvement of Roads, 51
Pennsylvania Society for the Promotion of Internal Improvements, 131, 133, 136–38
Perkins, W., 178
Perry County, 125, 134, 163, 241
Pettit, Thomas, 109, 110, 300
Philadelphia, 7, 12, 44, 50, 51, 59, 105–107, 112, 117, 131, 134, 135, 192, 195, 212, 222, 224, 225, 228, 229, 230, 234, 240, 253, 272, 273, 302, 313
   and Pennsylvania Railroad, 11, 12, 97, 105, 107–09, 112, 116, 121, 268
   and public works, 11, 139, 148, 149, 162, 290, 300
   charters of, 109, 111, 115
   competition of, 9, 10, 12, 42, 50, 107, 114, 116, 129, 136, 139, 205, 270, 290, 300
   investments by, 88, 93, 96, 97, 106, 109, 111, 114–16
   labor conditions in, 137, 187, 189, 190, 192
   representatives in legislature, 42, 43, 124, 275
   rivalry with Pittsburgh, 11, 44, 268, 271, 276
Philadelphia and Columbia Railroad, 146, 149, 161
Philadelphia Board of Trade, 271, 275
Philadelphia Contributionship for the Insuring of Houses, 39
Philadelphia County, 29, 45, 49, 117, 125, 134, 163, 241, 244
Philadelphia Domestic Society for the Encouragement of Manufactures, 57
Philadelphia, Easton and Water-Gap Railroad, 114, 115
Philadelphia Ice Company, 259
Pike County, 125, 134, 163, 241
Pittsburgh, 9, 13, 44, 48, 49, 116, 117, 129, 190, 212
   and public works, 133, 135, 148, 162
   and the Baltimore and Ohio Railroad, 11, 43
   and the Pennsylvania Railroad, 46, 271, 272, 273
   investments by, 88, 106, 114
   rivalry with Philadelphia, 11, 44, 268, 271, 276
Pittsburgh and Connelsville Railroad, 88, 269
Pittsburgh and Erie Railroad, 96
Pittsburgh Board of Trade, 271, 275, 277, 284
Pittsburgh, Lawrenceville, and McKeesport Railroad, 88
Pittsburgh Manufacturing Association, 57
Plebiscite, 164, 211, 213, 245, 314
Plumer, Arnold, 176

Pollock, Governor, 114, 175, 176, 213, 278, 279
Poor relief, 301
Popular sovereignty, 25, 28, 29, 299, 303, 304, 310
    See also "Will of the people"
Port Carbon (Pa.), 61
Porter, Governor James, 19, 25, 47, 56, 73, 80, 99, 100, 103, 150, 151, 155, 157, 170, 171, 246, 247, 250, 256, 257, 263, 267
Potter County, 87, 125, 163, 241
Pottsville (Pa.), 21, 59, 62, 134, 194
Powell, Robert, 193
Pressure groups, 26, 72, 76, 113, 126, 132, 142, 146, 160, 221, 249, 292, 313
Price, Eli K., 124, 213
Price fixing, 4, 7, 8, 9, 206, 259, 291, 308
Primogeniture, 70
Prison Discipline Society (Boston), 221
Private enterprise, 147, 166, 169, 252, 253, 295, 299, 303, 315, 317, 318
    See also Businessmen; Entrepreneurs
Privileged creditors, 193, 194, 292
Profit motive, 89–93, 96, 121, 138, 145, 299, 300, 303, 307, 308
Profits, 98, 100, 138, 146, 190, 198, 238, 301, 309
Prohibition, 204, 210–15, 217, 218, 283, 292, 306, 311, 314
    See also Liquor trade
Prohibitory function of state, 292, 295, 306
Promoters, 41, 105, 106
Promotional role of state, 4, 39, 56, 57, 75, 89, 93–96, 116, 202, 216, 236, 289, 290, 296, 300, 303
Property rights, 113, 117, 184, 186, 198, 214–16, 218, 234, 248, 252, 302, 306, 308, 312
Protectionism, 15, 16, 39, 56, 57
    See also "American system"
Proxy system, 75, 255, 256, 263
Public credit
    See State credit
Public enterprise, 66, 168, 170, 173, 180, 214, 216, 296–98, 300, 302, 303, 307, 308, 312, 315, 319
Public lands, 290
Public ownership, 129, 130, 146, 166, 167, 169, 171, 173, 195, 294, 317, 318
Public welfare, 237, 305, 312
Public works, 118, 120, Chap. IV, 214, 216, 218, 264, 268, 277, 311, 312, 313, 316, 317
    financial condition of, 135, 155–57, 313
    loans for, 17, 55, 64
    policy, 181, 203, 204, 235, 267, 298, 299, 308
    program, 4, 23, 51–53, 98, 126, 290–95, 298
    sale of, 161, 163, 164, 166, 172, 268, 270, 278, 279, 281, 295, 298, 315, 318
Pump priming 142–48, 301, 303

Quaker influence, 181
Quarrying, 40, 257

Raguet, Condy, 15, 17, 80, 137, 231, 301
Railroads, 10, 14, 21, 41, 52, 93, 106, 107, 238, 252, 267
    and public works, 145, 149, 161, 317
    and tax exemption, 276, 280, 281
    promotion, 11, 18, 64, 75, 92, 108, 113, 131
    state and municipal investment in, 85–88, 92, 104, 116, 119, 120, 122, 300, 301
    state's regulatory policy of, 258, 260, 263, 264
Randall, Josiah, 131
Rate regulation, 259, 291, 296
Rates, 260, 268–71, 273, 275
    See also Tolls
Read, John M., 109, 111, 115, 116, 119, 120, 128, 301, 302, 317
Reading (Pa.), 48, 117
Reading and Norristown Railroad, 108
Reading Railroad, 171, 270
Reed, William B., 313
Regionalism
    See Sectionalism
Regulation, of factory conditions, 190, 201, 306
    See also Factory, legislation
    of liquor trade, 208, 213, 235, 295
    state power of, 4, 6, 7, 9, 203–205, 213, 214, 217, 291, 294, 303, 305–308
    state power challenged, 295, 296, 312
Regulator, state as, 236, 254–62
Reservation, state power of, 130, 238, 240, 242, 244, 247, 253, 267, 291, 296

INDEX 365

Revocation power of state, 238, 241–44, 246, 249, 252, 253, 269, 303, 308, 314
Revolution, 5, 7, 8, 185, 208, 306
Right to work, 198, 306
Ritner, Governor, 56, 61, 65–67, 148, 242
Rogers, Evans, 104
Rotation-in-office principle, 30–33, 156, 157, 170, 173, 247, 252, 254, 310
Rousseau, J. J., 118
Rush, Benjamin, 23, 183

Sale of state-held stock
  See Liquidation of state investment
Salt, 40, 136
School system, 138, 141
  See also Education
Schuylkill County, 62, 125, 134, 163, 193, 194, 211, 241, 270
Schuylkill Navigation Company, 85
Schuylkill River, 51
Schuylkill Water-works, 112
Scotch-Irish element, 22
Scott, George, 176, 253
Second Bank of the United States
  See Bank of the United States (Second)
Secretary of state, 96, 264
Sectionalism, 10, 11, 12, 13, 14, 15, 20, 22, 26, 27, 33, 41–47, 49–53, 56, 63, 64, 66, 78, 95, 118, 126, 129, 130, 133–35, 139, 140, 148, 149, 153, 161, 169, 268, 281, 289, 292, 293, 295, 300, 308, 309, 313
Sergeant, John, 29–31, 33, 109, 110, 112, 139–42, 200, 302
Sharpless Case, 113–23, 126, 128, 280, 281, 302, 311, 313, 314, 317
Shippen, Justice, 242
Shunk, Governor, 57, 65, 71, 73, 76, 80, 146, 256, 267
Silk manufacturing, 40, 189
Simpson, Stephen, 21, 195–97, 223, 306
Sinking fund, 179, 277
Slate and slate quarrying, 40, 136
Slavery, 181–84, 186, 202, 218, 224, 291, 305
  See also Abolition
Smith, Adam, 5, 80, 116, 196
Smith, Sidney, 19, 313
Smith, William, 95
Snyder, Governor, 65
Snyder County, 125, 241

Social Compact, 29, 69, 199, 203, 251
Social reform and vested rights, 181–235
Socialism, Skidmorian, 118, 120
Society for the Relief of Free Negroes, 182, 183
Somerset County, 77, 125, 163, 194, 241
Southwark (Pa.), 112
Sovereignty, 71ff, 81, 139, 140, 244, 245, 247, 251, 283, 305
Specie reserves, 258
Spring Garden (Pa.), 97, 112
State Bank of Ohio v. *Knoop*, 280
State, economic action of, 6, 7, 9, 17, 297–309
State credit, 18, 19, 44, 98, 120, 149, 161, 164, 262
Stay laws, 229, 231–33, 235, 292
Stevens, Thaddeus, 27, 43, 64
Stockholder liability, 61, 70, 256, 257, 267, 291
Stokes, William A., 272, 273, 284, 311, 312, 315
Store-order payments, 194, 319
Story, Justice Joseph, 245
Strickland, William, 132
"Strict construction" policy, 242, 243, 248, 267, 291, 304
Strikes, 187, 190, 194
Subscriptions
  See Investments, public
Sullivan, J. L., 139, 301
Sullivan County, 125, 241
Sumner, William Graham, 47, 320
Sunbury and Erie Railroad, 11, 109, 165, 179, 296, 318
Supreme Court, federal, 213, 229, 232, 239, 275, 280, 281, 304
Supreme Court, state, 12, 58, 76, 93, 95, 99, 114, 126, 214, 229, 231, 232, 238, 242, 246, 268, 295, 296, 304
Supreme Executive Council, 185, 206, 207
Suspension of specie payments, 248, 258, 263
Susquehanna and Tidewater Canal, 172
Susquehanna County, 125, 163, 241
Susquehanna River, 10, 42, 51, 133, 136, 149, 205

Tamaqua (Pa.), 61
Taney, Roger B., 213, 248
Tariff, 15, 23, 24, 62
  See also Free trade, Protectionism

Taxation, 6, 17, 18, 44, 144, 261, 281, 296, 302, 303, 308, 312
  and public investments, 106–109, 111, 117, 118
  and public works, 53, 138, 141, 164, 168, 175, 177
  corporate, 262, 272, 295
  exemption of Pennsylvania R.R., 164, 165, 179, 278–81, 296
  revenue from, 150, 299, 301
Taylor, George, 59
Telegraph companies, 259, 260
Temperance movement, 208, 209, 306
  See also Prohibition
Tender laws, 229
Textiles, 4, 6, 188, 197, 309, 319
Thomson, President (of Pennsylvania R.R.), 161, 164, 178
Tilghman, Chief Justice William, 131, 229, 242, 243
Tioga County, 125, 133, 163, 241
Tolls, 94, 95, 102, 135, 138, 139, 145, 146, 149, 152, 158, 159, 162, 175, 259, 274
  See also Rates
Tonnage tax, 52, 267–79, 284, 296, 313, 314, 316, 319
Transportation, 40–42, 46–47, 50, 56, 58, 59, 66, 70, 83, 93–95, 100–103, 120, 121, 126, 129–31, 135, 138–40, 146–49, 167, 168, 171, 175, 210, 245, 257, 259, 265, 268, 289, 290, 292, 298–301, 308, 319
  See also Bridges; Canals; Pennsylvania Railroad; Railroads; Turnpikes and turnpike companies
Treasurer of state, 33, 96, 265, 301
Turnpikes and turnpike companies, 9, 14, 44, 45, 46, 47, 51, 83–87, 88, 92, 94, 95, 97, 102, 104, 129–31, 134–36, 141, 166, 171, 238, 252, 260, 263
Tyson, Job, 14, 20, 31, 112, 161, 300, 312

Union Canal, 85, 96, 133, 135, 171
Union County, 125, 134, 163, 241

Vaux, Roberts, 271

Venango County, 88, 125, 163, 241
Virginia, 133, 190

Wagoners, 135, 206, 301
Warren and Pine Grove Railroad, 46
Warren County, 125, 163, 241
Washington County, 45, 125, 163, 194, 241
Water companies, 238, 259, 260
Wayne County, 57, 125, 134, 163, 241
Webster, Pelatiah, 80, 196, 237
West Newton (Pa.), 114
Westmoreland County, 45, 114, 125, 134, 136, 163, 194, 241, 272, 311
Wharton, Thomas, 109, 112, 300, 302
Wheeling (W. Va.), 11, 114
Whig party, 22, 24, 25, 62, 64, 65, 77, 78, 105, 106, 164, 165, 189, 190
Whig-Anti-Masonic coalition, 63
White, John, 61
White, Josiah, 59
Whitestown Manufacturing Company, 254
Wilde, James, 61
"The will of the people," 25–27, 29, 30, 32
  See also Popular sovereignty
Williams, Thomas, 116–18, 120, 121, 126, 311, 320
Williamsport and Elmira Railroad, 46
Wilson, James, 6, 23, 237
Wiston, E. V., 227, 306
Wolf, Governor, 65, 67, 80, 145, 171, 262, 263
Woodward, Justice George, 27, 122, 123, 128, 176, 232, 233, 247, 304
Wool manufacturing, 40, 188, 189
Wright, Frances, 70
Wyoming County, 125, 241

York (Pa.), 136
York County, 8, 10, 45, 125, 133, 134, 163, 211, 241
York County Manufacturing Company, 254

DATE DUE	
~~NOV~~	~~1962~~
~~AUG 19 1974~~	NOV 1 8 1999
~~SEP 1974~~	
~~OCT 21 1974~~	
~~MAR 2 8 1977~~	
~~U D MAR 2 9 1988~~	
U D APR 1 9 1988	
~~SEP 07 1999~~	